T0258591

Advanced Speech Recognition: Concepts and Case Studies

Advanced Speech Recognition: Concepts and Case Studies

Edited by **Marcus Hintz**

LANRYE INTERNATIONAL

New Jersey

Published by Clanrye International,
55 Van Reypen Street,
Jersey City, NJ 07306, USA
www.clanryeinternational.com

Advanced Speech Recognition: Concepts and Case Studies
Edited by Marcus Hintz

© 2015 Clanrye International

International Standard Book Number: 978-1-63240-027-7 (Hardback)

This book contains information obtained from authentic and highly regarded sources. Copyright for all individual chapters remain with the respective authors as indicated. A wide variety of references are listed. Permission and sources are indicated; for detailed attributions, please refer to the permissions page. Reasonable efforts have been made to publish reliable data and information, but the authors, editors and publisher cannot assume any responsibility for the validity of all materials or the consequences of their use.

The publisher's policy is to use permanent paper from mills that operate a sustainable forestry policy. Furthermore, the publisher ensures that the text paper and cover boards used have met acceptable environmental accreditation standards.

Trademark Notice: Registered trademark of products or corporate names are used only for explanation and identification without intent to infringe.

Printed in the United States of America.

Contents

Preface

Every book is a source of knowledge and this one is no exception. The idea that led to the conceptualization of this book was the fact that the world is advancing rapidly; which makes it crucial to document the progress in every field. I am aware that a lot of data is already available, yet, there is a lot more to learn. Hence, I accepted the responsibility of editing this book and contributing my knowledge to the community.

This book majorly emphasizes on speech recognition and the associated tasks like speech optimization and modeling. Renowned veteran researchers from across the globe have contributed significant information in this profound book. The aim of this book is to serve as a comprehensive source of information and assist a broad spectrum of readers.

While editing this book, I had multiple visions for it. Then I finally narrowed down to make every chapter a sole standing text explaining a particular topic, so that they can be used independently. However, the umbrella subject sinews them into a common theme. This makes the book a unique platform of knowledge.

I would like to give the major credit of this book to the experts from every corner of the world, who took the time to share their expertise with us. Also, I owe the completion of this book to the never-ending support of my family, who supported me throughout the project.

Editor

Speech Recognition

Speech Recognition for Agglutinative Languages

R. Thangarajan

Additional information is available at the end of the chapter

1. Introduction

Speech technology is a broader area comprising many applications like speech recognition, Text to Speech (TTS) Synthesis, speaker identification and verification and language identification. Different applications of speech technology impose different constraints on the problem and these are tackled by different algorithms. In this chapter, the focus is on automatically transcribing speech utterances to text. This process is called Automatic Speech Recognition (ASR). ASR deals with transcribing speech utterances into text of a given language. Even after years of extensive research and development, ASR still remains a challenging field of research. But in the recent years, ASR technology has matured to a level where success rate is higher in certain domains. A well-known example is human-computer interaction where speech is used as an interface along with or without other pointing devices. ASR is fundamentally a statistical problem. Its objective is to find the most likely sequence of words, called hypothesis, for a given sequence of observations. The sequence of observations involves acoustic feature vectors representing the speech utterance. The performance of an ASR system can be measured by aligning the hypothesis with the reference text and by counting errors like deletion, insertion and substitution of words in the hypothesis.

ASR is a subject involving signal processing and feature extraction, acoustics, information theory, linguistics and computer science. Speech signal processing helps in extracting relevant and discriminative information, which is called features, from speech signal in a robust manner. Robustness involves spectral analysis used to characterize time varying properties of speech signal and speech enhancement techniques for making features resilient to noise. Acoustics provides the necessary understanding of the relationship between speech utterances and the physiological processes in speech production and speech perception. Information theory provides the necessary procedures for estimating parameters of statistical models during training phase. Computer science plays a major role in ASR with its implementation of efficient algorithms in software or hardware for decoding speech in real-time.

Currently, an important area in speech recognition is Large Vocabulary Continuous Speech Recognition (LVCSR). A large vocabulary means that system has a vocabulary ranging from 5,000 to 60,000 words. Continuous speech means that the utterances have words which are run together naturally. This is different from isolated word speech recognition where each word is demarcated with initial and final silence. Speech recognition algorithms can also be speaker independent, i.e. they are even able to recognize the speech of new users with whom the system is not exposed. Xuedong et al (2001) present a very good reference on algorithms and techniques in speech processing.

1.1. Issues in speech variability

Even though state-of-the-art speech recognition systems cannot match human performance, still they can recognize spoken input accurately but with some constraints. Some of the constraints may be speaker dependency, language dependency, speaking style, and applicability to a particular task and environment. Therefore, building a speech recognizer that could recognize the speech of any speaker, speaking in any language, style, domain and environment is far from realization.

a. Context variability

In any language, words with different meanings have the same phonetic realization. Their usage depends on the context. There is even more context dependency at the phone level. The acoustic realization of a phone is dependent on its neighboring phones. This is because of the physiology of articulators involved in speech production.

b. Style variability

In isolated speech recognition with a small vocabulary, a user pauses between every word while speaking. Thus it is easy to detect the boundary between words and decode them using the silence context. This is not possible in continuous speech recognition. The speaking rate affects the word recognition accuracy. That is, the higher the speaking rate, the higher the WER.

c. Speaker variability

Every speaker's utterance is unique per se. The speech produced by a speaker is dependent on a number of factors, namely vocal tract physiologies, age, sex, dialect, health, education, etc. For speaker independent speech recognition, more than 500 speakers from different age groups, their sex, educational background, and dialect are necessary to build a combined model. The speaker independent system includes a user enrollment process where a new user can train his voice with the system for 30 minutes before using it.

d. Environment variability

Many practical speech recognizers lack robustness against changes in the acoustic environment. This has always been a major limitation of speech based interfaces used in mobile communication devices. The acoustic environment variability is highly unpredictable and it cannot be accounted for during training of models. A mismatch will always occur between the trained speech models and test speech.

1.2. Measure of performance

The ultimate measures of success for any speech recognition algorithms are accuracy and robustness. Therefore, it is important to evaluate the performance of such a system. The WER is one of the most widely used measures for accuracy. The system may be tested on sample utterances from the training data for understanding the system and identification of bugs during the development process. This would result in a better performance than what one can get with test data. In addition, a development set can also be used to test the system and also fine-tune its parameters. Finally, the system can be tested on a test set comprising around 500 speech utterances of 5-10 different users in order to reliably estimate accuracy. This test set should be completely new with respect to training and development. There are three types of word recognition errors in speech recognition:

- Substitution (*Subs*): An incorrect word substituted for a correct word.
- Insertion (*Ins*): An extra word added in the recognized sentence.
- Deletion (*Dels*): A correct word omitted in the recognized sentence.

Generally, a hypothesis sentence is aligned with the correct reference sentence. The number of insertions, substitutions and deletions are computed using maximum substring matching. This is implemented using dynamic programming. The WER is computed as shown in equation (1):

$$WER = \frac{Subs + Dels + Ins}{N} \times 100 \qquad (1)$$

Other performance measures are speed and memory footprints. The speed is an important factor which quantifies the turn around time of the system once the speech is uttered. It is calculated as shown in equation (2):

$$speed = \frac{time\ taken\ for\ processing}{utterance\ duration} \times real\ time \qquad (2)$$

Obviously, the time taken for processing should be shorter than the utterance duration for a quicker response from the system. Memory footprints show the amount of memory required to load the model parameters.

There are a number of well-known factors which affect the accuracy of an ASR system. The prominent factors are those which include variations in context, speakers and noise in the environment. Research in ASR is classified into different types depending on the nature of the problems, like a small or a large vocabulary task, isolated or continuous speech, speaker dependent or independent and robustness to environmental variations. The state-of-the-art speech recognition systems can recognize spoken input accurately with some constraints. The constraints can be speaker dependency, language dependency, speaking style, task or environment. Therefore, building an automatic speech recognizer which can recognize the speech of different speakers, speaking in different languages, with a variety of accent, in any domain and in any ambience environmental background is far from reality.

ASR for languages like English, French and Czech is well matured. A lot of research and development have also been reported for oriental languages like Chinese and Japanese. But in the Indian scenario, ASR is still in its nascent stage due to the inherent agglutinative nature of most of its official languages. Agglutination refers to the extensive morphological inflection in which one can find a one-to-one correspondence between affixes and syntactic categories. This nature results in a large number of words in the dictionary which hinders modeling and training of utterances, and also creates Out-Of-Vocabulary (OOV) words when deployed.

2. Speech units

The objective of this chapter is to discuss a few methods to improve the accuracy of ASR systems for agglutinative languages. The language presented here as a case study is Tamil (ISO 639-3 *tam*). Tamil is a Dravidian language spoken predominantly in the state of Tamilnadu in India and in Sri Lanka. It is the official language of the Indian state of Tamilnadu and also has official status in Sri Lanka, Malaysia and Singapore. With more than 77 million speakers, Tamil is one of the widely spoken languages in the world. Tamil language has also been conferred the status of classical language by the government of India.

Currently, there is a growing interest among Indian researchers for building reliable ASR systems for Indian languages like Hindi, Telegu, Bengali and Tamil. Kumar et al (2004) reported the implementation of a Large Vocabulary Continuous Speech Recognition (LVCSR) system for Hindi. Many efforts have been put to build continuous speech recognition systems for Tamil language with a limited and restricted vocabulary (Nayeemulla Khan and Yegnanarayana 2001, Kumar and Foo Say Wei 2003, Saraswathi and Geetha 2004, Plauche et al 2006). Despite repeated efforts, a LVCSR system for the foresaid languages is yet to be explored to a significant level. Keeping agglutination apart, there are other issues to be addressed like aspirated and un-aspirated consonants, and retroflex consonants.

2.1. Phones, phonemes and syllables

Before embarking on the concepts, it is always better to review a few terminologies pertaining to linguistics. In any language, there are acoustic properties of speech units and symbolic representation of lexical units. For more information, please refer (Xuedong et al, 2001).

a. Phonemes and phones

From the acoustics point of view, a phoneme is defined as the smallest segmental unit of sound employed to tell apart meaningfully between utterances. A phoneme can be considered as a group of slightly different sounds which are all perceived to have the same function by the speakers of a language or a dialect. An example of a phoneme is the /k/ sound in the words *kit* and *skill*. It is customary to place phonemes between slashes in transcriptions. However, the phoneme /k/ in each of these words is actually pronounced differently i.e. it has different realizations. It is because the articulators which generate the phoneme cannot move from one position to another instantaneously. Each of these different realizations of the phoneme is called a phone or technically an allophone (in transcriptions, a phone is placed inside a square bracket like [k]). A phone can also be defined as an instance of a phoneme. In *kit* [k] is aspirated while in *skill* [k] is un-aspirated. Aspiration is a period of voiceless-ness after a stop closure and before the onset of voicing of the following vowel. Aspiration sounds like a puff of air after the [k] and before the vowel. An aspirated phone is represented as [k^h]. In some languages, aspirated and un-aspirated consonants are treated as different phonemes. Hindi, for instance, has four realizations for [k] and they are considered as different phonemes. Tamil does not discriminate them and treats them as allophones.

b. Words

Next comes the representation in symbolic form. According to linguistics, word is defined as a sequence of morphemes. The sequence is determined by the morpho-tactics. A morpheme is an independent unit which makes sense in any language. It could refer to the root word or any of the valid prefixes or suffixes. Therefore what is called a word is quite arbitrary and depends on the language in context. In agglutinative languages a word could consists of a root along with its suffixes – a process known as inflectional morphology. Syntax deals with sentence formation using lexical units. Agglutinative languages, on one hand, exhibit inflectional morphology to a higher extent. On the other hand, the syntactic structure is quite simple which enables free-word ordering in a sentence. The English language, which is not agglutinative, has simpler lexical morphology but the complexity of the syntactic structure is significantly higher.

c. Syllables

A syllable is a unit of organization for a sequence of speech sounds. It is composed of three parts: the onset, the nucleus and the coda. A syllable has a hierarchical structure as shown in Figure 1. It can also be expressed in Backus-Naur Form (BNF) as follows:

<syllable> ::= <onset> <rhyme>

<rhyme> ::= <nucleus> <coda>

A vowel forms the nucleus of the syllable while an optional consonant or consonant cluster forms the onset and coda. In some syllables, the onset or the coda will be absent and the syllables may start and/or end with a vowel.

Generally speaking, a syllable is a vowel-like sound together with some of the surrounding consonants that are most closely associated with it. For example, in the word *parsley*, there are two syllables [**pars.ley**] – CVCC and CVC. In the word *tarragon*, there are three syllables [**tar.ra.gon**] – CVC, CV and CVC. The process of segmenting a word into syllables is called *syllabification*. In English, the syllabification is a hard task because there is no agreed upon definition of syllable boundaries. Furthermore, there are some words like *meal, hour* and *tire* which can be viewed as containing one syllable or two (Ladefoged 1993).

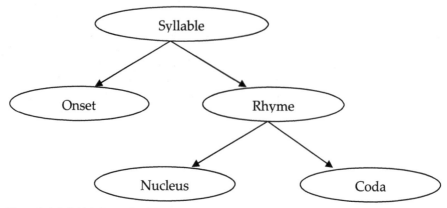

Figure 1. A Syllable's Hierarchical Structure

A syllable is usually a larger unit than a phone, since it may encompass two or more phonemes. There are a few cases where a syllable may only consist of single phoneme. Syllables are often considered the phonological building blocks of words. Syllables have a vital role in a language's rhythm, prosody, poetic meter and stress.

The syllable, as a unit, inherently accounts for the severe contextual effects among its phones as in the case of words. Already it has been observed that a syllable accounts for pronunciation variation more systematically than a phone (Greenberg 1998). Moreover, syllables are intuitive and more stable units than phones and their integrity is firmly based on both the production and perception of speech. This is what sets a syllable apart from a triphone. Several research works using syllable as a speech unit have been successfully carried out for English and other oriental languages like Chinese and Japanese by researchers across the world.

In Japanese language, for instance, the number of distinct syllables is 100, which is very small (Nakagawa et al 1999). However in a language like English, syllables are large in number. In some studies, it is shown that they are of the order of 30,000 syllables in English. The number of lexically attested syllables is of the order of 10,000. When there are a large number of syllables, it becomes difficult to train syllable models for ASR (Ganapathiraju et al 2001).

3. Agglutinative languages – Tamil

Tamil language, for instance, employs agglutinative grammar, where suffixes are used to mark noun class, number, and case, verb tense and other grammatical categories. As a result, a large number of inflectional variants for each word exist. The use of suffixes is governed by morpho-tactic rules. Typically, a *STEM* in Tamil may have the following structure.

STEM +negative+participle +nominalization +plural +locative +ablative +inclusive

For each stem, there are at least $2^7 = 128$ inflected word forms, assuming only two affixes of each type. Actually, there may be more than two options, but there may be gaps. In contrast, English has maximally 4 word forms for a verb as in *swim*, *swims*, *swam* and *swum*, and for nouns as in *man*, *man's*, *men* and *men's*. Hence, for a lexical vocabulary of 1,000, the actual Tamil words list of inflected forms will be of the order of 1,28,000.

3.1. Inflectional morphology

The Parts of Speech (POS) categories in Tamil take different forms due to inflections. According to Rajendran (2004) morphological inflections on nouns include gender and number. Prepositions take either independent or noun combined forms with various cases like accusative, dative, instrumental, sociative, locative, ablative, benefactive, genitive, vocative, clitics and selective. Table 1 arrays a list of examples of cases and their possible suffixes.

Cases	Suffixes
Accusative	ஏ, ஐ
Dative	க்கு, ற்கு
Instrumental	ஆல்
Sociative	ஒடு, உடன்
Locative	இல், உள், இடம்
Ablative	இருந்து
Benefactive	க்காக, ற்காக
Genetive	இன், அது, உடைய
Vocative	ஏ
Clitics	உம், ஓ, தான்
Selective	ஆவது
Interrogative	ஆ, ஓ

Table 1. Case Suffixes used with Noun in Tamil

The verbs in Tamil take various forms like simple, transitive, intransitive, causative, infinitive, imperative and reportive. Verbs are also formed with a stem and various suffix patterns. Some of the verbal suffix patterns are shown in Table 2. Rajendran et al (2003) had done a detailed study on computational morphology of verbal patterns in Tamil.

Suffix	Categories	Sub categories	Suffixes
Tense	Present		கிறு, கின்று, ஆனின்று
	Past		த் , ந் , ற் , இன்
	Future		ப் , வ்
Person	First	Singular	ஏன்
		Plural	ஓம்
	Second	Singular	ஆய்
		Plural	ஈர்கள்
		Honorific	ஈர்
	Third	Male Singular	ஆன் ,அன்
		Female Singular	ஆள், அள்
		Common Plural	ஆர்கள்
		Honorific	ஆர் , அர்
		Neutral Singular	அது
		Neutral Plural	அன
Others	Causative		இ
	Verbal Noun Untensed		அல்
	Infinitive		உ
	Imperative	Plural	உங்கள்
		Negative	ஆதே, ஆது
	Passive		படு
	Future	Negative	மாட், இல்லை
	Optative		முடியும், வேண்டும், கூடும், ஆம்
		negative	முடியாது, கூடாது, வேண்டாம்
	Morpho-phonology (*Sandhi*)		ந், க், ம், ச், த்
	Plural		கள்

Table 2. Verbal Suffixes in Tamil

Adjectives and adverbs are generally obtained by attaching the suffix – ஆன and ஆக to noun forms respectively. Tamil often uses a verb, an adjective or an adverb as the head of a noun phrase. This process is called nominalization where a noun is produced from another POS with morphological inflections.

3.2. Morpho-phonology

Morpho-phonology, also known as *sandhi*, wherein two consecutive words combine by deletion, insertion or substitution of phonemes at word boundaries to form a new word is very common in Tamil. In English, one can find morpho-phonology to a limited extent. For example, the negative prefix (*in*) when attached to different words, changes according to the first letter of the word.

in + proper → *improper*

in + logical → *illogical*

in + rational → *irrational*

in + mature → *immature*

However in Tamil, use of morpho-phonology is more common among two adjacent words. The last phoneme of the first word and the first phoneme of the following word combine and undergo a transformation. Based on certain phono-tactic rules and context, there may be no transformation, or an insertion of a consonant, or a deletion of a vowel/consonant, or a substitution of a vowel/consonant.   The following examples illustrate this phenomenon.

அரசு (*government*) + பணி (*service*) → அரசுப்பணி

ஆபரணம் (*ornament*) + தங்கம் (*gold*) → ஆபரணத்தங்கம்

ஒன்று (*first*) + ஆவது (*selective case suffix*) → ஒன்றாவது

In the first example, there is an insertion of a consonant (ப்) between the two words. The second example shows a substitution of the last consonant (ம்) of the first word by another consonant (த்). In the third example, there is a deletion of the last vowel (உ i.e. று → ற் + உ) of the first word and the consonant (ற்) merges with the incoming vowel (ஆ i.e. ற் + ஆ → றா) of the second word. As a result of morpho-phonology, two distinct words combine and sound as a single word. In fact, Morpho-phonology has evolved as a result of context dependencies among the phonetic units at the boundary of adjacent words or morphemes.

To a certain extent morpho-phonology is based on phono-tactics. The following rules encompass most of them.

- 'உ' removal rule: This rule states that when one morpheme ends in the vowel 'உ' and the following morpheme starts with a vowel, then the 'உ' would be removed from the combination.
- 'வ்' and 'ய்' addition rule: When one morpheme ends with a vowel from a particular a set of vowels and the morpheme it joins starts with a vowel then the morpheme 'வ்' or 'ய்' would be added to the end of the first morpheme.
- Doubling rule: According to this rule, when one morpheme ends with either 'ண்', 'ன்', 'ம்' or 'ய்' and the next morpheme starts with a vowel then the 'ண்', 'ன்', 'ம்' or 'ய்' is doubled.
- Insertion of க், ச், ட் or ப்: This rule states that when one morpheme ends with a vowel and the next morpheme begins with either க், ச், ட் or ப் followed by a vowel there is a doubling of the corresponding க், ச், ட் or ப்.

Apart from these rules, there are instances of morpho-phonology based on the context. For example, **பழங் கூடை** (old basket) and **பழக் கூடை** (fruit basket). Therefore, modelling morpho-phonology in Tamil is still a challenging issue for research.

3.3. Pronunciation in Tamil

Generally languages structure the utterance of words by giving greater prominence to some constituents than others. This is true in English where one or more syllables standout as more prominent than the rest. This is typically known as word stress. The same is true for higher level prosody in a sentence where one or more syllables may bear sentence stress or accent. Spoken Tamil language has a number of dialects. People from different parts of Tamilnadu state in India speak different accents. Harold Schiffman (2006) is a good reference for studying the grammar of spoken Tamil. As far as formal Tamil language is concerned, it is assumed that there is no stress or accent (Arden 1934, Arokianathan 1981, Soundaraj 2000) at word level and all syllables are pronounced with the same emphasis. However, there are other opinions that the position of stress in the word is by no means fixed to any syllable of individual word (Marthandan 1983). In connected speech, the stress is found more often in the initial syllable (Balasubramaniam 1980). In some studies (Asher and Keane 2005) it is shown that there is a marked reduction in vowel's duration of non-initial syllables compared to initial syllables.

4. Novel methods for improving accuracy of ASR systems

This section concentrates on two novel approaches adopted in ASR systems for agglutinative languages. In the first approach, an enhanced bi-gram or tri-gram morpheme based language model is designed to reduce the vocabulary size and reliably predict the strings in an agglutinative language. The second approach leverages the syllabic structure of the word and builds a syllable based acoustic model.

4.1. Language models

A language model is defined as the probability distribution over strings in a language. Frequencies of patterns of words as they occur in any training corpus are recorded as probability distributions. A language model is an indispensable part of ASR and machine translation systems. Language model helps in reducing the decoder's search space and in generating optimal sequence of words. For strict word-order languages like English, statistical language models have been effectively used because *trigram* or *bigram* models accurately model short distance relationship in a sentence. Other sophisticated language models also exist like class based model, distance based model and dependency based model. The performance of a statistical language model is measured in terms of *perplexity*. The perplexity refers to the branching factor in the search graph. If the perplexity is low, better the performance of a language model.

Owing to resource deficiency in text and annotated corpora in Tamil, building reliable statistical language models is a difficult task. Even with the available corpus, the agglutinative nature of the language further deepens the problem. Statistical studies using large corpora are still in the nascent stage. However, Rajendran (2006) has given a review of various recent works carried out in morphological analysis, morphological disambiguation, shallow parsing, POS tagging and syntactic parsing in Tamil.

For instance, let W_{i-1} and W_i be two consecutive words in a text. The probability $P(W_i|W_{i-1})$ is the bi-gram that measures the correlation between the words W_{i-1} and W_i. This bi-gram measure is sufficient for modeling strings of words in a language where inflectional morphology is low. However in agglutinative languages, like Tamil, a more minute measure is warranted. This issue has been successfully resolved by Saraswati and Geetha (2007) with their enhanced morpheme based language model. The size of the vocabulary was reduced by decomposing the words into stems and endings. These sub-word units (morphemes) are stored in the vocabulary separately. The enhanced morpheme-based language model is designed and trained on the decomposed corpus. A Tamil text corpus is decomposed into stem and its associated suffixes using an existing Tamil morphological analyzer (Anandan P et al, 2002). The decomposition helps reduce the number of distinct words by around 40% on two different corpora namely News and Politics. The stems and its endings are marked with a special character '#' for stems and '$' for suffixes in order to co-join them back after recognition is done.

A general morpheme based language model is one where the stem and suffixes are treated as independent words. No distinction is made between a stem and a morpheme. Figure 2 depicts the various probability measures involved in a morpheme based language model. The word W_{i-1} is split into the stem S_{i-1} and suffix E_{i-1}, and the word W_i is split into the stem S_i and suffix E_i.

In this case, the prediction of suffix E_{i-1} will be based on S_{i-1} which is strongly correlated since a stem can have a few suffixes among the possible 7 suffixes. This information is modeled in $P(E_{i-1}|S_{i-1})$ and $P(E_i|S_i)$ which can be reliably gathered from a corpus. However, the correlation between stem S_i and the suffix of the previous word E_{i-1} is weak, because the suffix bears very little information of the next word in a sentence. But when it comes to *stem to stem* correlation, the probability $P(S_i|S_{i-1})$ can be reliably used, since there is contextual information that exists between adjacent words in a sentence and stem is the primary part of a word. In Tamil language there is strong subject-predicate agreement which leads to contextual information between suffixes of words in a sentence. This information is available in $P(E_i|E_{i-1})$

The perplexity and WER are obtained using a Tamil speech recognition system. While figure 3.a portrays the perplexity of the language models, figure 3.b compares the WER of the ASR system employing both language models.

The results has confirmed that the modified morpheme-based trigram language model with Katz back-off smoothing technique is better perplexity and lower WER on two Tamil corpora. The results confirm that the proposed enhanced morpheme-based language model is much better than the word-based language models for agglutinative languages.

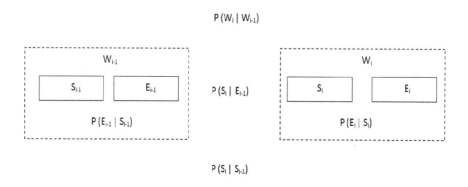

Figure 2. Morpheme based language Modeling

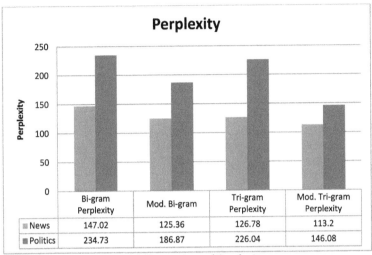

(a) Comparison of Perplexity

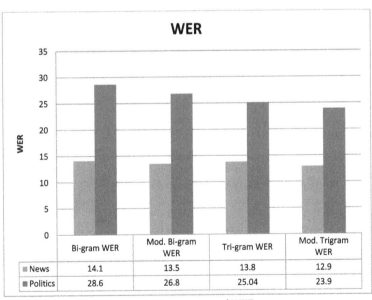

(b) Comparison of WER

Figure 3.

4.2. Syllable modeling

The importance of syllable as a unit in ASR was felt in early researches starting with (Fujimura 1975) where irregularities in phonemes have been discussed and it has been claimed that a syllable will serve as the viable minimal unit of speech in time domain.

In the paper (Greenberg 1998), it is stated that pronunciation variation in Switchboard corpus is more systematic at the level of a syllable. It has been emphasized that the onset and nucleus of a syllable do not show much contextual dependencies while the coda may still be susceptible to some contextual effects with the following syllable. Greenberg (1998) proposed that syllables are frequently realized in their standard or canonical form but in the case of phones, canonical realization is mostly unusual.

In the paper by Ganapathiraju et al (2001), the first successful robust LVCSR system that used syllable level acoustic unit in telephone bandwidth spontaneous speech is reported. The paper begins with a conjecture that syllable based system would perform better than existing triphone systems and concludes with experimental verification after comparing a syllable based system performance with that of a word-internal and a cross-word triphone system on publicly available databases, viz. Switchboard and Alphadigits. A number of syllable based experiments involving syllables and CI phones, syllables and CD phones, syllables, mono-syllabic words and CD phones have been reported in that paper. However, this system is deficient especially in the integration of syllable and phone models as mixed-word entry. It is because mixing models of different lengths and context might result only in marginal improvements.

4.2.1. Justification for using prosodic syllable as a speech unit

Thangarajan et al (2008a) have proposed a syllable based language model for combating the agglutinative nature of Tamil language. The basic syllable consonant-vowel phono-tactics in Tamil is characterized by a regular expression shown in equation (3). There are constraints on which consonants can appear in each of the three consonant positions and in combination with vowels. With no constraints, the maximum number of syllables will be $183 \times 12 = 69,984$. However, because of constraints the actual number of possible syllables is in order of magnitude smaller. The number of lexically attested syllable is smaller still. In addition, there are constraints on stress patterning in Tamil words.

$$RE(S) = [C]V[C[C]] \tag{3}$$

Properties that constitute prosody are fundamental frequency or formant f0 (perceived pitch), duration, intensity (perceived loudness) and to some extent vowel quality. Prosodic properties of speech are also used in detection of word boundaries and in other higher tasks of speech understanding like encoding or decoding pragmatic differences like a statement vs. a question, emotion and so on. At the word level, prosodic properties encode lexical tone, lexical stress and lexical pitch accent.

There are two types of prosodic syllables namely *Ner-acai* and *Nirai-acai*. *Ner-acai* is monosyllabic. It may consist of either one short vowel or one long vowel, either of which may be open or closed, i.e. ending in a vowel or consonant(s) respectively. *Nirai-acai* is always disyllabic with an obligatorily short vowel at first position, while the second phoneme is unrestricted. Like *Ner-acai*, *Nirai-acai* may also be of open or closed type. The prosodic syllable representation can take any of the following eight patterns as shown in Table 3. An uninflected Tamil word may comprise one to four prosodic syllables.

Description	Pattern	Example (with Romanized Tamil and meaning)
Short vowel, long vowel followed by consonant(s)* (Nirai)	SV + LV + C(s)	புலால் (pulal) (meat)
Short vowel followed by a long vowel, (Nirai)	SV + LV	விழா (vizha) (function)
Two short vowels followed by consonant(s)*, (Nirai)	SV + SV + C(s)	களம் (kaLam) (field)
Two short vowels, (Nirai)	SV + SV	கல (kala) (echo sound)
Short vowel followed by consonant(s)*, (Ner)	SV + C(s)	கல் (kal) (stone)
Long vowel followed by consonant(s)*, (Ner)	LV + C(s)	வாள் (vaL) (sword)
Long vowel, (Ner)	LV	வா (va) (come)
Short vowel, (Ner)	SV	க (ka)

* At the maximum, two consonants can occur

Table 3. The Linguistic Rules of Tamil Prosodic Syllables

4.2.2. Formal representations of prosodic syllables

Prosodic syllables are composed of phonemes. Based on the linguistic rules tabulated in Table 3, a regular expression can be formulated as shown in equation (4).

$$RE(S) = [SV](SV|LV)[C[C]] \qquad (4)$$

This expression describes all the possible patterns of prosodic syllables. In other words, an optional short vowel is followed obligatorily by either a short vowel or a long vowel, and zero or one or two consonants.

Theoretically, the number of prosodic syllables will be quite larger (of the order of 3,674,160), since there are 90 (18 times 5) short vowels, 126 (18 times 7) long vowels and 18 consonants. But, the actual number will be smaller due to constraints like phono-tactics and morpho-tactics. Hence, it is essential to estimate the number of prosodic syllables with the help of a corpus.

4.2.3. Analysis of Tamil text corpus

In this section, a Tamil text corpus provided by Central Institute for Indian Languages (CIIL) with 2.6 million words is taken and useful statistics about prosodic syllables is collected. This corpus is a collection of Tamil text documents collected from various domains, viz. agriculture, biographies, cooking tips and news articles. A simple algorithm to segment prosodic syllables from a word is proposed whose pseudo code is given below.

```
Function Syllabify (Word[0..n-1])

    k ← 0 // Index of current letter in the WORD
    m ← 0 // Index of syllable array
    // for each letter in the 'Word' categorize it as
    // short vowel, long vowel or consonant
    for k ← 0 to n-1
        if (Word[k] is a short vowel)
                CharCategory[k] ← 0
        else if (Word[k] is a long vowel)
                CharCategory[k] ← 1
        else
                CharCategory[k] ← 2    // it is a consonant
    end for

    for k ← 0 to n-1
        if ((k+2) <= n and CharCategory[k] = 0 and
                CharCategory[k + 1] = 1 or

                CharCategory[k + 1] = 0))
                copy(Syllable[m], Word[k], Word[k+1]);
                k ← k + 2;
        else if (CharCategory[k] = 1 || CharCategory[k] = 0)
                copy(Syllable[m], Word[k]);
                k ← k + 1;
        end if

        while(k < n && CharCategory[k] = 2)
            copy(Syllable[m], Word[k]);
                k ← k + 1;
        end while
        m ← m + 1;
    end for
        return m; // returns the no. of syllables; syllables
                  // are stored Syllable[]
end function
```

The algorithm works in two stages. Initially, grapheme to phoneme conversion (phonetisation) is done by scanning all the letters of a word and categorizing them as vowels and consonants. The next step of the algorithm combines the letters into syllables with the help of linguistic rules which are presented in Table 3. This step is called syllabification. Syllable patterns are checked from the biggest syllable to the smallest one. The algorithm stores the syllables in an array and returns their count.

After applying the algorithm to the text corpus, the frequency counts of various prosodic syllable patterns were gathered. The algorithm segmented 26,153 numbers of unique prosodic syllables in the corpus. Since the text corpus used here was not clean, it contained a lot of abbreviations, digits and other foreign characters. Therefore, the prosodic syllable patterns with frequency less than 10 were eliminated. Then, it was found that there were only 10,015 numbers of unique prosodic syllables as shown in Table 4.

Details	Frequency
Documents	686
Sentences	455,504
Words	2,652,370
No. of unique prosodic syllables segmented by the algorithm	26,153
No. of unique prosodic syllables validated by the DFA	10,015

Table 4. Prosodic Syllables in CIIL Corpus

4.2.4. Creating context independent syllable models

A lexicon based on prosodic syllables was created with the aid of the algorithm where every word in the dictionary was segmented into its constituent prosodic syllables. Along with the dictionary, a list of prosodic syllable models and continuous speech with sentence aligned transcription were given as input to the training program. The transcription were force-aligned with *Baum-Welch* training followed by Viterbi alignment.

In order to keep the complexity low, it was preferable to model CI syllable units with single Gaussian continuous density HMM. The continuous speech was transformed into a sequence of feature vectors. This sequence was matched with the optimal/best concatenated HMM sequence found using Viterbi algorithm. The time stamps of segmented syllable boundaries were obtained as a by-product of Viterbi decoding. The duration of the prosodic syllables was found to vary from 290 *ms* to 315 *ms*. Even though a prosodic syllable is either monosyllabic or disyllabic, the duration was more or less equal to 300 *ms* on average. This may be due to vowel duration reduction which occurs in non-initial syllables as reported by Asher and Keane (2005).

Based on these considerations, eight states per HMM were decided to be adequate for the experiment. Figure 4 shows the schematic block diagram of a syllable based recognizer.

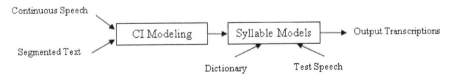

Figure 4. The Syllable Modeling and Recognition System

4.2.5. Results and discussions

For simplicity, an acoustic model was trained with 1,398 unique prosodic syllables drawn from agriculture domain. These prosodic syllables almost covered the agriculture data and the test set completely. In the experiment, the number of models to be trained was significantly reduced compared to the triphone models. The baseline triphone model had 3,171 numbers of unique triphones extracted from the transcript. The experiment was carried out using syllable based continuous speech recognition for Tamil. The dictionary and the transcripts were segmented into prosodic syllables with the proposed algorithm and models were trained. The syllable based acoustic model was deployed on a conventional continuous speech recognizer and tested with the same test set comprising 400 sentences. When comparing the WER, it is found that the WER of syllable models were considerably reduced (by 10%) compared to word models. However the triphone models performed well with a WER of 9.44%

It was also observed that in the prosodic syllable models, there were larger number of substitution errors than that of insertions and deletions whereas in the case of word models, there was a majority of deletion errors. This comparison is shown in Figure 5. The majority of deletion errors in word models signify OOV rate due to morphological inflections. The OOV words in syllable models significantly got reduced. This proves the fact that syllables are effective as sub-word units according to Thangarajan et al (2008b)

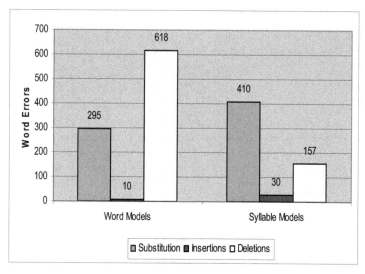

Figure 5. The Types of Word Errors in Word Models and Syllable Models

The increase in WER by 10% approximately in syllable models compared to triphone models can be attributed to the large number of syllables to be modeled with the available limited training set. This also indicates the presence of a little contextual effect between syllables. This is an avenue for future research.

5. Summary

In this chapter, the nature of agglutinative languages is discussed with Tamil language taken as a case study. The inflectional morphology of Tamil language is described in great detail. The challenges that are faced in ASR systems for such languages are highlighted. Two different approaches – enhanced morpheme based languages model and syllable based models - used in ASR for agglutinative languages are elaborated along with their results. The merits and scope for further research is also discussed.

Author details

R. Thangarajan
Department of Computer Science and Engineering,
Kongu Engineering College, Perundurai, Erode, Tamilnadu, India

6. References

[1] Anandan P., Saravanan K., Parthasarathy R., and Geetha T.V., (2002), 'Morphological Analyzer for Tamil', in the proceedings of ICON 2002, Chennai.

[2] Arden A. H. (1934), 'A progressive grammar of common Tamil' 4th edition, Christian Literature Society, Madras, India, pp. 59.

[3] Arokianathan S. (1981), 'Tamil clitics', Dravidian Linguistics Association, Trivandrum, India, pp. 5

[4] Asher R.E. and Keane E.L. (2005), 'Diphthongs in colloquial Tamil', (Hardcastle W.J. and Mackenzie Beck J. eds.), pp. 141-171.

[5] Balasubramanian T. (1980), 'Timing in Tamil', Journal of Phonetics, Vol. 8, pp.449-467.

[6] Fujimura O. (1975), 'Syllable as a unit of Speech Recognition', IEEE Transactions on Acoustics, Speech and Signal Processing, Vol. ASSP-23, No. 1, pp. 82-87.

[7] Ganapathiraju A., Jonathan Hamaker, Joseph Picone, Mark Ordowski and George R. Doddington (2001), 'Syllable Based Large Vocabulary Continuous Speech Recognition', IEEE Transactions on Speech and Audio Processing, Vol. 9, No. 4, pp. 358-366.

[8] Greenberg S. (1998), 'Speaking in Short Hand - A Syllable Centric Perspective for Understanding Pronunciation Variation', Proceedings of the ESCA Workshop on Modeling Pronunciation Variation for Automatic Speech Recognition, Kekrade, pp. 47-56.

[9] Harold F. Schiffman (2006), 'A Reference Grammar of Spoken Tamil', Cambridge University Press (ISBN-10: 0521027527).

[10] Kumar C.S. and Foo Say Wei (2003), 'A Bilingual Speech Recognition System for English and Tamil', Proceedings of Joint Conference of the Fourth International Conference on Information, Communications and Signal Processing, 2003 and the Fourth Pacific Rim Conference on Multimedia, Vol. 3, pp. 1641-1644.

[11] Kumar M., Rajput N. and Verma A. (2004), 'A large-vocabulary continuous speech recognition system for Hindi', IBM Journal of Research and Development, Vol. 48, No.5/6, pp. 703-715.

[12] Ladefoged, Peter. (1993), 'A course in phonetics.' 3rd edition, Fort Worth, TX: Harcourt, Brace, and Jovanovich

[13] Marthandan, C.R. (1983), 'Phonetics of casual Tamil', Ph.D. Thesis, University of London.

[14] Nakagawa S. and Hashimoto Y. (1988), 'A method for continuous speech segmentation using HMM', presented at IEEE International Conference on Pattern Recognition.

[15] Nakagawa S., Hanai K., Yamamoto K. and Minematsu N. (1999), 'Comparison of syllable-based HMMs and triphone-based HMMs in Japanese speech recognition', Proceedings of International Workshop Automatic Speech Recognition and Understanding, pp. 393-396.

[16] Nayeemulla Khan A. and Yegnanarayana B. (2001), 'Development of Speech Recognition System for Tamil for Small Restricted Task', Proceedings of National Conference on Communication, India.

[17] Plauche M., Udhyakummar N., Wooters C., Pal J. and Ramachadran D. (2006), 'Speech Recognition for Illiterate Access to Information and Technology', Proceedings of First International Conference on ICT and Development.

[18] Rajendran S, Viswanathan S and Ramesh Kumar (2003) 'Computational Morphology of Tamil Verbal Complex', Language in India, Vol. 3:4

[19] Rajendran S (2004) 'Strategies in the Formation of Compound Nouns in Tamil', Languages in India, Volume 4:6

[20] Rajendran S (2006) 'Parsing In Tamil: Present State of Art', Language in India, Vol. 6:8.

[21] Saraswathi S. and Geetha T.V. (2004), 'Implementation of Tamil Speech Recognition System Using Neural Networks', Lecture Notes in Computer Science, Vol. 3285.

[22] Saraswathi S. and Geetha T. V. (2007), 'Comparison of Performance of Enhanced Morpheme-based language Model with Different Word-based Language Models for Improving the Performance of Tamil Speech Recognition System', ACM Transaction on Asian Language Information Processing Vol. 6 No. 3, Article 9.

[23] Soundaraj F. (2000) 'Accent in Tamil: Speech Research for Speech Technology', In: (Nagamma Reddy K. ed.), Speech Technology: Issues and implications in Indian languages International School of Dravidian Linguistics, Thiruvananthapuram, pp. 246-256.

[24] Thangarajan R., Natarajan A. M. and Selvam M. (2008a), 'Word and Triphone based Approaches in Continuous Speech Recognition for Tamil Language', WSEAS Transactions on Signal Processing, Issue 3, Vol.4, 2008, pp. 76-85.

[25] Thangarajan R. and Natarajan A. M. (2008b), 'Syllable Based Continuous Speech Recognition for Tamil Language', South Asian Language Review (SALR), Vol. XVIII, No. 1, pp. 71-85.

[26] Xuedong Huang, Alex Acero and Hsiao-Wuen Hon (2001), 'Spoken Language Processing - A Guide to Theory, Algorithm and System Development', Prentice Hall PTR (ISBN 0-13-022616-5).

## Chapter 2

Robust Speech Recognition for Adverse Environments

Chung-Hsien Wu and Chao-Hong Liu

Additional information is available at the end of the chapter

1. Introduction

As the state-of-the-art speech recognizers can achieve a very high recognition rate for clean speech, the recognition performance generally degrades drastically under noisy environments. Noise-robust speech recognition has become an important task for speech recognition in adverse environments. Recent research on noise-robust speech recognition mostly focused on two directions: (1) removing the noise from the corrupted noisy signal in signal space or feature space - such as noise filtering: spectral subtraction (Boll 1979), Wiener filtering (Macho et al. 2002) and RASTA filtering (Hermansky et al. 1994), and speech or feature enhancement using model-based approach: SPLICE (Deng et al. 2003) and stochastic vector mapping (Wu et al. 2002); (2) compensating the noise effect into acoustic models in model space so that the training environment can match the test environment - such as PMC (Wu et al. 2004) or multi-condition/multi-style training (Deng et al. 2000). The noise filtering approaches require some assumption of prior information, such as the spectral characteristic of the noise. The performance will degrade when the noisy environment vary drastically or under unknown noise environment. Furthermore, (Deng et al. 2000; Deng et al. 2003) have shown that the use of denoising or preprocessing are superior to retraining the recognizers under the matched noise conditions with no preprocessing.

Stochastic vector mapping (SVM) (Deng et al. 2003; Wu et al. 2002) and sequential noise estimation (Benveniste et al. 1990; Deng et al. 2003; Gales et al. 1996) for noise normalization have been proposed and achieved significant improvement in noisy speech recognition. However, there still exist some drawbacks and limitations. First, the performance of sequential noise estimation will decrease when the noisy environment vary drastically. Second, the environment mismatch between training data and test data still exists and results in performance degradation. Third, the maximum-likelihood-based stochastic vector mapping (SPLICE) requires annotation of environment type and stereo training data. Nevertheless, the stereo data are not available for most noisy environments.

In order to overcome the insufficiency of tracking ability in the sequential expectation-maximization (EM) algorithm, in this chapter, the prior models were introduced to provide more information in sequential noise estimation. Furthermore, an environment model adaptation is constructed to reduce the mismatch between the training data and the test data. Finally, minimum classification error (MCE)-based approach (Wu et al. 2002) was employed without the stereo training data and an unsupervised frame-based auto-clustering was adopted to automatically detect the environment type of the training data (Hsieh et al. 2008).

For recognition of disfluent speech, a number of cues can be observed when edit difluency occurs in the spontaneous speech. These cues can be detected from linguistic features, acoustic features (Shriberg et al. 2000) and integrated knowledge sources (Bear et al. 1992). (Shriberg et al. 2005) outlined phonetic consequences of disfluency to improve models for disfluency processing in speech applications. Four types of disfluency based on intonation, segment duration and pause duration were presented in (Savova et al. 2003). Soltau et al. used a discriminatively trained full covariance Gaussian system for rich transcription (Soltau et al. 2005). (Furui et al. 2005) presented the approaches to corpus collection, analysis and annotation for conversational speech processing.

(Charniak et al. 2001) proposed an architecture for parsing the transcribed speech using an edit word detector to remove edit words or fillers from the sentence string, and then a standard statistical parser was used to parse the remaining words. The statistical parser and the parameters estimated by boosting were employed to detect and correct the disfluency. (Heeman et al. 1999) presented a statistical language model that is able to identify POS tags, discourse markers, speech repairs and intonational phrases. A noisy channel model was used to model the disfluency in (Johnson et al. 2004). (Snover et al. 2004) combined the lexical information and rules generated from 33 rule templates for disfluency detection. (Hain et al. 2005) presented the techniques in front-end processing, acoustic modeling, language and pronunciation modeling for transcribing the conversational telephone speech automatically. (Liu et al. 2005) compared the HMM, maximum entropy, and conditional random fields for disfluency detection in detail.

In this chapter an approach to the detection and correction of the edit disfluency based on the word order information is presented (Yeh et al. 2006). The first process attempts to detect the interruption points (IPs) based on hypothesis testing. Acoustic features including duration, pitch and energy features were adopted in hypothesis testing. In order to circumvent the problems resulted from disfluency especially in edit disfluency, a reliable and robust language model for correcting speech recognition errors was employed. For handling language-related phenomena in edit disfluency, a cleanup language model characterizing the structure of the cleanup sentences and an alignment model for aligning words between deletable region and correction part are proposed for edit disfluency detection and correction.

Furthermore, multilinguality frequently occurs in speech content, and the ability to process speech in multiple languages by the speech recognition systems has become increasingly desirable due to the trend of globalization. In general, there are different approaches to achieving multilingual speech recognition. One approach employing external language identification (LID) systems (Wu et al. 2006) to firstly identify the language of the input utterance and the corresponding monolingual system is then selected to perform the speech recognition (Waibel et al. 2000). The accuracy of the external LID system is the main factor to the overall system performance.

Another approach to multilingual speech recognition is to run all the monolingual recognizers in parallel and select the output generated by the recognizer that obtains the maximum likelihood score. The performance of the multilingual speech recognition depends on the post-end selection of the maximum likelihood sequence. The popular approaches to multilingual speech recognition are the utilization of a multilingual phone set. The multilingual phones are usually created by merging the phones across the target languages that are acoustically similar in an attempt to obtain a minimal phone set that covers all the sounds existing in all the target languages (Kohler 2001).

In this chapter, an approach to phonetic unit generation for mixed-language or multilingual speech recognition is presented (Huang et al. 2007). The International Phonetic Alphabet (IPA) representation is employed for phonetic unit modeling. Context-dependent triphones for Mandarin and English speech are constructed based on the IPA representation. Acoustic and contextual analysis is investigated to characterize the properties among the multilingual context-dependent phonetic units. Acoustic likelihood is adopted for the pair-wise similarity estimation of the context-dependent phone models to construct a confusing matrix. The hyperspace analog to language (HAL) model is used for contextual modeling and then used for contextual similarity estimation between phone models.

The organization of this paper is as follows. Section 2 presents two approaches to cepstral feature enhancement for noisy speech recognition using noise-normalized stochastic vector mapping. Section 3 describes an approach to edit disfluency detection and correction for rich transcription. In Section 4, fusion of acoustic and contextual analysis is described to generate phonetic units for mixed-language or multilingual speech recognition. Finally the conclusions are provided in the last section.

2. Speech recognition in noisy environment

In this section, an approach to feature enhancement for noisy speech recognition is presented. Three prior models are introduced to characterize clean speech, noise and noisy speech, respectively. The framework of the system is shown in Figure 1. Sequential noise estimation is employed for prior model construction based on noise-normalized stochastic vector mapping (NN-SVM). Therefore, feature enhancement can work without stereo training data and manual tagging of background noise type based on auto-clustering on the estimated noise data. Environment model adaptation is also adopted to reduce the mismatch between the training data and the test data.

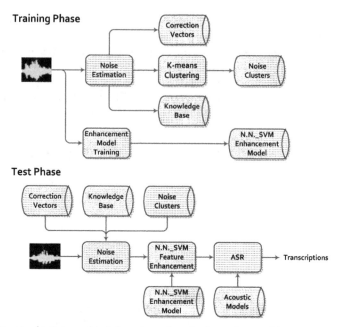

Figure 1. Diagram of training and test phases for noise-robust speech recognition

2.1. NN-SVM for cepstral feature enhancement

2.1.1. Stochastic Vector Mapping (SVM)

The SVM-based feature enhancement approach estimates the clean speech feature $\hat{x}$ from the noisy speech feature y through an environment-dependent mapping function $F\left(y;\Theta^{(e)}\right)$, where $\Theta^{(e)}$ denotes the mapping function parameters and e denotes the corresponding environment of noisy speech feature y.

Assuming that the training data of the noisy speech Y can be partitioned into N_e different noisy environments, the feature vectors of Y under an environment e can be modeled by a Gaussian mixture model (GMM) with N_k mixtures:

$$p\left(y\mid e;\Omega_e\right)=\sum_{k=1}^{N_k}p\left(k\mid e\right)p\left(y\mid k,e\right)=\sum_{k=1}^{N_k}\omega_k^e\cdot N\left(y;\xi_k^e,R_k^e\right) \tag{1}$$

where Ω_e represents the environment model. The clean speech feature $\hat{x}$ can be estimated using a stochastic vector mapping function which is defined as follows:

$$\hat{x}\triangleq F\left(y;\Theta^{(e)}\right)=y+\sum_{e=1}^{N_E}\sum_{k=1}^{N_k}p\left(k\mid y,e\right)r_k^e \tag{2}$$

where the posterior probability $p(k|y,e)$ can be estimated using the Bayes theory based on the environment model Ω_e as follows:

$$p(k|y,e) = \frac{p(k|e)p(y|k,e)}{\displaystyle\sum_{j=1}^{N_k} p(j|e)p(y|j,e)} \qquad (3)$$

and $\Theta^{(e)} = \left\{ r_k^{(e)} \right\}_{k=1}^{N_k}$ denotes the mapping function parameters. Generally, $\Theta^{(e)}$ are estimated from a set of training data using maximum likelihood criterion.

For the estimation of the mapping function parameter $\Theta^{(e)}$, if the stereo data, which contain a clean speech signal and the corrupted noisy speech signal with the identical clean speech signal, are available, the SPLICE-based approach can be directly adopted. However, the stereo data are not easily available in real-life applications. In this chapter an MCE-based approach is proposed to overcome the limitation. Furthermore, the environment type of the noisy speech data is needed for training the environment model $\Theta^{(e)}$. The noisy speech data are manually classified into N_E noisy environments types. This strategy assigns each noisy speech file to only one environment type and is very time consuming. Actually, each noisy speech file contains several segments with different types of noisy environment. Since the noisy speech annotation affects the purity of the training data for the environment model $\Theta^{(e)}$, this section introduces a frame-based unsupervised noise clustering approach to construct a more precise categorization of the noisy speech.

2.1.2. Noise-Normalized Stochastic Vector Mapping (NN-SVM)

In (Boll 1979), the concept of noise normalization is proposed to reduce the effect of background noise in noisy speech for feature enhancement. If the noise feature vector $\tilde{n}$ of each frame can be estimated first, the NN-SVM is conducted from Eq.**Error! Reference source not found.**(2) by replacing y and $\hat{x}$ with $y - \tilde{n}$ and $\hat{x} - \tilde{n}$ as

$$\hat{x} - \tilde{n} \triangleq F\left(y - \tilde{n}; \Theta^{(e)}\right) = y - \tilde{n} + \sum_{e=1}^{N_F}\sum_{k=1}^{N_k} p\left(k|y - \tilde{n}, e\right) r_k^e \qquad (4)$$

The process for noise normalization makes the environment model Ω_e more noise-tolerable. Obviously, the estimation algorithm of noise feature vector $\tilde{n}$ plays an important role in noise-normalized stochastic vector mapping.

2.2. Prior model for sequential noise estimation

This section employs a frame-based sequential noise estimation algorithm (Benveniste et al. 1990; Deng et al. 2003; Gales et al. 1996) by incorporating the prior models. In the procedure, only noisy speech feature vector of the current frame is observed. Since the noise and clean speech feature vectors are missing simultaneously, the relation among clean speech, noise and noisy speech is required first. Then the sequential EM algorithm is introduced for online noise estimation based on the relation. In the meantime, the prior models are involved to provide more information for noise estimation.

2.2.1. The acoustic environment model

The nonlinear acoustic environment model is introduced first for noise estimation in (Deng et al. 2003). Given the cepstral features of a clean speech x, an additive noise n and a channel distortion h, the approximated nonlinear relation among x, n, h and the corrupted noisy speech y in cepstral domain is estimated as:

$$y \approx h + x + g(n - h - x), \ g(z) = C\ln\left(I + \exp\left[C^T(z)\right]\right) \tag{5}$$

where C denotes the discrete cosine transform matrix. In order to linearize the nonlinear model, the first order Taylor series expansion was used around two updated operating points n_0 and μ_0^x denoting the initial noise feature and the mean vector of the prior clean speech model, respectively. By ignoring the channel distortion effect, for which $h = 0$, Eq.**Error! Reference source not found.**(5) is then derived as:

$$y \approx \mu_0^x + g\left(n_0 - \mu_0^x\right) + G\left(n_0 - \mu_0^x\right)\left(x - \mu_0^x\right) + \left[I - G\left(n_0 - \mu_0^x\right)\right]\left(n - n_0\right) \tag{6}$$

where $G(z) = -Cdiag\left(\dfrac{I}{I + \exp\left[C^T z\right]}\right)C^T$.

2.2.2. The prior models

The three prior models Φ_n, Φ_x and Φ_y, which denotes noise, clean speech and noisy speech models respectively, can provide more information for sequential noise estimation. First, the noise and clean speech prior models are characterized by GMMs as:

$$p(n;\Phi_n) = \sum_{d=1}^{N_d} w_d^n \cdot N\left(n;\mu_d^n,\Sigma_d^n\right), \ p(x;\Phi_x) = \sum_{m=1}^{N_m} w_m^x \cdot N\left(x;\mu_m^x,\Sigma_m^x\right) \tag{7}$$

where the pre-training data for noisy and clean speech are required to train the model parameters of the two GMMs, Φ_n and Φ_x.

While the prior noisy speech model is needed in sequential noise estimation, the noisy speech model parameters are derived according to the prior clean speech and noise models using the approximated linear model around two operating points μ_0^n and μ_0^x as follows:

$$p\left(y;\Phi_y\right) = \sum_{m=1}^{N_m}\sum_{d=1}^{N_d} w_{m,d}^y \cdot N\left(y;\mu_{m,d}^y, \Sigma_{m,d}^y\right) \tag{8}$$

$$\mu_{m,d}^y = \mu_0^x + g\left(\mu_0^n - \mu_0^x\right) + G\left(\mu_0^n - \mu_0^x\right)\left(\mu_m^x - \mu_0^x\right) + \left[I - G\left(\mu_0^n - \mu_0^x\right)\right]\left(\mu_d^n - \mu_0^n\right)$$

$$\Sigma_{m,d}^y = \left[I + G\left(\mu_0^n - \mu_0^x\right)\right]\Sigma_m^x\left[I + G^T\left(\mu_0^n - \mu_0^x\right)\right]^T \tag{9}$$

$$\mu_0^n = E[\mu_d^n], \quad \mu_0^x = E[\mu_m^x], \quad w_{m,d}^y = w_m \cdot w_d$$

The noisy speech prior model will be employed to search the most similar clean speech mixture component and noise mixture component in sequential noise estimation.

2.2.3. Sequential noise estimation

Sequential EM algorithm is employed for sequential noise estimation. In this section, the prior clean speech, noise and noisy speech model are considered to construct a robust noise estimation procedure. Based on the sequential EM algorithm, the estimated noise is obtained from $n_{t+1} = \arg\max_n Q_{t+1}(n)$. In the E-step of the sequential EM algorithm, an objective function is defined as:

$$Q_{t+1}(n) \triangleq E\left[\ln p(y_1^{t+1}, M_1^{t+1}, D_1^{t+1} \mid n) \mid y_1^{t+1}, n_1^t\right] \tag{10}$$

where M_1^{t+1} and D_1^{t+1} denote the mixture index sequence of the clean speech GMM and the noise GMM in which the noisy speech y occurs from frame 1 to frame t+1. The objective function is simplified for the M-step as:

$$\begin{aligned}
Q_{t+1}(n) &\triangleq E\left[\ln p(y_1^{t+1}, M_1^{t+1}, D_1^{t+1} \mid n) \mid y_1^{t+1}, n_1^t\right] \\
&= E\left[\ln p(y_1^{t+1} \mid M_1^{t+1}, D_1^{t+1}, n) + \ln p(M_1^{t+1} \mid D_1^{t+1}, n) + \ln p(D_1^{t+1} \mid n) \mid y_1^{t+1}, n_1^t\right] \\
&\approx E\left[\ln p(y_1^{t+1} \mid M_1^{t+1}, D_1^{t+1}, n) \mid y_1^{t+1}, n_1^t\right] + Const \\
&= \sum_{\tau=1}^{t+1} E\left[\left(\sum_{m=1}^{N_m}\sum_{d=1}^{N_d}\ln p(y_\tau \mid m, d, n)\cdot\delta_{m_\tau,m}\cdot\delta_{d_\tau,d}\right) \mid y_1^{t+1}, n_1^t\right] + Const \\
&= \sum_{\tau=1}^{t+1}\sum_{m=1}^{N_m}\sum_{d=1}^{N_d} E\left[\delta_{m_\tau,m}\delta_{d_\tau,d} \mid y_1^{t+1}, n_1^t\right]\ln p(y_\tau \mid m, d, n) + Const \\
&= \sum_{\tau=1}^{t+1}\sum_{m=1}^{N_m}\sum_{d=1}^{N_d}\gamma_\tau(m,d)\cdot\ln p(y_\tau \mid m, d, n) + Const
\end{aligned} \tag{11}$$

where $\delta_{m_\tau,m}$ denotes the Kronecker delta function and $\gamma_\tau(m,d)$ denotes the posterior probability. $\gamma_\tau(m,d)$ can be estimated according to the Bayes rule as:

$$\gamma_\tau(m,d) \equiv E\left[\delta_{m_\tau,m}\delta_{d_\tau,d} \mid y_1^{t+1}, n_1^t\right]$$

$$= \sum_{M_1^{t+1}} \sum_{D_1^{t+1}} p\left(M_1^{t+1}, D_1^{t+1} \mid y_1^{t+1}, n_1^t\right)\delta_{m_\tau,m}\delta_{d_\tau,d}$$

$$= p\left(m,d \mid y_\tau, n_{\tau-1}\right) \tag{12}$$

$$= \frac{p\left(y_\tau \mid m,d,n_{\tau-1}\right)p\left(m,d \mid n_{\tau-1}\right)}{\displaystyle\sum_{m=1}^{N_m}\sum_{d=1}^{N_d} p\left(y_\tau \mid m,d,n_{\tau-1}\right)p\left(m,d \mid n_{\tau-1}\right)}$$

$$= \frac{p\left(y_\tau \mid m,d,n_{\tau-1}\right)\cdot w_m \cdot w_d}{\displaystyle\sum_{m=1}^{N_m}\sum_{c=1}^{N_d} p\left(y_\tau \mid m,d,n_{\tau-1}\right)\cdot w_m \cdot w_d}$$

where the likelihood $p\left(y_\tau \mid m,d,n_{\tau-1}\right)$ can be approximated using the approximated linear model as:

$$p\left(y_\tau \mid m,d,n_{\tau-1}\right) \sim N\left[y_\tau; \mu_{m,c}^y\left(n_{\tau-1}\right), \Sigma_{m,d}^y\right]$$

$$\mu_{m,d}^y\left(\mu_{\tau-1}^n\right) = \mu_0^x + g\left(n_0 - \mu_0^x\right) + G\left(n_0 - \mu_0^x\right)\left(\mu_m^x - \mu_0^x\right) + \left[I - G\left(n_0 - \mu_0^x\right)\right]\left(n_{\tau-1} - n_0\right) \tag{13}$$

$$\Sigma_{m,d}^y = \left[I + G\left(n_0 - \mu_0^x\right)\right]\Sigma_m^x\left[I + G^T\left(n_0 - \mu_0^x\right)\right]^T$$

Also, a forgetting factor is employed to control the effect of the features of the preceding frames.

$$Q_{t+1}(n) = \sum_{\tau=1}^{t+1}\varepsilon^{t+1-\tau}\sum_{m=1}^{N_m}\sum_{d=1}^{N_d}\gamma_\tau(m,d)\cdot\ln p(y_\tau \mid m,d,n) + Const$$

$$\tilde{Q}_{t+1}(n) = -\sum_{\tau=1}^{t+1}\varepsilon^{t+1-\tau}\sum_{m=1}^{N_m}\sum_{d=1}^{N_d}\gamma_\tau(m,d)\cdot\left[y_\tau - \mu_{m,d}^y\left(n_\tau\right)\right]^T\left(\Sigma_{m,d}^y\right)^{-1}\left[y_\tau - \mu_{m,d}^y\left(n_\tau\right)\right]$$

$$= \varepsilon\tilde{Q}_t(n) - R_{t+1}(n) \tag{14}$$

$$R_{t+1}(n) = \sum_{m=1}^{N_m}\sum_{d=1}^{N_d}\gamma_{t+1}(m,d)\cdot\left[y_\tau - \mu_{m,d}^y\left(n_\tau\right)\right]^T\left(\Sigma_{m,d}^y\right)^{-1}\left[y_\tau - \mu_{m,d}^y\left(n_\tau\right)\right]$$

In the M-step, the iterative stochastic approximation is introduced to derive the solution. Finally, sequential noise estimation is performed as follows:

$$n_{t+1} = n_t + (K_{t+1})^{-1} s_{t+1} \quad K_{t+1} = -\frac{\partial^2 Q_{t+1}}{\partial^2 n}\big|_{n=n_t} \quad s_{t+1} = -\frac{\partial R_{t+1}}{\partial n}\big|_{n=n_t}$$

$$K_{t+1} = -\frac{\partial^2 Q_{t+1}}{\partial^2 n}\big|_{n=n_t}$$

$$= \sum_{\tau=1}^{t+1} \varepsilon^{t+1-\tau} \sum_{m=1}^{N_m} \sum_{d=1}^{N_d} \gamma_\tau(m,d)\left[I - G\left(n_0 - \mu_0^x\right)\right]^T \left(\Sigma_{m,d}^y\right)^{-1}\left[I - G\left(n_0 - \mu_0^x\right)\right] \tag{15}$$

$$s_{t+1} = -\frac{\partial R_{t+1}}{\partial n}\big|_{n=n_t}$$

$$= \sum_{m=1}^{N_m} \sum_{d=1}^{N_d} \gamma_{t+1}(m,d)\left[I - G\left(n_0 - \mu_0^x\right)\right]^T \left(\Sigma_{m,d}^y\right)^{-1}\left[y_{t+1} - \mu_{m,d}^y(n_t)\right]$$

The prior models are used to search the most similar noise or clean speech mixture component. Given the two mixture components, the estimation of the posterior probability $\gamma_\tau(m,d)$ will be more accurate.

2.3. Environment model adaptation

Because the prior models are usually not complete enough to represent the universal data, the environment mismatch between the training data and the test data will result in the degradation on feature enhancement performance. In this section, an environment model adaptation strategy is proposed before the test phase to deal with the problem. The environment model adaptation procedure contains two parts: The first one is model parameter adaptation on noise prior model Φ_n and noisy speech prior model Φ_y in the training phase and adaptation phase. The second is on noise-normalized SVM function $\Theta^{(e)}$ and environment model Ω_e in the adaptation phase.

2.3.1. Model adaptation on noise and noisy speech prior models

For noise and noisy speech prior model adaptation, MAP adaptation is applied to the noise prior model Φ_n first. The adaptation equations for the noise prior model parameters given T frames of the adaptation noise data z, which is estimated using the un-adapted prior models, are defined as:

$$\widetilde{w}_d = \left(v_d - 1\right) + \sum_{t=1}^{T} s_{d,t} \Big/ \sum_{d=1}^{N_d}\left(v_d - 1\right) + \sum_{d=1}^{N_d}\sum_{t=1}^{T} s_{d,t}$$

$$\widetilde{\mu}_d^n = \tau_d \rho_d + \sum_{t=1}^{T} s_{d,t} \cdot z_t \Big/ \tau_d + \sum_{t=1}^{T} s_{d,t} \tag{16}$$

$$\widetilde{\Sigma}_d^{n^{-1}} = \upsilon_d + \sum_{t=1}^{T} s_{d,t}\left(z_t - \widetilde{\mu}_d^n\right)\left(z_t - \widetilde{\mu}_d^n\right)^T + \tau_d\left(\rho_d - \widetilde{\mu}_d^n\right)\left(\rho_d - \widetilde{\mu}_d^n\right)^T \Big/ \left(\alpha_d - p\right) + \sum_{t=1}^{T} s_{d,t}$$

where the conjugate prior density of the mixture weight is the Dirichlet distribution with hyper-parameter v_d and the joint conjugate prior density of mean and variance parameters is the Normal-Wishart distribution with hyper-parameters τ_d, ρ_d, α_d, and υ_d. The two distributions are defined as follows:

$$g\left(w_1,...,w_{N_d} \mid v_1,...,v_{N_d}\right) \propto \prod_{d=1}^{N_d} w_d^{v_d-1}$$

$$g\left(\mu_d^n, \Sigma_d^n \mid \tau_d, \rho_d, \alpha_d, \upsilon_d\right) \propto \left|\Sigma_d^n\right|^{(\alpha_d-p)/2} \exp\left[-\frac{\tau_d}{2}\left(\mu_d^n - \rho_d\right)^T \tau_d \left(\mu_d^n - \rho_d\right)\right] \exp\left[-\frac{1}{2}\text{tr}\left(\upsilon_d \Sigma_d^n\right)\right] \tag{17}$$

where $v_d > 0$, $\alpha_k > p-1$ and $\tau_k > 0$. After adaptation of noise prior model, the noisy speech prior model Φ_y is then adapted using the clean speech prior model Φ_x and the newly adapted noise prior model Φ_n based on Eq.**Error! Reference source not found.**(8).

2.3.2. Model adaptation of noise-normalized SVM (NN-SVM)

For NN-SVM adaptation, model parameters Ω_e and mapping function parameters in $F\left(y; \Theta^{(e)}\right)$ need to be adapted in the adaptation phase. First, adaptation of model parameter Ω_e is similar to that of noise prior model. Second, the adaptation of $\Theta^{(e)} = \left\{r_k^{(e)}\right\}_{k=1}^{N_k}$ is an iterative procedure. While $\Theta^{(e)} = \left\{r_k^{(e)}\right\}_{k=1}^{N_k}$ is not a random variable and does not follow any conjugate prior density, a maximum likelihood (ML)-based adaptation which is similar to the correction vector estimation of SPLICE is employed as:

$$\widetilde{r_k^{(e)}} = \sum_t p\left(k \mid y_t - \tilde{n}, e\right)\left(\tilde{x}_t - y_t\right) \Big/ \sum_t p\left(k \mid y_t - \tilde{n}, e\right) \tag{18}$$

where the temporal estimated clean speech $\tilde{x}_t$ are estimated using the un-adapted noise normalized stochastic mapping function in Eq.(4).

2.4. Experimental results

Table 1 shows the experimental results of the proposed approach on AURORA2 database. The AURORA2 database contains both clean and noisy utterances of the TIDIGITS corpus and is available from ELDA (Evaluations and Language resources Distribution Agency). Two results of previous research were illustrated for comparison and three experiments were conducted for different experimental conditions: no denoising, SPLICE with recursive EM using stereo data (Deng et al. 2003), the proposed approach using manual annotation without adaptation, and the proposed approach using auto-clustered training data without and with adaptation. The overall results show that the proposed approach slightly outperformed the SPLICE-based approach with recursive EM algorithm under the lack of stereo training data and manual annotation. Furthermore, based on the results in Set B with 0.11% improvement (different background noise types to the training data) and Set C with

0.04% improvement (different background noise types and channel characteristic to the training data), the environment model adaptation can slightly reduce the mismatch between the training data and test data.

Methods	Training-Mode	Set A	Set B	Set C	Overall
No Denoising	Multi-condition	87.82	86.27	83.78	86.39
	Clean only	61.34	55.75	66.14	60.06
MCE	Multi-condition	92.92	89.15	90.09	90.85
	Clean only	87.82	85.34	83.77	86.02
SPLICE with Recursive-EM	Multi-condition	91.49	89.16	89.62	90.18
	Clean only	87.82	87.09	85.08	86.98
Proposed approach (manual tag, no adaptation)	Multi-condition	91.42	89.18	89.85	90.21
	Clean only	87.84	86.77	85.23	86.89
Proposed approach (auto-clustering, no adaptation)	Multi-condition	91.06	90.79	90.77	90.89
	Clean only	87.56	87.33	86.32	87.22
Proposed approach (auto-clustering, with adaptation)	Multi-condition	91.07	90.90	90.81	90.95
	Clean only	87.55	87.44	86.38	87.27

Table 1. Experimental results (%) on AURORA2

2.5. Conclusions

In this section two approaches to cepstral feature enhancement for noisy speech recognition using noise-normalized stochastic vector mapping are presented. The prior model was introduced for precise noise estimation. Then the environment model adaptation is constructed to reduce the environment mismatch between the training data and the test data. Experimental results demonstrate that the proposed approach can slightly outperform the SPLICE-based approach without stereo data on AURORA2 database.

3. Speech recognition in disfluent environment

In this section, a novel approach to detecting and correcting the edit disfluency in spontaneous speech is presented. Hypothesis testing using acoustic features is fist adopted to detect potential interruption points (IPs) in the input speech. The word order of the utterance is then cleaned up based on the potential IPs using a class-based cleanup language model. The deletable region and the correction are aligned using an alignment model. Finally, a log linear weighting mechanism is applied to optimize the performance.

3.1. Edit disfluency ANalsis

In conversational utterances, several problems such as interruption, correction, filled pause, and ungrammatical sentence are detrimental for speech recognition. The definitions of disfluencies have been discussed in SimpleMDE. Edit disfluencies are portions of speech in which a speaker's utterance is not complete and fluent; instead the speaker corrects or alters the utterance, or abandons it entirely and starts over. In general, edit disfluencies can be divided into four categories: repetitions, revisions, restarts and complex disfluencies. Since complex disfluencies consist of multiple or nested edits, it seems reasonable to consider the complex disfluencies as a combination of the other simple disfluencies: repetitions, revisions, and restarts. Edit disfluencies have a complex internal structure, consisting of the deletable region (delreg), interruption point (IP) and correction. Editing terms such as fillers, particles and markers are optional and follow the IP in edit disfluency.

In spontaneous speech, acoustic features such as short pause (silence and filler), energy and pitch reset generally appear along with the occurrence of edit dislfuency. Based on these features, we can detect the possible IPs. Furthermore, since IPs generally appear at the boundary of two successive words, we can exclude the unlikely IPs whose positions are within a word. Besides, since the structural patterns between the deletable word sequence and correction word sequence are very similar, the deletable word sequence in edit disfluency is replaceable by the correction word sequence.

3.2. Framework of edit disfluency transcription system

The overall transcription task for conversational speech with edit disfluency in the proposed method is composed of two main mechanisms; IP detection module and edit disfluency correction module. The framework is shown in Figure 2. IP detection module predicts the potential IPs first. Edit disfluency correction module generates the rich transcription that contains information of interruption, text transcription from the speaker's utterances and the cleaned-up text transcription without disfluencies. Figure 3 shows the correction process for edit disfluency.

The speech signal is fed to both acoustic feature extraction module and speech recognition engine in IP detection module. Information about durations of syllables and silence from speech recognition is provided for acoustic feature extraction. Combined with side information from speech recognition, duration-, pitch-, and energy-related features are extracted and used to model the IPs using a Gaussian mixture model (GMM). Besides, in order to perform hypothesis testing on IP detection, an anti-IP GMM is also constructed based on the extracted features from the non-IP regions. The hypothesis testing verifies if the posterior probability of the acoustic features of a syllable boundary is above a threshold and therefore determines if the syllable boundary is an IP. Since IP is an event that happens in interword location, we can remove the detected IPs that do not appear in the word boundary.

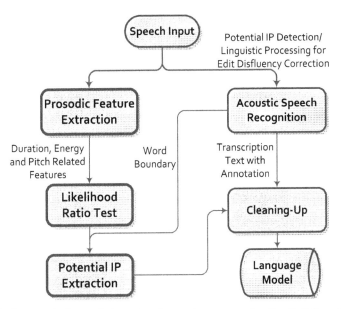

Figure 2. The framework of transcription system for spontaneous speech with edit disfluencies

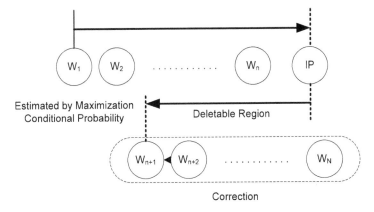

Figure 3. The correction process for the edit disfluency

There are two processing stages in the edit disfluency correction module: cleanup and alignment. As shown in Figure 4, cleanup process divides the word string into three parts: deletable region (delreg), editing term, and correction according to the locations of potential IPs detected by the IP detection module. Cleanup process is performed by shifting the correction part and replaces the deletable region to form a new cleanup transcription. The edit disfluency correction module is composed of an n-gram language model and the alignment model. The n-gram model regards the cleanup transcriptions as fluent utterances and models their word order information. The alignment model finds the optimal correspondence between deletable region and correction in edit disfluency.

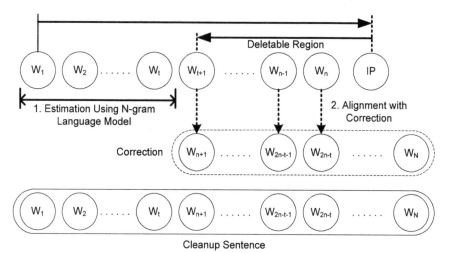

Figure 4. The cleanup language model for the edit disfluency

3.3. Potential interruption point detection

For IP detection, instead of detecting exact IP, potential IPs are selected for further processing. Since the IP is the point at which the speaker breaks off the deletable region, some acoustic events will go along with it. For syllabic languages like Chinese, every character is pronounced as a monosyllable, while a word is composed of one to several syllables. The speech input of the syllabic languages with n syllables can be described as a sequence,

$$Seq_{syllable\_silence} \equiv syllable_1, silence_1, syllable_2, silence_2, ..., silence_{n-1}, syllable_n,$$

and then this sequence can be separated into a syllable sequence

$$Seq_{syllable} \equiv syllable_1, syllable_2, ..., syllable_n,$$

and a silence sequence

$$Seq_{silence} \equiv silence_1, silence_2, ..., silence_{n-1}.$$

We model the interruption detection problem as choosing between H_0, which is termed the IP not embedded in the silence hypothesis, and H_1 which is the IP embedded in the silence hypothesis. The likelihood ratio test is employed to detect the potential IPs. The function $L\left(Seq_{syllable\_silence}\right)$ is termed the likelihood ratio since it indicates for each value of $Sequence_{syllable\_silence}$ the likelihood of H_1 versus the likelihood of H_0.

$$L\left(Seq_{syllable\_silence}\right) = \frac{P\left(Seq_{syllable\_silence}; H_1\right)}{P\left(Seq_{syllable\_silence}; H_0\right)} \tag{19}$$

By introducing the threshold γ to adjust the precision and recall rates, $H_1 : L\left(Seq_{syllable\_silence}\right) \geq \gamma$ means the IP is embedded in $silence_k$. Conceptually, $silence_k$ is a potential IP. Under the assumption of independence, the probability of IP appearing in $silence_k$ can be regarded as the product of probabilities obtained from $silence_k$ and the syllables around it. The probability density functions (PDFs) under each hypothesis are denoted and estimated as

$$\begin{aligned} P\left(Seq_{syllable\_silence}; H_1\right) &= P\left(Seq_{syllable\_silence} \mid E_{ip}\right) \\ &= P\left(Seq_{silence} \mid E_{ip}\right) \times P\left(Seq_{syllable} \mid E_{ip}\right) \end{aligned} \tag{20}$$

and

$$\begin{aligned} P\left(Seq_{syllable\_silence}; H_0\right) &= P\left(Seq_{syllable\_silence} \mid \neg E_{ip}\right) \\ &= P\left(Seq_{silence} \mid \neg E_{ip}\right) \times P\left(Seq_{syllable} \mid \neg E_{ip}\right) \end{aligned} \tag{21}$$

Where E_{ip} denotes that IP is embedded in $silence_k$ and $\neg E_{ip}$ means that IP does not appear in $silence_k$, that is,

E_{ip} : Interuption point $\in silence_k$

$\neg E_{ip}$: Interuption point $\notin silence_k$

3.3.1. IP detection using posterior probability of silence duration

Since IPs always appear at the inter-syllable position, the n-1 silence positions between n syllables will be considered as the IP candidates. By this, we can take the IP detection as the problem to verify whether each of the n-1 silence positions is an IP or not. In conversation, speakers may hesitate to find the correct words when disfluency appears. Hesitation is usually realized as a pause. Since the length of silence is very sensitive to disfluency, we use normal distributions to model the posterior probabilities of that IP appears and does not appear in $silence_k$, respectively.

$$P\left(Seq_{silence} \mid E_{ip}\right) = \frac{2}{\sqrt{2\pi}\sigma_{ip}} \exp\left(-\frac{\left(Seq_{silence} - \mu_{ip}\right)^2}{2\sigma_{ip}^{\,2}}\right) \tag{22}$$

$$P\left(Seq_{silence} \mid \neg E_{ip}\right) = \frac{2}{\sqrt{2\pi}\sigma_{nip}} \exp\left(-\frac{\left(Seq_{silence} - \mu_{nip}\right)^2}{2\sigma_{nip}^{\,2}}\right) \tag{23}$$

Where μ_{ip}, μ_{nip}, σ_{nip}^2 and σ_{ip}^2 denote the means and variances of the silence duration containing and not containing the IP, respectively.

3.3.2. Syllable-based acoustic features extraction

Acoustic features including duration, pitch, and energy for each syllable (Soltau et al. 2005) are adopted for IP detection. A feature vector of the syllables within an observation window around the silence is formed as the input of the GMM. That is, we are interested in the syllables around the silence that may appear as an IP. A window of $2w$ syllables with w syllables after and before $silence_k$ is used. First, the subscript will be translated according to the position of silence as $Syl_{n-k} \leftarrow Syl_n$. And we then extract the features of syllables within the observation windows.

Since the durations of syllables are not the same even for the same syllable, the duration ratio is defined as the average duration of the syllable normalized by the average duration over all syllables.

$$nf_{duration_i} \equiv \frac{\sum\limits_{j=1}^{n_i} duration\left(syllable_{i.j}\right)}{\sum\limits_{i=1}^{|syllable|} \sum\limits_{j=1}^{n_i} duration\left(syllable_{i.j}\right)} \tag{24}$$

Where $syllable_{i.j}$ means the j-th samples of syllable i in the corpus. $|syllable|$ means the number of the syllable. n_i is the number of syllable i in the corpus. Similarly, for energy and pitch, frame-based statistics are used to calculate the normalized features for each syllable.

Considering the result of speech recognition, the features are normalized to be the first order features. For modeling the speaking rate and variation in the energy and pitch during the utterance, the 2nd order feature called delta-duration, delta-energy and delta-pitch are obtained from the forward difference of the 1st order features. The following equation shows the estimation for delta-duration, which can also be applied for the estimation of delta-energy and delta-pitch.

$$\Delta nf_{duration_i} = \begin{cases} nf_{duration_{i+1}} - nf_{duration_i} & if \ -w < i < w \\ 0 & others \end{cases} \tag{25}$$

Where w is half of the observation window size. Totally, there are three kinds of two orders features after feature extraction. We combine these features to form a vector with $24w-6$ features to be the observation vector of the GMM. The acoustic features are denoted as the syllable-based observation sequence that corresponds to the potential IP, $silence_k$, by

$$\left\{O = \left[O_D, O_P, O_E\right] \in R^{dim}\right\} \tag{26}$$

Where $O_s \in R^{\dim_s}$, $S \in \{D, P, E\}$ represents the single kind feature vectors and *dim* means the dimensions of the feature vector consisting of duration-related, pitch-related and energy-related features. The following equation shows the estimation for duration-related features.

$$O_D \equiv \begin{bmatrix} nf_{duration_{-w+1}}, \ldots, nf_{duration_{-1}}, nf_{duration_0}, nf_{duration_{+1}}, nf_{duration_{+2}}, \ldots, nf_{duration_{+w}} \\ \Delta nf_{duration_{-w+1}}, \ldots, \Delta nf_{duration_{-1}}, \Delta nf_{duration_0}, \Delta nf_{duration_{+1}}, \Delta nf_{duration_{+2}}, \ldots, \Delta nf_{duration_{+w-1}} \end{bmatrix}^T \quad (27)$$

3.3.3. Gaussian mixture model for interruption point detection

The GMM is adopted for IP detection using the acoustic features.

$$P\left(Seq_{syllable} \mid C_j\right) \equiv P\left(O_t \mid \lambda_j\right) = \sum_{i=1}^{W} \omega_i N\left(O_t; \mu_i, \Sigma_i\right) \quad (28)$$

Where $C_j = \left\{E_{ip}, \neg E_{ip}\right\}$ means the hypothesis set for *silencek* containing and not containing the IP. λ_j is the GMM for class C_j and ω_i is a mixture weight which must satisfy the constraint $\sum_{i=1}^{W} \omega_i = 1$, where W is the number of mixture components, and $N(\cdot)$ is the Gaussian density function:

$$N\left(O_t; \mu_i, \Sigma_i\right) = \frac{1}{\left(2\pi\right)^{\dim/2} |\Sigma_i|^{1/2}} \exp\left(-\frac{1}{2}\left(O_t - \mu_i\right)^T \Sigma_i^{-1}\left(O_t - \mu_i\right)\right) \quad (29)$$

where μ_i and Σ_i are the mean vector and covariance matrix of the *i*-th component. O_t denotes the *t*-th observation in the training corpus. The parameters $\theta = \left[\omega_i, \mu_i, \Sigma_i\right]$, $i = 1..M$ can be estimated iteratively using the EM algorithm for mixture *i*

$$\hat{\omega}_i = \frac{1}{N} \sum_{t=1}^{N} P\left(i \mid O_t, \lambda\right) \quad (30)$$

$$\hat{\mu}_i = \frac{\sum_{t=1}^{N} P\left(i \mid O_t, \lambda\right) O_t}{\sum_{t=1}^{N} P\left(i \mid O_t, \lambda\right)} \quad (31)$$

$$\hat{\Sigma}_i = \frac{\sum_{t=1}^{N} P\left(i \mid O_t, \lambda\right)\left(O_t - \hat{\mu}_i\right)\left(O_t - \hat{\mu}_i\right)^T}{\sum_{t=1}^{N} P\left(i \mid O_t, \lambda\right)} \quad (32)$$

Where $P(i \mid O_t, \lambda) = \dfrac{P(O_t \mid \lambda)\omega_i}{\sum\limits_{j=1}^{W} P(O_t \mid \lambda)\omega_j}$ and N denote the total number of feature observations.

3.3.4. Potential interruption point extraction

Based on the assumption that IP appears generally at the boundary of two successive words, we can remove the detected IPs that do not appear in the word boundary. After the removal of unlikely IPs, the remaining IPs will be kept for further processing. Since the word graph or word lattice is obtained from speech recognition module, every path in the word graph or word lattice form its potential IP set for an input utterance.

3.4. Lingusitic processing for edit disfluency correction

In previous section, potential IPs has been detected from the acoustic features. However, correcting edit disfluency using the linguistic features is, in fact, one of the keys for rich transcription. In this section, the edit disfluency is detected by maximizing the likelihood of the language model for the cleaned-up utterances and the word correspondence between the deletable region and the correction given the position of the IP. Consider the word sequence W in the word lattice generated by the speech recognition engine. We can model the word string W using a log linear mixture model in which language model and alignment are both included.

$$
\begin{aligned}
W^* &= \underset{W, IP}{\arg\max}\, P(W; IP) \\
&= \underset{W, IP}{\arg\max}\, P(w_1, w_2, \ldots w_t, w_{t+1}, \ldots w_n, w_{n+1}, \ldots w_{2n-t}, w_{2n-t+1}, \ldots w_N; IP) \\
&= \underset{W, n, t}{\arg\max}\left(\begin{array}{l} P(w_1, w_2, \ldots w_t, w_{n+1}, \ldots w_{2n-t}, w_{2n-t+1}, \ldots w_N)^{\alpha} \\ \times P(w_{t+1}, \ldots w_n \mid w_{n+1}, \ldots w_{2n-t}, w_{2n-t+1}, \ldots w_N)^{(1-\alpha)} \end{array} \right) \\
&= \underset{W, n, t}{\arg\max}\left(\begin{array}{l} \alpha \log\big(P(w_1, w_2, \ldots w_t, w_{n+1}, \ldots w_{2n-t}, w_{2n-t+1}, \ldots w_N)\big) \\ +(1-\alpha)\log\big(P(w_{t+1}, \ldots w_n \mid w_{n+1}, \ldots w_{2n-t}, w_{2n-t+1}, \ldots w_N)\big) \end{array} \right)
\end{aligned}
\tag{33}
$$

where α and $1-\alpha$ are the combination weight for cleanup language model and alignment model. IP means the interruption point obtained from the IP detection module and n is the position of the potential IP.

3.4.1. Language model of cleanup utterance

In the past, statistical language models have been applied to speech recognition and have achieved significant improvement in the recognition results. However, probability estimation of word sequences can be expensive and always suffers from the problem of data sparseness. In practice, the statistical language model is often approximated by the class-based *n*-gram model with modified Kneser-Ney discounting probabilities for further smoothing.

$$P\left(w_1, w_2, \ldots w_t, w_{n+1}, \ldots w_{2n-t}, w_{2n-t+1}, \ldots w_N\right)$$
$$= \prod_{i=1}^{t} P\left(w_i \mid Class\left(w_1^{i-1}\right)\right) P\left(w_{n+1} \mid Class\left(w_1^t\right)\right) \prod_{j=n+2}^{N} P\left(w_j \mid Class\left(w_1^t w_{n+1}^{j-1}\right)\right) \tag{34}$$

Where $Class(\cdot)$ means the conversion function that translates a word sequence into a word class sequence. In this section, we employ two word classes: semantic class and parts-of-speech (POS) class. A semantic class, such as the synsets in WordNet (http://wordnet.princeton.edu/) or concepts in the UMLS (http://www.nlm.nih.gov/research/umls/), contains the words that share a semantic property based on semantic relations, such as hyponym and hypernym. POS is called syntactic or grammatical categories defined as the role that a word plays in a sentence such as noun, verb, adjective… etc.

The other essential issue of *n*-gram model for correcting edit disfluency is the number of orders in Markov model. Since IP is the point at which the speaker breaks off the deletable region and the correction consists of the portion of the utterance that has been repaired by the speaker and can be considered fluent. By removing part of the word string will lead to a shorter string and result in the condition that higher probability is obtained for shorter word string. As a result, short word string will be favored. To deal with this problem, we can increase the order to constrain the perplexity and normalize the word length by aligning the deletable region and the correction.

3.4.2. Alignment model between the deletable region and the correction

In conversational speech, the structural pattern of a deletable region is usually similar to that of the correction. Sometimes, the deletable region appears as a substring of the correction. Accordingly, we can find the structural pattern in the starting point of the correction which generally follows the IP. Then, we can take the potential IP as the center and align the word string before and after it. Since the correction is used for replacing the deletable region and ending the utterance, there exists a correspondence between the words in the deletable region and the correction. We may, therefore, model the alignment assuming the conditional probability of the correction given the possible deletable region. According to this observation, class-based alignment is proposed to clean up edit disfluency. The alignment model can be described as

$$P\left(w_{n+1}, \ldots w_{2n-t}, w_{2n-t+1}, \ldots w_N \mid w_{t+1}, \ldots w_n\right)$$
$$= \prod_{k=t+1}^{n} \left(P\left(f_k \mid Class\left(w_k\right)\right) \prod_{l=1}^{f_k} P\left(Class\left(w_l\right) \mid Class\left(w_k\right)\right) \right) \prod_{k,l,m} P\left(l \mid k, m\right) \tag{35}$$

where fertility f_k means the number of words in the correction corresponding to the word w_k in the deletable region. k and l are the positions of the words w_k and w_l in the deletable region and the correction, respectively. m denotes the number of words in the deletable region. The alignment model for cleanup contains three parts: fertility probability, translation or corresponding probability and distortion probability. The fertility probability of word w_k is defined as

$$P\left(f_k \mid Class\left(w_k\right)\right) = \frac{\displaystyle\sum_{w_{i \in Class\left(w_k\right)}} \delta\left(f_i = f_k\right)}{\displaystyle\sum_{p=0}^{N} \sum_{w_{j \in Class\left(w_k\right)}} \delta\left(f_j = p\right)} \qquad (36)$$

where $\delta(\cdot)$ is an indicator function and N means the maximum value of fertility. The translation or corresponding probability is measured according to (Wu et al. 1994).

$$P\left(Class\left(w_l\right) \mid Class\left(w_k\right)\right) = \frac{2 \times Depth\left(LCS\left(Class\left(w_l\right), Class\left(w_k\right)\right)\right)}{Depth\left(Class\left(w_l\right)\right) + Depth\left(Class\left(w_k\right)\right)} \qquad (37)$$

where $Depth(\cdot)$ denotes the depth of the word class and $LCN(\cdot)$ denotes the lowest common subsumer of the words. The distortion probability $P(l \mid k, m)$ is the mapping probability of the word sequence between the deletable region and the correction.

3.5. Experimental results and discussion

To evaluate the performance of the proposed approach, a transcription system for spontaneous speech with edit dsifluencies in Mandarin was developed. A speech recognition engine using Hidden Markov Model Toolkit (HTK) was constructed as the syllable recognizer using 8 states (3 states for initial, and 5 states for final in Mandarin).

3.5.1. Experimental data

The Mandarin Conversational Dialogue Corpus (MCDC), collected from 2000 to 2001 at the Institute of Linguistics of Academia Sinica, Taiwan, consists of 30 digitized conversational dialogues of a total length of 27 hours. 60 subjects were randomly chosen from daily life in Taiwan area. It was annotated according to (Yeh et al. 2006) that gives concise explanations and detailed operational definitions of each tag in Mandarin. Corresponding to SimpleMDE, direct repetitions, partial repetitions, overt repairs and abandoned utterances are taken as edit disfluency in MCDC. The dialogs tagged as number 01, 02, 03 and 05 are used as the test corpus. For training the parameters in the speech recognizer, MAT Speech Database, TCC-300 and MCDC were employed.

3.5.2. Potential interruption point detection

According to the observation of the MCDC, the probability density function (pdf) of the duration of the silences with or without IPs is obtained. The average duration of the silences with IP is larger than that of the silences without IP. According to this result, we can estimate the posterior probability of silence duration using a GMM for IP detection. For hypothesis testing, an anti-IP GMM is also constructed.

Since IP detection can be regarded as a position determination problem, an observation window over several syllables is adopted. In this observation window, the values of pitch and energy of the syllables just before an IP are usually larger than that after the IP. This phenomenon means the pitch reset and energy reset co-occur with IP in the edit disfluency. This generally happens in the syllables of the first word just after the IP. The pitch reset event is very obvious when the disfluency type is repair. Similar to the pitch, energy plays the same role when edit disfluency appears, but the effect is not so obvious compared to the pitch. The filler words or phrase after IP will be lengthened to strive for the time for the speaker to construct the correction and attract the listener to pay attention to. This factor can achieve significant improvement in IP detection rate.

The hypothesis testing, combined with the GMM model with four mixture components using the syllable features, will determine if the silence contains the IP. The parameter γ should be determined to achieve a better result. The overall IP error rate defined in RT'04F will be simply the average number of missed IP detections and falsely detected IPs per reference IP:

$$Error_{IP} = \frac{n_{M-IP} + n_{FA-IP}}{n_{IP}} \tag{38}$$

Where n_{M-IP} and n_{FA-IP} denote the numbers of missed and false alarm IPs respectively. n_{IP} means the number of reference IPs. We can adjust the threshold γ for n_{M-IP} and n_{FA-IP}.

Since the goal of the IP detection module is to detect the potential IPs, false alarm for IP detection is not a serious problem compared to miss error. That is to say, we want to obtain high recall rate without much increase in false alarm rate. Finally, the threshold γ was set to 0.25. Since the IP always appears in word boundary, this constraint can be used to remove unlikely IPs.

3.5.3. Clean-up disfluency using linguistic information

For evaluating the edit disfluency correction model, two different types of transcriptions were used: human generated transcription (REF) and speech-to-text recognition output (STT). Using the reference transcriptions provides the best case for the evaluation of the edit disfluency correction module because there are no word errors in the transcription. For practicability, the syllable lattice from speech recognition is fed to the edit disfluency correction module for performance assessment.

For class-based approach, part of speech (POS) and semantic class are employed as the word class. Herein, semantic class is obtained based on Hownet (http://www.keenage.com/) that defines the relation "IS-A" as the primary feature. There are 26 and 30 classes in POS class and semantic class respectively. By this, we can categorize the words according to their hypernyms or concepts, and every word can map to its own semantic class.

The edit word detection (EWD) task is to detect the regions of the input speech containing the words in the deletable regions. One of the primary metrics for edit disfluency correction is to use the edit word detection method defined in RT'04F (Chen et al. 2002), which is similar to the metric for IP detection shown in Eq. (38).

Due to the lack of structural information, unigram does not obtain any improvement. Bigram provides more significant improvement combined with POS class-based alignment than semantic class-based alignment. Using 3-gram and semantic class-based alignment outperforms other combinations. The reason is that 3-gram with more strict constraints can reduce the false alarm rate for edit word detection. In fact, we also tried using 4-gram to gain more improvement than 3-gram, but the excess computation makes the light improvement not conspicuous as we expected. Besides, the statistics of 4-gram is too spare compared to 3-gram model. The best combination in edit disfluency correction module is 3-gram and semantic class.

According to the analysis of the results shown in Table 2, we can find the values of the probabilities of the n-gram model are much smaller than that of the alignment model. Since the alignment can be taken as the penalty for edit words, we should balance the effects between the 3-gram and the alignment with semantic class using a log linear combination weight α. For optimizing the performance, we estimate α empirically based on the minimization of the edit word errors.

	Human generated transcription (REF)			Speech-to-text recognition output (STT)		
	$\dfrac{n_{M-EWD}}{n_{EWD}}$	$\dfrac{n_{FA-EWD}}{n_{EWD}}$	$Error_{EWD}$	$\dfrac{n_{M-EWD}}{n_{EWD}}$	$\dfrac{n_{FA-EWD}}{n_{EWD}}$	$Error_{EWD}$
1-gram+alignment[1]	0.15	0.17	0.32	0.58	0.65	1.23
1-gram+alignment[2]	0.23	0.12	0.35	0.62	0.42	1.04
2-gram+alignment[1]	0.09	0.15	0.24	0.46	0.43	0.87
2-gram+alignment[2]	0.10	0.11	0.21	0.38	0.36	0.74
3-gram+alignment[1]	0.12	0.04	0.16	0.39	0.23	0.62
3-gram+alignment[2]	**0.11**	**0.04**	**0.15**	0.36	0.24	0.60

[1]: word class based on the part of speech (POS) [2]: word class based on the semantic class

Table 2. Results (%) of linguistic module with equal weight $\alpha = (1-\alpha) = 0.5$ for edit word detection on REF and STT conditions

3.6. Conclusion and future work

This investigation has proposed an approach to edit disfluency detection and correction for rich transcription. The proposed theoretical approach, based on a two stage process, aims to model the behavior of edit disfluency and cleanup the disfluency. IP detection module using hypothesis testing from the acoustic features is employed to detect the potential IPs. Word-based linguistic module consists of a cleanup language model and an alignment model is used for verifying the position of the IP and therefore correcting the edit disfluency. Experimental results indicate that the IP detection mechanism is able to recall IPs by adjusting the threshold in hypothesis testing. In an investigation of the linguistic properties of edit disfluency, the linguistic module was explored for correcting disfluency based on the potential IPs. The experimental results indicate a significant improvement in performance was achieved. In the future, this framework will be extended to deal with the problem resulted from subword to improve the performance of the rich transcription system.

4. Speech recognition in multilingual environment

This section presents an approach to generating phonetic units for mixed-language or multilingual speech recognition. Acoustic and contextual analysis is performed to characterize multilingual phonetic units for phone set creation. Acoustic likelihood is utilized for similarity estimation of phone models. The hyperspace analog to language (HAL) model is adopted for contextual modeling and contextual similarity estimation. A confusion matrix combining acoustic and contextual similarities between every two phonetic units is built for phonetic unit clustering. Multidimensional scaling (MDS) method is applied to the confusion matrix for reducing dimensionality.

4.1. Introduction

In multilingual speech recognition, it is very important to determine a global phone inventory for different languages. When an authentic multilingual phone set is defined, the acoustic models and pronunciation lexicon can be constructed (Chen et al. 2002). The simplest approach to phone set definition is to combine the phone inventories of different languages together without sharing the units across the languages. The second one is to map language-dependent phones to the global inventory of the multilingual phonetic association based on phonetic knowledge to construct the multilingual phone inventory. Several global phone-based phonetic representations such as International Phonetic Alphabet (IPA) (Mathews 1979), Speech Assessment Methods Phonetic Alphabet (Wells 1989) and Worldbet (Hieronymus 1993) are generally used. The third one is to merge the language-dependent phone models using a hierarchical phone clustering algorithm to obtain a compact multilingual inventory. In this approach, the distance measure between acoustic models, such as Bhattacharyya distance (Mak et al. 1996) and Kullback-Leibler (KL) divergence (Goldberger et al. 2005), is employed to perform the bottom-up clustering. Finally, the multilingual phone models are generated with the use of a phonetic top-down clustering procedure (Young et al. 1994).

4.2. Multilingual phone set definition

From the viewpoint of multilingual speech recognition, a phonetic representation is functionally defined by the mapping of the fundamental phonetic units of languages to describe the corresponding pronunciation. In this section, IPA-based multilingual phone definition is suitable and consistent for phonetic representation. Using phonetic representation of the IPA, the recognition units can be effectively reduced for multilingual speech recognition. Considering the co-articulated pronunciation, context-dependent triphones are adopted in the expansion of IPA-based phonetic units.

In multilingual speech recognition, misrecognition generally results from incorrect pronunciation or confusable phonetic set. For examples, in Mandarin speech, the "ei_M" and "zh_M" is usually pronounced as "en_M" and "z_M", respectively. In this section, statistical methods are proposed to deal with the problem of misrecognition caused by the confusing characteristics between phonetic units in multilingual speech recognition. Based on the analysis of confusing characteristics, confusing phones due in part to the confusable phonetic representation are redefined to alleviate the misrecognition problem.

4.2.1. Acoustic likelihood

For the estimation of the confusion between two phone models, the posterior probabilities obtained from the phone-based hidden Markov model (HMM) are employed. Given two phone models, ω_k and ω_l, trained with the corresponding training data, x_i^k, $1 \leq i \leq I$ and x_j^l, $1 \leq j \leq J$, the symmetric acoustic likelihood (ACL) between two phone models, ω_k and ω_l, are estimated as follows.

$$a_{k,l} = \frac{\sum_{i=1}^{I} P(x_i^l \mid \omega_k) + \sum_{j=1}^{J} P(x_j^k \mid \omega_l)}{I + J} \tag{39}$$

where I and J represent the number of training data for phone models, ω_k and ω_l, respectively. The acoustic confusing matrix $A = (a_{k,l})_{N \times N}$ is obtained from the pairwise similarities between every two phone models, and N denotes the number of phone models.

4.2.2. Contextual analysis

A co-articulation pattern can be considered as a semantically plausible combination of phones. This section presents a text mining framework to automatically induce co-articulation patterns from a mixed-language or a multilingual corpus. A crucial step to induce the co-articulation patterns is to represent speech intonation as well as combination of phones. To achieve this goal, the hyperspace analog to language (HAL) model constructs a high-dimensional contextual space for the mixed-language or multilingual corpus. Each context-dependent triphone in the HAL space is represented as a vector of its context phones, which represents that the sense of a phone can be co-articulated through its context phones. Such notion is derived from the observation of articulation behavior. Based on the co-articulation behavior, if two phones share more common context, they are more similarly articulated.

The HAL model represents the multilingual triphones based on a vector representation. Each dimension of the vector is a weight representing the strength of association between the target phone and its context phone. The weights are computed by applying an observation window of length ℓ over the corpus. All phones within the window are considered as the co-articulated pronunciation with each other. For any two phones of distance d within the window, the weight between them is defined as $\ell - d + 1$. After moving the window by one phone increment over the sentence, the HAL space $G = (g_{k,l})_{N \times N}$ is constructed. The resultant HAL space is an $N \times N$ matrix, where N is the number of triphones.

Table 3 presents the HAL space for the example of English and Mandarin mixed sentence " 查一下<look up> (CH A @ I X I A) Baghdad (B AE G D AE D)." For each phone in Table 3, the corresponding row vector represents its left contextual information, i.e. the weights of the phones preceding it. The corresponding column vector represents its right contextual information. $w_{k,l}$ indicates the k-th weight of the l-th triphone φ_l. Furthermore, the weights in the vector are re-estimated as described as follows.

$$\overline{w}_{k,l} = w_{k,l} \times \log \frac{N}{N_l} \tag{40}$$

where N denotes the total number of phone vectors and N_l represents the number of vectors of phone φ_l with nonzero dimension. After each dimension is re-weighted, the HAL space is transformed into a probabilistic framework, and thus each weight can be redefined as

$$\hat{w}_{k,l} = \frac{\overline{w}_{k,l}}{\sum\limits_{k=1}^{N} \overline{w}_{k,l}} \tag{41}$$

To generate a symmetric matrix, the weight is averaged as

$$g_{k,l} = \frac{\hat{w}_{k,l} + \hat{w}_{l,k}}{2}, \quad 1 \leq k, l \leq N$$

4.2.3. Fusion of confusing matrices and dimensional reduction

The multidimensional scaling (MDS) method is used to project multilingual triphones to the orthogonal axes where the ranking distance relation between them can be estimated using Euclidean distance. MDS is generally a procedure which characterizes the data in terms of a matrix of pairwise distances using Euclidean distance estimation. One of the purposes of

MDS is to reduce the data dimensionality into a low-dimensional space. The IPA-based phone alphabet is 55 for English and Mandarin. This makes around 166,375 ($55 \times 55 \times 55$) triphone numbers. When the number of target languages is increased, the dimension of the confusing matrix becomes huge. Another purpose of multidimensional scaling is to project the elements in the matrix to the orthogonal axes where the ranking distance relation between elements in the confusion matrix can be estimated. Compared to the hierarchical clustering method (Mak et al. 1996), this section applies MDS to the global similarity measure of multilingual triphones.

	CH	A	@	I	X	B	AE	G	D
CH									
A	3			4	1				
@	2	3							
I	1	2	4		3				
X		1	2	3					
B	3			2	1				
AE	2			1		3		2	3
G	1					2	3		
D						1	5	4	

Table 3. Example of multilingual sentence "查一下<look up>(CH A @ I X I A) Baghdad (B AE G D AE D)" in HAL space

In this section, the multidimensional scaling method suitable to represent the high dimensionality relation is adopted to project the confusing characteristic of multilingual triphones onto a lower-dimensional space for similarity estimation. Multidimensional scaling approach is similar to the principal component analysis (PCA) method. The difference is that MDS focuses on the distance relation between any two variables and PCA focuses on the discriminative principal component in variables. MDS is applied for estimating the similarity of pairwise triphones. The similarity matrix $V = (v_{k,l})_{N \times N}$ contains pairwise similarities between every two multilingual triphones. The element of row k and column l in the similarity matrix is computed as

$$v_{k,l} = -(\alpha \times \log(a_{k,l}) + (1-\alpha) \times \log(g_{k,l})) \qquad 1 \le k, l \le N \qquad (42)$$

where α denotes the combination weight. The sum rule of data fusion is indicated to combine acoustic likelihood (ACL) and contextual analysis (HAL) confusing matrices as shown in Figure 5.

MDS is then adopted to project the triphones onto the orthogonal axes where the ranking distance relation between triphones can be estimated based on the similarity matrices of triphones. The first step of MDS is to obtain the following matrices

$$B = HSH \qquad (43)$$

where $H = I - \dfrac{1}{n}11'$ is the centralized matrix. I indicates the diagonal matrix and 1 means the indicator vector. The elements in matrix B is computed as

$$b_{kl} = s_{kl} - \bar{s}_{k\bullet} - \bar{s}_{\bullet l} - \bar{s}_{\bullet\bullet} \tag{44}$$

where

$$\bar{s}_{k\bullet} = \sum_{l=1}^{N} \frac{s_{kl}}{N} \tag{45}$$

is the average similarity values over the kth row,

$$\bar{s}_{\bullet l} = \sum_{k=1}^{N} \frac{s_{kl}}{N} \tag{46}$$

denotes the average similarity values over the lth column, and

$$\bar{s}_{\bullet\bullet} = \sum_{k=1}^{N} \sum_{l=1}^{N} \frac{s_{kl}}{N^2} \tag{47}$$

are the average similarity values over all rows and columns of the matrix B. The eigenvector analysis is applied to matrix B to obtain the axis of each triphone in a low dimension. The singular value decomposition (SVD) is applied to solve the eigenvalue and eigenvector problems. Afterwards, the first z nonzero eigenvalues for each phone in a descending order, i.e. $\lambda_1 \geq \lambda_2 \geq \ldots \geq \lambda_z > 0$, is obtained. The corresponding ordered eigenvectors are denoted as u. Then, each triphone is represented by a projected vector as

$$Y = [\sqrt{\lambda_1}u_1, \sqrt{\lambda_2}u_2, \ldots, \sqrt{\lambda_z}u_z] \tag{48}$$

4.2.4. Phone clustering

This section presents how to cluster the triphones with similar acoustic and contextual properties into a multilingual triphone cluster. Cosine measure between triphones Y_k and Y_l is adopted as follows.

$$C(Y_k, Y_l) = \frac{\vec{y}_k \bullet \vec{y}_l}{\|\vec{y}_k\| \cdot \|\vec{y}_l\|} = \frac{\sum_{i=1}^{z} y_{k,i} \times y_{l,i}}{\sqrt{\sum_{i=1}^{z} y_{k,i}^2} \times \sqrt{\sum_{i=1}^{z} y_{l,i}^2}} \tag{49}$$

where $y_{k,i}$ and $y_{l,i}$ are the element of the triphone vectors Y_k and Y_l. The modified k-means (MKM) algorithm is applied to cluster all the triphones into a compact phonetic set. The convergence of closeness measure is determined by a pre-set threshold.

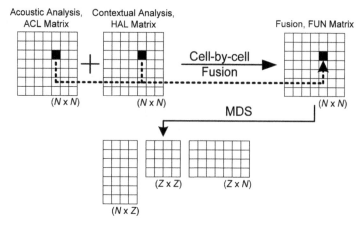

Figure 5. An illustration of fusion of acoustic likelihood (ACL) and contextual analysis (HAL) confusing matrices for the MDS process

4.3. Experimental evaluations

For evaluation, an in-house multilingual speech recognizer was implemented and experiments were conducted to evaluate the performance of the proposed approach on an English-Mandarin multilingual corpus.

4.3.1. Multilingual database

In Taiwan, English and Mandarin are popular in conversation, culture, media, and everyday life. For bilingual corpus collection, the English across Taiwan (EAT) project (EAT [online] http://www.aclclp.org.tw/) sponsored by National Science Council, Taiwan prepared 600 recording sheets. Each sheet contains 80 reading sentences, including English long sentences, English short sentences, English words and mixed English and Mandarin sentences. Each sheet was used for speech recording individually for English-major students and non-English-major students. Microphone corpus was recorded as sound files with 16 kHz sampling rate and 16 bit sample resolution. The summarized recording information of EAT corpus is shown in Table 4. In this section, we applied mixed English-Mandarin sentences in microphone application. The average sentence length is around 12.62 characters.

	English-Major		Non-English-Major	
	male	female	male	female
No. of Sentences	11,977	30,094	25,432	15,540
No. of Speakers	166	406	368	224

Table 4. EAT-MIC Multilingual Corpus Information

4.3.2. Evaluation of the phone set generation based on acoustic and contextual analysis

In this section, the phone recognition rate was adopted for the evaluation of acoustic modeling accuracy. Three classes of speech recognition errors, including insertion errors (*Ins*), deletion errors (*Del*) and substitution errors (*Sub*), were considered. This section applied the fusion of acoustic and contextual analysis approaches to generating the multilingual triphone set. Since the optimal clustering number of acoustic models was unknown, several sets of HMMs were produced by varying the MKM convergence threshold during multilingual triphone clustering. There are three different approaches including acoustic likelihood (ACL), contextual analysis (HAL) and fusion of acoustic and contextual analysis (FUN). It is evident that the proposed fusion method achieves a better result than individual ACL or HAL methods. The comparison of acoustic analysis and contextual analysis, HAL achieves a higher recognition rate than ACL. It denotes that contextual analysis is more significant than acoustic analysis for multilingual confusing phone clustering. The curves shows that phone accuracy will increase with the increase in state number, and finally decrease due to the confusing triphone definition and the requirement of a large size of multilingual training corpus. The proposed multilingual phone generation approach can get an improved performance than the ordinary multilingual triphone sets. In this section, the English and Mandarin triphone sets is defined based on the expansion of the IPA definition. The multilingual speech recognition system for English and Mandarin contains 924 context-dependent triphone models. The best phone recognition accuracy was 67.01% for the HAL window size = 3. Therefore, this section applied this setting in the following experiments.

4.3.3. Comparison of acoustic and language models for multilingual speech recognition

Table 5 shows the comparisons on different acoustic and language models for multilingual speech recognition. For the comparison of monophone and triphone-based recognition, different phone inventory definitions including direct combination of language-dependent phones (MIX), language-dependent IPA phone definition (IPA), tree-based clustering procedure (TRE) (Mak et al. 1996) and the proposed methods (FUN) were considered. The phonetic units of Mandarin can be represented as 37 fundamental phones and English can be represented as 39 fundamental phones. The phone set for the direct combination of English and Mandarin is 78 phones with two silence models. The phone set for IPA definition of English and Mandarin contains 55 phones.

	Monophone		Triphone	
	MIX	IPA	TRE	FUN
Phone models	78	55	1172	924
With language model	45.81%	66.05%	76.46%	78.18%
Without language model	32.58%	51.98%	65.32%	67.01%

Table 5. Comparison of acoustic and language models for multilingual speech recognition

In acoustic comparison, multilingual context-independent (MIX and IPA) and context-dependent (TRE and FUN) phone sets were investigated. With the language model of English and Mandarin, the approach based on MIX achieved 45.81% phone accuracy and the IPA method achieved 66.05% phone accuracy. The IPA performance is evidently better than MIX approach. TRE method achieved 76.46% phone accuracy and our proposed approach achieved 78.18%. It is obvious that triphone models achieved better performance than monophone models. There is around 2.25% relative improvement from 76.46% accuracy for the baseline system based on TRE to 78.18% accuracy for the approach using acoustic and contextual analysis.

In order to evaluate the acoustic modeling performance, the experiments were conducted without using language model. Without the language model, the MIX approach achieved 32.58%, IPA method achieved 51.98%, TRE method achieved 65.32%, and the proposed approach achieved 67.01% phone accuracies. In conclusion, multilingual speech recognition can obtain the best performance using FUN approach for the context-dependent phone definition with language model.

4.3.4. Comparison of monolingual and multilingual speech recognition

In this experiment, the utterances of English word and English sentence in the EAT corpus were collected for the evaluation of monolingual speech recognition. A comparison of monolingual and multilingual speech recognition using EAT corpus was shown in Table 6. Totally, 2496 English words, 3072 English sentences and 5884 mixed English and Mandarin utterances were separately used for training. Other 200 utterances were applied for evaluation. In the context-dependent without language model condition, the performance of monolingual English word achieved 76.25% which is higher than 67.42% for monolingual English sentences. The phone recognition accuracy of monolingual English sentences is 67.42% slightly better than 67.01% for mixed English and Mandarin sentences.

	Monolingual		Multilingual
	English word	English sent.	English and Mandarin mixed sent.
Training corpus	2496	3072	5884
Phone recognition accuracy	76.25%	67.42%	67.01%

Table 6. Comparison of monolingual and multilingual speech recognition

4.4. Conclusions

In this section, the fusion of acoustic and contextual analysis is proposed to generate phonetic units for mixed-language or multilingual speech recognition. The context-dependent triphones are defined based on the IPA representation. Furthermore, the confusing characteristics of multilingual phone sets are analyzed using acoustic and contextual information. From the acoustic analysis, the acoustic likelihood confusing matrix is constructed by the posterior probability of triphones. From the contextual analysis, the hyperspace analog to language (HAL) approach is employed. Using the multidimensional scaling and data fusion approaches, the combination matrix is built and each phone is represented as a vector. Furthermore, the modified k-means algorithm is used to cluster the multilingual triphones into a compact and robust phone set. Experimental results show that the proposed approach gives encouraging results.

5. Conclusions

In this chapter speech recognition techniques in adverse environments are presented. For speech recognition in noisy environments, two approaches to cepstral feature enhancement for noisy speech recognition using noise-normalized stochastic vector mapping are described. Experimental results show that the proposed approach outperformed the SPLICE-based approach without stereo data on AURORA2 database. For speech recognition in disfluent environments, an approach to edit disfluency detection and correction for rich transcription is presented. The proposed theoretical approach, based on a two stage process, aims to model the behavior of edit disfluency and cleanup the disfluency. Experimental results indicate that the IP detection mechanism is able to recall IPs by adjusting the threshold in hypothesis testing. For speech recognition in multilingual environments, the fusion of acoustic and contextual analysis is proposed to generate phonetic units for mixed-language or multilingual speech recognition. The confusing characteristics of multilingual phone sets are analyzed using acoustic and contextual information. The modified k-means algorithm is used to cluster the multilingual triphones into a compact and robust phone set. Experimental results show that the proposed approach improves recognition accuracy in multilingual environments.

Author details

Chung-Hsien Wu* and Chao-Hong Liu
Department of Computer Science and Information Engineering, National Cheng Kung University, Tainan, Taiwan, R.O.C.

Acknowledgement

This work was partially supported by NCKU Project of Promoting Academic Excellence & Developing World Class Research Centers.

6. References

Bear, J., J. Dowding and E. Shriberg (1992). *Integrating multiple knowledge sources for detection and correction of repairs in human-computer dialog. Proc. of ACL.* Newark, Deleware, USA, Association for Computational Linguistics: 56-63.

* Corresponding Author

Benveniste, A., M. Métivier and P. Priouret (1990). *Adaptive Algorithms and Stochastic Approximations. Applications of Mathematics.* New York, Springer. 22.

Boll, S. (1979). Suppression of acoustic noise in speech using spectral subtraction. *IEEE Transactions on Acoustics, Speech and Signal Processing,* Vol. 27. No. 2. pp. 113-120.

Charniak, E. and M. Johnson (2001). *Edit detection and parsing for transcribed speech. Proc. of NAACL,* Association for Computational Linguistics: 118-126.

Chen, Y. J., C. H. Wu, Y. H. Chiu and H. C. Liao (2002). Generation of robust phonetic set and decision tree for Mandarin using chi-square testing. *Speech Communication,* Vol. 38. No. 3-4. pp. 349-364.

Deng, L., A. Acero, M. Plumpe and X. Huang (2000). Large-vocabulary speech recognition under adverse acoustic environments. *Proc. ICSLP-2000,* Beijing, China.

Deng, L., J. Droppo and A. Acero (2003). Recursive estimation of nonstationary noise using iterative stochastic approximation for robust speech recognition. *Speech and Audio Processing, IEEE Transactions on,* Vol. 11. No. 6. pp. 568-580.

Furui, S., M. Nakamura, T. Ichiba and K. Iwano (2005). Analysis and recognition of spontaneous speech using Corpus of Spontaneous Japanese. *Speech Communication,* Vol. 47. No. 1-2. pp. 208-219.

Gales, M. J. F. and S. J. Young (1996). Robust continuous speech recognition using parallel model combination. *IEEE Transactions on Speech and Audio Processing,* Vol. 4. No. 5. pp. 352-359.

Goldberger, J. and H. Aronowitz (2005). *A distance measure between gmms based on the unscented transform and its application to speaker recognition. Proc. of EUROSPEECH.* Lisbon, Portugal: 1985-1988.

Hain, T., P. C. Woodland, G. Evermann, M. J. F. Gales, X. Liu, G. L. Moore, D. Povey and L. Wang (2005). Automatic transcription of conversational telephone speech. *IEEE Transactions on Speech and Audio Processing,* Vol. 13. No. 6. pp. 1173-1185.

Heeman, P. A. and J. F. Allen (1999). Speech repairs, intonational phrases, and discourse markers: modeling speakers' utterances in spoken dialogue. *Computational Linguistics,* Vol. 25. No. 4. pp. 527-571.

Hermansky, H. and N. Morgan (1994). RASTA processing of speech. *IEEE Transactions on Speech and Audio Processing,* Vol. 2. No. 4. pp. 578-589.

Hieronymus, J. L. (1993). ASCII phonetic symbols for the world's languages: Worldbet. *Journal of the International Phonetic Association,* Vol. 23.

Hsieh, C. H. and C. H. Wu (2008). Stochastic vector mapping-based feature enhancement using prior-models and model adaptation for noisy speech recognition. *Speech Communication,* Vol. 50. No. 6. pp. 467-475.

Huang, C. L. and C. H. Wu (2007). Generation of phonetic units for mixed-language speech recognition based on acoustic and contextual analysis. *IEEE Transactions on Computers,* Vol. 56. No. 9. pp. 1225-1233.

Johnson, M. and E. Charniak (2004). *A TAG-based noisy channel model of speech repairs. Proc. of ACL,* Association for Computational Linguistics: 33-39.

Kohler, J. (2001). Multilingual phone models for vocabulary-independent speech recognition tasks. *Speech Communication*, Vol. 35. No. 1-2. pp. 21-30.

Liu, Y., E. Shriberg, A. Stolcke and M. Harper (2005). *Comparing HMM, maximum entropy, and conditional random fields for disfluency detection*. Proc. of Eurospeech: 3313-3316.

Macho, D., L. Mauuary, B. Noé, Y. M. Cheng, D. Ealey, D. Jouvet, H. Kelleher, D. Pearce and F. Saadoun (2002). Evaluation of a noise-robust DSR front-end on Aurora databases. *Proc. ICSLP-2002*, Denver, Colorado, USA.

Mak, B. and E. Barnard (1996). *Phone clustering using the Bhattacharyya distance. Proc. ICSLP*, IEEE. 4: 2005-2008.

Mathews, R. H. (1979). *Mathews' Chinese-English Dictionary*, Harvard university press.

Savova, G. and J. Bachenko (2003). *Prosodic features of four types of disfluencies. Proc. of DiSS*: 91–94.

Shriberg, E., L. Ferrer, S. Kajarekar, A. Venkataraman and A. Stolcke (2005). Modeling prosodic feature sequences for speaker recognition. *Speech Communication*, Vol. 46. No. 3-4. pp. 455-472.

Shriberg, E., A. Stolcke, D. Hakkani-Tur and G. Tur (2000). Prosody-based automatic segmentation of speech into sentences and topics. *Speech Communication*, Vol. 32. No. 1-2. pp. 127-154.

Snover, M., B. Dorr and R. Schwartz (2004). *A lexically-driven algorithm for disfluency detection*. *Proc. of HLT/NAACL*, Association for Computational Linguistics: 157-160.

Soltau, H., B. Kingsbury, L. Mangu, D. Povey, G. Saon and G. Zweig (2005). The IBM 2004 conversational telephony system for rich transcription. *Proc. of IEEE International Conference on Acoustics, Speech, and Signal Processing (ICASSP '05)*, Philadelphia, USA.

Waibel, A., H. Soltau, T. Schultz, T. Schaaf and F. Metze (2000). Multilingual Speech Recognition. *Verbmobil: foundations of speech-to-speech translation*, Springer-Verlag.

Wells, J. C. (1989). Computer-coded phonemic notation of individual languages of the European Community. *Journal of the International Phonetic Association*, Vol. 19. No. 1. pp. 31-54.

Wu, C. H., Y. H. Chiu, C. J. Shia and C. Y. Lin (2006). Automatic segmentation and identification of mixed-language speech using delta-BIC and LSA-based GMMs. *IEEE Transactions on Audio, Speech, and Language Processing*, Vol. 14. No. 1. pp. 266-276.

Wu, C. H. and G. L. Yan (2004). Acoustic Feature Analysis and Discriminative Modeling of Filled Pauses for Spontaneous Speech Recognition. *Journal of VLSI Signal Processing Systems*, Vol. 36. No. 2. pp. 91-104.

Wu, J. and Q. Huo (2002). An environment compensated minimum classification error training approach and its evaluation on Aurora2 database. *Proc. ICSLP-2002*, Denver, Colorado, USA.

Wu, Z. and M. Palmer (1994). *Verbs semantics and lexical selection. Proc. 32nd ACL*, Association for Computational Linguistics: 133-138.

Yeh, J. F. and C. H. Wu (2006). Edit disfluency detection and correction using a cleanup language model and an alignment model. *IEEE Transactions on Audio, Speech, and Language Processing*, Vol. 14. No. 5. pp. 1574-1583.

Young, S. J., J. Odell and P. Woodland (1994). *Tree-based state tying for high accuracy acoustic modelling. Proc. ARPA Human Language Technology Conference.* Plainsboro, USA, Association for Computational Linguistics: 307-312.

## Chapter 3

Robust Distributed Speech Recognition Using Auditory Modelling

Ronan Flynn and Edward Jones

Additional information is available at the end of the chapter

1. Introduction

The use of the Internet for accessing information has expanded dramatically over the past few years, while the availability and use of mobile hand-held devices for communication and Internet access has greatly increased in parallel. Industry has reacted to this trend for information access by developing services and applications that can be accessed by users on the move. These trends have highlighted a need for alternatives to the traditional methods of user data input, such as keypad entry, which is difficult on small form-factor mobile devices. One alternative is to make use of automatic speech recognition (ASR) systems that act on speech input from the user. An ASR system has two main elements. The first element is a front-end processor that extracts parameters, or features, that represent the speech signal. These features are processed by a back-end classifier, which makes the decision as to what has been spoken.

In a fully embedded ASR system [1], the feature extraction and the speech classification are carried out on the mobile device. However, due to the computational complexity of high-performance speech recognition systems, such an embedded architecture can be impractical on mobile hand-held terminals due to limitations in processing and memory resources. On the other hand, fully centralised (server-based) ASR systems have fewer computational constraints, can be used to share the computational burden between mobile users, and can also allow for the easy upgrade of speech recognition technologies and services that are provided. However, in a centralised ASR system the recognition accuracy can be compromised as a result of the speech signal being distorted by low bit-rate encoding at the codec and a poor quality transmission channel [2, 3].

A distributed speech recognition (DSR) system is designed to overcome some of the difficulties described above. In DSR, the terminal (the mobile device) includes a local front-end processor that extracts, directly from the speech, the features to be sent to the remote server (back-end) where recognition is performed. In mobile environments, the speech features can be sent over an error protected data channel rather than a voice channel, making the DSR system more robust to channel errors.

However, DSR systems generally operate in high levels of background noise (particularly in mobile environments). For mobile users in noisy environments (airports, cars, restaurants etc.) the speech recognition accuracy can be reduced dramatically as a consequence of additive background noise. A second source of error in DSR systems is the presence of transmission errors in the form of random packet loss and packet burst loss during transmission of speech features to the classifier. Packet loss can arise in wireless and packet switched (IP) networks, both networks over which a DSR system would normally be expected to operate. Packet loss, in particular packet burst loss, can have a serious impact on recognition performance and needs to be considered in the design of a DSR system.

This chapter addresses the issue of robustness in DSR systems, with particular reference to the problems of background noise and packet loss, which are significant bottlenecks in the commercialisation of speech recognition products, particularly in mobile environments. The layout of the chapter is as follows. Section 2 discusses the DSR architecture and standards in more detail. This is followed by an overview of the auditory model used in this chapter as an alternative front-end to those published in the DSR standards. The Aurora 2 database and a description of the speech recognition system used are also discussed in Section 2. Section 3 addresses the problem of robustness of speech recognition systems in the presence of additive noise, in particular, by examining in detail the use of speech enhancement techniques to reduce the effects of noise on the speech signal. The performance of a DSR system in the presence of both additive background noise and packet loss is examined in Section 4. The feature vectors produced by the auditory model are transmitted over a channel that is subject to packet burst loss and packet loss mitigation to compensate for missing features is investigated. Conclusions are presented in Section 5.

2. Distributed speech recognition systems

2.1. DSR architecture and standards

A DSR system is designed as a compromise between local and centralised recognition, in order to alleviate the issues associated with these approaches [2, 3]. In DSR, the speech recognition task is split between the terminal or client, where the front-end feature extraction is performed, and the network or server, where the back-end recognition is performed. The features that represent the speech are sent by means of an error protected data channel to the classifier for processing. DSR avoids both the speech encoding and decoding stages associated with centralised recognition and so eliminates the degradations that originate from the speech compression algorithms. The bandwidth required to transmit the extracted features to the server is much less than what is required to send the encoded speech signal. DSR systems offer some advantages over other architectures. Recent comparative studies have shown the superior performance of DSR to codec-based ASR [4]. However, in a DSR system, transmission errors in the form of random packet loss and packet burst loss still need to be taken into consideration. Such transmission errors can have a significant impact on recognition accuracy.

Furthermore, it is well known that the presence of noise severely degrades the performance of speech recognition systems, and much research has been devoted to the development of techniques to alleviate this effect; this is particularly important in the context of DSR where mobile clients are typically used in high-noise environments (though the same problem also exists for local embedded, or centralised architectures in noisy conditions). One approach that can be used to improve the robustness of ASR systems is to enhance the speech signal itself before feature extraction. Speech enhancement can be particularly useful in cases where a significant mismatch exists between training and testing conditions, such as where a recognition system is trained with clean speech and then used in noisy conditions. A significant amount of research has been carried out on speech enhancement, and a number of approaches have been well documented in the literature [5]. There has also been much interest in DSR in recent years, within the research community, and in international standardisation bodies, in particular, the European Telecommunications Standards Institute (ETSI) [6-9], which has developed a number of different recommendations for front-end processors of different levels of complexity.

The ETSI basic front-end [6] was developed for implementation over circuit-switched channels and this implementation is also considered in the other three standards. The advanced front-end [7] produces superior performance to the basic front-end, and was designed to increase robustness in background noise. The implementation of the front-ends over packet-switched Internet Protocol (IP) networks has been specified in two documents published by the Internet Engineering Task Force (IETF). The first of these [10] specifies the real-time transport protocol (RTP) payload format for the basic front-end while the second [11] specifies the RTP payload format for the advanced front-end.

The ETSI basic and advanced front-ends both implement MFCC-based parameterisation of the speech signal. The stages involved in feature extraction based on MFCCs are shown in Figure 1. The speech signal first undergoes pre-emphasis in order to compensate for the unequal sensitivity of human hearing across frequency. Following pre-emphasis, a short-term power spectrum is obtained by applying a fast Fourier transform (FFT) to a frame of Hamming windowed speech. Critical band analysis is carried out using a bank of overlapping, triangular shaped, bandpass filters, whose centre frequencies are equally spaced on the mel scale. The FFT magnitude coefficients are grouped into the appropriate critical bands and then weighted by the triangular filters. The energies in each band are summed, creating a filter bank vector of spectral energies on the mel scale. The size of this vector of spectral energies is equal to the number of triangular filters used. A non-linearity in the form of a logarithm is applied to the energy vector. The final step is the application of a discrete cosine transform (DCT) to generate the MFCCs.

In the ETSI DSR front-ends, speech, sampled at 8 kHz, is blocked into frames of 200 samples with an overlap of 60%. A logarithmic frame energy measure is calculated for each frame before any processing takes place. In the case of the basic front-end, pre-emphasis is carried out using a filter coefficient equal to 0.97 while the advanced front-end uses a value of 0.9. A Hamming window is used in both the ETSI basic and advanced front-ends prior to taking an FFT. In the ETSI advanced front-end a power spectrum estimate is calculated before performing the filter bank integration. This results in higher noise robustness when compared with using a magnitude spectrum estimate as used in the ETSI basic front-end [12]. The two front-ends both generate a feature vector consisting of 14 coefficients made up of the frame log-energy measure (determined prior to pre-emphasis) and cepstral coefficients C_0 to C_{12}. In order to introduce robustness against channel variations, the ETSI advanced front-end carries out post-processing in the cepstral domain on coefficients C_1 to C_{12} in the form of blind equalisation [13].

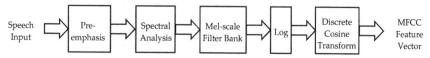

Figure 1. MFCC feature extraction

2.2. Auditory modelling as an alternative front-end

Many computational auditory models have been proposed for use in speech recognition systems, often with excellent results, particularly in the presence of noise. In the work presented here, the auditory model of Li *et al.* [14] is used. The choice of this auditory front-end is motivated by previous work carried out by the authors [15] where a number of auditory front-ends were investigated in a comparative study of robust speech recognition with the widely-used Aurora 2 database [16]. In that study, there was no pre-processing or enhancement of the speech utterances. The front-ends investigated were perceptual linear prediction (PLP) proposed by Hermansky [17], the PEMO algorithm proposed by Tchorz and Kollmeier [18], and the front-end processor proposed by Li *et al.* [14]. For the task of connected digit recognition using the Aurora 2 database, the front-end proposed by Li *et al.* gave the best overall recognition results of all the auditory models examined, and with an overall reduction in recognition error compared to the ETSI basic front-end [6] which was used as a baseline for comparison.

The steps involved in feature extraction in the Li *et al.* auditory model are shown in Figure 2. Speech is sampled at 8 kHz and blocked into frames of 240 samples. Frame overlap is 66.7% and a Hamming window is used prior to taking a FFT. An outer/middle ear transfer function that models pressure gain in the outer and middle ears is applied to the spectrum magnitude. After conversion of the spectrum to the Bark scale, the transfer function output is processed by an auditory filter that is derived from psychophysical measurements of the frequency response of the cochlea. A non-linearity in the form of a logarithm followed by a DCT is applied to the filter outputs to generate the cepstral coefficients. The recognition experiments use vectors that include energy and 12 cepstral coefficients (C_1 to C_{12}) along with velocity and acceleration coefficients. This results in vectors with an overall dimension equal to 39.

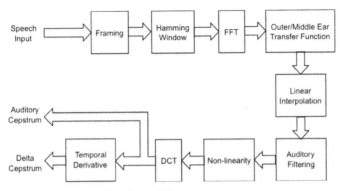

Figure 2. Feature extraction proposed by Li *et al.* [14].

2.3. Aurora 2 database

The recognition problem examined in this work is connected digit recognition using the Aurora 2 database [16]. The motivation behind the creation of the Aurora database was to provide a framework that allowed for the evaluation and comparison of speech recognition algorithms in noisy conditions, thus providing a good basis for comparison between researchers. It has been widely used in the development and evaluation of DSR systems. The speech database is derived from utterances of isolated digits and connected digit sequences spoken by US-American adults originally included in the well-known TIDigits database. The speech in the TIDigits database is sampled at 20 kHz and is down-sampled to 8 kHz in the Aurora database. Some additional filtering is applied to the down-sampled data in order to take into account the frequency characteristics of equipment used in telecommunications systems. The channel characteristics used are G.712 and modified intermediate reference system (MIRS). The down-sampled, filtered speech corresponds to "clean" data in the Aurora database. The Aurora database also contains "noisy" data. This corresponds to clean data with noise artificially added at SNRs of 20 dB, 15 dB, 10 dB, 5 dB, 0 dB and –5 dB. The noise signals added are chosen to reflect environments in which telecommunication terminals are used. In total there are eight different noise types: subway, babble, car, exhibition hall, restaurant, street, airport and train station.

The Aurora framework includes a set of standard test conditions for evaluation of front-end processors. For the purpose of training the speech recogniser, two modes are defined. The first mode is training on clean data and the second mode is multi-condition training on noisy data. The same 8440 utterances, taken from the training part of the TIDigits, are used for both modes. For the multi-condition training, the clean speech signals are used, as well as speech with four different noise types (subway, babble, car and exhibition hall), added at SNRs of 20 dB, 15 dB, 10 dB and 5 dB. There are three different test sets defined for recognition testing, with the test utterances taken from the testing part of the TIDigits database. Test Set A (28028 utterances) employs the same four noises as used for the multi-condition training. Test Set B uses the same utterances as Test Set A but uses four different noise types (restaurant, street, airport and train station). In both Test Sets A and B, the frequency characteristic used in the filtering of the speech and noise is the same as that used in the training sets, namely G.712. The frequency characteristic of the filter used in Test Set C (14014 utterances) is the MIRS, and is different from that used in the training sets. Subway and street noises are used in Test Set C.

2.4. Speech recognition system

The classifier used for the recognition experiments in the work presented in this chapter is the HMM-based recogniser architecture specified for use with the Aurora 2 database [16], and implemented with the widely-used HTK package [19]. The use of a well-known specification provides a common framework with which to compare different front-ends and feature vectors for the purpose of connected digit recognition. There are eleven whole word HMMs each with 16 states; each state has 3 Gaussian mixtures. The topology of the models is left-to-right without any skips over states. This topology is suitable for modelling the sequential nature of speech and the consecutive states represent the consecutive speech states in a particular utterance. Two pause models, "sil" and "sp", are defined. The "sil" model has 3 states and each state has 6 mixtures. The "sp" model has a single state. The Baum-Welch re-estimation algorithm is applied in the training of the word models. An utterance can be modelled by any sequence of digits with the possibility of a "sil" model at both ends and adjacent digits separated by a "sp" model.

The method used to measure the performance of a speech recognition system is dependent on the type of utterance that is to be recognised, i.e. isolated word or continuous speech. There are three error types associated with the recogniser in a continuous speech recognition system:

Substitutions (S) – A word in the original sentence is recognised as a different word.

Deletions (D) – A word in the original sentence is missed.

Insertions (I) – A new word is inserted between two words of the original sentence.

The performance measure used throughout the work presented here, and also used in [16], is the word accuracy as defined by (1):

$$Word\ accuracy = \frac{N-(S+D+I)}{N} \times 100\% \tag{1}$$

where N is the total number of evaluated words. The word accuracies for each of the Aurora test sets presented throughout this chapter are calculated according to [16], which defines the performance measure for a test set as the word accuracy averaged over all noises and over all SNRs between 0 dB and 20dB. The overall word accuracy for the two training modes, clean training and multi-condition training, is calculated as the average over the three test sets A, B and C.

3. Speech enhancement

Additive noise from interfering noise sources, and convolutional noise arising from transmission channel characteristics both contribute to a degradation of performance in automatic speech recognition systems. This section addresses the problem of robustness of speech recognition systems in the first of these conditions, namely additive noise. As noted previously, speech enhancement is one way in which the effects of noise on the speech signal can be reduced. Enhancement of noisy speech signals is normally used to improve the perception of the speech by human listeners however, it may also have benefits in enhancing robustness in ASR systems. Speech enhancement can be particularly useful in cases where a significant mismatch exists between training and testing conditions, such as where a recognition system is trained with clean speech and then used in noisy conditions, as inclusion of speech enhancement can help to reduce the mismatch. This approach to improving robustness is considered in this section.

In the speech recognition system described here, the input speech is pre-processed using an algorithm for speech enhancement. A number of different methods for the enhancement of speech, combined with the auditory front-end of Li *et al.* [14], are evaluated for the purpose of robust connected digit recognition. The ETSI basic [6] and advanced [7] front-ends proposed for distributed speech recognition are used as a baseline for comparison.

3.1. Speech enhancement overview

The enhancement of noisy speech can be described as an estimation problem in which the original clean signal is estimated from a degraded version of the signal. A significant amount of research has been carried out on speech enhancement, and a number of approaches have been well documented in the literature. A survey of a number of approaches to speech enhancement using a single microphone is presented in [5].

Two measures that can be used to perceptually evaluate speech are its *quality* and its *intelligibility* [5]. Speech quality is a subjective measure and is dependent on the individual preferences of listeners. It is a measure of how comfortable a listener is when listening to the speech under evaluation. The intelligibility of the speech can be regarded as an objective measure, and is calculated based on the number or percentage of words that can be correctly recognised by listeners. The intelligibility and the quality of speech are not correlated [5] and it is well known that improving one of the measures can have a detrimental effect on the other one. Speech enhancement algorithms give a trade-off between noise reduction and signal distortion. A reduction in noise can lead to an improvement in the subjective quality of the speech but a decrease in the measured speech intelligibility [5].

When using speech enhancement in an ASR system, the speech is enhanced before feature extraction and recognition processing. The advantage of this is that there is no impact on the computational complexity of the feature extraction or the recognition processes as the enhancement is independent of both, and the speech enhancement can be implemented as an add-on without significantly affecting existing parts of the system. However, every speech enhancement process will introduce some form of signal distortion and it is important that the impact of this distortion on the recognition process is minimised.

3.2. Speech enhancement algorithms

In this section, the various speech enhancement algorithms that were examined are briefly described. The algorithms range from well-established algorithms like that of Ephraim and Malah [20], to more recently proposed ones like that of Rangachari and Loizou [21]. Furthermore, the algorithms cover a range of paradigms, including spectral subtraction-based algorithms using the FFT for spectral analysis, as well as methods based on auditory filter banks.

Ephraim and Malah [20] present a minimum mean-square error short-time spectral amplitude (MMSE STSA) estimator. The estimator is based on modelling speech and noise spectral components as statistically independent Gaussian random variables. The enhanced speech is constructed using the MMSE STSA estimator combined with the original phase of the noisy signal. Analysis is carried out in the frequency domain and the signal spectrum is estimated using an FFT.

Westerlund *et al.* [22] present a speech enhancement technique in which the input signal is first divided into a number of sub-bands. The signal in each sub-band is individually multiplied by a gain factor in the time domain based on an estimate of the short term SNR in each sub-band at every time instant. High SNR values indicate the presence of speech and the sub-band signal is amplified. Low SNR values indicate the presence of noise only and the sub-band signal remains unchanged.

Martin [23] presented an algorithm for the enhancement of noisy speech signals by means of spectral subtraction, in particular through a method for estimation of the noise power on a sub-band basis. Martin's noise estimation method is based firstly on the independence of speech and noise, and secondly on the observation that speech energy in an utterance falls to a value close to or equal to zero for brief periods. Such periods of low speech energy occur between words or syllables in an utterance and during speech pauses. The energy of the signal during these periods reflects the noise power level. Martin's minimum statistics noise estimation method tracks the short-term power spectral density estimate of the noisy speech signal in each frequency bin separately. The minimum power within a defined window is used to estimate the noise floor level. The minimum tracking method requires a bias compensation since the minimum power spectral density of the noisy signal is smaller than the average value. In [24], Martin further developed the noise estimation algorithm by using a time- and frequency-dependent smoothing parameter when calculating the smoothed power spectral density. A method to calculate an appropriate time and frequency dependent bias compensation is also described in [24] as part of the algorithm.

Rangachari and Loizou [21] proposed an algorithm for the estimation of noise in highly non-stationary environments. The noisy speech power spectrum is averaged using time and frequency dependent smoothing factors. This new averaged value is then used to update the noise estimate. Signal-presence probability in individual frequency bins is calculated in order to update the smoothing factors. Signal presence is determined by computing the ratio of the noisy speech power spectrum to its local minimum, which is updated continuously by averaging past values of the noisy speech power spectra with a look-ahead factor. The results in [21] indicate that the local minimum estimation algorithm adapts very quickly to highly non-stationary noise environments.

A technique for the removal of noise from degraded speech using two filtering stages was proposed by Agarwal and Cheng [25]. The first filtering stage coarsely reduces the noise and whitens any residual noise while the second stage attempts to remove the residual noise. Filtering is based on the Wiener filter concept and filter optimisation is carried out in the mel-frequency domain. The algorithm, described as a two-stage mel-warped Wiener filter noise reduction scheme, is a major component of the ETSI advanced front-end standard for DSR [7]. The implementation of noise reduction in the ETSI advanced front-end is summarised in [12].

3.3. Tests and results

This section presents recognition results from tests on the Aurora 2 database [16], using the combination of the speech enhancement algorithms described previously and the auditory model proposed by Li *et al.* (see Section 2.2). In the analysis, two versions of the Li *et al.* front-end are used. The first, referred to as Li *et al.* (I), generates a feature vector consisting of 13 coefficients made up of the frame log-energy measure and the cepstral coefficients C_1 to C_{12}. The second version, referred to as Li *et al.* (II), generates a feature vector that contains the cepstral coefficients C_1 to C_{12} along with a weighted combination of cepstral coefficient C_0 and the frame log-energy measure. The reason for investigating two versions of the Li *et al.* front-end, Li *et al.* (I) and Li *et al.* (II), is to allow for a closer comparison with the ETSI basic front-end [6] and the ETSI advanced front-end [7] respectively. In all cases training was carried out using clean data, so that the effect of the speech enhancement in removing mismatch could be examined. The speech enhancement algorithms were used on both the (clean) training speech as well as the (noisy) test speech. Feature vectors were extracted directly from the enhanced speech with no intermediate processing. The recognition experiments used vectors that include 13 static coefficients along with velocity and acceleration coefficients. This results in vectors with an overall dimension equal to 39. The word accuracies detailed in the tables of results were calculated as previously described in Section 2.4.

In the comparison of Li *et al.* (I) and the ETSI basic front-end, there was no post-processing of the feature vectors carried out. The recognition results using the Aurora 2 database for Li *et al.* (I), for each speech enhancement algorithm, are given in Table 1 and the corresponding results for the ETSI basic front-end (the baseline for this test) are given in Table 2.

The performance of Li *et al.* (II) was compared with the performance of the ETSI advanced front-end. The ETSI advanced front-end includes a SNR-dependent waveform processing block that is applied after noise reduction and before feature extraction. The purpose of this

Enhancement	Absolute word accuracy %			
	Set A	Set B	Set C	Overall
None	62.16	64.31	57.76	62.14
Ephraim & Malah	78.85	79.38	74.78	78.25
Westerlund et al.	75.87	76.32	70.45	74.97
Martin	72.47	71.96	70.21	71.81
Rangachari & Loizou	74.50	73.16	74.29	73.92
Agarwal & Cheng	86.33	84.87	81.86	84.85

Table 1. Recognition results for the Li et al. (I) front-end.

Enhancement	Absolute word accuracy %			
	Set A	Set B	Set C	Overall
None	61.34	55.75	66.14	60.06
Ephraim & Malah	76.34	75.91	73.71	75.64
Westerlund et al.	76.04	72.54	72.36	73.90
Martin	67.98	67.57	68.24	67.87
Rangachari & Loizou	63.58	61.57	67.82	63.62
Agarwal & Cheng	84.39	82.75	78.72	82.60

Table 2. Recognition results for the ETSI basic front-end.

Enhancement	Absolute word accuracy %			
	Set A	Set B	Set C	Overall
None	67.34	69.18	63.44	67.30
Ephraim & Malah	80.36	81.03	79.34	80.42
Westerlund et al.	78.70	80.02	78.44	79.18
Martin	73.07	72.93	72.17	72.83
Rangachari & Loizou	76.08	76.16	75.94	76.08
Agarwal & Cheng	87.03	86.85	84.58	86.47

Table 3. Recognition results for the Li et al. (II) front-end.

block is to improve the noise robustness in the front-end of an ASR system by enhancing the high SNR period portion and attenuating the low SNR period portion in the waveform time domain, thus increasing the overall SNR of noisy speech [26]. However, the evaluation here is looking primarily at the effect of speech enhancement or noise reduction alone on the connected digit recognition accuracy. Therefore, the waveform processing block in the ETSI advanced front-end was disabled. In addition, the ETSI advanced front-end carries out post-processing in the cepstral domain in the form of blind equalisation as described in [13]. To ensure a closer match with the ETSI advanced front-end, the feature vectors produced by Li *et al.* (II) undergo post-processing in the cepstral domain by means of cepstral mean subtraction (CMS). The recognition results for Li *et al.* (II), for each speech enhancement algorithm, are detailed in Table 3 and the recognition results for the ETSI advanced front-end are detailed in Table 4.

	Absolute word accuracy %			
Enhancement	Set A	Set B	Set C	Overall
None	65.92	65.48	70.07	66.57
Ephraim & Malah	77.92	77.61	78.64	77.94
Westerlund *et al.*	79.09	79.13	79.70	79.23
Martin	71.26	72.91	72.71	72.21
Rangachari & Loizou	73.77	73.35	78.85	74.62
Agarwal & Cheng	85.92	85.66	83.89	85.41

Table 4. Recognition results for the ETSI advanced front-end.

Table 5 provides an overall view of the relative performance of the different speech enhancement algorithms for each of the four front-end versions considered.

Rank	Li *et al.* (I) FE	ETSI basic FE	Li *et al.* (II) FE	ETSI advanced FE
1	Agarwal & Cheng	Agarwal & Cheng	Agarwal & Cheng	Agarwal & Cheng
2	Ephraim & Malah	Ephraim & Malah	Ephraim & Malah	Westerlund *et al.*
3	Westerlund *et al.*	Westerlund *et al.*	Westerlund *et al.*	Ephraim & Malah
4	Rangachari & Loizou	Martin	Rangachari & Loizou	Rangachari & Loizou
5	Martin	Rangachari & Loizou	Martin	Martin

Table 5. Performance ranking of enhancement algorithms.

3.4. Discussion

Ignoring speech enhancement, and comparing Tables 1 and 2, the performance of Li *et al.* (I) exceeds the baseline ETSI front-end [6] by 2.08% overall. From Table 3 and Table 4, again without speech enhancement applied, there is a difference in recognition accuracy of 0.73% in favour of Li *et al.* (II) when compared with the ETSI advanced front-end [7].

The other results in Tables 1 to 4 show that enhancement of the speech prior to feature extraction significantly improves the overall recognition performance. This improvement in recognition accuracy is observed for both the ETSI basic [6] and advanced [7] front-ends and the front-end proposed by Li *et al.* [14]. A comparison of Table 1 with Table 2 shows that Li *et al.* (I) outperforms the ETSI basic front-end for all of the speech enhancement techniques evaluated. Furthermore, from Tables 3 and 4, it is seen that Li *et al.* (II) again outperforms the ETSI advanced front-end for all speech enhancement methods except Westerlund *et al.* [22], for which the overall recognition results are quite close.

For Li *et al.* (I), Li *et al.* (II), the ETSI basic front-end and the ETSI advanced front-end, the best overall recognition accuracy is obtained for speech enhancement using the algorithm proposed by Agarwal and Cheng [25]. The combination of auditory front-end and the two-stage, mel-warped, Wiener filter noise reduction scheme results in an overall recognition accuracy that is approximately 6% better overall compared with the next ranked front-end and speech enhancement combination. After Agarwal and Cheng [25], the next best performance across the board is obtained using Ephraim and Malah [20], and Westerlund *et al.* [22]. This suggests that the choice of speech enhancement algorithm for best speech recognition performance is somewhat independent of the choice of front-end (though this would have to be validated by further testing with other front ends).

4. Robustness to noise and packet loss

In the previous section, the benefit of speech enhancement prior to feature extraction in a speech recognition system was demonstrated. However, in a DSR system, transmission errors can still have a significant impact on recognition performance. Such transmission errors in the form of bit errors, random packet loss and packet burst loss need to be taken into consideration. This is particularly important in the context of increasing use of packet-based networks for transmission of speech and data in mobile environments. This section examines the performance of a DSR system in the presence of both background noise and packet loss.

4.1. Channel models and loss compensation

A DSR client and server may be interconnected over either a circuit-switched channel or a packet-switched channel. Approaches used in the literature to simulate different channel types fall into two categories. The first makes use of physical layer models that simulate transmission phenomena that occur on the physical channel. The second category involves the use of statistical models that model unconditional packet loss probability and conditional packet loss burst lengths. This is the approach used in this chapter.

To simulate packet loss and error bursts, the 2-state Gilbert model is widely used. In [27-29], a voice over IP (VoIP) channel is simulated using such a model. References [30, 31] simulate IP channels and use a 2-state Gilbert model to simulate burst type packet loss on the channel. Statistical models have also been used to simulate the physical properties of the communication channel. The Gilbert model was found in [3] to be inadequate for simulating a GSM channel and instead a two-fold stochastic model is used in which there are two processes, namely shadowing and Rayleigh fading. This same model was used by [32], again to model a GSM network. Reference [33] compares three models of packet loss and examines their effectiveness at simulating different packet loss conditions. The models are a 2-state Markov chain, the Gilbert-Elliot model and a 3-state Markov chain. The 2-state Markov chain in [33] uses State 1 to model a correctly received packet and State 2 to model a lost packet. While the Gilbert-Elliot model is itself a 2-state Markov model, there is only a probability of packet loss when in State 2. The three models in [33] are all validated for GSM and wireless local area network (WLAN) channels. Results indicate that the 3-state Markov model gives the best results overall and this model is used in the work described here; the model is described in more detail later in this chapter.

There are a number of techniques documented that are used within DSR systems for the purpose of reducing transmission error degradation and so increasing the robustness of the speech recognition. Error-robustness techniques are categorised in [4] under the headings client-based error recovery, and server-based error concealment. Client-based techniques include retransmission, interleaving and forward error correction (FEC). While retransmission and FEC may result in recovering a large amount of transmission errors, they have the disadvantage of requiring additional bandwidth and introducing additional delays and computational overhead. Server-based methods include feature reconstruction, by means of repetition or interpolation, and error correction in the ASR-decoding stage. Reference [4] provides a survey of robustness issues related to network degradations and presents a number of analyses and experiments with a focus on transmission error robustness.

The work described in [34-38] is focused on burst-like packet loss and how to improve speech recognition in the context of DSR. The importance of reducing the average burst length of lost feature vectors rather than reducing the overall packet loss rate is central to the work in these papers. By minimising the average burst length, the estimation of lost feature vectors is more effective. Reference [34] compared three different interleaving mechanisms (block, convolutional and decorrelated) and found that increasing the degree of interleaving increases the speech recognition performance but that this comes with the cost of a higher delay. It is further suggested in [38] that, for a DSR application, it is more beneficial to trade delay for accuracy rather than trading bit-rate for accuracy as in forward error correction schemes. Reference [35] combines block interleaving to reduce burst lengths on the client side with packet loss compensation at the server side. Two compensation mechanisms are examined: feature reconstruction by means of nearest neighbour repetition, interpolation and maximum a-posteriori (MAP) estimation; and a decoder-based strategy using missing feature theory. The results suggest that for packet loss compensation, the decoder-based strategy is best. This is especially true in the presence of large bursts of losses as the accuracy of reconstruction methods falls off rapidly as burst length increases. Interleaving, feature estimation and decoder based strategies are combined in [36] in order to improve the recognition performance in the presence of packet loss in DSR.

In this section, the 3-state model proposed in [33] is used to simulate packet loss and loss bursts. To compensate for missing packets, two error-concealment methods are examined, namely nearest neighbour repetition and interpolation. Error mitigation using interleaving is also considered.

4.2. Packet loss framework

4.2.1. Packet loss model

The packet loss model used in this work is the 3-state Markov chain proposed by [33]. This 3-state model was found to be more effective at simulating different packet loss conditions in comparison with a 2-state Markov chain and the Gilbert-Elliot model. The model is detailed in Figure 3, showing the three states and the transition probabilities. Occupancy of states 1 and 3 indicate no packet loss while occupancy of state 2 indicates packet loss. In Figure 3, Q, q and Q' are the self-loop probabilities of states 1, 2 and 3 respectively. The model parameters are designed so that state 1 models long duration periods of no loss and state 3 models short periods of no loss, which occur in between packet loss in burst-like conditions. The following four parameters define the model, and from these parameters the transition probabilities of the 3-state model can be determined:

α = overall probability of a packet being lost

β = average packet loss burst length

N_1 = average length, in packets, of loss-free periods

N_3 = average length, in packets, of no-loss periods inside loss periods

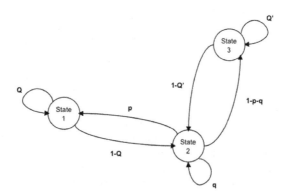

Figure 3. Packet Loss Model [33].

The transition probabilities are calculated from the following equations:

$$q = 1 - \frac{1}{\beta}$$

(2)

$$Q = 1 - \frac{1}{N_1} \tag{3}$$

$$Q' = 1 - \frac{1}{N_3} \tag{4}$$

$$p = \frac{1-Q}{Q-Q'} \left[\frac{1-Q'}{\alpha} + q + Q' - 2 \right] \tag{5}$$

The authors in [33] suggest that an alternative to performing speech recognition tests using simulated channels is to define a set of packet loss characteristics, thus enabling recognition performance to be analysed across a range of different packet loss conditions. References [34-37] define four channels with different characteristics in order to simulate packet loss. These same four channels are used here to determine the effect of packet loss on speech recognition performance. The parameter values for the four channels are detailed in Table 6. These parameters result from work in [33] on IP and wireless networks. These are network environments over which a DSR system would typically operate. In an IP network, packet loss arises primarily due to congestion at the routers within the network, due to high levels of IP traffic. The nature of IP traffic is that it can be described as being 'bursty' in nature with the result that packet loss occurs in bursts. Signal fading, where the signal strength at a receiving device is attenuated significantly, is also a contributing factor to packet loss in a wireless network. Long periods of fading in a wireless network can result in bursts of packet loss. The authors in [33] measured the characteristics of an IP network and a WLAN, and the results showed the packet loss rate (α) and the burst length (β) to be highly variable. At one point or another, most channel conditions occurred, although not necessarily for long. Based on the experimental measurements, a set of packet loss characteristics was defined in [33] and these are used to analyse recognition performance for different network conditions. The parameters in Table 6 are taken from this defined set of packet loss characteristics.

	α	β	N_1	N_3
Channel A	10%	4	37	1
Channel B	10%	20	181	1
Channel C	50%	4	5	1
Channel D	50%	20	21	1

Table 6. Packet loss parameters.

4.2.2. Packet loss mitigation

Two error concealment methods are examined, namely nearest neighbour repetition and interpolation. These methods attempt to reconstruct the feature vector stream when packet loss is detected. Missing feature vectors are estimated solely from correctly received feature vectors. In a DSR system, nearest neighbour repetition and interpolation would both be implemented on the server side. Additionally, interleaving, a technique used to reduce feature vector loss burst lengths (with a penalty of additional delay), is also briefly discussed. Interleaving is carried out on the client side of a DSR system, with de-interleaving on the server side.

4.2.2.1. Nearest neighbour repetition

The ETSI advanced front-end [7] specifies that where missing feature vectors occur due to transmission errors, they should be substituted with the nearest correctly received feature vector in the receiver. If there are $2B$ consecutive missing feature vectors, the first B speech vectors are substituted by a copy of the last good speech vector before the error, and the last B speech vectors are substituted by a copy of the first good speech vector received after the error. The speech vector includes the 12 static cepstral coefficients C_1-C_{12}, the zeroth cepstral coefficient C_0 and the log energy term, and all are replaced together. A disadvantage of this method is that if B is large then long stationary periods can arise.

4.2.2.2. Interpolation

The disadvantage of stationary periods that arise with nearest neighbour repetition can be alleviated somewhat by polynomial interpolation between the correctly received feature vectors either side of a loss burst. Reference [34] found that non-linear interpolation using cubic Hermite polynomials gives the best estimates for missing feature vectors. Equation (6) is used to calculate the nth missing feature vector in a loss burst of length β packets, which is equivalent to a loss burst length of 2β feature vectors if each packet contains two feature vectors as defined by the ETSI advanced front-end [7]. The parameter n in (6) is the missing feature vector index.

$$\hat{x}_{b+n} = a_0 + a_1\left(\frac{n}{\beta+1}\right) + a_2\left(\frac{n}{\beta+1}\right)^2 + a_3\left(\frac{n}{\beta+1}\right)^3 \quad 1 \leq n \leq 2\beta \tag{6}$$

The coefficients a_0, a_1, a_2 and a_3 in (6) are determined from the two correctly received feature vectors either side of the loss burst, x_b and x_{b+n+1}, and their first derivatives, x'_b and x'_{b+n+1}. Equation (6) can be rewritten as

$$\hat{x}_{b+n} = x_b\left(1 - 3t^2 + 2t^3\right) + x_{b+\beta+1}\left(3t^2 - 2t^3\right) + x'_b\left(t - 2t^2 + t^3\right) + x'_{b+\beta+1}\left(t^3 - t^2\right) \quad 1 \leq n \leq 2\beta \tag{7}$$

where $t = n/(\beta+1)$. It was found in [34] that performance was better when the derivative components in (7) are set to zero. These components are also set to zero for the work presented in this chapter.

4.2.2.3. Interleaving

Research has shown that by minimising the average burst length of lost vectors the estimation of lost feature vectors is more effective [34]. The aim of interleaving is to break a long loss burst into smaller loss bursts by distributing them over time and so making it appear that the errors are more randomly distributed.

In a DSR system, the interleaver on the client side takes a feature vector sequence X_i, where i is the order index, and changes the order in which the vectors are transmitted over the channel. The result is to generate a new vector sequence Y_i that is related to X_i by

$$Y_i = X_{\pi(i)} \tag{8}$$

where $\pi(i)$ is the permutation function. On the server side, the operation is reversed by de-interleaving the received vector sequence as follows:

$$X_i = Y_{\pi^{-1}(i)} \tag{9}$$

where $\pi(\pi^{-1}(i))=i$.

In order for the interleaver to carry out the reordering of the feature vectors, it is necessary to buffer the vectors, which introduces a delay. On the server side, in order to carry out the de-interleaving, buffering of the incoming feature vectors takes place and a second delay is introduced. The sum of these two delays is known as the latency of the interleaving/de-interleaving process.

The spread S of an interleaver is a metric that indicates how good an interleaver is at breaking up error bursts. A burst of length L vectors will be broken into bursts of length 1 if $S \geq L$. For $S < L$ the full distribution of the burst cannot be guaranteed and some sets of consecutive feature vectors may be lost.

For the work in this chapter, block interleaving is implemented. A block interleaver of degree d changes the order of transmission of a $d \times d$ block of input vectors. An example of a block interleaver of degree $d = 4$ and spread $S = 4$ is given in Figure 4.

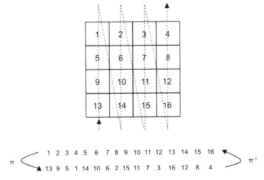

Figure 4. $d \times d$ block interleaver where $d = 4$, with permutation function.

4.3. Tests and results

The primary purpose of this section is to investigate the performance of the auditory model proposed by Li *et al.* [14] in combination with speech enhancement in the presence of noise and packet loss. As a baseline for comparison, results are also presented for the ETSI advanced front-end [7]. In all cases, training was carried out using clean data. The speech enhancement algorithm of Agarwal and Cheng [25] was used on both the (clean) training speech as well as the (noisy) test speech. The ETSI advanced front-end includes a SNR-dependent waveform processing block that is applied after noise reduction and before feature extraction. The waveform processing block in the ETSI advanced front-end is also implemented in the front-end of Li *et al.* in order to ensure a closer match between the two front-ends. Feature vectors are extracted from the output of this waveform processing block. A detailed description of the waveform processing block can be found in [26]. The ETSI advanced front-end carries out post-processing in the cepstral domain in the form of blind equalization as described by [13]. The feature vectors produced by Li *et al.* undergo post-processing in the cepstral domain by means of cepstral mean subtraction (CMS). As defined by the ETSI advanced front-end [7], each packet transmitted over the communication channel carries two feature vectors.

In [7] a distributed speech recognition front-end feature vector compression algorithm is defined. The algorithm makes use of the parameters from the front-end feature extraction algorithm of the ETSI advanced front-end. The purpose of the algorithm is to reduce the number of bits needed to represent each front-end feature vector and so reduce the bit rate required over the communications channel. The feature vector is directly quantized with a split vector quantiser. The 14 coefficients (C_1 to C_{12}, C_0 & ln$E$) are grouped into pairs, and each pair is quantized using its own vector quantisation (VQ) codebook. The resulting set of index values is then used to represent the feature vector. The results documented in this paper are based on feature vectors that have undergone split vector quantisation.

The baseline recognition results for the two front-ends, without vector quantisation and with no packet loss but with noise, are detailed in Table 7. The word accuracies in the following tables are calculated as described in Section 2.4.

| | Absolute word accuracy % | | | |
Front-end	Set A	Set B	Set C	Overall
ETSI AFE	87.74	87.09	85.44	87.02
Li *et al.*	88.62	88.09	86.89	88.06

Table 7. Baseline recognition results.

In order to implement split vector quantization it is necessary to design VQ codebooks for each of the seven coefficient pairs. ETSI has made available script files for the ETSI advanced front-end and included with these are the VQ codebooks for the coefficient pairs. The recognition results for the ETSI advanced front-end with feature vector quantization using the ETSI supplied VQ codebooks are given in Table 8.

To allow for close comparison between the ETSI advanced front end and the front-end proposed by Li *et al.*, the VQ codebooks for Li *et al.* should be determined in the same manner as the VQ codebooks for the ETSI advanced front-end. However, this was not possible as the detail of how the ETSI advanced front-end VQ codebooks were calculated is not publicly available at this time. Therefore, an implementation of the Generalized Lloyd Algorithm (GLA), described by [39], was used to design the VQ codebooks for both the ETSI advanced front-end and the front-end of Li *et al.* The recognition results for the two front-ends using the VQ codebooks generated by the GLA implementation are detailed in Table 9. The overall word accuracies in Table 9, with vector quantization, compare well with the baseline accuracies, without vector quantization, in Table 7. There is also close correlation between the recognition results in Table 8 and Table 9 for the ETSI advanced front-end, indicating that the VQ codebooks generated by the GLA implementation used for this work are a good substitute for the VQ codebooks provided by ETSI with the advanced front-end.

Front-end	Absolute word accuracy %			
	Set A	Set B	Set C	Overall
ETSI AFE	87.81	87.11	85.74	87.12

Table 8. Recognition results using ETSI VQ codebooks.

Front-end	Absolute word accuracy %			
	Set A	Set B	Set C	Overall
ETSI AFE	87.73	86.92	85.41	86.94
Li *et al.*	88.22	87.59	86.55	87.63

Table 9. Recognition results with VQ codebooks designed using implementation of the GLA.

Packet loss (where each packet contains two feature vectors) is introduced on the communication channel by using the packet loss model described in Section 4.2.1. The four different packet loss channels investigated are defined in Table 6. Recognition tests, in the presence of packet loss, were carried out for each of the following conditions:

- no speech enhancement, no loss mitigation (Table 10);
- speech enhancement, no loss mitigation (Table 11);
- speech enhancement, nearest neighbour repetition (Table 12);
- speech enhancement, interpolation (Table 13);
- speech enhancement, interleaving, interpolation (Table 14).

Tests were first carried out for packet loss with no steps taken to recover the missing features or to minimise the loss burst length. The test results for both front-ends when no speech enhancement is used are given in Table 10, while recognition results with speech enhancement are given in Table 11. A comparison of Table 10 with Table 11 illustrates the benefit of using speech enhancement in improving recognition performance. Comparing Table 11 with Table 9 (no packet loss) it is seen that packet loss has a significant impact on the recognition results, in particular for channels C and D where the probability of packet loss is 50%.

Loss parameters	ETSI AFE absolute word accuracy %			
	Set A	Set B	Set C	Overall
Channel A	60.56	60.96	64.36	61.48
Channel B	59.31	59.49	63.67	60.25
Channel C	36.45	37.62	37.66	37.16
Channel D	35.38	35.89	37.68	36.04
Loss parameters	Li *et al.* absolute word accuracy %			
	Set A	Set B	Set C	Overall
Channel A	66.66	68.39	63.85	66.79
Channel B	65.59	67.35	62.93	65.76
Channel C	38.27	39.60	36.29	38.41
Channel D	37.78	39.25	36.07	38.03

Table 10. No speech enhancement, no error mitigation.

Loss parameters	ETSI AFE absolute word accuracy %			
	Set A	Set B	Set C	Overall
Channel A	80.17	80.09	77.97	79.70
Channel B	79.86	79.28	77.61	79.18
Channel C	42.50	42.87	40.50	42.25
Channel D	44.07	44.25	42.21	43.77
Loss parameters	Li *et al.* absolute word accuracy %			
	Set A	Set B	Set C	Overall
Channel A	81.08	80.64	79.37	80.56
Channel B	80.33	79.85	78.85	79.84
Channel C	43.35	43.53	41.91	43.13
Channel D	44.46	44.30	43.44	44.19

Table 11. Speech enhancement, no error mitigation.

Two methods, nearest neighbour repetition and Hermite interpolation, are used to reconstruct the feature vector stream as a result of missing features due to packet loss. Table 12 details the recognition results obtained when using nearest neighbour repetition while

Table 13 details the results obtained when Hermite interpolation is implemented (speech enhancement is used in both cases). Both reconstruction methods show improvements in recognition testing over no error mitigation for all four channels. In particular, with feature reconstruction channel C shows improvements in recognition accuracy greater than 55% for both front-ends. Channel D also shows good improvement. Nearest neighbour repetition gives a slightly higher performance compared to Hermite interpolation.

| Loss parameters | ETSI AFE absolute word accuracy % | | | |
	Set A	Set B	Set C	Overall
Channel A	84.04	83.34	81.69	83.29
Channel B	80.85	80.37	78.89	80.26
Channel C	68.90	68.25	66.83	68.23
Channel D	50.95	50.82	50.67	50.84
Loss parameters	Li *et al.* absolute word accuracy %			
	Set A	Set B	Set C	Overall
Channel A	84.57	84.00	82.67	83.96
Channel B	81.10	80.89	79.78	80.75
Channel C	68.81	68.60	66.87	68.34
Channel D	50.33	51.10	49.86	50.54

Table 12. Speech enhancement, nearest neighbour repetition.

| Loss parameters | ETSI AFE absolute word accuracy % | | | |
	Set A	Set B	Set C	Overall
Channel A	83.87	83.28	82.01	83.26
Channel B	80.81	80.21	78.78	80.17
Channel C	67.62	68.03	66.28	67.52
Channel D	50.33	50.16	48.91	49.98
Loss parameters	Li *et al.* absolute word accuracy %			
	Set A	Set B	Set C	Overall
Channel A	84.23	83.69	82.56	83.68
Channel B	80.87	80.60	79.64	80.51
Channel C	67.05	67.03	65.32	66.70
Channel D	50.33	50.16	48.91	49.98

Table 13. Speech enhancement, Hermite interpolation.

When interleaving is introduced, the receive side perceives that the average loss burst length is reduced [37]. Table 14 shows the recognition results obtained when interleaving, with an interleaving depth of 4, is used in conjunction with Hermite interpolation. Comparing the results in Table 14 with the results in Table 13 it is seen that feature reconstruction is improved when interleaving is employed.

Loss parameters	ETSI AFE absolute word accuracy %			
	Set A	Set B	Set C	Overall
Channel A	86.59	85.66	84.25	85.75
Channel B	82.65	81.89	80.51	81.92
Channel C	78.35	77.92	76.67	77.84
Channel D	58.52	58.77	59.88	58.89
Loss parameters	Li et al. absolute word accuracy %			
	Set A	Set B	Set C	Overall
Channel A	86.91	86.29	85.20	86.32
Channel B	82.84	82.15	81.50	82.30
Channel C	78.14	77.92	76.73	77.77
Channel D	57.95	58.13	57.05	57.84

Table 14. Speech enhancement, Hermite interpolation with interleaving ($d = 4$).

4.4. Discussion

The results in Table 7 show that the front-end proposed by Li et al. [14], when combined with the speech enhancement algorithm proposed by [25], reduces the overall word error rate of the ETSI advanced front-end [7] by 8%. Looking at Table 9, the vector quantisation has a lesser impact on the overall recognition performance of the ETSI advanced front-end compared with the impact of vector quantisation on the Li et al. front-end. The Li et al. front-end, combined with speech enhancement, still outperforms the ETSI advanced front-end in the presence of vector quantisation although the improvement in overall word error rate is reduced from 8% (without vector quantisation) to 5.3%. In the presence of packet loss, with no speech enhancement and with no packet loss compensation, a comparison of Table 10 shows that the front-end of Li et al. gives better overall recognition results than the ETSI advanced front-end. The benefit of speech enhancement in the presence of packet loss, without any missing feature reconstruction, can be seen by comparing Table 10 and Table 11. With speech enhancement and no packet loss compensation, Table 11 shows that Li et al. outperforms the ESTI advanced front-end for all four channels, and for all three test sets. Comparing Table 9 with Table 11, a significant reduction in recognition performance is observed in the presence of packet loss, in particular for channels C and D where the probability of packet loss is 50%. When nearest neighbour repetition is used to reconstruct missing features, Table 12 shows that there is a significant increase in recognition performance across all channels when compared to the results presented in Table 11. Looking at Table 12, the recognition results for the two front-ends under evaluation are similar across all channels and test sets. The front-end of Li *et al.* performs marginally better overall than the ETSI advanced front-end for channels A, B and C; however, for channel D, the overall recognition performance of the ETSI advanced front-end is better than that of Li *et al.* A comparison of Table 13 with Table 12 shows a slight decrease in recognition performance when Hermite interpolation is used to reconstruct the feature vector stream instead of nearest neighbour repetition. With Hermite interpolation, Table 13 shows that the front-end of Li *et al.* outperforms the ETSI advanced front-end for the packet loss conditions of channels A and B, however, for channel C the reverse is the case. The overall performance of both front-ends is the same for channel D. Interleaving the feature vectors prior to transmission on the channel gives the perception on the receive side that the loss bursts are shorter than they actually are. The advantage of interleaving can be seen by a comparison of Table 14 with Table 13, where overall recognition results are improved for both front-ends when interleaving is introduced. Looking at Table 14 it is seen that Li *et al.* gives the better overall recognition performance for channels A and B while the ETSI advanced front-end gives the better performance for channels C and D. The results indicate that, in the presence of packet loss and environmental noise, the overall recognition performance of the front-end of Li *et al.* is better than that of the ETSI advanced front-end for all channel conditions when there are no packet loss mitigation techniques implemented. For each of the error mitigation techniques used, Li *et al.* outperforms the ETSI advanced front-end for channel conditions when the probability of packet loss is 10%. For packet loss probabilities of 50%, Li *et al.* gives better results than the ETSI advanced front-end for short average burst lengths (4 packets) when nearest neighbour repetition is used. However, the ETSI advanced front-end gives better recognition performance than Li *et al.* for the same channel conditions when Hermite interpolation is used, with and without interleaving. When the average burst length is increased to 20 packets and the probability of packet loss is 50%, the overall recognition performance of the ETSI advanced front-end is better than that of the front-end of Li *et al.*

5. Conclusions

This chapter has examined the speech recognition performance of both a speech enhancement algorithm combined with the auditory model front-end proposed by Li *et al.* [14], and the ETSI advanced front-end [7], in the presence of both environmental noise and packet loss. A number of speech enhancement techniques were first examined, including well-established techniques such as Ephraim and Malah [20] and more recently-proposed techniques such as Rangachari and Loizou [21]. Experiments using the Aurora connected-digit recognition framework [16] found that the best performance was obtained using the method of Agarwal and Chang [25]. The test results also suggest that the choice of speech enhancement algorithm for best speech recognition performance is independent of the choice of front-end.

Packet loss modelling using statistical modelling was also examined, and packet loss mitigation was discussed. Following initial testing with no packet loss compensation, a number of existing packet loss mitigation techniques were investigated, namely nearest neighbour repetition and interpolation. Results show that the best recognition performance was obtained using nearest neighbour repetition to reconstruct missing features. The advantage of interleaving at the sender's side to minimise the average burst length of lost vectors was also demonstrated.

In summary, the experiments and results outlined in this chapter show the benefit of combining speech enhancement and packet loss mitigation to combat both noise and packet loss. Furthermore, the performance of the auditory model of Li *et al.* was generally shown to be superior to that of the standard ETSI advanced front-end.

Author details

Ronan Flynn
School of Engineering, Athlone Institute of Technology, Athlone, Ireland

Edward Jones
College of Engineering and Informatics, National University of Ireland, Galway, Ireland

6. References

[1] V. Digalakis, L. Neumeyer and M. Perakakis, "Quantization of cepstral parameters for speech communication over the world wide web", *IEEE Journal on Selected Areas in Communications*, vol. 17, pp. 82-90, Jan. 1999.

[2] D. Pearce, "Enabling new speech driven services for mobile devices: an overview of the ETSI standards activities for distributed speech recognition front-ends", in *Proc. AVIOS 2000: The Speech Applications Conference*, San Jose, CA, USA, May 2000.

[3] G. Gallardo-Antolín, C. Peláez-Moreno and F. Díaz-de-María, "Recognizing GSM digital speech", *IEEE Trans. on Speech and Audio Processing*, vol. 13, pp. 1186-1205, Nov. 2005.

[4] Z.H. Tan, P. Dalsgaard and B. Lindberg, "Automatic speech recognition over error-prone wireless networks", *Speech Communication*, vol. 47, pp. 220-242, 2005.

[5] Y. Ephraim and I. Cohen, "Recent advancements in speech enhancement", in *The Electrical Engineering Handbook*, 3rd ed., R.C. Dorf, Ed., Boca Raton, FL: CRC Press, 2006, pp. 15-12 to 15-26.

[6] "Speech Processing, Transmission and Quality Aspects (STQ); Distributed speech recognition; Front-end feature extraction algorithm; Compression algorithms", in *ETSI ES 201 108, Ver. 1.1.3*, Sept. 2003.

[7] "Speech Processing, Transmission and Quality Aspects (STQ); Distributed speech recognition; Advanced front-end feature extraction algorithm; Compression algorithms", in *ETSI ES 202 050, Ver. 1.1.5*, Jan. 2007.

[8] "Speech Processing, Transmission and Quality Aspects (STQ); Distributed speech recognition; Extended front-end feature extraction algorithm; Compression algorithms; Back-end speech reconstruction algorithm", in *ETSI ES 202 211, Ver. 1.1.1*, Nov. 2003.

[9] "Speech Processing, Transmission and Quality Aspects (STQ); Distributed speech recognition; Extended advanced front-end feature extraction algorithm; Compression

algorithms; Back-end speech reconstruction algorithm", in *ETSI ES 202 212, Ver. 1.1.2*, Nov. 2005.

[10] "RTP Payload Format for European Telecommunications Standards Institute (ETSI) European Standard ES 210 108 Distributed Speech Recognition Encoding", in *RFC 3557*, July 2003.

[11] "RTP Payload Formats for European Telecommunications Standards Institute (ETSI) European Standard ES 202 050, ES 202 211, and 202 212 Distributed Speech Recognition Encoding", in *RFC 4060*, May 2005.

[12] D. Macho, L. Mauuary, B. Noe, Y. M. Cheng, D. Ealey, D. Jouvet, H. Kelleher, D. Perace, and F. Saadoun, "Evaluation of a noise-robust DSR front-end on Aurora databases", in *Proceedings of International Conference on Speech and Language Processing*, Denver, Colorado, USA, Sept. 2002, pp. 17-20.

[13] L. Mauuary, "Blind equalization in the cepstral domain for robust telephone based speech recognition", in *Proc. EUSIPCO 98*, Sept. 1998, pp. 359-363.

[14] Q. Li, F. K. Soong and O. Siohan, "A high-performance auditory feature for robust speech recognition", in *Proc. of 6th International Conference on Spoken Language Processing (ICSLP)*, Beijing, China, Oct. 2000, pp. 51-54.

[15] R. Flynn and E. Jones, "A comparative study of auditory-based front-ends for robust speech recognition using the Aurora 2 database", in Proc. IET Irish Signals and Systems Conference, Dublin, Ireland, 28-30 June 2006, pp. 111-116.

[16] H. G. Hirsch and D. Pearce, "The Aurora experimental framework for the performance evaluation of speech recognition systems under noisy conditions", in *Proc. ISCA ITRW ASR-2000*, Paris, France, Sept. 2000, pp. 181-188.

[17] H. Hermansky, "Perceptual linear prediction (PLP) analysis of speech", *J. Acoust. Soc. Amer.*, vol. 87, pp. 1738-1752, 1990.

[18] J. Tchorz and B. Kollmeier, "A model of auditory perception as front end for automatic speech recognition", *J. Acoust. Soc. Amer.*, vol. 106, pp. 2040-2050, 1999.

[19] *HTK speech recognition toolkit.* Available: http://htk.eng.cam.ac.uk/. Accessed March 2011.

[20] Y. Ephraim and D. Malah, "Speech enhancement using a minimum mean-square error short-time spectral amplitude estimator", *IEEE Trans. on Acoustics, Speech and Signal Processing*, vol. 32, pp. 1109-1121, Dec. 1984.

[21] S. Rangachari and P. Loizou, "A noise-estimation algorithm for highly non-stationary environments", *Speech Communication*, vol. 48, pp. 220-231, 2006.

[22] N. Westerlund, M. Dahl and I. Claesson, "Speech enhancement for personal communication using an adaptive gain equalizer", *Speech Communication*, vol. 85, pp. 1089-1101, 2005.

[23] R. Martin, "Spectral subtraction based on minimum statistics", in *Proc. Eur. Signal Processing Conference*, 1994, pp. 1182-1185.

[24] R. Martin, "Noise power spectral density estimation based on optimal smoothing and minimum statistics", *IEEE Trans. on Speech and Audio Processing*, vol. 9, pp. 504-512, July 2001.

[25] A. Agarwal and Y.M. Cheng, "Two-stage mel-warped wiener filter for robust speech recognition", in *Proceedings of Automatic Speech Recognition and Understanding Workshop*, Keystone, Colorado, USA, 1999, pp. 67-70.

[26] D. Macho and Y. M. Cheng, "SNR-dependent waveform processing for improving the robustness of ASR front-end", in *Proc. of IEEE International Conference on Acoustics, Speech and Signal Processing (ICASSP)*, May 2001, pp. 305-308.

[27] C. Peláez-Moreno, G. Gallardo-Antolín and F. Díaz-de-María, "Recognizing voice over IP: A robust front-end for speech recognition on the world wide web", *IEEE Trans. on Multimedia*, vol. 3, pp. 209-218, June 2001.

[28] C. Peláez-Moreno, G. Gallardo-Antolín, D.F. Gómez-Cajas and F. Díaz-de-María, "A comparison of front-ends for bitstream-based ASR over IP", *Signal Processing*, vol. 86, pp. 1502-1508, July 2006.

[29] J. Van Sciver, J. Z. Ma, F. Vanpoucke and H. Van Hamme, "Investigation of speech recognition over IP channels", in *Proc. of IEEE International Conference on Acoustics, Speech and Signal Processing (ICASSP)*, May 2002, pp. 3812-3815.

[30] D. Quercia, L. Docio-Fernandez, C. Garcia-Mateo, L. Farinetti and J. C. DeMartin, "Performance analysis of distributed speech recognition over IP networks on the AURORA database", in *Proc. of IEEE International Conference on Acoustics, Speech and Signal Processing (ICASSP)*, May 2002, pp. 3820-3823.

[31] P. Mayorga, L. Besacier, R. Lamy and J. F. Serignat, "Audio packet loss over IP and speech recognition", in *Proc. of IEEE Workshop on Automatic Speech Recognition and Understanding (ASRU)*, Nov. 2003, pp. 607-612.

[32] J. Vicente-Peña, G. Gallardo-Antolín, C. Peláez-Moreno and F. Díaz-de-María, "Band-pass filtering of the time sequences of spectral parameters for robust wireless speech recognition", *Speech Communication*, vol. 48, pp. 1379-1398, Oct. 2006.

[33] B.P. Milner and A.B. James, "An analysis of packet loss models for distributed speech recognition", in *Proc. of 8th International Conference on Spoken Language Processing (ICSLP)*, Jeju Island, Korea, Oct. 2004, pp. 1549-1552.

[34] A. B. James and B. P. Milner, "An analysis of interleavers for robust speech recognition in burst-like packet loss", in *Proc. of IEEE International Conference on Acoustics, Speech and Signal Processing (ICASSP)*, May 2004, pp. 853-856.

[35] A. B. James and B. P. Milner, "Towards improving the robustness of distributed speech recognition in packet loss", in *Proc. Second COST278 and ISCA Tutorial and Research Workshop (ITRW) on Robustness Issues in Conversational Interaction*, University of East Anglia, U.K., Aug. 2004, p. paper 42.

[36] A. B. James and B. P. Milner, "Combining packet loss compensation methods for robust distributed speech recognition", in *Proc. of Interspeech-2005*, Lisbon, Portugal, Sept. 2005, pp. 2857-2860.

[37] A. B. James and B. P. Milner, "Towards improving the robustness of distributed speech recognition in packet loss", *Speech Communication*, vol. 48, pp. 1402-1421, Nov. 2006.

[38] B. P. Milner and A. B. James, "Robust speech recognition over mobile and IP networks in burst-like packet loss", in *IEEE Trans. on Audio, Speech and Language Processing* vol. 14, ed, Jan. 2006, pp. 223-231.

[39] Y. Linde, A. Buzo and R. Gray, "An algorithm for vector quantizer design", *IEEE Trans. on Communications*, vol. COM-28, pp. 84-95, Jan. 1980.

## Chapter 4

A Particle Filter Compensation Approach to Robust Speech Recognition

Aleem Mushtaq

Additional information is available at the end of the chapter

1. Introduction

The speech production mechanism goes through various stages. First, a thought is generated in speakers mind. The thought is put into a sequence of words. These words are converted into a speech signal using various muscles including face muscles, chest muscles, tongue etc. This signal is distorted by environmental factors such as background noise, reverberations, channel distortions when sent through a microphone, telephone channel etc. The aim of Automatic Speech Recognition Systems (ASR) is to reconstruct the spoken words from the speech signal. From information theoretic [1] perspective, we can treat what is between the speaker and machine as a distortion channel as shown in figure 1.

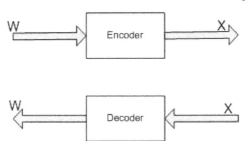

Figure 1. Information theoretic view of Speech Recognition

Here, W represent the spoken words and X is the speech signal. The problem of extracting W from X can be viewed as finding the words sequence that most likely resulted in the observed signal X as given in equation (1)

$$\hat{W} = \arg\max_{W} p(X \mid W) \tag{1}$$

Like any other Machine Learning/Pattern Recognition problem, the posterior $p(X|W)$ plays a fundamental role in the decoding process. This distribution is parametric and its parameters are found from the available training data. Modern ASR systems do well when environment of speech signal being tested matches well with that of the training data. This is so because the parameter values correspond well to the speech signal being decoded. However, if the environments of training and testing data do not match well, the performance of the ASR systems degrade. Many schemes have been proposed to overcome this problem but humans still outperform these systems, especially in adverse conditions.

The approaches to overcome this problem falls under two categories. One way is to adapt the parameters of $p(X|W)$ such that they match better with the testing environment and the other is to choose features X such that they are more robust to environment variations. The features can also be transformed to make them more suited to the parameters of $(X|W)$, obtained from training data.

1.1. Typical ASR system

Typical ASR systems for small vocabulary are comprised of three main components as shown in figure 2. Speech data is available in waveform which is first converted into feature vectors. Mel Frequency Cepstrum Coefficients (MFCC) [2] features have been widely used in speech community for the task of speech recognition due to their superior discriminative capability.

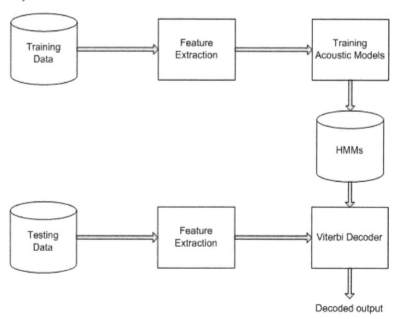

Figure 2. Typical ASR System

The features from an available training speech corpus are used to estimate the parameters of Acoustic Models. An acoustic model for a particular speech unit, say a phoneme or a word is the likelihood of observing that unit based on the features as given in equation 1.1. Most commonly used structure for the acoustic models in ASR systems is the Hidden Markov Models (HMM). These models capture the dynamics and variations of speech signal well. The test speech signal is then decoded using Viterbi Decoder.

1.2. Distortions in speech

The distortions in speech signal can be viewed in signal space, feature space and the model space [3] as shown in figure 3. Resilience to environmental distortions can be added in the feature extraction process, by modifying the distorted features or adapting the acoustic models to better match the environment from which test signal has emanated. S_X and F_X represent speech signal and speech feature respectively. M_X represent the acoustic models.

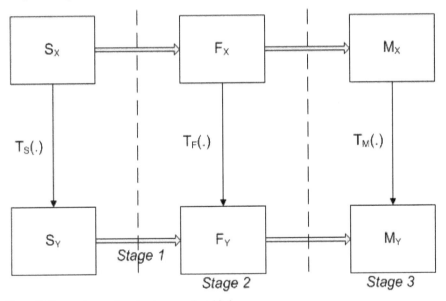

Figure 3. Stages where noise robustness can be added

In stage 1, the feature extraction process is improved so that the features are robust to distortions. In stage 2, the features are modified to match them better with the training environment. The mismatch in this stage is usually modeled by nuisance parameters. These are estimated from the environment and test data and their effect is minimized based on some optimality criteria. In stage 3, the acoustic models are improved to match better with the testing environment. One way to achieve this is to use Multi-Condition training i.e. use data from diverse environments to train the models. Another way is find transform the models where transformation matrix is obtained from the test environment.

1.3. Speech and noise tracking for noise compensation

A sequential Monte Carlo feature compensation algorithm was initially proposed [4-5] in which the noise was treated as a state variable while speech was considered as the signal corrupting the observation noise and a VTS approximation was used to approximate the clean speech signal by applying a minimum mean square error (MMSE) procedure. In [5] extended Kalman filters were used to model a dynamical system representing the noise which was further improved by using Polyak averaging and feedback with a switching dynamical system [6]. These were initial attempts to incorporate particle filter for speech recognition in more indirect fashion as it was used for tracking of noise instead of the speech signal itself. Since the speech signal is treated as corrupting signal to the noise, limited or no information readily available from the HMMs or the recognition process can be utilized efficiently in the compensation process.

Particle filters are powerful numerical mechanisms for sequential signal modeling and is not constrained by the conventional linearity and Gaussianity [7] requirements. It is a generalization of the Kalman filter [8] and is more flexible than the extended Kalman filter [9] because the stage-by-stage linearization of the state space model in Kalman filter is no longer required [7]. One difficulty of using particle filters lies in obtaining a state space model for speech as consecutive speech features are usually highly correlated. Just like in the Kalman filter and HMM frameworks, state transition is an integral part of the particle filter algorithms.

In contrast to the previous particle filter attempts [4-6] we describe a method in this chapter where we treat the speech signal as the state variable and the noise as the corrupting signal and attempt to estimate clean speech from noisy speech. We incorporate statistical information available in the acoustic models of clean speech, e.g., the HMMs trained with clean speech, as an alternative state transition model[10-11]. The similarity between HMMs and particles filters can be seen from the fact that an observation probability density function corresponding to each state of an HMM describes, in statistical terms, the characteristics of the source generating a signal of interest if the source is in that particular state, whereas in particle filters we try to estimate the probability distribution of the state the system is in when it generates the observed signal of interest. Particle filters are suited for feature compensation because the probability density of the state can be updated dynamically on a sample-by-sample basis. On the other hand, state densities of the HMMs are assumed independent of each other. Although they are good for speech inference problems, HMMs do not adapt well in fast changing environments.

By establishing a close interaction of the particle filters and HMMs, the potentials of both models can be harnessed in a joint framework to perform feature compensation for robust speech recognition. We improve the recognition accuracy through compensation of noisy speech, and we enhance the compensation process by utilizing information in the HMM state transition and mixture component sequences obtained in the recognition process. When state sequence information is available we found we can attain a 67% digit error reduction from multi-condition training in the Aurora-2 connected digit recognition task. If the missing parameters are estimated in the operational situations we only observe a 13% error reduction in the current study. Moreover, by tracking the speech features, compensation can be done using only partial information about noise and consequently good recognition performance can be obtained despite potential distortion caused by non-stationary noise within an utterance.

The remainder of the chapter is organized as follows. In section 2, a tracking scheme in general is described followed by the explanation of the well known Kalman filter tracking algorithm. Particle Filters, which form the backbone of PFC are also described in this section. In section 3, the steps involved in tracking and then extracting the clean speech signal from the noisy speech signal are laid out. We also discuss various methods to obtain information required to couple the particle filters and the HMMs in a joint framework. Finally, the experimental results and performance comparison for PFC is given before drawing the conclusions in section 4.

2. Tracking algorithms

Tracking is the problem of estimating the trajectory of an object in a space as it moves through that space. The space could be an image plane captured directly from a camera or it could be synthetically generated from a radar sweep. Generally, tracking schemes can be applied to any system that can be represented by a time dynamical system which consists of a state space model and an observation

$$x_t = f(x_{t-1}, w_t)$$
$$y_t = h(x_t, n_t)$$

(2)

Where n_t is the observation noise and w_t is called the process noise and represents the model uncertainties in the state transition function $f(.)$. What is available is an observation y_t which is function of x_t. We are interested in finding a good estimate of current state given observations till current time t i.e. $p(x_t|y_t, y_{t-1}, y_{t-2}, \cdots y_0)$. The state space model $f(.)$ represents the relation between states adjacent in time. The model in equation (2) assumes that state sequence is one step Markov process

$$f(x_{t+1} \mid x_t, x_{t-1}, ... x_0) = f(x_{t+1} \mid x_t)$$

(3)

It is further assumed that observations are independent of one another

$$f(y_{t+1} \mid x_{t+1}, y_t, ... y_0) = f(y_{t+1} \mid x_{t+1})$$

(4)

Tracking is a two step process. The first step is to obtain density x_t at time $t-1$. This is called the prior density of x_t. Once it is available, we can construct a posterior density upon availability of observation y_t. The propagation step is given in equation (5). The update step is obtained using Bayesian theory (equation (6)).

$$f(x_t \mid y_{t-1}, ..., y_0) = \int f(x_t \mid x_{t-1}) f(x_{t-1} \mid y_{t-1}, ..., y_0) dx_{t-1}$$

(5)

$$f(x_t \mid y_t, y_{t-1}, ..., y_0) = \frac{f(y_t \mid x_t, y_{t-1}, ..., y_0) f(x_t \mid y_{t-1}, ..., y_0)}{f(y_t \mid y_{t-1}, ..., y_0)} \tag{6}$$

2.1. Kalman filter as a recursive estimation tracking algorithm

Kalman Filter is the optimal recursive estimation solution for posterior density $p(x_{t+1}|y_t, ..., y_0)$ if the time dynamical system is linear

$$x_{t+1} = A_t x_t + w_t$$
$$y_t = C_t x_t + n_t \tag{7}$$

where A_t and C_t are known as state transition matrix and observation matrix respectively. Subscript t indicates that both can vary with time. Under the assumption that both process noise w_t and observation noise n_t are Gaussian with zero mean and covariance Q_t and R_t respectively, $p(x_{t+1}|x_t)$ can be readily obtained.

$$mean(x_{t+1} \mid x_t) = E(A_t x_t + w_t) = A_t x_t$$
$$covariance(x_{t+1} \mid x_t) = E(w_t w_t^T) = Q_t \tag{8}$$

and therefore

$$p(x_{t+1} \mid x_t) \sim N(A_t x_t, Q_t) \tag{9}$$

To obtain the propagation step, we need $p(x_t|y_t, ..., y_0)$ in addition to $(x_{t+1}|x_t)$. Since this is an iterative step, the estimate of x_t given observations up to time t is available at $t+1$ and let's call it $x_{t|t}$. Let covariance of $x_{t|t}$ be $P_{t|t}$. Then

$$p(x_t \mid y_t, y_{t-1}, ..., y_0) \sim N(\hat{x}_{t|t}, P_{t|t}) \tag{10}$$

where $P_{t|t}$ is the covariance of $x_t|y_t, ..., y_0$ and is given by $E[(x_t - E[x_t])(x_t - E[x_t])^T|y_t, ..., y_0]$. Now both components of the integral in equation (5) are available in equation (9) and (10). Solving the integral using expanding and completing the squares [12] we get

$$p(x_{t+1} \mid y_t, y_{t-1}, ..., y_0) \sim N(A_t \hat{x}_{t|t}, A_t P_{t|t} A_t^T + Q_t) \tag{11}$$

This is the propagation step and is sometimes is also written as

$$p(x_{t+1} \mid y_t, y_{t-1}, ..., y_0) \sim N(\hat{x}_{t+1|t}, P_{t+1|t}) \tag{12}$$

To get the update step, we note that the distributions of $x_{t+1}|y_t, ..., y_0$ and y_{t+1} are both Gaussian. For two random variables say x and y that are jointly Gaussian, the distribution of one of them given the other for example $x|y$ is also Gaussian. Consequently, $x_{t+1}|y_{t+1}, y_t, ..., y_0$ is a Gaussian distribution with following mean and variance

$$\hat{x}_{t+1} \mid x_{t+1} = E[x_{t+1} \mid y_{t+1}, y_t, ..., y_0] = \hat{x}_{t+1} \mid x_t + R_{xy} R_{yy}^{-1} (y_{t+1} - E[y_{t+1} \mid y_t, ..., y_0]) \tag{13}$$

where

$$R_{xy} = E[(x_{t+1} - E[x_{t+1}])(y_{t+1} - E[y_{t+1}])^T \mid y_t, y_{t-1}, ..., y_0]$$
$$= E[(x_{t+1} - \hat{x}_{t+1|t})(C_{t+1}(x_{t+1} - \hat{x}_{t+1|t}) + n_{t+1})^T \mid y_t, y_{t-1}, ..., y_0] \qquad (14)$$
$$= P_{t+1|t} C_{t+1}^T$$

Similarly

$$R_{yy} = C_{t+1} P_{t+1|t} C_{t+1}^T + R_{t+1} \qquad (15)$$

Back substituting equation (14) and equation (15) in equation (13), we get

$$\hat{x}_{t+1} \mid x_{t+1} = \hat{x}_{t+1|t} + K_{t+1}(y_{t+1} - C_{t+1}\hat{x}_{t+1|t}) \qquad (16)$$

where K is called the Kalman gain and is given by

$$K_{t+1} = P_{t+1|t} C_{t+1}^T (C_{t+1} P_{t+1|t} C_{t+1}^T + R_{t+1})^{-1} \qquad (17)$$

Covariance can also be obtained by referring to the fact that covariance of $x|y$, the two jointly Gaussian random variables, is given by

$$\text{cov}(X \mid Y) = R_{xx} - R_{xy} R_{yy}^{-1} R_{yx} \qquad (18)$$

we thus obtain the covariance of estimate of $\hat{x}_{t+1|t+1}$ as follows

$$P_{t+1|t+1} = P_{t+1|t} - P_{t+1|t} C_{t+1}^T (C_{t+1} P_{t+1|t} C_{t+1}^T + R_{t+1})^{-1} C_{t+1} P_{t+1|t} \qquad (19)$$
$$= (1 - K_{t+1} C_{t+1}^T) P_{t+1|t}$$

The block diagram in Figure 4 below shows a general recursive estimation algorithm steps starting from some initial state estimate x_0. The block labeled Kalman filter summarizes the steps specific to Klaman filter algorithm.

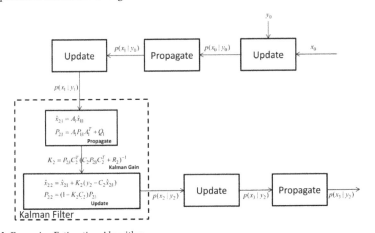

Figure 4. Recursive Estimation Algorithm

2.2. Grid based methods

It is hard to obtain analytical solutions to most recursive estimation algorithms. If the state space for a problem is discrete, then we can use grid based methods and can still obtain the optimal solution. Considering that state x takes N_s possible values, we can represent discrete density $p(y|x)$ using N_s samples[7].

$$p(x_k \mid y_k, y_{k-1}, ..., y_0) = \sum_{i=1}^{N_s} w_{k|k} \delta(x_k - x_k^i) \tag{20}$$

where the weights are computed as follows

$$w_{k|k}^i \sim \frac{1}{C} w_{k|k-1}^i p(y_k \mid x_k^i)$$

$$w_{k|k-1}^i \sim \sum_{j=1}^{N_s} w_{k-1|k-1}^i p(x_k^i \mid x_{k-1}^j) \tag{21}$$

Here C is the normalizing constant to make total probability equal one. The assumption that state can be represented by finite number of points gives us the ability to sample the whole state space. The weight w_k^i represents the probability of being in state x_k^i when observation at time k is y_k. In grid based method we construct the discrete density at every time instant in two steps. First we estimate the weights at k without the current observation $w_{k|k-1}^i$ and then update them when observation is available and obtain $w_{k|k}^i$. In the propagation step we take into account probabilities (weights) for all possible state values at $k-1$ to estimate the weights at time k as shown in figure 5.

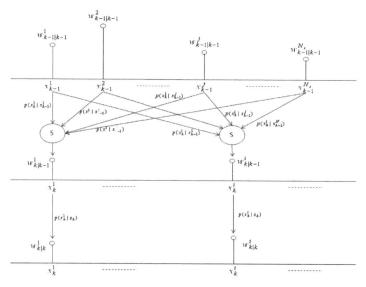

Figure 5. Grid based method

If the prior $p(x_k^i|x_k^j)$ and the observation probability $p(z_k|x_k)$ are available, the grid based method gives us the optimal solution for tracking the state of the system. If the state of the system is not discrete, then we can obtain an approximate solution using this method. We divide the continuous space into say J cells and for each cell we compute the prior and posterior in a way that takes into account the range of the whole cell:

$$p(x_k^i \mid x_{k-1}^j) = \int_{x \in x_k^i} p(x \mid \bar{x}_{k-1}^j)dx$$

$$p(y_k \mid x_k^i) = \int_{x \in x_k^i} p(y_k \mid x)dx \qquad (22)$$

where $\bar{x}_k$ is the center of jth cell at time $k-1$. The weight update in equation (21) subsequently remains unchanged.

2.3. Particle filter method

Particle filtering is a way to model signals emanating from a dynamical system. If the underlying state transition is known and the relationship between the system state and the observed output is available, then the system state can be found using Monte Carlo simulations [13]. Consider the discrete time Markov process such that

$$\begin{aligned} X_1 &\sim \mu(x_1) \\ X_t \mid X_{t-1} = x_t &\sim p(x_t \mid x_{t-1}) \\ Y_t \mid X_t = x_t &\sim p(y_t \mid x_t) \end{aligned} \qquad (23)$$

We are interested in obtaining $p(x_t|y_t, ..., y_0)$ so that we have a filtered estimate of x_t from the measurements available so far, $y_t, ..., y_0$. If the state space model for the process is available, and both the state and the observation equations are linear, then Kalman filter described above can be used to determine the optimal estimate of x_t given observations $y_t, ..., y_0$. This is so under the condition that process and observation noises are white Gaussian noise with zero mean and mutually independent. In case the state and observation equations are nonlinear, the Extended Kalman Filter (EKF) [9], which is a modified form of the Kalman Filter can be used. Particle filter algorithm estimates the state's posterior density, $p(x_t|y_t, ..., y_0)$ represented by a finite set of support points [7]:

$$p(x_t \mid y_t, y_{t-1}, ..., y_1) = \sum_{i=1}^{N_s} w_t^i \delta(x_t - x_t^i) \qquad (24)$$

where x_t^i for $i = 1, ..., N_s$ are the support points and w_t^i are the associated weights. We thus have a discretized and weighted approximation of the posterior density without the need of an analytical solution. Note the similarities with Grid based method. In that, support points for discrete distribution were predefined and covered the whole space. In particle filter algorithm, the support points are determined based on the concept of importance sampling in which instead of drawing from $p(.)$, we draw points from another distribution $q(.)$ and compute the weights using the following:

$$w^i = \frac{\pi(x^i)}{q(x^i)} \qquad (25)$$

where $\pi(.)$ is the distribution of $p(.)$ and $q(.)$ is an importance density from which we can draw samples. For the sequential case, the weight update equation can be computed one by one,

$$w_t^i = w_{t-1}^i \frac{p(y_t \mid x_t^i)p(x_t^i \mid x_{t-1}^i)}{q(x_t^i \mid x_{t-1}^i, y_t)} \qquad (26)$$

The density $q(.)$ propagates the samples to new positions at t given samples at time $t-1$ and is derived from the state transition model of the system.

3. Tracking algorithms for noise compensation

State transition information is an integral part of the particle filter algorithm and is used to propagate the particle samples through time transitions of the signal being processed. Specifically, the state transition is important to be able to position the samples at the right locations. To solve this problem, statistics from HMMs can be used. Although we only have discrete states in HMMs, each state is characterized by a continuous density Gaussian mixture model (GMM) and therefore it enables us to capture part of the variation in speech features to generate particle samples for feature compensation. Using particle filter algorithms with side information about the statistics of clean speech available in the clean HMMs we can perform feature compensation. If the clean speech is corrupted by an additive noise, n, and a distortion channel, h, then we can represent the noise corrupted speech with an additive noise model [14], assuming known statistics of the noise parameters,

$$y = x + h + \log(1 + \exp(n - x - h)) \qquad (27)$$

where $y = \log(S_y(m_p))$, $x = \log(S_x(m_p))$ and $h = \log(|H(m_p)|^2)$ and $S(m_p)$ denotes the pth mel spectrum.

$$S_y(m_p) = S_x(m_p) \mid H(m_p) \mid^2 + S_N(m_p) \qquad (28)$$

The additional side information needed for feature compensation is a set of nuisance parameters, Φ similar to *stochastic matching* [3], we can iteratively find Φ followed by decoding as shown in Figure 6:

$$\Phi' = \arg\max_{\Phi} P(Y' \mid \Phi, \Lambda) \qquad (29)$$

where Y' is the noisy or compensated utterance.

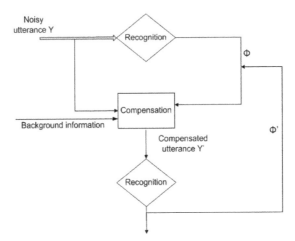

Figure 6. General feature compensation scheme

The clean HMMs and the background noise information enable us to generate appropriate samples from $q(.)$ in equation (26). The parameters Φ in equation (30) in our particle filter compensation (PFC) implementation, correspond to the corresponding correct HMM state sequence and mixture component sequence. These sequences provide critical information for density approximation in PFC. As shown in Figure 6 this can be done in two stages. We first perform a front-end compensation of noisy speech. Then recognition is done in the second stage to generate the side information Φ so as to improve compensation. This process can be iterated similar to what's done in maximum likelihood stochastic matching [3]. During compensation, the observed speech y is mapped to clean speech features x. For this purpose clean speech alone cannot be represented by a finite set of points and therefore HMMs by themselves cannot be used directly for tracking of x. Now if an HMM λ_m is available that adequately represents the speech segment under consideration for compensation along with an estimated state sequence $s_1, s_2, ..., s_T$ that correspond to T feature vectors to be considered in the segment, then we can generate the samples from the ith sample according to

$$p(x_t \mid x_{t-1}^i) \sim \sum_{k=1}^{K} c_{k,s_t} N(\mu_{k,s_t}, \Sigma_{k,s_t})$$ (30)

where $N(\mu_{k,s_t}, \Sigma_{k,s_t})$ is the kth Gaussian mixture for the state s_t in λ_m and c_{k,s_t} is its corresponding weight for the mixture. The total number of particles is fixed and the contribution from each mixture, computed at run time, depends on its weight. We have chosen the importance sampling density, $q(x_t|x_{t-1}^i, y_t)$ in equation (26) to be $p(x_t|x_{t-1}^i)$ in equation (31). This is known as the sampling importance resampling (SIR) filter [7]. It is one of the simplest implementation of particle filters and it enables the generation of samples independently from the observation. For the SIR filter, we only need to know the state and the observation equations and should be able to sample from the prior as in Eq. (3). Also, the resampling step is applied at every stage and the weight assigned to the i-th support point of the distribution of the speech signal at time t is updated as:

$$w_t^i \propto p(y_t \mid x_t^i) \tag{31}$$

The procedure for obtaining HMMs and the state sequence will be described in detail later. To obtain $p(y_t|x_t^i)$, the distribution of the log spectra of noise for each channel is assumed Gaussian with mean μ_n and variance σ_n^2. Assuming there is additive noise only with no channel effects

$$y = x + \log(1 + e^{n-x}) \tag{32}$$

We are interested in evaluating $p(y|x)$ where x represents clean speech and n is the noise with density $N(\mu_n, \sigma_n)$. Then

$$p[Y < y \mid x] = p[x + \log(1 + e^{N-x}) < y \mid x]$$
$$p(y \mid x) = F'(u) = p(u)\frac{e^{y-x}}{e^{y-x} - 1} \tag{33}$$

Where $F(\mu)$ is the Gaussian cumulative density function with mean μ_n and variance σ_n^2 and $u = \log(e^{y-x} - 1) + x$. In the case of MFCC features, the nonlinear transformation is [14]

$$y = x + D\log(1 + e^{D^{-1}(n-x)}) \tag{34}$$

Consequently,

$$p(y \mid x) = p_N(g^{-1}(y))J_{g^{-1}}(y) \tag{35}$$

where $P_N(.)$ is a Gaussian pdf, $J_{g^{-1}}(y)$ is the corresponding Jacobian and D is a discrete cosine transform matrix which is not square and thus not invertible. To overcome this problem, we zero-pad the y and x vectors and extend D to be a square matrix. The variance of the noise density is obtained from the available noise samples. Once the point density of the clean speech features is available, we estimate of the compensated features using discrete approximation of the expectation as

$$x_t = \sum_{i=1}^{N_s} w_t^i x_t^i \tag{36}$$

where N_s is the total number of particle samples at time t.

3.1. Estimation of HMM side information

As described above, it is important to obtain $\Phi \in \{\lambda_m, S\}$ where λ_m is an HMM that faithfully represents the speech segment being compensated and $S = s_1, s_2, \ldots, s_T$ is the state sequence corresponding to the utterance of length T. To obtain λ_m for the mth word W_m in the utterance, we chose the N-best models $\lambda_{m_1}, \lambda_{m_2}, \dots, \lambda_{m_N}$ from HMMs trained using 'clean speech data'. The N models are combined together to obtain a single model λ_m as follows.

3.1.1. Gaussian Mixtures Estimation

To obtain the observation model for each state j of model λ_m, we concatenate mixtures from the corresponding states of all component models,

$$\hat{b}_j^{(m)}(o) = \sum_{l=1}^{L}\sum_{k=1}^{K} c_{k,j}^{(m_l)} N(\mu_{k,j}^{(m_l)}, \Sigma_{k,j}^{(m_l)}) \tag{37}$$

where K is the number of Gaussian mixtures in each original HMM and L is the number of different words $m_1, m_2, \dots, m_L$ in the N-best hypothesis. $\mu_{k,j}^{m_l}$ and $\Sigma_{k,j}^{m_l}$ are mean and covariance from the k-th mixture in the j-th state of model m_l. The mixture weights are normalized by scaling them according to the likelihood of the occurrence of the model, from which they come from,

$$c_{k,j}^{(m_l)} = c_{k,j}^{(m_l)} \times p(W_m = \lambda_{m_i}) \tag{38}$$

The mixture weight is an important parameter because it determines the number of samples that will be generated from the corresponding mixture. The state transition coefficients for λ_m are computed using the following:

$$\hat{a}_{ij}^{(m)} = \sum_{l=1}^{L} p[s_t^{(m_l)} = i, s_{t-1}^{(m_l)} = j \mid W_m = \lambda_{m_i}] p[W_m = \lambda_{m_i}]$$

$$\hat{a}_{ij}^{(m)} = \sum_{l=1}^{L} [a_{ij}^{(m_l)} \mid W_m = \lambda_{m_i}] p[W_m = \lambda_{m_i}] \tag{39}$$

3.1.2. State sequence estimation

The recognition performance can be greatly improved if a good estimate of the HMM state sequence S is available. But obtaining this sequence in a noisy operational environment in ASR is very challenging. The simplest approach is to use the decoded state sequence obtained with multi-condition trained models in an ASR recognition process as shown in the bottom of Figure 6. However, these states could often correspond to incorrect models and deviate significantly from the optimal one. Alternatively, we can determine the states (to generate samples from) sequentially during compensation. For left-to-right HMMs, given the state s_{t-1} at time $t - 1$, we chose s_t using equation (41) as follows:

$$s_t \sim a_{s_t, s_{t-1}}$$

$$s_t = \arg\max_i (a_{ij}) \tag{40}$$

where a comes from the state transition matrix for λ_m. The mixture indices are subsequently selected from amongst the mixtures corresponding to the chosen state.

3.1.3. Experiments

To investigate the properties of the proposed approach, we first assume that a decent estimate of the state is available at each frame. Moreover, we assume that speech boundaries are marked and therefore the silence and speech sections of the utterance are known. To obtain this information, we use a set of digit HMMs (18 states, 3 Gaussian mixtures) that have been trained using clean speech represented by 23 channel mel-scale log spectral feature. The speech boundaries and state information for a particular noisy utterance is then captured through digit recognition performed on the corresponding clean speech utterance. The speech boundary information is critical because the noise statistics have to be estimated from the noisy section of the utterance. To get the HMM needed for particle filter compensation L models $\lambda_1, \lambda_2, \ldots, \lambda_L$ are selected based on the N-best hypothesis list. For our experiments, we set $L = 3$. We combine these models to get λ'_m for the m-th word in the utterance. Best results are obtained if the correct word model is present in the pool of models that contribute to λ'_m. Upon availability of this information, the compensation of the noisy log spectral features is done using the sequential importance sampling. To see the efficacy of the compensation process, we consider the noisy, clean and compensated filter banks (channel 8) for the whole utterances shown in Figure 7. The SNR for this particular case is 5 dB. It is clear that the compensated feature matches well with the clean feature. It should be noted however that such a good restoration of the clean speech signal from the noisy signal is achievable only when a good estimate of the side information about the state and mixture component sequences is available.

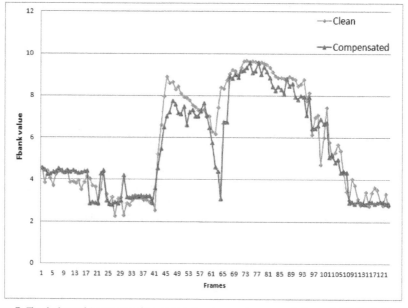

Figure 7. Fbank channel 8 corresponding underlying clean and compensated speech (SNR = 5 dB).

Assuming all such information were given (the ideal oracle case) recognition can be performed on MFCCs (39 MFCCs with 13 MFCCs and their first and second time derivatives) extracted from these compensated log spectral features. The HMMs used for recognition are trained with noisy data that has been compensated in the same way as the testing data. The performance compared to multi-condition (MC) and clean condition training (Columns 5 and 6 in Table 1) is given in Column 2 of Table 1 (Adapted Model I). It is clearly noted that a very significant 67% digit error reduction was attained if the missing information were made available to us.

Word Accuracy	Adapted Models I	Adapted Models II	Adapted Models III	MC Training	Clean Training
clean	99.10	99.10	99.10	98.50	99.11
20dB	97.75	96.46	97.38	97.66	97.21
15dB	97.61	95.98	96.47	96.95	92.36
10dB	96.66	94.00	94.40	95.16	75.14
5dB	95.20	90.64	88.02	89.14	42.42
0dB	92.13	82.62	68.28	64.75	22.57
-5dB	89.28	72.13	32.92	27.47	NA
0-20dB	95.86	90.23	88.91	88.73	65.94

Table 1. ASR accuracy comparisons for Aurora-2

In the case of the actual operational scenarios, when no side information is available, models were chosen from the N-Best list while the states were computed using Viterbi decoding. Of course, the states would correspond to only one model which might not be correct, and there might be a significant mismatch between actual and computed states. Moreover the misalignment of words also exacerbated the problem. The results for this case (Adapted Model III as shown in Table 1 Column 4) were only marginally better than those obtained with the multi-condition trained models. To see the effects of the improvements for the case where the states are better aligned, we made use of whatever information we could get. The boundaries of words were extracted from the N-Best list using exhaustive search and the states for the words between these boundaries were assigned by splitting the digits into equal-sized segments and assigning one state to each segment. This limited the damage done by state misalignment, and it can be seen that a 13% digit error reduction from MC training was observed (Adapted Model II in Table 1 Column 3).

3.2. A clustering approach to obtaining correct HMM information

HMM states are used to spread the particles at the right locations for subsequent estimation of the underlying clean speech density. If the state is incorrect, the location of particles will be wrong and the density estimate will be erroneous. One solution is to merge the states into clusters. Since the total number of clusters can be much less than the number of states, the problem of choosing the correct information block for sample generation is simplified. A tree structure to group the Gaussian mixtures from clean speech HMMs into clusters can be built with the following distance measure [15]:

$$d(m,n) = \int g_m(x) \log \frac{g_m(x)}{g_n(x)} dx + \int g_n(x) \log \frac{g_n(x)}{g_m(x)} dx \tag{41}$$

$$= \sum_i [\frac{\sigma_m^2(i) - \sigma_n^2(i) + (\mu_n(i) - \mu_m(i))^2}{\sigma_n^2(i)} \\ + \frac{\sigma_n^2(i) - \sigma_m^2(i) + (\mu_n(i) - \mu_m(i))^2}{\sigma_m^2(i)}] \tag{42}$$

where $\mu_m(i)$ is the i-th element of the mean vector μ_m and $\sigma_m^2(i)$ is the i-th diagonal element of the covariance matrix Σ_m. The parameters of the single Gaussian representing the cluster, $g_c^k(X) = N(X|\mu_k, \sigma_k^2)$, is computed as follows:

$$\mu_k(i) = \frac{1}{M_k} \sum_{m=1}^{M_k} E(x_m^{(k)}(i)) = \frac{1}{M_k} \sum_{m=1}^{M_k} \mu_m^{(k)}(i) \tag{43}$$

$$\sigma_k^2(i) = \frac{1}{M_k} \sum_{m=1}^{M_k} E((x_m^{(k)}(i) - \mu_k(i))^2 \\ = \frac{1}{M_k} \sum_{m=1}^{M_k} \sigma_m^{2(k)}(i) + \sum_{m=1}^{M_k} \mu_m^{(k)2}(i) - M_k \mu_k^2(i) \tag{44}$$

Alternatively, we can group the components at the state level using the following distance measure [16]:

$$d(n,m) = -\frac{1}{S} \sum_{s=1}^{S} \frac{1}{P} \sum_{p=1}^{P} \log[b_{ms}(\mu_{nsp})] + \log[b_{ns}(\mu_{msp})] \tag{45}$$

where S is the total number of states in the cluster, P is the number of mixtures per state and b(.) is the observation probability. This method makes it easy to track the state level composition of each cluster. In both cases, the clustering algorithm proceeds as follows:

1. Create one cluster for each mixture up to k clusters.
2. While $k > M_k$, find n and m for which $d(n,m)$ is minimum and merge them.

Once clustering is complete, it is important to pick the most suitable cluster for feature compensation at each frame. The particle samples are then generated from the representative density of the chosen cluster. Two methods can be explored. The first is to decide the cluster based on the N-best transcripts obtained from recognition using multi-condition trained models. Denote the states obtained from the N-best transcripts for noisy speech feature vectors at time t as $s_{t1}, s_{t2,...}, s_{tN}$. If state s_{ti} is a member of cluster c_k, we increment $M(c_k)$ by one, where $M(c_k)$ is a count of how many states from the N-best list belong to cluster c_k. We choose the cluster based on $\text{argmax}_k M(c_k)$ and generate samples from it. If more than one cluster satisfies this criterion, we merge their probability density functions. In the second method, we chose the cluster that maximizes the likelihood of the MFCC vector at time t, O_t, belonging to that cluster as follows:

$$C \sim \arg\max_k g_{mc}(O_t | C_k) \tag{46}$$

It is important to emphasize here that g_{mc} is derived from multi-condition speech models and has a different distribution from the one used to generate the samples. The relationship between clean clusters and multi-condition clusters is shown in figure 1. Clean clusters are obtained using methods described in section 3. The composition information of these clusters is then used to build a corresponding multi-condition cluster set from multi-condition HMMs. A cluster C_j in clean clusters represents statistical information of a particular section of clean speech. The multi-condition counterpart C_j represents statistics of the noisy version of the same speech section.

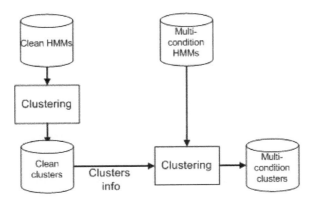

Figure 8. Clustering of multi-condition trained HMMs

Clean clusters are necessary to track clean speech because we need to generate samples from clean speech distributions. However, they are not the best choice for estimating equation (46) because the observation is noisy and has a different distribution. The best candidate for computing equation (46) is the multi-condition cluster set. It is constructed from multi-condition HMMs that match more closely with noisy speech. A block diagram of the overall compensation and recognition process is shown in Figure 9. We make inference about the cluster to be used for observation vector O_t using both the N-best transcripts and equation (46) combined together. Samples at frame t are then generated using the pdf of chosen cluster. The weights of the samples are computed using equation (46) and compensated features are obtained using equation (36). Once the compensated features are available for the whole utterance, recognition is performed again using retrained HMMs with compensated features.

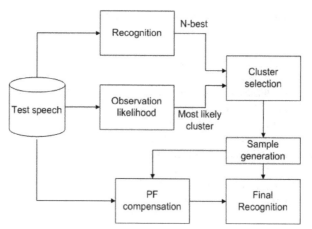

Figure 9. Complete recognition process

3.2.1. Experiments

To evaluate the proposed framework we experimented on the Aurora 2 connected digit task. We extracted features (39 elements with 13 MFCCs and their first and second time derivatives) from test speech as well as 23 channel filter-bank features thereby forming two streams. One-best transcript was obtained from the MFCC stream using the multi-condition trained HMMs. PFC is then applied to the filter-bank stream (stream two). We chose two clusters, one based on 1-best and the other selected with equation (46). The multi-condition clusters used in equation (46) were from 23 channel fbank features so that the test features from stream two can be directly used to evaluate the likelihood of the observations. For results in these experiments, clusters were formed using method two, i.e., tracking the state-wise composition of each cluster. The number of clusters and particles were varied to evaluate the performance of the algorithm under different settings. From the compensated filter-bank features of stream two, we extracted 39-element MFCC features. Final recognition on these models was done using the retrained HMMs, i.e., multi-condition training data compensated in a similar fashion as described above.

Word Accy	20 Clust.	25 Clust.	30 Clust.	MC Trained	Clean Trained
clean	99.11	99.11	99.11	98.50	99.11
20dB	97.76	98.00	97.93	97.66	97.21
15dB	97.00	97.14	96.69	96.80	92.36
10dB	95.21	95.41	93.88	95.32	75.14
5dB	89.48	89.59	87.08	89.14	42.42
0dB	70.16	70.38	68.84	64.75	22.57
-5dB	36.30	36.63	36.94	27.47	NA
0-20dB	89.92	90.10	88.88	88.73	65.94

Table 2. Variable number of clusters (100 particles)

The results for a fixed number of particles (100) are shown in Table 1. The number of clusters was 20, 25 or 30. To set the specific number of clusters, HMM states were combined and clustering was stopped when the specified number was reached. HMM sets for all purposes were 18 states, with each state represented by 3 Gaussian mixtures. For the 11-digit vocabulary, we have a total of approximately 180 states. In case of, for example, 20 clusters, we have a 9 to 1 reduction of information blocks to choose from for plugging in the PF scheme.

It is interesting to note that best results were obtained for 25 clusters. Increasing the number of clusters beyond 25 did not improve the accuracy. The larger the number of clusters, the more specific speech statistics each cluster contains. If the number of clusters is large, then each cluster encompasses more specific section of the speech statistics. Having more specific information in each cluster is good for better compensation and recognition because the particles can be placed more accurately. However, due to the large number of clusters to choose from, it is difficult to pick the correct cluster for generation of particles. More errors were made in the cluster selection process resulting in degradation in the overall performance.

This is further illustrated in Figure 10. If the correct cluster is known, having large number of clusters and consequently more specific information per cluster will only improve the performance. The results are for 20, 25 and 30 clusters. In the known cluster case, one cluster is obtained using equation (46) and the second cluster is the correct one. Correct cluster means the one that contains the state (obtained by doing recognition on the clean version of the noisy utterance using clean HMMs) to which the observation actually belongs to. For the unknown cluster case, the clusters are obtained using equation (46) and 1 − best. It can readily be observed from the known cluster case that if the choice of cluster is always correct, the recognition performance improves drastically. Error rate was reduced by 54%, 59% and 61.4% for 20, 25 and 30 clusters, respectively. Moreover, improvement faithfully follows the number of clusters used. This was also corroborated by the fact that if the cluster is specific down to the HMM state level, i.e., the exact HMM state sequence was assumed known and each state is a separate cluster (total of approximately 180 clusters), the error rate was reduced by as much as 67% [10].

For the results in Table 2, we fixed the number of clusters and varied the number of particles. As we increased the number of particles, the accuracy of the algorithm improves for set A and B combined i.e. for additive noise. The error reduction is 17% over MC trained models. Using a large number of particles implies more samples were utilized to construct the predicted densities of the underlying clean speech features, which is now denser and thus better approximated. Thus, a gradual improvement in the recognition results was observed as the particles increased. In case of Set C, however, the performance was worse when more particles were used. This is so because the underlying distribution is different due to the distortions other than additive noise.

	Set A	Set B	Set C	Average
100 particles	90.02	91.03	89.26	90.1
500 particles	90.03	91.10	89.07	90.07
1000 particles	90.02	91.13	89.07	90.07
MC Trained	88.41	88.82	88.97	88.73
Clean Trained	64.00	67.46	65.39	65.73

Table 3. Variable number of particles (25 clusters)

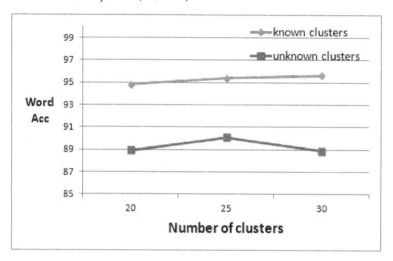

Figure 10. Accuracy when correct cluster known vs. unknown

4. Conclusions

In this chapter, we proposed a particle filter compensation approach to robust speech recognition, and show that a tight coupling and sharing of information between HMMs and particle filters has a strong potential to improve recognition performance in adverse environments. It is noted that we need an accurate alignment of the state and mixture sequences used for compensation with particle filters and the actual HMM state sequences that describes the underlying clean speech features.   Although we have observed an improved performance in the current particle filter compensation implementation there is still a considerable performance gap between the oracle setup with correct side information and what's achievable in this study with the missing side information estimated from noisy speech. We further developed a scheme to merge statistically similar information in HMM states to enable us to find the right section of HMMs to dynamically plug in the particle filter algorithm. Results show that if we use information from HMMs that match specifically well with section of speech being compensated, significant error reduction is possible compared to multi-condition HMMs.

Author details

Aleem Mushtaq

School of ECE, Georgia Institute of Technology, Atlanta, USA

5. References

[1] C.-H. Lee and Q. Huo, "On adaptive decision rules and decision parameter adaptation for automatic speech recognition", *Proc. IEEE*, vol. 88, pp. 1241-1269, 2000.

[2] S.Davis and P. Mermelstein, "Comparison of parametric representations for monosyllable word recognition in continuously spoken sentences," Proc. ICASSP 1980ol. 28, no.4, pp. 357-366, 1980.

[3] A. Sankar and C.-H. Lee, "A maximum-likelihood approach to stochastic matching for robust speech recognition," IEEE Trans. Speech Audio Processing, vol. 4, pp.190-202, May.1996.

[4] B. Raj, R. Singh, and R. Stern, "On tracking noise with linear dynamical system models." Proc. ICASSP, 2004.

[5] M. Fujimoto and S. Nakamura, "Particle Filter based non-stationary noise tracking for robust speech recognition," Proc. ICASSP, 2005.

[6] M. Fujimoto and S. Nakamura, "Sequential non-stationary noise tracking using particle filtering with switching dynamical system," Proc. ICASSP, 2006.

[7] M .S. Arulampalam, S. Maskell, N. Gordon, and T. Clapp, "A Tutorial on Particle Filters for Online Nonlinear/Non-Gaussian Bayesian Tracking," IEEE Trans. Signal Proc., 2002.

[8] Robert Grover Brown and Patrick Y. C. Hwang. 1996. Introduction to Random Signals and Applied Kalman Filtering, 3rd edition, Prentice Hall.

[9] Simon Haykin. 2009. Adaptive Filter Theory, 4th edition, Prentice Hall.

[10] A. Mushtaq, Y. Tsao and C.-H. Lee, "A Particle Filter Compensation Approach to Robust Speech Recognition." Proc. Interspeech, 2009.

[11] A. Mushtaq and C.-H. Lee, "An integrated approach to feature compensation combining particle filters and Hidden Markov Model for robust speech recognition." Proc. ICASSP, 2012.

[12] Todd K. Moon and Wynn C. Stirling. 2007. Mathematical Methods and Algorithms for Signal Processing, Pearson Education.

[13] N Arnaud, Doucet, and Johansen, "A tutorial on particle filtering and smoothing: Fifteen years later," Tech. Rep., 2008. [Online].
http://www.cs.ubc.ca/~arnaud/doucet_johansen_tutorialPF.pdf

[14] A. Acero, L. Deng, T. Kristjansson, and J. Zhang, "HMM adaptation using vector Taylor series for noisy speech recognition," Proc. ICSLP, pp. 869-872, 2002.

[15] T. Watanbe, K. Shinoda, K. Takagi, and E. Yamada, "Speech recognition using tree-structured probability sensity function," in Proc. Int. Conf. Speech Language Processing '94, 1994, pp. 223-226.

[16] S. J. Young, J. J. Odell, and P. C. Woodland, "Tree-based state tying for high accuracy acoustic modeling, " Proc. ARPA Human Language Technology Workshop, pp. 307–312, 1994.

## Chapter 5

Improvement Techniques for Automatic Speech Recognition

Santiago Omar Caballero Morales

Additional information is available at the end of the chapter

1. Introduction

Research on spoken language technology has led to the development of Automatic Speech Recognition (ASR), Text-To-Speech (TTS) synthesis, and dialogue systems. These systems are now used for different applications such as in mobile telephones for voice dialing, GPS navigation, information retrieval, dictation, translation, and assistance for handicapped people.

To perform Automatic Speech Recognition (ASR) there are different techniques such as Artificial Neural Networks (ANNs), Support Vector Machines (SVMs), Weighted Finite State Transducers (WFSTs), and Hidden Markov Models (HMMs). In the case of HMMs there are algorithms such as Viterbi, Baum - Welch / Forward - Backward, that adjust their parameters and the decoding/recognition process itself. However these algorithms do not guarantee optimization of these parameters as the recognition process is stochastic.

Main challenges arise when the structures used to describe the stochastic process (i.e., a three-state left-to-right HMM) are not enough to model the acoustic features of the speech. Also, when training data to build robust ASR systems is sparse. In practice, both situations are met, which leads to decrease in rates of ASR accuracy. Thus, research has focused on the development of techniques to overcome these situations and thus, to improve ASR performance. In the fields of heuristic optimization, data analysis, and finite state automata, diverse techniques have been proposed for this purpose. In this chapter, the theoretical bases and application details of these techniques are presented and discussed.

Initially, the optimization approach is reviewed in Section 2, where the application of heuristic methods as Genetic Algorithms and Tabu Search for structure and parameter optimization of HMMs is presented. This continues in Section 3, where the application of WFSTs and discrete HMMs for statistical error modelling of an ASR system's response is presented. This approach is proposed as a corrective method to improve ASR performance. Also, the use of a data analysis algorithm as Non-negative Matrix Factorization (NMF) is presented as a mean to improve the information obtained from sparse data. Then, case studies where these techniques are applied, and statistically significant improvements on ASR performance is achieved, are presented and discussed in Section 4. Finally, in Section 5 the main conclusions and observations about the techniques and their performance on ASR development are presented.

2. Techniques for optimization of parameters

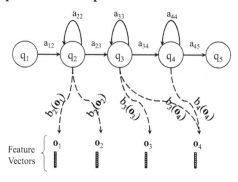

Figure 1. Parameters of an HMM.

In Figure 1 the standard structure and parameters of an HMM for acoustic modelling at the phonetic level are shown [10]. The notation $\lambda = (A, B, \pi)$ is used to indicate these parameters, where π is an initial state distribution [1]. There are three main problems associated with HMMs, and thus, with the estimation of these parameters:

- The evaluation problem. Given the parameters of a model (λ), estimate the probability of a particular observation sequence ($Pr(\mathbf{O}|\lambda)$).

- The learning problem. Given a sequence of observations o_t from a training set, estimate/adjust the transition (A) and the emission (B) probabilities of an HMM to describe the data more accurately.

- The decoding problem. Given the parameters of the model, find the most likely sequence of hidden states $Q^* = \{q_1, q_2, ..., q_n\}$ that could have generated a given output sequence $\mathbf{O} = \{\mathbf{o}_1, \mathbf{o}_2, ..., \mathbf{o}_t\}$.

Standard algorithms such as Viterbi (for decoding) and Baum-Welch (learning) are widely used for these problems [1]. However, heuristics such as Tabu Search (TS) and Genetic Algorithms (GA) have been proposed to further improve the performance of HMMs and the parameters estimated by Viterbi/Baum-Welch.

A GA is a search heuristic that mimics the process of natural evolution and generates useful solutions to optimization problems [2]. In Figure 2 the general diagram of a GA used for HMM optimization is show, where the solutions for an optimization problem receive values based on their quality or "fitness", which determine their opportunities for reproduction. It is expected that parent solutions of very good quality will produce offsprings (by means of reproduction operators such as crossover or mutation) with similar or better characteristics, improving their fitness after some generations. Hence, fitness evaluation is a mechanism used to determine the confidence level of the optimized solutions to the problem [9]. In Figure 3 a general "chromorome" representation of an individual of the GA population, or parent solution, is shown. This array contains the elements of an HMM (presented in Figure 1), which can be coded into binary format to perform reproduction of solutions.

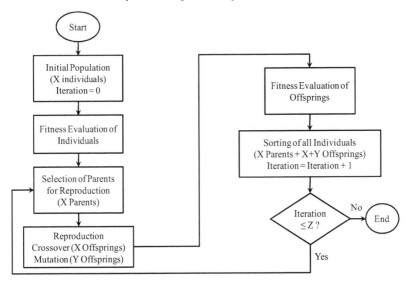

Figure 2. General diagram of a GA for optimization of HMMs.

		Transition Matrix				Observation Probabilities				Initial State Distribution			
N	M	a_{11}	...	...	...	a_{NN}	b_{11}	...	...	...	b_{NM}	π_1	...	...	...	π_N

Figure 3. Chromosome array of the elements of an HMM, where N defines the number of states, and M the number of mixture components of the observation probabilities' distributions.

In [3], GA optimization was performed for the observation probabilities and transition states for word HMMs, while in [8] finding an optimal structure was the objective. In [8], the fitness of individuals (HMM structures) was measured considering (1) the log-likelihood sum of the HMM calculated by the Viterbi algorithm over a training set of speech data, and (2) a penalization based on the error rate obtained with the HMM when performing Viterbi over a sub-set of test data. [9] used a GA to optimize the number of states in the HMM and its parameters for web information extraction, obtaining important increases in precision rates when compared with Baum-Welch training. Fitness was measured on the likelihood $(Pr(\boldsymbol{O}|\lambda))$ over a training set.

On the other hand, TS is a metaheuristic that can guide a heuristic algorithm from a local search to a global space to find solutions beyond the local optimality [11]. It can avoid loops in the search process by restricting certain "moves" that would make the algorithm to revisit a previously explored space of solutions. These moves are kept hidden or reserved (are being kept "Tabu") in a temporal memory (a Tabu List) which can be updated with new moves or released with different criteria. While in a GA the diversification of the search process is performed by the reproduction operators, in TS this is performed by "moves" which consist of perturbances (changes) in the parameter values of an initial solution (i.e., observation or transition probabilities). These changes can be defined by a function, or by adding or substracting small randomly generated quantities to the initial solution's values.

This approach was explored by [27] for HMM optimization. As in other studies, the log probability indicating the HMM likelihood over a training set was used to measure the fitness of a solution. The "moves" consisted in adding randomly generated values to each HMM's parameters. In the next section, improvement techniques based on statistical error modelling of phoneme confusions are presented and discussed.

3. Statistical error modelling techniques

Modelling of phoneme confusions has been explored to estimate error patterns in the articulation and automatic recognition of speech. The statistical modelling of this information has led to achieve improvements in the performance of ASR systems. In [17] a word confusion-matrix was used to predict the performance of a speaker-dependent ASR system. This allowed the removal of words more likely to be confused from a selected vocabulary, and to form a better set of command-words for control applications.

A similar "vocabulary design" approach was also used in [18], where a phoneme confusion - matrix was used to incorporate alternative transcriptions of a word in the dictionary, and thus, reduce its confusion probability with other words. A chinese - character confusion - matrix was used in [23] to get more accurate "candidates" to increase recognition of chinese scripts. In [20], the modelling of phoneme confusions was performed to correct phoneme recognition errors. In this section, three main techniques to perform statistical modelling of phoneme-confusions patterns are presented:

- Non-negative Matrix Factorization, NMF (Section 3.1.1). Application case in Section 4.2 (with Metamodels).

- Metamodels (Section 3.2). Application case in Section 4.1 (with GA), 4.2 (with NMF), and 4.3 (with WFSTs).

- Weighted Finite State Transducers, WFSTs (Section 3.3). Application case in Section 4.3 (with Metamodels).

3.1. Phoneme confusion-matrix as resource for error modelling

In the field of artificial intelligence, a confusion-matrix is a visualization tool typically used in supervised learning. Each column of the matrix represents the instances in a recognized class, while each row represents the instances in an actual class [15]. One benefit of a confusion matrix is that it is easy to see if the system is confusing two classes (e.g., commonly mislabelling or classifying one as another).

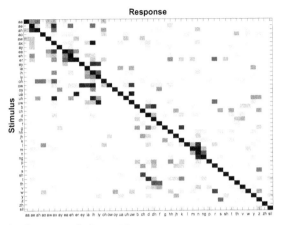

Figure 4. Example of a phoneme confusion-matrix.

As shown in Figure 4, in a phoneme confusion-matrix, rows represent the phonemes intended or uttered by the speaker (*stimulus phonemes*), and the columns represent the decoded phonemes given by the ASR system (*response*)[1]. The classification of phonemes to estimate a phoneme confusion - matrix is performed by the alignment of two phoneme strings (or sequences):

- P, the reference (correct) phoneme transcription of the sequence of words W uttered by a speaker.
- $\tilde{P}^*$, the sequence of phonemes decoded by the ASR system.

As $\tilde{P}^*$ is the system's output, it might contain several errors. Based on the classification performed by the aligner, these are identified as substitution (S), insertion (I), and deletion (D) errors. Thus, the performance of ASR systems is measured based on these errors, and two metrics are widely used for phoneme and word ASR performance:

$$Word\_Accuracy(WAcc) = \frac{N - D - S - I}{N}, \quad Word\_Error\_Rate(WER) = 1 - WAcc \quad (1)$$

where N is the number of elements (words or phonemes) in the reference string (P). Thus, the objective of the statistical modelling of the phoneme confusion-matrix is to estimate W from $\tilde{P}^*$. This can be accomplished by the following expression [22]:

$$W^* = \max_P \prod_j^M Pr(p_j)Pr(\tilde{p}_j^*|p_j) \quad (2)$$

---

[1] In this case, each class is a phoneme in the British-English BEEP pronunciation dictionary [13] which considers 45 phonemes (vowels and consonants).

where p_j is the j'th phoneme in the postulated phoneme sequence P, and $\tilde{p}_j^*$ the j'th phoneme in the decoded sequence $\tilde{P}^*$ (of length M). Equation 2 indicates that the most likely word sequence is the sequence that is most likely given the observed phoneme sequence from a speaker. The term $Pr(\tilde{p}_j^*|p_j)$ represents the probability that the phoneme $\tilde{p}_j^*$ is recognized when p_j is uttered, and is obtained from a speaker's confusion-matrix. This element is integrated into the recognition process as presented in Figure 5.

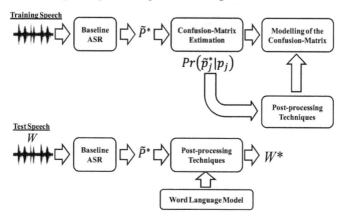

Figure 5. Training and testing process of error modelling techniques.

This information then can be modelled by post-processing techniques to improve the baseline ASR's output. Evaluation is performed when $\tilde{P}^*$ (which now is obtained from test speech) is decoded by using the "trained" techniques into sequences of words W^*. The correction process is done at the phonetic level, and by incorporating a word-language model a more accurate estimate of W is obtained. In the sections 3.2 and 3.3, the foundations of two post-processing techniques are explained.

3.1.1. Non-negative matrix factorization to improve phoneme confusion - matrix estimates

An important problem is observed when the data available for confusion-matrix estimation is small, which leads to poor estimates, and in practice, this is the normal situation. An approach presented by [28] and [30] made use of Non-negative Matrix Factorization (NMF) to find structure within confusion-matrices from a set of "training" speakers, which then could be used to make improved estimates for a "test" speaker given only a few samples from his/her speech. An advantage of this technique is that it was able to remove some of the noise present in the sparse estimates, while retaining the particular speaker's confusion-matrix patterns. This approach is reviewed in this section.

NMF is more suitable to estimate confusion-matrix probabilities (e.g., $Pr(\tilde{p}_i^*|p_i)$), as these are non-negative. This is a property not shared by similar methods as Principal Component Analysis (PCA) and Singular Value Decomposition (SVD). Note that, although there is no guarantee that the NMF estimates will be in the range [0,1], the normalizations required are less severe than those required if negative estimates are present.

NMF seeks to approximate an $n \times m$ non-negative matrix V by the product of two non-negative matrices W and H:

$$V \approx WH. \tag{3}$$

where W is a $n \times r$ matrix, H is a $r \times m$ matrix, and $r \leq min(n,m)$. When $r < min(n,m)$, the estimate of V, $\hat{V} = WH$, can be regarded as having being projected into and out of a lower-dimensional space r [6]. The columns of W are regarded as forming a set of (non-orthogonal) basis vectors that efficiently represent the structure of V, with the columns of H acting as weights for individual column vectors of V [28]. Estimation of V is accomplished by minimizing a distance function between WH and V, which is defined by the Frobenius norm [6].

In this case, for a speaker S_y, it is assumed that two types of confusion-matrices exist, (1) a **target** confusion-matrix, which is estimated using all the available utterances from that speaker and is designated as CM^y, and (2) **partial** confusion-matrices, defined as CM_U^y, which are estimated by using some U utterances. Thus, for NMF each column of V is a **target** confusion-matrix CM^x (written out column by column) from a training-set speaker S_x. To estimate a **target** confusion-matrix CM^y from a **partial** confusion-matrix CM_U^y of a "test" speaker S_y, CM_U^y is added as an extra column to V. When NMF is applied to V, the estimated confusion-matrix $\widehat{CM}^y$ is retrieved from $\hat{V}$ and is re-normalized so that its rows sum to 1.0. A weighted distance squared difference measure $D(CM^y, \widehat{CM}^y)$ can be used to assess the quality of the estimates of $\widehat{CM}^y$. The process, presented in Figure 6 is iterated until the obtained estimates converge.

If the data available from a speaker is very small, the **partial** confusion-matrix CM_U^y will be too sparse to make an improved estimate using NMF. Hence, CM_U^y can be smoothed by using a speaker-independent confusion-matrix $\overline{CM}$, which is well estimated from the training data. If the total number of non-zero elements in CM_U^y is less than a given threshold (TH), the row can be replaced by the equivalent row of $\overline{CM}$.

3.2. Metamodels

In practice, it is too restrictive to use only the confusion-matrix to model $Pr(\tilde{p}_j^*|p_j)$ as this cannot model insertions well. Instead, a Hidden Markov model (HMM) can be constructed for each of the phonemes in the phoneme inventory. These HMMs, termed as *metamodels* [22, 24], can be best understood by comparison with a "standard" acoustic HMM: a standard acoustic HMM estimates $Pr(O'|p_j)$, where O' is a subsequence of the complete sequence of observed acoustic vectors in the utterance, O, and p_j is a postulated phoneme in P. A metamodel estimates $Pr(\tilde{P}'|p_j)$, where $\tilde{P}'$ is a subsequence of the complete sequence of observed (decoded) phonemes in the utterance $\tilde{P}$.

The architecture of the metamodel of a phoneme is shown in Figure 7 [22, 24]. Each state of a metamodel has a discrete probability distribution over the symbols for the set of phonemes, plus an additional symbol labelled DELETION. The central state (2) of a metamodel for a certain phoneme models correct decodings, substitutions and deletions of this phoneme made by the phoneme recognizer. States 1 and 3 model (possibly multiple) insertions before and after the phoneme. If the metamodel were used as a generator, the output phone sequence produced could consist of, for example:

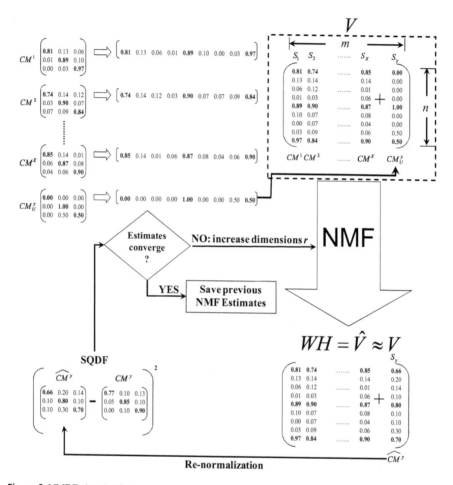

Figure 6. NMF Estimation Process.

- a single phone which has the same label as the metamodel (a correct decoding) or a different label (a substitution);

- a single phone labelled DELETION (a deletion);

- two or more phones (one or more insertions).

As an example of the operation of a metamodel, consider a hypothetical phoneme that is always decoded correctly without substitutions, deletions or insertions. In this case, the discrete distribution associated with the central state would consist of zeros except for the probability associated with the symbol for the phoneme itself, which would be 1.0. In addition, the transition probabilities a_{02} and a_{24} would be set to 1.0 so that no insertions could

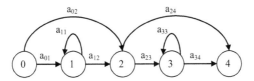

Figure 7. Metamodel of a phoneme.

be made. When used as a generator, this model can produce only one possible phoneme sequence: a single phoneme which has the same label as the metamodel.

The discrete probability distributions of each metamodel can be refined by using embedded re-estimation with the Baum-Welch Algorithm [10] over the $\{P, \tilde{P}^*\}$ pairs of all the utterances. When performing speech recognition, the language model is used to compile a "meta-recognizer" network, which is identical to the network used in a standard word recognizer except that the nodes of the network are the appropriate metamodels rather than the acoustic models used by the word recognizer. As shown in Figure 5, the output test phoneme sequence $\tilde{P}^*$ is passed to the meta-recognizer to produce a set of word hypotheses.

3.2.1. Extended metamodels

An extension to the original metamodel was presented by [29], noting that only one state is used to model multiple insertions in the original metamodel. Because of the first-order Markov property, this would not be able to model patterns within insertions. In order to cover a higher number of insertions, and identify their pattern of substitutions, the insertion-states were extended as shown in Figure 8.

Having information about the pattern of substitutions of an insertion can provide support to the modelling of the "insertion-context" of a phoneme. B_j represents the j-th *insertion-before* the phoneme, and A_k is the k-th *insertion-after* the phoneme. These $j = 1 \dots J$ and $k = 1 \dots K$ indexes identify the contexts of such insertions, where J and K represent the length of the contexts.

For the modelling of the insertions **"before"** a phoneme, consider the Figure 9(a). As the "insertion-context" is taken with reference of the central state (C), state B_1 models the first-order insertions, state B_2 the second-order insertions, and so until state B_J, where J is the length of the context. From left-to-right, state B_{J+1} is the "initial" state, and B_0 is the central state (as state 0 and state 2 in Figure 7).

While the probabilities within each state are estimated from the normalized confusion - matrices, the transition probabilities a between states are estimated from the non - normalized confusion - matrices. Figure 9(a) shows a general example of the counts (ocurrences of phonemes) within each state B_j, where $C(B_j)$ represents the total counts in that state. Note that $C(B_0) = C(C)$, and $C(B_{J+1}) = 0$, as the initial state has null observations (non-emitting state). ΔB_j represents the number of elements that do the *transition* to a particular state B_j, and is expressed as:

$$\Delta B_j = C(B_j) - C(B_{j+1}) \tag{4}$$

The transition probabilities a_B for the "insertion-before" states are then computed as:

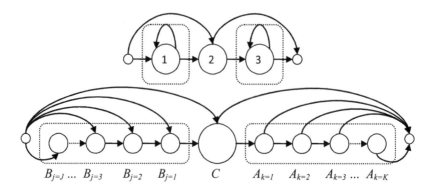

Figure 8. Extended metamodel of a phoneme. The states A_k and B_j represent the k-th insertion-after, and the j-th insertion-before, of a phoneme.

> **for** $j = 0$ to J **do**
> $$a\_B_{J+1,j} = \frac{C(B_j) - C(B_{j+1})}{C(B_0)} = \frac{\Delta B_j}{C(B_0)}$$
> **end for**

The above algorithm also gives the transition probability from the initial state to the central state when $j = 0$ ($a\_B_{J+1,0}$). When a transition ends into an insertion state (B_j), the next transition must be to the preceding insertion state (B_{j-1}) because there is a dependency on their ocurrences, so:

> **for** $j = 0$ to J-1 **do**
> $$a\_B_{j+1,j} = 1$$
> **end for**

The modelling of the insertions **"after"** a phoneme is performed in a slightly different way as the transition sequences change. As shown in Figure 9(b), the "insertion-context" is taken with reference of the central state (C), where state A_1 models the first-order insertions, state A_2 the second-order insertions, and so until state A_K, where K is the length of the context. From left-to-right, state A_0 is the central state, and A_{K+1} is the final or end state (as state 2 and state 4 in Figure 7). $C(A_0) = C(B_0) = C(C)$, and $C(A_{K+1}) = 0$ as the final state is non-emitting.

When starting on the central state there must be a sequence for the next transitions, thus either going to the final state A_{K+1} or to the first-order insertion-after state A_1. If the above transition ended in A_1, then the next transition could be to the second-order insertion-after state A_2, or to the final state A_{K+1}, and so on. ΔA_k represents the number of elements or observations that move from an insertion-after state A_k to the final state A_{K+1} and is expressed as:

$$\Delta A_k = C(A_k) - C(A_{k+1}) \tag{5}$$

The remaining observations, $C(A_k)$-ΔA_k, do the transition to the state A_{k+1}, as the elements in A_{k+1} are dependent on the same number of elements in A_k. The transition probabilities a_A for each insertion-after state are computed as:

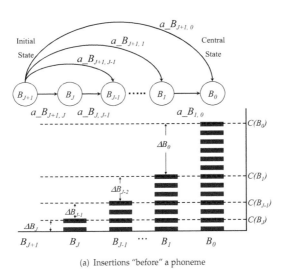

(a) Insertions "before" a phoneme

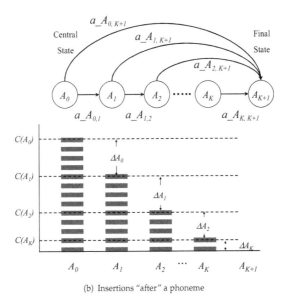

(b) Insertions "after" a phoneme

Figure 9. Extended insertion states of a metamodel.

for $k = 0$ to K+1 **do**

$$a\_A_{k,K+1} = \frac{C(A_k) - C(A_{k+1})}{C(A_k)} = \frac{\Delta A_k}{C(A_k)}$$

end for

for $k = 0$ to K **do**

$$a\_A_{k,k+1} = \frac{C(A_{k+1})}{C(A_k)}$$

end for

3.3. Weighted finite state transducers

As presented by [25] and [26] , a network of Weighted Finite-State Transducers (WFSTs) is an alternative for the task of estimating W from $\tilde{P}^*$. This is because the speech recognition process can be realized as a composition of WFSTs.

WFSTs can be regarded as a network of automata, each of which accepts an input symbol and outputs one of a finite set of outputs, each of which has an associated probability. The outputs are drawn (in this case) from the same alphabet as the input symbols and can be single symbols, sequences of symbols, or the deletion symbol ϵ . The automata are linked by a (typically sparse) set of arcs and there is a probability associated with each arc.

The WFSTs can be used to model a speaker's phonetic confusions. In addition, a composition of such transducers can model the mapping from phonemes to words, and the mapping from words to a word sequence described by a grammar. The usage proposed here complements and extends the work presented by [20], in which WFSTs were used to correct phoneme recognition errors. Here, the technique is extended to convert noisy phoneme strings into word sequences.

Hence, for this approach, the following transducers to decode $\tilde{P}^*$ into a sequence of words W^* are defined:

1. C, the confusion matrix transducer, which models the probabilities of phoneme insertions, deletions and substitutions.

2. D, the dictionary transducer, which maps sequences of decoded phonemes from $\tilde{P}^* \circ C$ into words in the dictionary.

3. G, the language model transducer, which defines valid sequences of words from D.

Thus, the process of estimating the most probable sequence of words W^* given $\tilde{P}^*$ can be expressed as:

$$W^* = \tau^*(\tilde{P}^* \circ C \circ D \circ G) \tag{6}$$

where τ^* denotes the operation of finding the most likely path through a transducer and $\circ$ denotes composition of transducers [25]. Details of each transducer are presented in the following section.

3.3.1. Confusion matrix transducer C

In this section, the formation of the confusion-matrix transducer C is described. In Section 3.1, $\tilde{p}_j^*$ as the j'th phoneme in $\tilde{P}^*$ and p_j as the j'th phoneme in P were defined, where $Pr(\tilde{p}_j^*|p_j)$

is estimated from the speaker's confusion-matrix, which is obtained from an alignment of many sequences of $\tilde{P}^*$ and P. While single substitutions are modelled in the same way by both metamodels and WFSTs, insertions and deletions are modelled in a different way, taking advantage of the characteristics of the WFSTs. Here, the confusion-matrix transducer C can map single and multiple phoneme insertions and deletions.

$$P: \quad /ax\ b\ aa\ th\ ih \quad\quad ax\ z\ \ w\ ey\ \ ih\ ng\ dh\ ax\ b\ \ eh\ t/$$
$$\tilde{P}^*: /ax \quad\quad r\ \ ih\ ng\ dh\ ax\ ng\ dh\ ax\ l\ ih\ ng\ dh\ ax\ b/$$

Table 1. Example of an alignment of transcription P, and recognized output $\tilde{P}^*$, for estimation of a Confusion-Matrix Transducer C.

Consider Table 1, where the top row of phonemes represents the transcription of a word sequence, and the bottom row the output from the speech recognizer. It can be seen that the phoneme sequence /b aa/ is deleted after /ax/, and this can be represented in the transducer as a multiple substitution/insertion: /ax/→/ax b aa/. Similarly the insertion of /ng dh/ after /ih/ is modelled as /ih ng dh/→/ih/. The probabilities of these multiple substitutions / insertions / deletions are estimated by counting. In cases where a multiple insertion or deletion is made of the form $A{\rightarrow}/B\ C/$, the appropriate fraction of the unigram probability mass $Pr(A{\rightarrow}B)$ is subtracted and given to the probability $Pr(A{\rightarrow}/B\ C/)$, and the same process is used for insertions or deletions of higher order.

A fragment of the confusion-matrix transducer that represents the alignment of Table 1 is presented in Figure 10. For computational convenience, the weight for each confusion in the transducer is represented as $-logPr(\tilde{p}_j^*|p_j)$. In practice, an initial set of transducers are built directly from the speaker's "unigram" confusion matrix, which is estimated using each transcription/output alignment pair available from that speaker, and then to add extra transducers that represent multiple substitution/insertion/deletions. The complete set of transducers are then determinized and minimized, as described in [25]. The result of these operations is a single transducer for the speaker as shown in Figure 10.

3.3.2. Dictionary and language model transducer (D, G)

The transducer D maps sequences of phonemes into valid words. Although other work has investigated the possibility of using WFSTs to model pronunciation in this component [12], here the pronunciation modelling is done by the transducer C. A small fragment of the dictionary entries is shown in Figure 11, where each sequence of phonemes that forms a word is listed as an FST. The minimized union of all these word entries is also shown. The single and multiple pronunciations of each word were taken from the British English BEEP pronouncing dictionary [13].

The language model FSA (Finite State Automata) G can be represented as in Figure 12, where $<\ s\ >$ represents the state for a starting word, and $\{w_1, w_2\}$ a word bigram. A backoff state is added for when a bigram probability is not in the model, in which case $P(w_2|w_1) = P(w_2)B(w_1)$.

In the following sections, applications and results of the techniques reviewed in this section will be presented and discussed.

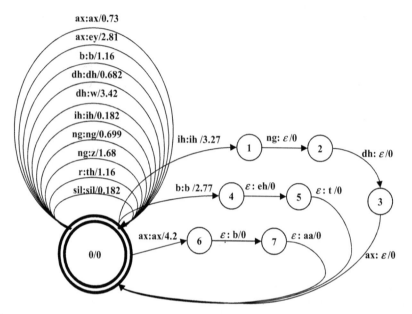

Figure 10. Example of the Confusion-Matrix Transducer C for the alignment of Table 1.

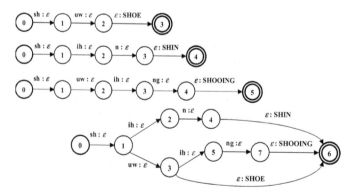

Figure 11. Dictionary transducer D: individual entries, and minimized network of entries.

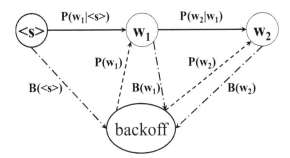

Figure 12. Weighted FSA for a bigram [19].

4. Case studies

4.1. Structure optimization of metamodels with GA

In this section the use of a Genetic Algorithm (GA) to optimize the structure of a set of metamodels and further improve ASR performance is presented [29]. The experiments were performed with speakers from the british-english Wall Street Journal (WSJ) speech database [14], and the metamodels were built with the libraries of the HTK Toolkit[10] from the University of Cambridge.

4.1.1. Chromosome representation

Considering the extended architecture of a metamodel of Figure 8, the length of the insertion contexts and the non-normalized phoneme confusion-matrix are the parameters that will be optimized by the GA. The phoneme confusion-matrix has dimension 47x47 because the database used for this work, the WSCAM0 speech database, consists phonetically of 46 phonemes [13, 14], plus the phoneme $/DEL/$ to identify deletions. The chromosome representation of the parameters of the metamodels is shown in Figure 13.

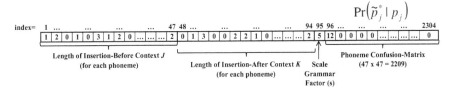

Figure 13. Chromosome representation of the parameters of the extended metamodels.

Because an insertion context exists for each phoneme, there are 2x47 = 94 insertion contexts in total. This information is arranged in a single vector of dimension 1x94, which is saved in genes 1-94 of the chromosome vector (see Figure 13). In gene 95 the value of the scale grammar factor (s), which controls the influence of the language model over the recognition process, is placed [10]. From genes 96 to 2304 the elements of the confusion-matrix are placed. Hence, each chromosome vector represents all the parameters of the metamodels for all phonemes in the speech set.

The integer values for each set of genes are: K, $J = 0$ to 3; $s = 0$ to 10; phoneme confusion - matrix = 0 to 100 (number of occurrences of each aligned pair $\{p_j^*, p_j\}$) before being normalized as probabilities $Pr(\tilde{p}_j^* | p_j)$).

The general structure of the GA is the one presented in Figure 2. For this, the initial population consists of 10 individuals, where the first element is the initial extended metamodel and the remaining elements are randomly generated within the range of values specified above. Fitness of each individual was measured on the word recognition accuracy (WAcc, Eq. 1) achieved with the resulting metamodels on a training set.

4.1.2. Operators

- **Selection**: The selection method (e.g., how to choose the eligible parents for reproduction) was based on the Roulette Wheel and was implemented as follows:
  - For each of the 10 best individuals in the population, compute its fitness value.
  - Compute the selection probability for each x_i individual as: $p_i = \frac{f_i}{\sum_{k=1}^{N} f_k}$, where N is the size of the population (sub-set of 10 individuals), and f_i the fitness value of the individual x_i.
  - Compute the accumulated probability q_i for each individual as: $q_i = \sum_{j=1}^{i} p_j$.
  - Generate a uniform random number $r \in \{0, 1\}$.
  - If $r < q_i$, then select the first individual (x_1), otherwise, select x_i such that $q_{i-1} < r \leq q_i$.
  - Repeat Steps 4 and 5 N times (until all N individuals are selected).

- **Crossover**: Uniform crossover was used for reproduction of parents chosen by the Roulette Wheel method. A template vector of dimension 1x2304 was used for this, where each of its elements received a random binary value (0, 1). Offspring 1 is produced by copying the corresponding genes from Parent 1 where the template vector has a value of 0, and copying the genes from Parent 2 where the template vector has a value of 1. Offspring 2 is obtained by doing the inverse procedure. 10 offsprings are obtained by crossover from the 10 individuals in the initial population. This increases the size of the population to 20.

- **Mutation**: The mutation scheme consisted in randomly changing values in the best 5 individuals as follows:
  - change 5 genes in the sub-vector that includes the length of the insertion contexts (genes 1 to 94);
  - change the scale grammar factor (gene 95);
  - change 94 genes in the sub-vector that represents the phoneme confusion-matrix (genes 96 to 2304).

  In this way, a population of 25 individuals is obtained for the GA.

- **Stop condition**: The GA is repeated until convergence through generations is achieved. A boundary of 15 iterations was set for the GA as it was observed that minimum variations were observed after that.

4.1.3. Experiments and results

A speaker-independent ASR system was built with the HTK Toolkit [10] using the WSJCAM0 speech database [14]. 92 speakers from the set *si_tr* were used for acoustic model training (three-state left-to-right HMMs, with eight Gaussian components per state). The front-end used 12 MFCCs plus energy, delta, and acceleration coefficients.

The experiments were done with speech data from 10 speakers of the development set *si_dt* of the same database. From each speaker, 74 sentences were selected, discarding adaptation sentences that were the same for all speakers. From this set, 30 were selected for testing-only purposes and 44 for confusion-matrix estimation (training of metamodels) and fitness evaluation for the GA. The metamodels were trained with three different sets of sentences: 5, 10, and 14 sentences, and fitness evaluation and metamodels re-estimation were performed with 15, 30, and 44 sentences respectively. This formed the *training schemes 5-15*, *10-30*, and *14-44* (e.g., if 5 sentences were used for metamodel training, fitness evaluation of the GA and metamodel re-estimation were performed with 15 sentences). Word bigram language models were estimated from the transcriptions of the *si_dt* speakers, and were the same for all the systems (baseline and metamodels).

Figure 14(a) shows the graph of fitness convergence of the GA when the scheme *14-44* was used. The baseline performance is around 78% while the initial extended metamodel achieved a performance of 87.3%. The mean fitness of the populations starts at 85% and, as the individuals evolve, increases to up to 87.4%. The best individual from each generation achieves a fitness of up to 88.20%. For the metamodels trained with the schemes *5-15* and *10-30* the pattern of converge was very similar.

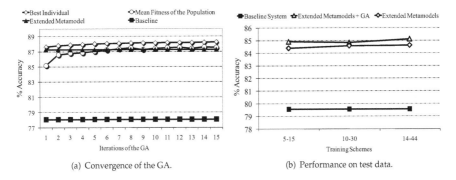

(a) Convergence of the GA.   (b) Performance on test data.

Figure 14. Results of the GA optimized metamodels.

Figure 14(b) shows the mean performance of the optimized metamodels on the testing set when all training schemes were used. On average, the optimized metamodels showed an increase of around 0.50% when compared with the initial extended metamodels. These gains were statistically significant as shown in Table 2. The matched pairs test described by [32] was used to test for statistical significant difference.

When the extended metamodels were optimized with a GA, a significant gain was achieved with schemes *5-15* and *14-44*. The use of the GA also reduced the size of the metamodels by 10% for all cases, thus eliminating unnecessary states and transitions. Finally, with a used vocabulary of 3000 words and 740 sentences (300 for testing), there is an important confidence about the significance of these results.

Training Scheme	Metamodel	Errors in Test Set	p-value	Conclusion
5-15	Initial	773	0.0591	<0.1 Significant
	Optimized	748		
10-30	Initial	764	0.2479	Not Significant
	Optimized	752		
14-44	Initial	761	0.0567	<0.1 Significant
	Optimized	737		

Table 2. Significance test for the initial and the optimized extended metamodels.

4.2. Estimation of phoneme confusion patterns with NMF

In this section, an application of the NMF approach to phoneme confusion-matrix estimation to improve ASR performance is presented [30]. The NMF estimates are integrated into the original metamodels (see Figure 7), and in this application, the NMF technique is extended to estimate also insertion patterns. The results obtained with NMF show statistically significant gains in recognition accuracy when compared with an adapted baseline ASR system and the performance of the original metamodels.

The procedure presented in Figure 6 was used for confusion-matrix estimation. A threshold $CT = 2$ was set for smoothing purposes, and the partial confusion-matrices CM_U^y were estimated from accurate alignments of P and $\tilde{P}^*$ from training speech data.

4.2.1. Experiments and results

The Wall Street Journal (WSJ) database, and the baseline ASR system described in Section 4.1.3 were used for the NMF experiments. The training-speakers S_x for V (see Section 3.1.1) consisted of 85 speakers from the si_tr set, which were also used to estimate $\overline{CM}$. 10 test-speakers S_y for V were selected from the set si_dt of the same database. Note that from the training-speakers, only **target** confusion-matrices CM^x were estimated. For the test-speakers, **partial** CM_U^y and **target** CM^y confusion-matrices were estimated in order to evaluate the quality of the NMF estimates of $\widehat{CM}^y$.

Supervised Maximum Likelihood Linear Regression (MLLR) adaptation [33] was implemented using the same sets of utterances U selected for confusion-matrix estimation. A regression class tree with 32 terminal nodes was used for this purpose. As shown in Table 3, the mean number of MLLR transformations increased as more U utterances were used. The adapted acoustic models represent the baseline for the experiments.

Adaptation Data (U)	5	10	15	20	30
Mean No. of MLLR Transformations	4	7	10	11	12

Table 3. Mean number of MLLR transformations across all test speakers using different sets of adaptation data.

A word-bigram language model, estimated from the data of the si_tr speakers, was used to obtain $\tilde{P}^*$ and estimate CM^x with the unadapted baseline system. In order to keep these sequences independent from those of the test-set speakers, the word-bigram language model used to decode $\tilde{P}^*$ for CM^y and CM_U^y, was estimated from the data of the selected test-speakers of the *si_dt* set. In all cases, a grammar scale factor *s* of 10 was used. The metamodels were tested using all the utterances available from the speakers S_y.

Figure 15 shows the performance of the metamodels using MLLR adapted acoustic models. The metamodels trained with **partial** estimates improved over the adapted baseline. When the NMF estimates were used, the accuracy of the metamodels improved when the training data was small. As presented in Table 4, these improvements were statistically significant when 5, 10, and 15 utterances were used for training/estimation.

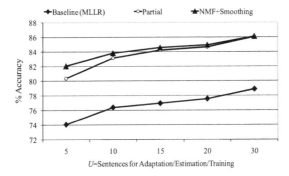

Figure 15. Mean word recognition accuracy of the metamodels and the adapted baseline across all test-speakers.

U	Metamodel	Errors in Test Set	*p*-value	Conclusion
5	Partial	2608	0.000000	< 0.001, 0.01, 0.05, 0.1 Significant
	NMF	2383		
10	Partial	2240	0.005603	< 0.01, 0.05, 0.1 Significant
	NMF	2151		
15	Partial	2093	0.102104	< 0.105 Significant
	NMF	2045		
20	Partial	2033	0.198040	Not Significant
	NMF	1996		
30	Partial	1847	0.888571	Not Significant
	NMF	1843		

Table 4. Significance test for the metamodels trained with partial and NMF estimates.

4.3. Metamodels and WFSTs to improve ASR performance for disordered speech

Dysarthria is a motor speech disorder characterized by weakness, paralysis, or poor coordination of the muscles responsible for speech. Although ASR systems have been developed for disordered speech, factors such as low intelligibility and limited phonemic repertoire decrease speech recognition accuracy, making conventional speaker adaptation algorithms perform poorly on dysarthric speakers.

In the work presented by [22], rather than adapting the acoustic models, the errors made by the speaker are modelled to attempt to correct them. For this, the metamodels and WFSTs techniques are applied to correct the errors made at the phonetic level and make use of a language model to find the best estimate of the correct word sequence. Experiments performed with dysarthric speech of different levels of severity showed that both techniques outperformed standard adaptation techniques.

4.3.1. Limited phonemic repertoire

Among the identified factors that give rise to ASR errors in dysarthric speech [16], the most important are decreased intelligibility (because of substitutions, deletions and insertions of phonemes), and limited phonemic repertoire, the latter leading to phoneme substitutions. To illustrate the effect of reduced phonemic repertoire, Figure 16 shows an example phoneme confusion-matrix for a dysarthric speaker from the NEMOURS Database of Dysarthric Speech (described in Section 4.3.2). This confusion-matrix is estimated by a speaker-independent ASR system, and so it may show confusions that would not actually be made by humans. From Figure 16 the following observations are made:

- A small set of phonemes (in this case the phonemes /ua/, /uw/, /m/, /n/, /ng/, /r/, and /sil/) dominates the speaker's output speech.
- Some vowel sounds and the consonants /g/, /zh/, and /y/, are never recognized correctly. This suggests that there are some phonemes that the speaker apparently cannot enunciate at all, and for which he or she substitutes a different phoneme, often one of the dominant phonemes mentioned above.

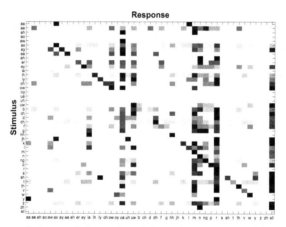

Figure 16. Phoneme confusion-matrix from a dysarthric speaker.

These observations differ from the pattern of confusions seen in a normal speaker as shown in Figure 4. This confusion-matrix shows a clearer pattern of correct recognitions, and few confusions of vowels with consonants.

Most speaker adaptation algorithms are based on the principle that it is possible to apply a set of transformations to the parameters of a set of acoustic models of an "average" voice to move them closer to the voice of an individual (e.g., MLLR). Whilst this has been shown to be successful for normal speakers, it may be less successful in cases where the phoneme uttered is not the one that was intended but is substituted by a different phoneme or phonemes, as often happens in dysarthric speech. In this situation, it is suggested that a more effective approach is to combine a model of the substitutions likely to have been made by the speaker with a language model to infer what was said. So rather than attempting to adapt the system, we model the insertion, deletion, and substitution errors made by a speaker and attempt to correct them.

4.3.2. Speech data, baseline recognizer, and adaptation technique

While the baseline ASR system was built with the WSJ database as in [29] and [30], the dysarthric speech data was provided by the NEMOURS Database [21]. This database is a collection of 814 short sentences spoken by 11 speakers (74 sentences per speaker) with varying degrees of dysarthria (data from only 10 speakers was used as some data is missing for one speaker). The sentences are nonsense phrases that have a simple syntax of the form "the X is Y the Z", where X and Z are usually nouns and Y is a verb in present participle form (for instance, the phrases "The shin is going the who", "The inn is heaping the shin", etc.). Note that although each of the 740 sentences is different, the vocabulary of 112 words is shared.

Speech recognition experiments were implemented by using the baseline recognizer on the dysarthric speech. For these experiments, a word-bigram language model was estimated from the (pooled) 74 sentences provided by each speaker.

The technique used for the speaker adaptation experiments was MLLR (Maximum Likelihood Linear Regression) [33]. From the complete set of 74 sentences per speaker, 34 sentences were used for adaptation and the remaining 40 for testing. The set of 34 was divided into sets to measure the performance of the adapted baseline system when using a different amount of adaptation data. Thus adaptation was implemented using 4, 10, 16, 22, 28, and 34 sentences. For future reference, the baseline system adapted with X sentences is termed as MLLR_X, and the baseline without any adaptation as BASE.

An experiment was done to compare the performance of the baseline and MLLR-adapted recognizer (using 16 utterances for adaptation) with a human assessment of the dysarthric speakers used in this study. Recognition was performed with a grammar scale factor and word insertion penalty as described in [10].

Figure 17 shows the intelligibility of each of the dysarthric speakers as measured using the Frenchay Dysarthria Assessment (FDA) test in [21], and the recognition performance (% Accuracy) when tested on the unadapted baseline system (BASE) and the adapted models (MLLR_16). The correlation between the FDA performance and the recognizer performance is 0.67 (unadapted models) and 0.82 (adapted). Both are significant at the 1% level, which gives some confidence that the recognizer displays a similar performance trend when exposed to different degrees of dysarthric speech as humans.

4.3.3. Experiments and results

The metamodels used in this case had the original architecture which was shown in Figure 7. In Figure 18 the results of the metamodels on the phoneme strings from the MLLR adapted acoustic models are shown. When a very small set of sentences, e.g., 4, is used for training of the metamodels, it is possible to get an improvement of approximately 1.5% over the MLLR

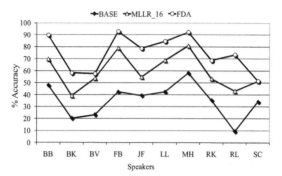

Figure 17. Comparison of recognition performance: Human assessment (FDA), unadapted (BASE) and adapted (MLLR_16) SI models.

adapted models. This gain in accuracy increases as the training/adaptation data is increased, obtaining an improvement of almost 3% when all 34 sentences are used.

The matched pairs test described by [32] was used to test for significant differences between the recognition accuracy using metamodels and the accuracy obtained with MLLR adaptation when a certain number of sentences were available for metamodel training. The results with the associated p-values are presented in Table 5.

In all the cases, metamodels improve MLLR adaptation with p-values less than 0.01 and 0.05. Note that the metamodels trained with only four sentences (META_04) decrease the number of word errors from 1174 (MLLR_04) to 1139.

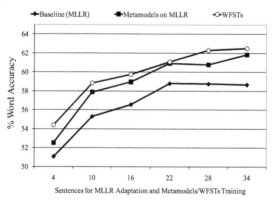

Figure 18. Mean word recognition accuracy of the MLLR adapted baseline, the metamodels, and the WFSTs across all dysarthric speakers.

The WFSTs were tested using the same conditions and speech data as the metamodels. The FSM Library [25] from AT&T was used for the experiments with WFSTs. Figure 18 shows clearly the gain in performance given by the WFSTs over both MLLR and the metamodels. This gain is statistically significant at the 0.1 level for all cases except when 22 and 34 sentences were used for training.

System	Errors in Test Set	p-value	Conclusion
MLLR_04	1174	0.00168988	< 0.01 Significant
META_04	1139		
MLLR_10	1073	0.00024590	< 0.001 Significant
META_10	1036		
MLLR_16	1043	0.00204858	< 0.01 Significant
META_16	999		
MLLR_22	989	0.00003510	< 0.001 Significant
META_22	941		
MLLR_28	990	0.00240678	< 0.01 Significant
META_28	952		
MLLR_34	992	0.00000014	< 0.001 Significant
META_34	924		

Table 5. Comparison of statistical significance of results over all dysarthric speakers using metamodels.

5. Conclusions

In this chapter the details and applications of techniques to improve ASR performance were presented. These consisted in heuristic and statistical post-processing techniques which made use of a speaker's phoneme confusion - matrix for error modelling, achieving correction at the phonetic level of an ASR's output for both, normal and disordered speech.

The first post-processing technique, termed as metamodels, incorporated the information of the speaker's confusion-matrix into the recognition process. The metamodels expanded the confusion-matrix modelling by incorporating information of the pattern of insertions associated with each phoneme. Deletions were modelled as a phoneme being substituted (or confused) by the "DELETION" symbol.

A metamodel's architecture, for which there was an extended version, was suitable for further optimization, and in Section 4.1 the application of a GA for this purpose was presented. The improvements in word recognition accuracy obtained on normal speech after optimization were statistically significant when compared with the previous performance of the metamodels. This corroborated the findings of other works [8, 9], where GA was applied to improve recognition performance by evolving the internal parameters of an HMM (state transitions, observation probabilities).

Also, in Section 4.2 was presented another application case, where the use of Non - negative Matrix Factorization (NMF) provided more accurate estimates of a speaker's phoneme confusion - matrix which, when incorporated into a set of metamodels, improved significantly the accuracy of an ASR system. This performance was also higher than the performance of the metamodels trained with original partial data (with no NMF estimates).

However, when tested with speakers with disordered speech, where significant increase in substitution, deletion, and insertion errors exists, two important issues were identified:

• The metamodels were unable to model specific phoneme sequences that were output in response to individual phoneme inputs. They were capable of outputting sequences, but the symbols (phonemes) in these sequences were conditionally independent, and so specific sequences could not be modelled. This also led to be unable to model deletion of sequences of phonemes, although the original and extended architecture ensures modelling of multiple insertions and single substitutions / deletions.

- Adding the "DELETION" symbol led to an increase in the size of the dictionary, because it could potentially substitute each phoneme in the network of metamodels during the recognition process. Not adding this symbol led to the problem of a "Tee" model in the HTK package [10]. In such case, a deletion is represented as a direct transition from the initial to the final state, thus allowing "skipping" the phoneme. The decoding algorithm failed because it was possible to traverse the complete network of metamodels without absorbing a single input symbol.

Hence, for modelling of deletions, a specific way to define a "missing" or "empty" observation was needed. An alternative to solve these issues, the second post-processing technique, a network of Weighted Finite State Transducers (WFSTs) was presented. In Section 4.3, a case of improving ASR performance for speakers with the speech disorder of dysarthria was presented, where both techniques, metamodels and WFSTs were used for that purpose. The main advantage of the WFSTs is the definition and use of the *epsilon* (ϵ) symbol, which in finite-state automata represents an "empty" observation. This allowed the modelling of multiple deletions, substitutions, and insertions. General improvement on ASR for dysarthric speech was obtained with this technique when compared to the metamodels and the adapted baseline system.

As conclusion it can be mentioned that the techniques presented in this chapter offer wide possibilities of application in the general field of speech recognition. Their robustness has been corroborated with case studies with normal and disordered speech, where higher performance was consistently achieved over unadapted and adapted baseline ASR systems. Also, these techniques are flexible enough to be optimized and integrated with other processes as in [30] and [5].

Author details

Santiago Omar Caballero Morales
Technological University of the Mixteca, Mexico

6. References

[1] Jurafsky, D. & Martin, J.H. (2009). *Speech and Language Processing*, Pearson: Prentice Hall, USA.

[2] Goldberg, D.E. (1989). *Genetic Algorithms in Search, Optimization and Machine Learning*, Addison-Wesley Publishing Co., USA.

[3] Chan, C.W.; Kwong, S.; Man, K.F. & Tang, K.S. (2001). Optimization of HMM Topology and its Model Parameters by Genetic Algorithms. *Pattern Recognition*, Vol. 34, pp. 509-522

[4] Hong, Q. Y. & Kwong, S. (2005). A Genetic Classification Method for Speaker Recognition. *Engineering Applications of Artificial Intelligence*, Vol. 18, pp. 13-19

[5] Matsumasa, H.; Takiguchi, T.; Ariki, Y.; LI, I-C. & Nakabayash, T. (2009). Integration of Metamodel and Acoustic Model for Dysarthric Speech Recognition. *Journal of Multimedia - JMM*, Vol. 4, No. 4, pp. 254-261

[6] Lee, D.D. & Seung, H.S. (1999). Learning the parts of objects by non-negative matrix factorization. *Nature*, Vol. 401, pp. 788-791

[7] Lee, D.D. & Seung, H.S. (2001). Algorithms for non-negative matrix factorization. *Advances in Neural Information Processing Systems*, Vol. 13, pp. 556-562

[8] Takara, T.; Iha, Y. & Nagayama, I. (1998). Selection of the Optimal Structure of the Continuous HMM using the Genetic Algorithm, *Proc. of the International Conference on Spoken Language Processing (ICSLP 98)*, Sydney, Australia.

[9] Xiao, J.; Zou, L. & Li, C. (2007). Optimization of Hidden Markov Model by a Genetic Algorithm for Web Information Extraction, *Proc. of the International Conference on Intelligent Systems and Knowledge Engineering (ISKE 2007)*, Chengdu, China, ISBN: 978-90-78677-04-8

[10] Young, S. & Woodland, P. (2006). *The HTK Book (for HTK Version 3.4)*, Cambridge University Engineering Department, United Kingdom.

[11] Reeves, C.R. (1993). *Modern Heuristic Techniques for Combinational Problems*, John Wiley & Sons Inc., USA.

[12] Bodenstab, N. & Fanty, M. (2007). Multi-pass pronunciation adaptation, *Proc. of the IEEE International Conference on Acoustics, Speech, and Signal Processing (ICASSP) 2007*, Honolulu, Hawaii, Vol. 4, pp. 865–868, ISBN: 1-4244-0728-1

[13] Robinson, T.; Mitton, R.; Wilson, M.; Foote, J.; James, D. & Donovan, R. (1997). *British English Example Pronunciation Dictionary (BEEP) v1.0*, University of Cambridge, Department of Engineering, Machine Intelligence Laboratory, United Kingdom

[14] Robinson, T.; Fransen, J.; Pye, D.; Foote, J. & Renals, S. (1995). WSJCAM0: A British English speech corpus for large vocabulary continuous speech recognition, *Proc. of the IEEE International Conference on Acoustics, Speech, and Signal Processing (ICASSP) 1995*, Detroit, USA, Vol.1., pp. 81-84, ISBN: 0-7803-2431-5

[15] Hamilton, H. J. (2007). *Notes of Computer Science 831: Knowledge Discovery in Databases*, University of Regina, Department of Computing Sciences, Canada.

[16] Rosen, K. & Yampolsky, S. (2000). Automatic speech recognition and a review of its functioning with dysarthric speech. *Augmentative and Alternative Communication*, Vol. 16, pp. 48-60

[17] Green, P.; Carmichael, J.; Hatzis, A.; Enderby, P.; Hawley, M.S. & Parker M.(2003). Automatic Speech Recognition with Sparse Training Data for Dysarthric Speakers, *Proc. of the 8th European Conference on Speech Communication Technology (Eurospeech)*, Geneva, Switzerland, pp. 1189-1192, ISSN: 1018-4074

[18] Torre, D.; Villarrubia, L.; Hernandez,L. & Elvira, J.M. (1997). Automatic Alternative Transcription Generation and Vocabulary Selection for Flexible Word Recognizers, *Proc. of the IEEE International Conference on Acoustics, Speech, and Signal Processing (ICASSP) 2007*, Honolulu, Hawaii, Vol. 2, pp. 1463-1466

[19] Fosler-Lussier, E. (2008). *Finite State Machines In Spoken Language Processing (FSM Tutorial)*, Speech and Language Technology Laboratory, Ohio State University, USA.

[20] Levit, M.; Alshawi, H.; Gorin, A. & Nöth, E. (2003). Context-Sensitive Evaluation and Correction of Phone Recognition Output, *Proc. of the 8th European Conference on Speech Communication Technology (Eurospeech)*, Geneva, Switzerland, pp. 925-928, ISSN: 1018-4074

[21] Bunnel, H.T.; Polikoff, J.B.; Menéndez-Pidal, X.; Peters, S.M. & Leonzio, J.E. (1996). The Nemours Database of Dysarthric Speech, *Proc. of the Fourth International Conference on Spoken Language Processing (ICSLP 96)*, Philadelphia, USA.

[22] Caballero-Morales, S.O. & Cox, S.J. (2009). Modelling Errors in Automatic Speech Recognition for Dysarthric Speakers. *EURASIP Journal on Advances in Signal Processing*, pp. 1-14, ISSN: 1687-6172

[23] Li, Y.X.; Tan, C.L.; Ding, X. & Liu, C. (2004). Contextual post-processing based on the confusion matrix in offline handwritten Chinese script recognition. *Pattern Recognition*, Vol. 37, No. 9, pp. 1901-1912

[24] Cox, S.J. & Dasmahapatra, S. (2002). High level approaches to confidence estimation in speech recognition. *IEEE Transactions on Speech and Audio Processing*, Vol. 10, No. 7, pp. 460-471,. ISSN: 1063-6676

[25] Mohri, M.; Pereira, F. & Riley, L. (2002). Weighted finite state transducers in speech recognition. *Computer Speech and Language*, Vol. 16, pp. 69-88, ISSN: 0885-2308

[26] Fosler-Lussier, E.; Amdal, I. & Kuo, H.-K.J. (2002). On the road to improved lexical confusability metrics, *ISCA Tutorial and Research Workshop on Pronunciation Modelling and Lexicon Adaptation (PMLA-2002)*, Estes Park, Colorado, USA.

[27] Thatphithakkul, N. & Kanokphara, S. (2004). HMM Parameter Optimization using Tabu Search, *International Symposium on Communications and Information Technologies (ISCIT) 2004*, Sapporo, Japan, pp. 904-908

[28] Cox, S. J. (2008). On Estimation of A Speaker's Confusion Matrix from Sparse Data, *Proc. of the 9th Annual Conference of the International Speech Communication Association (Interspeech 2008)*, Brisbane, Australia, pp. 2618-2621, ISSN: 1990-9772

[29] Caballero-Morales, S.O. (2011). Structure Optimization of Metamodels to Improve Speech Recognition Accuracy, *Proc. of the International Conference on Electronics Communications and Computers (CONIELECOMP) 2011*, pp. 125-130, ISBN: 978-1-4244-9557-3

[30] Caballero-Morales, S.O. & Cox, S.J. (2009). On the Estimation and the Use of Confusion-Matrices for Improving ASR Accuracy, *Proc. of the International Conference on Spoken Language Processing (Interspeech 2009)*, pp. 1599-1602, ISSN: 1990-9772

[31] Caballero-Morales, S.O. & Cox, S.J. (2007). Modelling confusion matrices to improve speech recognition accuracy, with an application to dysarthric speech, *Proc. of the International Conference on Spoken Language Processing (Interspeech 2007)*, pp. 1565-1568, ISSN: 1990-9772

[32] Gillick, L. & Cox, S.J. (1989). Some statistical issues in the comparison of speech recognition algorithms, *Proc. of the IEEE International Conference on Acoustics, Speech, and Signal Processing (ICASSP) 1989*, Glasgow , United Kingdom, pp. 532-535, ISSN: 1520-6149

[33] Leggetter, C.J. & Woodland, P.C. (1995). Maximum likelihood linear regression for speaker adaptation of continuous density hidden Markov models. *Computer Speech and Language*, Vol. 9, No. 2, pp. 171-185, ISSN: 0885-2308

Dereverberation Based on Spectral Subtraction by Multi-Channel LMS Algorithm for Hands-Free Speech Recognition

Longbiao Wang, Kyohei Odani, Atsuhiko Kai, Norihide Kitaoka
and Seiichi Nakagawa

Additional information is available at the end of the chapter

1. Introduction

In a distant-talking environment, channel distortion drastically degrades speech recognition performance because of a mismatch between the training and testing environments. The current approach focusing on automatic speech recognition (ASR) robustness to reverberation and noise can be classified as speech signal processing [1, 4, 5, 14], robust feature extraction [10, 20], and model adaptation [3, 25].

In this chapter, we focus on speech signal processing in the distant-talking environment. Because both the speech signal and the reverberation are nonstationary signals, dereverberation to obtain clean speech from the convolution of nonstationary speech signals and impulse responses is very hard work. Several studies have focused on mitigating the above problem [8, 9, 11, 12]. [1] explored a speech dereverberation technique whose principle was the recovery of the envelope modulations of the original (anechoic) speech. They applied a technique that they originally developed to treat background noise [11] to the dereverberation problem. [7] proposed a novel approach for multimicrophone speech dereverberation. The method was based on the construction of the null subspace of the data matrix in the presence of colored noise, employing generalized singular-value decomposition or generalized eigenvalue decomposition of the respective correlation matrices. A reverberation compensation method for speaker recognition using spectral subtraction in which the late reverberation is treated as additive noise was proposed by [16, 17]. However, the drawback of this approach is that the optimum parameters for spectral subtraction are empirically estimated from a development dataset and the late reverberation cannot be subtracted well since it is not modeled precisely. [18] proposed a novel dereverberation method utilizing multi-step forward linear prediction. They estimated the linear prediction coefficients in a time domain and suppressed the amplitude of late reflections through spectral subtraction in a spectral domain.

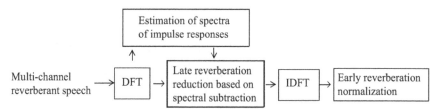

Figure 1. Schematic diagram of blind dereverberation method.

In this chapter, we propose a robust distant-talking speech recognition method based on spectral subtraction (SS) employing the multi-channel least mean square (MCLMS) algorithm. Speech captured by distant-talking microphones is distorted by the reverberation. With a long impulse response, the spectrum of the distorted speech is approximated by convolving the spectrum of clean speech with the spectrum of the impulse response as explained in the next section. This enables us to treat the late reverberation as additive noise, and a noise reduction technique based on spectral subtraction can be easily applied to compensate for the late reverberation. By excluding the phase information from the dereverberation operation, the dereverberation reduction in a power spectral domain provides robustness against certain errors that the conventional sensitive inverse filtering method cannot achieve [18]. The compensation parameter (that is, the spectrum of the impulse response) for spectral subtraction is required. An adaptive MCLMS algorithm was proposed to blindly identify the channel impulse response in a time domain [12–14]. In this chapter, we extend the method to blindly estimate the spectrum of the impulse response for spectral subtraction in a frequency domain. The early reverberation is normalized by CMN [6]. Power SS is the most commonly used SS method. A previous study has shown that generalized SS (GSS) with a lower exponent parameter is more effective than power SS for noise reduction [26]. In this chapter, both of power SS and GSS are employed to suppress late reverberation. A diagram of the proposed method is shown in Fig. 1.

In this chapter, we also investigate the robustness of the power SS-based dereverberation under various reverberant conditions for large vocabulary continuous speech recognition (LVCSR). We analyze the effect factors (numbers of reverberation windows and channels, length of utterance, and the distance between sound source and microphone) of compensation parameter estimation for dereverberation based on power SS in a simulated reverberant environment.

The remainder of this paper is organized as follows. Section 2 describes the outline of blind dereverberation based on spectral subtraction. A multi-channel method based on the LMS algorithm and used to estimate the power spectrum of the impulse response (that is, a compensation parameter for spectral subtraction) is described in Section 3. Section 4 describes the experimental results of hands-free speech recognition in both simulated and real reverberant environments. Finally, Section 5 summarizes the paper.

2. Outline of blind dereverberation

2.1. Dereverberation based on power SS

If speech $s[t]$ is corrupted by convolutional noise $h[t]$ and additive noise $n[t]$, the observed speech $x[t]$ becomes

$$x[t] = h[t] * s[t] + n[t]. \tag{1}$$

where $*$ denotes the convolution operation. In this chapter, additive noise is ignored for simplification, so Eq. (1) becomes $x[t] = h[t] * s[t]$.

To analyze the effect of impulse response, the impulse response $h[t]$ can be separated into two parts $h_{early}[t]$ and $h_{late}[t]$ as [16, 17]

$$h_{early}[t] = \begin{cases} h[t] & t < T \\ 0 & \text{otherwise} \end{cases},$$

$$h_{late}[t] = \begin{cases} h[t+T] & t \geq 0 \\ 0 & \text{otherwise} \end{cases}, \tag{2}$$

where T is the length of the spectral analysis window, and $h[t] = h_{early}[t] + \delta(t-T) * h_{late}[t]$. $\delta()$ is a dirac delta function (that is, a unit impulse function). The formula (1) can be rewritten as

$$x[t] = s[t] * h_{early}[t] + s[t-T] * h_{late}[t], \tag{3}$$

where the early effect is distortion within a frame (analysis window), and the late effect comes from previous multiple frames.

When the length of impulse response is much shorter than analysis window size T used for short-time Fourier transform (STFT), STFT of distorted speech equals STFT of clean speech multiplied by STFT of impulse response $h[t]$ (in this case, $h[t] = h_{early}[t]$). However, when the length of impulse response is much longer than an analysis window size, STFT of distorted speech is usually approximated by

$$X(f, \omega) \approx S(f, \omega) * H(\omega)$$

$$= S(f, \omega)H(0, \omega) + \sum_{d=1}^{D-1} S(f - d, \omega)H(d, \omega), \tag{4}$$

where f is frame index, $H(\omega)$ is STFT of impulse response, $S(f, \omega)$ is STFT of clean speech s and $H(d, \omega)$ denotes the part of $H(\omega)$ corresponding to frame delay d. That is to say, with long impulse response, the channel distortion is no more of multiplicative nature in a linear spectral domain, rather it is convolutional [25].

[17] proposed a far-field speaker recognition based on spectral subtraction. In this method, the early term of Eq. (3) was compensated by the conventional CMN, whereas the late term of Eq. (3) was treated as additive noise, and a noise reduction technique based on spectral subtraction was applied as

$$|\hat{S}(f, \omega)| = \max(|X(f, \omega)| - \alpha \cdot g(\omega)|X(f-1, \omega)|, \beta \cdot |X(f, \omega)|), \tag{5}$$

where α is the noise overestimation factor, β is the spectral floor parameter to avoid negative or underflow values, and $g(\omega)$ is a frequency-dependent value which is determined on a development and set as $|1 - 0.9e^{j\omega}|$ [17]. However, the drawback of this approach is that the optimum parameters α, β for the spectral subtraction are empirically estimated on a development dataset and the STFT of late effect of impulse response as the second term of the right-hand side of Eq. (4) is not straightforward subtracted since the late reverberation is not modelled precisely.

In this chapter, we propose a dereverberation method based on spectral subtraction to estimate the STFT of the clean speech $\hat{S}(f,\omega)$ based on Eq. (4), and the spectrum of the impulse response for the spectral subtraction is blindly estimated using the method described in Section 3. Assuming that phases of different frames is noncorrelated for simplification, the power spectrum of Eq. (4) can be approximated as

$$|X(f,\omega)|^2 \approx |S(f,\omega)|^2|H(0,\omega)|^2 + \sum_{d=1}^{D-1}|S(f-d,\omega)|^2|H(d,\omega)|^2. \qquad (6)$$

The estimated power spectrum of clean speech may not be very accurate due to the estimation error of the impulse response, especially the estimation error of early part of the impulse response. In addition, the unreliable estimated power spectrum of clean speech in a previous frame causes a furthermore estimation error in the current frame. In this chapter, the late reverberation is reduced based on the power SS, while the early reverberation is normalized by CMN at the feature extraction stage. A diagram of the proposed method is shown in Fig. 1. SS is used to prevent the estimated power spectrum obtained by reducing the late reverberation from being a negative value; the estimated power spectrum $|\hat{X}(f,\omega)|^2$ obtained by reducing the late reverberation then becomes

$$|\hat{X}(f,\omega)|^2 \approx max\{|X(f,\omega)|^2 - \alpha \cdot \frac{\sum_{d=1}^{D-1}\{|\hat{X}(f-d,\omega)|^2|\hat{H}(d,\omega)|^2\}}{|\hat{H}(0,\omega)|^2}, \beta \cdot |X(f,\omega)|^2\}, \qquad (7)$$

where $|\hat{X}(f,\omega)|^2 = |\hat{S}(f,\omega)|^2|\hat{H}(0,\omega)|^2$, $|\hat{S}(f,\omega)|^2$ is the spectrum of estimated clean speech, $\hat{H}(f,\omega)$ is the estimated STFT of the impulse response. To estimate the power spectra of the impulse responses, we extended the Multi-channel LMS algorithm for identifying the impulse responses in a time domain [14] to a frequency domain in Section 3.2.

2.2. Dereverberation based on GSS

Previous studies have shown that GSS with an arbitrary exponent parameter is more effective than power SS for noise reduction [26]. In this chapter, we extend GSS to suppress late reverberation. Instead of the power SS-based dereverberation given in Eq. (7), GSS-based dereverberation is modified as

$$|\hat{X}(f,\omega)|^{2n} \approx max\{|X(f,\omega)|^{2n} - \alpha \cdot \frac{\sum_{d=1}^{D-1}\{|\hat{X}(f-d,\omega)|^{2n}|\hat{H}(d,\omega)|^{2n}\}}{|\hat{H}(0,\omega)|^{2n}}, \beta \cdot |X(f,\omega)|^{2n}\}, (8)$$

where n is the exponent parameter. For power SS, the exponent parameter n is equal to 1. In this chapter, the exponent parameter n is set to 0.1 as this value yielded the best results [26].

The methods given in Eq. (7) and Eq. (8) are referred to *power SS-based* and *GSS-based dereverberation methods*, respectively.

2.3. Dereverberation and denoising based on GSS

The precision of impulse response estimation is drastically degraded when the additive noise is present. We present a dereverberation and denoising based on GSS. A diagram of the processing method is shown in Fig. 2. At first, the spectrum of additive noise is estimated and noise reduction is performed. Then the reverberation is suppressed using the estimated spectra of impulse responses. When additive noise is present, the power spectrum of Eq. (6) becomes

$$|X(f,\omega)|^2 \approx |S(f,\omega)|^2|H(0,\omega)|^2 + \sum_{d=1}^{D-1} |S(f-d,\omega)|^2|H(d,\omega)|^2 + |N(f,\omega)|^2, \quad (9)$$

where $N(f,\omega)$ is the spectrum of noise $n(t)$. To suppress the noise and reverberation

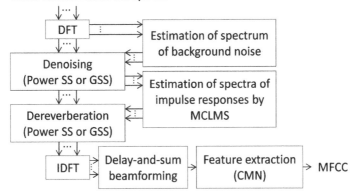

Figure 2. Schematic diagram of an SS-based dereverberation and denoising method.

simultaneously, Eq. (8) is modified as

$$|\hat{X}(f,\omega)|^{2n} \approx max\{|\hat{X}_N(f,\omega)|^{2n} - \alpha_1 \cdot \frac{\sum_{d=1}^{D-1}\{|\hat{X}(f-d,\omega)|^{2n}|\hat{H}(d,\omega)|^{2n}\}}{|\hat{H}(0,\omega)|^{2n}}, \beta_1 \cdot |\hat{X}_N(f,\omega)|^{2n}\}, \quad (10)$$

$$|\hat{X}_N(f,\omega)|^{2n} \approx max\{|X(f,\omega)|^{2n} - \alpha_2 \cdot |\hat{N}(\omega)|^{2n}, \beta_2 \cdot |X(f,\omega)|^{2n}\}, \quad (11)$$

where $\hat{N}(\omega)$ is the mean of noise spectrum $N(f,\omega)$, and $\hat{X}_N(f,\omega)$ is the spectrum obtained by subtracting the spectrum of the observed speech from the estimated mean spectrum of noise $\hat{N}(\omega)$ [1]. In this paper, we set parameter β_1 equal to β_2.

3. Compensation parameter estimation for spectral subtraction by multi-channel LMS algorithm

3.1. Blind channel identification in time domain

3.1.1. Identifiability and principle

An adaptive multi-channel LMS algorithm for blind Single-Input Multiple-Output (SIMO) system identification in time domain was proposed by [13, 14].

---

[1] In this study, stationary noise is assumed.

Before introducing the MCLMS algorithm for the blind channel identification, we express what SIMO systems are *blind identifiable*. A multi-channel FIR (Finite Impulse Response) system can be blindly primarily because of the channel diversity. As an extreme counter-example, if all channels of a SIMO system are identical, the system reduces to a Single-Input Single-Output (SISO) system, becoming unidentifiable. In addition, the source signal needs to have sufficient modes to make the channels fully excited. The following two assumptions are made to guarantee an identifiable system:

1. The polynomials formed from $h_n, n = 1, 2, \cdots, N$, where h_n is n-th impulse response and N is the channel number, are co-prime [2], i.e., the channel transfer functions $H_n(z)$ do not share any common zeros;

2. The autocorrelation matrix $\mathbf{R}_{ss} = E\{s(k)s^T(k)\}$ of input signal is of full rank (such that the single-input multiple-output (SIMO) system can be fully excited).

In the following, these two conditions are assumed to hold so that we will be dealing with a blindly identifiable FIR (Finite Impulse Response) SIMO system.

In the absence of additive noise, we can take advantage of the fact that

$$x_i * h_j = s * h_i * h_j = x_j * h_i, \quad i, j = 1, 2, \cdots, N, i \neq j, \tag{12}$$

and have the following relation at time t:

$$\mathbf{x}_i^T(t)\mathbf{h}_j(t) = \mathbf{x}_j^T(t)\mathbf{h}_i(t), \quad i, j = 1, 2, \cdots, N, i \neq j, \tag{13}$$

where $\mathbf{h}_i(t)$ is the i-th impulse response at time t and

$$\mathbf{x}_n(t) = [x_n(t) \ x_n(t-1) \ \cdots \ x_n(t-L+1)]^T,$$
$$n = 1, 2, \cdots, N, \tag{14}$$

where $\mathbf{x}_n(t)$ is speech signal received from the n-th channel at time t and L is the number of taps of the impulse response. Multiplying Eq. (13) by $\mathbf{x}_n(t)$ and taking expectation yields,

$$\mathbf{R}_{x_i x_i}(t+1)\mathbf{h}_j(t) = \mathbf{R}_{x_i x_j}(t+1)\mathbf{h}_i(t),$$
$$i, j = 1, 2, \cdots, N, i \neq j, \tag{15}$$

where $\mathbf{R}_{x_i x_j}(t+1) = E\{\mathbf{x}_i(t+1)\mathbf{x}_j^T(t+1)\}$. Eq. (15) comprises $N(N-1)$ distinct equations. By summing up the $N-1$ cross relations associated with one particuar channel $\mathbf{h}_j(t)$, we get

$$\sum_{i=1, i \neq j}^{N} \mathbf{R}_{x_i x_i}(t+1)\mathbf{h}_j(t) = \sum_{i=1, i \neq j}^{N} \mathbf{R}_{x_i x_j}(t+1)\mathbf{h}_i(t),$$
$$j = 1, 2, \cdots, N. \tag{16}$$

Over all channels, we then have a total of N equations. In matrix form, this set of equations is written as:

$$\mathbf{R}_{x+}(t+1)\mathbf{h}(t) = 0, \tag{17}$$

where

---

[2] In mathematics, the integers a and b are said to be co-prime if they have no common factor other than 1, or equivalently, if their greatest common divisor is 1.

$$\mathbf{R}_{x+}(t+1) = \begin{bmatrix} \sum_{n \neq 1} \mathbf{R}_{x_n x_n}(t+1) & -\mathbf{R}_{x_2 x_1}(t+1) & \cdots & -\mathbf{R}_{x_N x_1}(t+1) \\ -\mathbf{R}_{x_1 x_2}(t+1) & \sum_{n \neq 2} \mathbf{R}_{x_n x_n}(t+1) & \cdots & -\mathbf{R}_{x_N x_2}(t+1) \\ \vdots & \vdots & \ddots & \vdots \\ -\mathbf{R}_{x_1 x_N}(t+1) & -\mathbf{R}_{x_2 x_N}(t+1) & \cdots & \sum_{n \neq N} \mathbf{R}_{x_n x_n}(t+1) \end{bmatrix}, \tag{18}$$

$$\tilde{\mathbf{R}}_{x+}(t+1) = \begin{bmatrix} \sum_{n \neq 1} \tilde{\mathbf{R}}_{x_n x_n}(t+1) & -\tilde{\mathbf{R}}_{x_2 x_1}(t+1) & \cdots & -\tilde{\mathbf{R}}_{x_N x_1}(t+1) \\ -\tilde{\mathbf{R}}_{x_1 x_2}(t+1) & \sum_{n \neq 2} \tilde{\mathbf{R}}_{x_n x_n}(t+1) & \cdots & -\tilde{\mathbf{R}}_{x_N x_2}(t+1) \\ \vdots & \vdots & \ddots & \vdots \\ -\tilde{\mathbf{R}}_{x_1 x_N}(t+1) & -\tilde{\mathbf{R}}_{x_2 x_N}(t+1) & \cdots & \sum_{n \neq N} \tilde{\mathbf{R}}_{x_n x_n}(t+1) \end{bmatrix}, \tag{22}$$

$$\mathbf{h}(t) = [\mathbf{h}_1(t)^T \quad \mathbf{h}_2(t)^T \quad \cdots \quad \mathbf{h}_N(t)^T]^T, \tag{19}$$

$$\mathbf{h}_n(t) = [h_n(t,0) \quad h_n(t,1) \quad \cdots \quad h_n(t, L-1)]^T, \tag{20}$$

where $h_n(t,l)$ is the l-th tap of the n-th impulse response at time t. If the SIMO system is blindly identifiable, the matrix $\mathbf{R}_{x+}$ is rank deficient by 1 (in the absence of noise) and the channel impulse responses can be uniquely determined.

When the estimation of channel impulse responses is deviated from the true value, an error vector at time $t + 1$ is produced by:

$$\mathbf{e}(t+1) = \tilde{\mathbf{R}}_{x+}(t+1)\hat{\mathbf{h}}(t), \tag{21}$$

where $\tilde{\mathbf{R}}_{x_i x_j}(t+1) = \mathbf{x}_i(t+1)\mathbf{x}_j^T(t+1), i, j = 1, 2, \cdots, N$ and $\hat{\mathbf{h}}(t)$ is the estimated model filter at time t. Here we put a tilde in $\tilde{\mathbf{R}}_{x_i x_j}$ to distinguish this instantaneous value from its mathematical expectation $\mathbf{R}_{x_i x_j}$.

This error can be used to define a cost function at time $t + 1$

$$J(t+1) = \|\mathbf{e}(t+1)\|^2 = \mathbf{e}(t+1)^T \mathbf{e}(t+1). \tag{23}$$

By minimizing the cost function J of Eq. (23), the impulse response is blindly derived. There are various methods to minimize the cost function J, for example, constrained Multi-Channel LMS (MCLMS) algorithm, constrained Multi-Channel Newton (MCN) algorithm and Variable Step-Size Unconstrained MCLMS (VSS-UMCLMS) algorithm and so forth [12, 14]. Among these methods, the VSS-UMCLMS achieves a nice balance between complexity and convergence speed [14]. Moreover, the VSS-UMCLMS is more practical and much easier to use since the step size does not have to be specified in advance. Therefore, in this chapter, we apply VSS-UMCLMS algorithm to identify the multi-channel impulse responses.

3.1.2. Variable step-size unconstrained multi-channel LMS algorithm in time domain

The cost function $J(t+1)$ at time $t + 1$ diminishes and its gradient with respect to $\hat{\mathbf{h}}(t)$ can be approximated as

$$\Delta J(t+1) \approx \frac{2\tilde{\mathbf{R}}_{x+}(t+1)\hat{\mathbf{h}}(t)}{\|\hat{\mathbf{h}}(t)\|^2} \tag{24}$$

and the model filter $\hat{\mathbf{h}}(t+1)$ at time $t+1$ is

$$\hat{\mathbf{h}}(t+1) = \hat{\mathbf{h}}(t) - 2\mu\tilde{\mathbf{R}}_{x+}(t+1)\hat{\mathbf{h}}(t), \tag{25}$$

which is theoretically equivalent to the adaptive algorithm proposed by [2] although the cost functions are defined in different ways in these two adaptive blind SIMO identification algothrithms. In Eq. (25), μ is step size for Multi-channel LMS.

With such a simplified adaptive algorithm, the primary concern is whether it would converge to the trivial all-zero estimate. Fortunately this will not happen as long as the initial estimate $\hat{\mathbf{h}}(0)$ is not orthogonal to the true channel impulse response vector $\mathbf{h}$ [2].

Finally, an optimal step size for the unconstrained MCLMS at time $t+1$ is obtained by

$$\mu_{opt}(t+1) = \frac{\hat{\mathbf{h}}^T(t)\Delta J(t+1)}{\|\Delta J(t+1)\|^2}. \tag{26}$$

The details of the VSS-UMCLMS were described in [14].

3.2. Extending VSS-UMCLMS algorithm to compensation parameter estimation for spectral subtraction

To blindly estimate the compensation parameter (that is, the spectrum of impulse response), we extend the MCLMS algorithm mentioned in Section 3.1 from a time domain to a frequency domain in this section.

The spectrum of distorted signal is a convolution operation of the spectrum of clean speech and that of impulse response as shown in Eq. (4). The spectrum of the impulse response is dependent on frequency ω, and the varibale ω is omitted for simplification. Thus, in the absence of additive noise, the spectra of distorted signals have the following relation at frame f on the frequency domain:

$$\mathbf{X}_i^T(f)\mathbf{H}_j(f) = \mathbf{X}_j^T(f)\mathbf{H}_i(f), \quad i,j = 1,2,...,N, \quad i \neq j, \tag{27}$$

Where $\mathbf{X}_n(f) = [X_n(f) \quad X_n(f-1) \quad ... \quad X_n(f-D+1)]^T$ is a D-dimention vector of spectra of the distorted speech received from the n-th channel at frame f, $X_n(f)$ is the spectrum of the distorted speech received from the n-th channel at frame f for frequency ω, $\mathbf{H}_n(f) = [H_n(f,0) \quad H_n(f,1) \quad ... \quad H_n(f,d) \quad ... \quad H_n(f,D-1)]^T, d = 0,1,...,D-1$ is a D-dimensional vector of spectra of the impulse response, and $H_n(f,d)$ is the spectrum of the impulse response for frequency ω at frame f corresponding to frame delay d (that is, at frame $f+d$).

Using Eq. (27) in place of Eq. (13), the spectra of the impulse responses can be blindly estimated by the VSS-UMCLMS mentioned in Section 3.1.2.

4. Experiments

4.1. Experimental setup

The proposed dereverberation method based on spectral subtraction is evaluated on an isolated word recognition task in a simulated reverberant environment, and a large vocabulary continuous speech recognition task in both a simulated reverberant environment and a real reverberant environment, respectively.

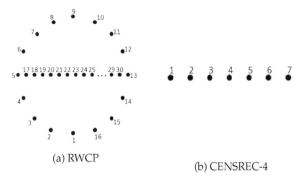

(a) RWCP

(b) CENSREC-4

Figure 3. Illustration of microphone array.

(a) RWCP database

Array no	Array type	Room	Angle	RT60 (S)
1	linear	Echo room (panel)	150°	0.30
2	circle	Echo room (cylinder)	30°	0.38
3	linear	Tatami-floored room (S)	120°	0.47
4	circle	Tatami-floored room (S)	120°	0.47
5	circle	Tatami-floored room (L)	90°	0.60
6	circle	Tatami-floored room (L)	130°	0.60
7	linear	Conference room	50°	0.78
8	linear	Echo room (panel)	70°	1.30

(b) CENSREC-4 database

Array no	Room	Room size	RT60 (s)
9	Office	9.0 Å 6.0 m	0.25
10	Japanese style room	3.5 Å 2.5 m	0.40
11	Lounge	11.5 Å 27.0 m	0.50
12	Japanese style bath	1.5 Å 1.0 m	0.60
13	Living room	7.0 Å 3.0 m	0.65
14	Meeting room	7.0 Å 8.5 m	0.65
15	Elevator hall	11.5 Å 6.5 m	0.75

RT60 (second): reverberation time in room; S: small; L: large

Table 1. Details of recording conditions for impulse response measurement

4.1.1. Experimental setup for isolated word recognition task

Multi-channel distorted speech signals simulated by convolving multi-channel impulse responses with clean speech were used to create artificial reverberant speech. Six kinds of multi-channel impulse responses measured in various acoustical reverberant environments were selected from the Real World Computing Partnership (RWCP) sound scene database [23]. Table 1 lists the details of recording conditions (impulse responses with array no 3-8 in RWCP

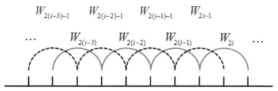

Figure 4. Illustration of the analysis window for spectral subtraction.

database were used in the isolated word recognition task). The illustration of microphone array is shown in Fig. 3. A four-channel circle or linear microphone array was taken from a circle + linear microphone array (30 channels). The four-channel circle type microphone array had a diameter of 30 cm, and the four microphones were located at equal 90° intervals. The four microphones of the linear microphone array were located at 11.32 cm intervals. Impulse responses were measured at several positions 2 m from the microphone array. The sampling frequency was 48 kHz.

For clean speech, 20 male speakers each with a close microphone uttered 100 isolated words. The 100 isolated words were phonetically balanced common isolated words selected from the Tohoku University and Panasonic isolated spoken word database [21]. The average time of all utterances was about 0.6 s. The sampling frequency was 12 kHz. The impulse responses sampled at 48 kHz were downsampled to 12 kHz so that they could be convolved with clean speech. The frame length was 21.3 ms, and the frame shift was 8 ms with a 256-point Hamming window. Then, 116 Japanese speaker-independent syllable-based HMMs (strictly speaking, mora-unit HMMs [22]) were trained using 27,992 utterances read by 175 male speakers from the Japanese Newspaper Article Sentences (JNAS) corpus [15]). Each continuous-density HMM had five states, four with probability density functions (pdfs) of output probability. Each pdf consisted of four Gaussians with full-covariance matrices. The acoustic model was common for the baseline and proposed methods, and it was trained in a clean condition. The feature space comprised 10 mel-frequency cepstral coefficients. First- and second-order derivatives of the cepstra plus first and second derivatives of the power component were also included (32 feature parameters in total).

The number of reverberant windows D in Eq. (4) was set to eight, which was empirically determined. In general, the window size D is proportional to RT60. However, the window size D is also affected by the reverberation property; for example, the ratio of power of the late reverberation to the power of the early reverberation. In our preliminary experiment with partial test data, the performance of our proposed method with a window size D = 2 to 16 outperformed the baseline significantly and the window size D = 8 achieved the best result. Automatic estimation of the optimum window size D is our future work. The length of the Hamming window for discrete Fourier transformation was 256 (21.3 ms), and the rate of overlap was 1/2. An illustration of the analysis window is shown in Fig. 4. For the proposed dereverberation based on spectral subtraction, the previous clean power spectra estimated with a skip window were used to estimate the current clean power spectrum [3]. The spectrum of the impulse response $\hat{H}(d,\omega)$ is estimated using the corresponding utterance to be recognized with average duration of about 0.6 second. No special parameters such as over-subtraction parameters were used in spectral subtraction ($\alpha = 1$), except that the

---

[3] Eq. (27) is true when using a skip window and the spectrum of the impulse response can be blindly estimated.

microphone	SONY ECM-C10
A/D board	Tokyo Electron device TD-BD-16ADUSB
recording room size [m]	7.1(D) ∆ 3.3(W) ∆ 2.5(H)
number of speakers	5 male speakers
number of utterances	100 utterances (about 20 utterances per speaker)
background noise	electric fan
sampling frequency	16 kHz
quantization bit rate	16 bits

Table 2. Conditions for recording in real environment.

subtracted value was controlled so that it did not become negative ($\beta = 0.15$). The speech recognition performance for clean isolated words was 96.0%.

4.1.2. Experimental setup for LVCSR task

In this study, both the artificial reverberant speech and real reverberant speech were used to evaluate our proposed method.

For artificial reverberant speech, multi-channel distorted speech signals simulated by convolving multi-channel impulse responses with clean speech were used. Fifteen kinds of multi-channel impulse responses measured in various acoustical reverberant environments were selected from the real world computing partnership (RWCP) sound scene database [23] and the CENSREC-4 database [24]. Table 1 lists the details of 15 recording conditions. The illustration of microphone array is shown in Fig. 3. For RWCP database, a 2–8 channel circle or linear microphone array was taken from a circle + linear microphone array (30 channels). The circle type microphone array had a diameter of 30 cm. The microphones of the linear microphone array were located at 2.83 cm intervals. Impulse responses were measured at several positions 2 m from the microphone array. For the CENSREC-4 database, 2 or 4 channel microphones were taken from a linear microphone array (7 channels) with the two microphones located at 2.125 cm intervals. Impulse responses were measured at several positions 0.5 m from the microphone array. The Japanese Newspaper Article Sentences (JNAS) corpus [15] was used as clean speech. Hundred utterances from the JNAS database convolved with the multi-channel impulse responses shown in Table 1 were used as test data. The average time for all utterances was about 5.8 s.

For reverberant speech in a real environment, we recorded multi-channel speech degraded simultaneously by background noise and reverberation. Table 2 gives the conditions and content of the recordings. One hundred utterances from the JNAS corpus, uttered by five male speakers seated on the chairs labeled A to E in Fig. 5, were recorded by a multi-channel recording device. The heights of the microphone array and the utterance position of each speaker were about 0.8 m and 1.0 m, respectively. An electric fan with high air volume located behind the speaker in position A was used as background noise. An average SNR of the speech was about 18 dB. We used a microphone array with 9 channels (Fig. 5) and a pin microphone to record speech in the distant-talking environment and close-talking environment, respectively.

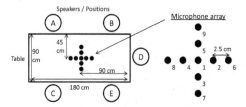

Figure 5. Illustration of recording settings and microphone array in real environment

Sampling frequency	16 kHz
Frame length	25 ms
Frame shift	10 ms
Acoustic model	5 states, 3 output probability left-to-right triphone HMMs
Feature space	25 dimensions with CMN (12 MFCCs + Δ + Δpower)

Table 3. Conditions for large vocabulary continuous speech recognition

method	Power SS		GSS	
	DN	DR	DN	DR
analysis window	Hamming			
window length	32 ms			
window shift	16 ms			
noise overestimation factor α	$\alpha_2=$ 3.0	$\alpha_1=$ 1.0	$\alpha_1=\alpha_2=$ 0.1	
spectral floor parameter β	$\beta_1=\beta_2=0.15$			

Table 4. Conditions for SS-based denoising and dereverberation. "DN": denoising. "DR": dereverberation.

Table 3 gives the conditions for speech recognition. The acoustic models were trained with the ASJ speech databases of phonetically balanced sentences (ASJ-PB) and the JNAS. In total, around 20K sentences (clean speech) uttered by 132 speakers were used for each gender. Table 4 gives the conditions for SS-based denoising and dereverberation. The parameters shown in Table 4 were determined empirically. For SS-based dereverberation method without background noise, the parameter α was equal to α_1 and β was equal to β_1. The number of reverberant windows D was set to 6 (192 ms). An illustration of the analysis window is shown in Fig. 4. An open-source LVCSR decoder software "Julius" [19] that is based on word trigram and triphone context-dependent HMMs is used.

4.2. Experimental results

4.2.1. Isolated word recognition results

Table 5 shows the isolated word recognition results in a simulated reverberant environment. "Distorted speech #" in Table 5 corresponds to "array no" in Table 1. Delay-and-sum

Distorted speech #	CMN	Power SS-based dereverberation
3	69.4	76.0
4	73.2	80.6
5	71.4	80.3
6	71.8	78.6
7	67.7	74.4
8	63.1	71.2
Ave.	69.4	76.9

Delay-and-sum beamforming was performed for all methods

Table 5. Isolated word recognition results (%).

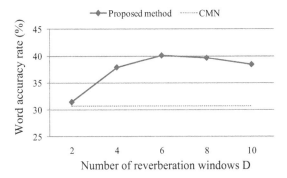

Figure 6. Effect of the number of reverberation windows D on power SS-based dereverberation for speech recognition.

beamforming [27] is performed for all methods in this chapter. The conventional CMN combined with delay-and-sum beamforming was used as a baseline.

The power SS-based dereverberation method by Eq. (7) improved speech recognition significantly compared with CMN for all severe reverberant conditions. The reason was that the proposed method compensated for both the late and early reverberation. The proposed method achieved an average relative error reduction rate of 24.5% in relation to conventional CMN with beamforming.

4.2.2. LVCSR results

(a) Effect factor analysis of power SS-based dereverberation in the simulated reverberant environment

In this section, we describe the use of four microphones to estimate the spectrum of the impulse responses without a particular explanation. Delay-and-sum beamforming (BF) was performed on the 4-channel dereverberant speech signals. For the proposed method, each speech channel was compensated by the corresponding estimated impulse response. Preliminary experimental results for isolated word recognition showed that the power SS-based dereverberation method significantly improved the speech recognition performance significantly compared with traditional CMN with beamforming. In this section, we

Array no #	Number of reverberation windows D				
	2	4	6	8	10
1	**81.45**	80.43	79.94	79.67	79.98
2	43.89	55.71	**57.69**	54.06	51.98
3	23.40	32.02	**33.46**	33.29	32.81
4	28.77	38.42	39.69	**39.88**	38.92
5	22.89	30.26	33.34	**33.59**	31.71
6	21.01	27.46	**31.79**	31.32	28.97
7	15.89	20.55	23.32	**23.92**	22.54
8	14.26	17.94	**21.41**	21.12	20.24
Ave	31.44	37.85	40.08	39.61	38.39

The results with bold font indicate the best result corresponding to each array

Table 6. Detail results based on different number of reverberation windows D and reverberant environments (%)

	Linear array	Circle array
2 channels	17, 29	1, 9
4 channels	17, 21, 25, 29	1, 5, 9, 13
8 channels	17, 19, 21, 23, 25, 27, 29, 30	1, 3, 5, 7, 9, 11, 13, 15, 17

Table 7. Channel number corresponding to Fig. 3(a) using for dereverberation and denoising (RWCP database)

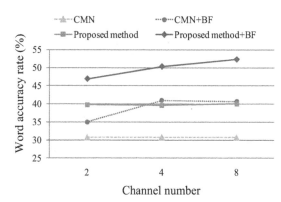

Figure 7. Effect of the number of channels on power SS-based dereverberation for speech recognition.

evaluated the power SS-based dereverberation method for LVCSR and analyzed the effect factor (number of reverberation windows D in Eq. (7), channel number, and length of utterance) for compensation parameter estimation based on power SS using RWCP database. The word accuracy rate for LVCSR with clean speech was 92.6%.

The effect of the number of reverberation windows on speech recognition is shown in Fig. 6. The detail results based on different number of reverberation windows D and reverberant environments (that is, different reverberation times) were shown in Table 6. The results shown on Fig. 6 and Table 6 were not performed delay-and-sum beamforming. The results show

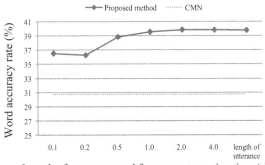

Length of utterance used for parameter estimation (s)

Figure 8. Effect of length of utterance used for parameter estimation on power SS-based dereverberation for speech recognition.

that the optimal number of reverberation windows D depends on the reverberation time. The best average result of all reverberant speech was obtained when D equals 6. The speech recognition performance with the number of reverberation windows between 4 and 10 did not vary greatly and was significantly better than the baseline.

We analyzed the influence of the number of channels on parameter estimation and delay-and-sum beamforming. Besides four channels, two and eight channels were also used to estimate the compensation parameter and perform beamforming. Channel numbers corresponding to Fig. 3(a) shown in Table 7 were used. The results are shown in Fig. 7. The speech recognition performance of the SS-based dereverberation method without beamforming was hardly affected by the number of channels. That is, the compensation parameter estimation is robust to the number of channels. Combined with beamforming, the more channels that are used and the better is the speech recognition performance.

Thus far, the whole utterance has been used to estimate the compensation parameter. The effect of the length of utterance used for parameter estimation was investigated, with the results shown in Fig. 8. The longer the length of utterance used, the better is the speech recognition performance. Deterioration in speech recognition was not experienced with the length of the utterance used for parameter estimation greater than 1 s. The speech recognition performance of the SS-based dereverberation method is better than the baseline even if only 0.1 s of utterance is used to estimate the compensation parameter.

We also compared the power SS-based dereverberation method on LVCSR in different simulated reverberant environments. The experimental results shown in Fig. 9. Naturally, the speech recognition rate deteriorated as the reverberation time increased. Using the SS-based dereverberation method, the reduction in the speech recognition rate was smaller than in conventional CMN, especially for impulse responses with a long reverberation time. For RWCP database, the SS-based dereverberation method achieved a relative word recognition error reduction rate of 19.2% relative to CMN with delay-and-sum beamforming. We also conducted an LVCSR experiment with SS-based dereverberation under different reverberant conditions (CENSREC-4), with the reverberation time between 0.25 and 0.75 s and the distance between microphone and sound source 0.5 m. A similar trend to the above results was observed. Therefore, the SS-based dereverberation method is robust to various reverberant

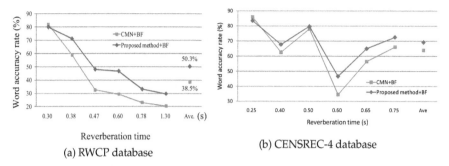

(a) RWCP database

(b) CENSREC-4 database

Figure 9. Word accuracy for LVCSR in different simulated reverberant environments.

conditions for both isolated word recognition and LVCSR. The reason is that the SS-based dereverberation method can compensate for late reverberation through SS using an estimated power spectrum of the impulse response.

(b) Results of GSS-based method in the simulated reverberant environment

In this section, reverberation and noise suppression using only 2 speech channels is described. In both power SS-based and GSS-based dereverberation methods, speech signals from two microphones were used to estimate blindly the compensation parameters for the power SS and GSS (that is, the spectra of the channel impulse responses), and then reverberation was suppressed by SS and the spectrum of dereverberant speech was inverted into a time domain. Finally, delay-and-sum beamforming was performed on the two-channel dereverberant speech.

The results of power SS-based method and the GSS-based method without background noise were compared in Table 8. "Distorted speech #" in Table 8 corresponds to "array no" in Table 1. The speech recognition performance was drastically degraded under reverberant conditions because the conventional CMN did not suppress the late reverberation. Delay-and-sum beamforming with CMN (41.91%) could not markedly improve the speech recognition performance because of the small number of microphones and the small distance between the microphone pair. In contrast, the power SS-based dereverberation using Eq. (7) markedly improved the speech recognition performance. The GSS-based dereverberation using Eq. (8) improved speech recognition performance significantly compared with the power SS-based dereverberation and CMN for all reverberant conditions. The GSS-based method achieved an average relative word error reduction rate of 31.4% compared to the conventional CMN and 9.8% compared to the power SS-based method.

Table 9 shows the speech recognition results for the power SS and GSS-based denoising and dereverberation methods for the simulated noisy and reverberant speech. "Distorted speech #", "DN" and "DNR" in Table 9 denote the "array #" in Table 1, "denoising", and "denoising and dereverberation", respectively. The speech recognition performance of conventional CMN was drastically degraded owing to the noisy and reverberant conditions and the fact that CMN did not suppress the late reverberation. The power SS-based DN improved speech recognition performance significantly compared to the CMN for all reverberant conditions. The GSS-based DN using Eq. (11), however, did not improve the speech recognition performance compared to the power SS-based DN. On the other hand, the power SS-based DNR achieved a marked improvement in the speech recognition performance compared with

Distorted speech #	CMN only	Power SS-based method	GSS-based method
2	44.35	63.34	65.95
4	27.59	40.79	49.16
5	25.61	42.55	49.29
11	73.90	79.26	80.77
12	27.06	42.28	45.38
13	29.62	50.78	56.13
15	65.24	71.67	74.35
Ave.	41.91	55.81	60.15

Delay-and-sum beamforming was performed for all methods

Table 8. Comparison of Word accuracy for LVCSR with power SS-based method and GSS-based method in the simulated reverberant environment (%)

Distorted Speech #	CMN only	Power SS		GSS	
		DN	DNR	DN	DNR
1	28.2	37.4	48.8	30.3	48.3
2	16.0	25.9	33.5	18.8	36.3
3	9.5	21.3	31.3	13.9	32.8
4	55.8	72.2	69.9	60.4	68.2
5	17.2	24.4	32.0	20.9	37.7
6	26.1	32.8	45.3	30.0	51.7
7	54.4	64.6	66.5	57.7	68.8
Average	29.6	39.8	46.7	33.1	49.1

Delay-and-sum beamforming was performed for all methods

Table 9. Word accuracy for LVCSR with the simulated noisy reverberant speech (%).

that of CMN. The GSS-based DNR using Eq. (10) improved speech recognition performance significantly compared to both the CMN method and the power SS-based DNR for almost all reverberant conditions.

(c) Results in the real noisy reverberant environment

Table 10 shows the speech recognition results for the real noisy reverberant speech under the same conditions as the simulated noisy reververant speech. The word accuracy rate for close-talking speech recorded in a real environment was 88.3%. We investigated the best channel combination in the real environment and the best speech recognition performance was obtained when channels 6, 7, 8, and 9 described in Fig. 5 were used. Therefore, this channel combination was used in this study. Power SS-based DN and GSS-based DN achieved a smaller improvement in recognition performance compared with the simulated noisy reverberant environment because the type of background noise in the real environment was different from that in the simulated environment. On the other hand, the power SS-based DNR markedly improved the speech recognition performance compared to CMN. The GSS-based DNR improved speech recognition performance significantly compared to

| Speakers / | CMN | Power SS | | GSS | |
Position	only	DN	DNR	DN	DNR
A	60.2	67.7	78.9	64.7	79.5
B	75.6	72.2	78.5	72.5	83.2
C	67.4	63.2	69.4	66.7	77.5
D	59.1	53.9	74.9	60.8	78.7
E	42.9	51.0	62.8	50.0	61.7
Average	60.9	61.6	73.1	62.9	76.2

Delay-and-sum beamforming was performed for all methods

Table 10. Word accuracy for LVCSR with the real noisy reverberant speech (%).

both the CMN method and the power SS-based DNR for almost all speakers. The GSS-based DNR achieved an average relative word error reduction rate of 39.1% and 11.5% compared to conventional CMN and power SS-based DNR, respectively. These results show that our proposed method is also effective in a real environment under the same denoising and dereverberation conditions as the simulated noisy reverberant environment.

5. Conclusion

In this chapter, we proposed a blind spectral subtraction based dereverberation method for hands-free speech recognition method. We treated the late reverberation as additive noise, and a noise reduction technique based on spectral subtraction was applied to compensate for the late reverberation. The early reverberation was normalized by CMN. The time-domain MCLMS algorithm was extended to blindly estimate the spectrum of the impulse response for spectral subtraction in a frequency domain. We evaluated our proposed methods on isolated word recognition task and LVCSR task. The proposed spectral subtraction based on multi-channel LMS significantly outperformed than the conventional CMN. For isolated word recognition task, a relative error reduction rate of 24.5% in relation to the conventional CMN was achieved. For LVCSR task without background noise, the proposed method achieved an average relative word error reduction rate of 31.5% compared to conventional CMN in the simulated reverberant environment. We also presented a denoising and dereverberation method based on spectral subtraction and evaluated it in both the simulated noisy reverberant environment and the real noisy reverberant environment. The GSS-based method achieved an average relative word error reduction rate of 39.1% and 11.5% compared to conventional CMN and power SS-based method, respectively. These results show that our proposed method is also effective in a real noisy reverberant environment.

In this chapter, we also investigated the effect factors (numbers of reverberation windows and channels, and length of utterance) for compensation parameter estimation. We reached the following conclusions: 1) the speech recognition performance with the number of reverberation windows between 4 and 10 did not vary greatly and was significantly better than the baseline; 2) the compensation parameter estimation was robust to the number of channels; and 3) degradation of speech recognition did not occur with the length of utterance used for parameter estimation longer than 1 s. We also compared the SS-based dereverberation method on LVCSR in different simulated reverberant environments. A similar trend was observed.

Author details

Longbiao Wang, Kyohei Odani and Atsuhiko Kai
Shizuoka University, Japan

Norihide Kitaoka
Nagoya University, Japan

Seiichi Nakagawa
Toyohashi University of Technology, Japan

6. References

[1] Avendano, C. & Hermansky, H. (1996). Study on the dereverberation of speech based on temporal envelope filtering. *Proceedings of ICSLP-1996*, pp. 889-892, Philadelphia, USA, October 1996.

[2] Chen, H., Cao, X., & Zhu, J. (2002). Convergence of stochastic-approximation-based algorithms for blind channel identification. *IEEE Trans. Information Theory*, Vol. 48, 2002, pp. 1214-1225.

[3] Couvreur, L. & Couvreur, C. (2004). Blind model selection for automatic speech recognition in reverberant environments. *Journal of VLSI Signal Processing*, Vol. 36, No. 2-3, February/March 2004, pp. 189-203.

[4] Delcroix, M., Hikichi, T. & Miyoshi, M. (1994). On a blind speech dereverberation algorithm using multi-channel linear prediction. *IEEE Transations on Fundamentals of Electronics, Communications and Computer Sciences*, Vol. E89-A, No. 10, October 2006, pp. 2837-2846.

[5] Delcroix, M., Hikichi, T. & Miyoshi, M. (1994). Precise dereverberation using multi-channel linear prediction. *IEEE Transations on Audio, Speech, and Language Processing*, Vol. 15, No. 2, February 2007, pp. 430-440.

[6] Furui, S. (1981). Cepstral analysis technique for automatic speaker verification. *IEEE Trans. Acous. Speech Signal Processing*, Vol. 29, No. 2, 1981, pp. 254-272.

[7] Gannot, S. & Moonen, M. (2003). Subspace methods for multimicrophone speech dereverberation. *EURASIP Journal on Applied Signal Processing*, October 2003, pp. 1074-1090.

[8] Gillespie, B. W., Malvar, H. S. & Florencio, D. A. F. (2001). Speech dereverberation via maximum-kurtosis subband adaptive filtering, *Proceedings of ICASSP-2001*, Vol. 6, pp. 3701-3704, Salt Lake City, USA, May 2001.

[9] Habets, E. A. P. (2004). Single-channel speech dereverberation based on spectral subtraction, *Proceedings of the 15th Annual Workshop on Circuits, Systems and Signal Processing (ProRISC-2004)*, pp. 250-254, Veldhoven, Netherlands, November 2004.

[10] Hermansky, H. & Morgan, N. (1994). RASTA processing of speech. *IEEE Transations on Speech and Audio Processing*, Vol. 2, No. 4, October 1994, pp. 578-589.

[11] Hermansky, H., Wan, E. A. & Avendano, C. (1995). Speech enhancement based on temporal processing, *Proceedings of ICASSP-1995*, pp. 405-408, Detroit, USA, May 1995.

[12] Huang, Y. & Benesty, J. (2002). Adaptive multichannel least mean square and Newton algorithms for blind channel identification. *Signal Processing*, Vol. 82, No. 8, August 2002, pp. 1127-1138.

[13] Huang, Y., Benesty, J. & Chen, J. (2005). Optimal step size of the adaptive multi-channel LMS algorithm for blind SIMO identification. *IEEE Signal Processing Letters*, Vol. 12, No. 3, March 2005, pp. 173-176.

[14] Huang, Y., Benesty, J. & Chen, J. (2006). *Acoustic MIMO Signal Processing*, Springer-Verlag, ISBN 978-3-540-37630-9, Berlin, Germany.

[15] Itou, K., Yamamoto, M., Takeda, K., Takezawa, T., Matsuoka, T., Kobayashi, T., Shikano, K. & Itahashi, S. (1999). JNAS: Japanese speech corpus for large vocabulary continuous speech recognition research. *Journal of the Acoustical Society of Japan (E)*, Vol. 20, No. 3, May 1999, pp. 199-206.

[16] Jin, Q., Pan, Y. & Schultz, t. (2006). Far-field speaker recognition, *Proceedings of ICASSP-2006*, pp. 937-940, Toulouse, France, May 2006.

[17] Jin, Q., Schultz, t. & Waibel, A. (2007). Far-field speaker recognition. *IEEE Transations on Audio, Speech, and Language Processing*, Vol. 15, No. 7, September 2007, pp. 2023-2032.

[18] Kinoshita, K., Delocroix, M., Nakatani, T. & Miyoshi, M. (2009). Suppression of late reverberation effect on speech signal using long-term multiple-step linear prediction. *IEEE Transations on Audio, Speech, and Language Processing*, Vol. 17, No. 4, May 2009, pp. 534-545.

[19] Lee, A., Kawahara, T. & Shikano, K. (2001). Julius—an open source real-time large vocabulary recognition engine. *Proceedings of European Conference on Speech Communication and Technology*, September 2001, pp. 1691-1694.

[20] Maganti, H. & Matassoni, M. (2010). An audiotry modulation spectral feature for reverberant speech recognition, *Proceedings of INTERSPEECH-2010*, pp. 570-573, Makuhari, Japan, September 2010.

[21] Makino, S., Niyada, K., Mafune, Y. & Kido, K. (1992). Tohoku University and Panasonic isolated spoken word database. *Journal of the Acoustical Society of Japan*, Vol. 48, No. 12, December 1992, pp. 899-905 (in Japanese).

[22] Nakagawa, S., Hanai, K., Yamamoto, K. & Minematsu, N. (1999). Comparison of syllable-based HMMs and triphone-based HMMs in Japanese speech recognition. *Proceedings of International Workshop on Automatic Speech Recognition and Understanding*, 1999, pp. 393-396.

[23] Nakamura, S., Hiyane, K., Asano, F. & Nishiura, T. (2000). Acoustical sound database in real environments for sound scene understanding and hands-free speech recognition, *Proceedings of IREC-2000*, pp. 965-971.

[24] Nakayama, M., Nishiura, T., Denda, Y., Kitaoka, N., Yamamoto, K., Yamada, T., Tsuge, S., Miyajima, C., Fujimoto, M., Takiguchi, T., Tamura, S., Ogawa, T., Matsuda, S., Kuroiwa, S., Takeda, K. & Nakamura, S. (2008). CENSREC-4: Development of evaluation framework for distant-talking speech recognition under reverberant environments, *Proceedings of INTERSPEECH-2008*, pp. 968-971, Brisbane, Australia, September 2008.

[25] Raut, C., Nishimoto, T. & Sagayama, S. (2006). Adaptation for long convolutional distortion by maximum likelihood based state filtering approach, *Proceedings of ICASSP-2006*, pp. 1133-1136, Toulouse, France, May 2006.

[26] Sim, B. L., Tong, Y. C. & Chang J. S. (1998). A parametric formulation of the generalized spectral subtraction method. *IEEE Transactions on Speech and Audio Processing*, Vol. 6, No. 4, July 1998, pp. 328-337.

[27] Van Veen, B. & Buckley, K. (1988). Beamforming: A versatile approach to spatial filtering. *IEEE ASSP Mag.*, Vol. 5, No. 2, March 2011, pp. 4-24.

## Chapter 7

Linear Feature Transformations in Slovak Phoneme-Based Continuous Speech Recognition

Jozef Juhár and Peter Viszlay

Additional information is available at the end of the chapter

1. Introduction

The most common acoustic front-ends in automatic speech recognition (ASR) systems are based on the state-of-the-art Mel-Frequency Cepstral Coefficients (MFCCs). The practice shows that this general technique is good choice to obtain satisfactory speech representation. In the past few decades, the researchers have made a great effort in order to develop and apply such techniques, which may improve the recognition performance of the conventional MFCCs. In general, these methods were taken from mathematics and applied in many research areas such as face and speech recognition, high-dimensional data and signal processing, video and image coding and many other. One group of mentioned methods is represented by linear transformations.

Linear feature transformations (also referred as subspace learning or dimensionality reduction methods) are used to convert the original data set to an alternative and more compact set with retaining of information as much as possible. They are also used to increase the robustness and the performance of the system. In speech recognition, the basic acoustic front-end based on MFCCs can be supplemented by some kind of linear feature transformation. The linear transformation is applied in feature extraction step. Then the whole feature extraction process is achieved in two steps: parameter extraction and feature transformation. Linear transformation is applied to a sequence of acoustic vectors obtained by some kind of preprocessing method. Usually, the spectral, log-spectral, Mel-filtered spectral or cepstral features are projected to a more relevant and more decorrelated subspace, which is directly used in acoustic modeling. During the transformation often a dimension reduction step is also done. This is achieved by retaining only the relevant dimensions after the transformation according to some optimization criterion. The dimension reduction step helps to solve the problem called the curse of dimensionality.

In practice, supervised and unsupervised subspace learning methods are used. The most popular data-driven unsupervised transformation used in ASR is Principal Component Analysis (PCA). It is known that the supervised methods need an information about the structure of the data, which are partitioned in the classes. Therefore, it is necessary to use appropriate class labels. A widely used supervised method is known as Linear Discriminant Analysis (LDA).

In numerous research works and publications it was proven that the above mentioned linear transformations were successfully applied in ASR to multiple languages with different characteristics of speech. The Slovak speech recognition research group tends to follow this trend. In this work, we present a practical methodology with adequate theoretical principles related to application of linear feature transformations in Slovak phoneme-based large vocabulary continuous speech recognition (LVCSR).

The main subject of this chapter is the application of LDA in Slovak ASR, but the core of most experiments is based on Two-dimensional LDA (2DLDA), which is an extension of LDA. Several context lengths of basic vectors are used in the discriminat analysis and different final dimensions of transformation matrix are utilized. The classical procedures by several our modifications are supplemented. The second part of the chapter is oriented to PCA and to our proposed method related to PCA training from limited amount of training data. The third part investigates the interaction of the above mentioned PCA and 2DLDA applied in one recognition task. The closing part compares and evaluates all experiments and concludes the chapter by presenting the best achieved results.

This chapter is divided into few basic units. Sections 2 and 3 describe LDA and 2DLDA used in speech recognition. Section 4 surveys PCA and also presents the proposed partial-data trained PCA method. Section 5 presents the setup of the system for continuous phoneme-based speech recognition. Section 6 presents extensive experiments and evaluations of the used methods in different configurations. Finally Section 7 concludes the chapter. Section 8 gives the future intentions in our research.

2. Conventional Linear Discriminant Analysis (LDA)

Linear discriminant analysis is a well-known dimensionality reduction and transformation method that maps the N-dimensional input data to p-dimensional ($p < N$) subspace while retaining maximum discrimination information. A general mathematical model of linear transformation can be written in the following manner:

$$\mathbf{y} = W^T\mathbf{x}, \tag{1}$$

where $\mathbf{y}$ is the output transformed feature set, W is the transformation matrix and $\mathbf{x}$ is the input feature set. The aim of LDA is to find this transformation matrix W with respect to some optimization criterion (information loss, class discrimination, ...). It can be obtained by applying an eigendecomposition to the covariance matrices. The p best functions resulted from the decomposition are used to transform the feature vectors to reduced representation.

2.1. Mathematical background

According to [1, 7, 11, 14, 19] LDA can be defined as follows. Suppose a training data matrix $X \in \Re^{N \times n}$ with n column vectors $\mathbf{x}_i$, where $1 \leq i \leq n$. LDA finds a linear transformation represented by transformation matrix $W \in \Re^{N \times p}$ that maps each column $\mathbf{x}_i$ of X to a column vector $\mathbf{y}_i$ in the p-dimensional space as:

$$\mathbf{y}_i = W^T \mathbf{x}_i; \; p < N. \tag{2}$$

Consider that the original data is partitioned into k classes as $X = \{\Pi_1, \ldots, \Pi_k\}$, where the class Π_i contains n_i elements (feature vectors) from the ith class. Notice that $n = \sum_{i=1}^{k} n_i$. The classes can be represented by *class mean vectors*

$$\mu_i = \frac{1}{n_i} \sum_{x \in \Pi_i} \mathbf{x} \tag{3}$$

and their *class covariance matrices*

$$\Sigma_i = \sum_{x \in \Pi_i} (\mathbf{x} - \mu_i)(\mathbf{x} - \mu_i)^T, \tag{4}$$

which are defined to quantify the quality of the cluster. Since LDA in ASR mostly in class-independent manner is used, we define the *within-class covariance matrix* as the sum of all class covariance matrices

$$\Sigma_W = \frac{1}{n} \sum_{i=1}^{k} \Sigma_i = \frac{1}{n} \sum_{i=1}^{k} \sum_{x \in \Pi_i} (\mathbf{x} - \mu_i)(\mathbf{x} - \mu_i)^T. \tag{5}$$

To quantify the covariance between classes, the *between-class covariance matrix* is used. It is defined as:

$$\Sigma_B = \frac{1}{n} \sum_{i=1}^{k} (\mu_i - \mu)(\mu_i - \mu)^T, \tag{6}$$

where

$$\mu = \frac{1}{n} \sum_{i=1}^{k} \sum_{x \in \Pi_i} \mathbf{x} \tag{7}$$

is the *global mean vector* (computed disregarding the class label information). Note that the variable $\mathbf{x}$ in speech recognition represents a *supervector* created by concatenating of acoustic vectors computed on successive speech frames. To build a supervector of J acoustic vectors (J is typically 3, 5, 7, 9 or 11 frames), the vector $\mathbf{x}_j$ at the current position j is spliced together with $\frac{J-1}{2}$ vectors on the left and right as

$$\mathbf{x} = \left[\mathbf{x}[j - \tfrac{J-1}{2}] \; \ldots \; \mathbf{x}[j] \; \ldots \; \mathbf{x}[j + \tfrac{J-1}{2}] \right]. \tag{8}$$

It should be noted that in case, when the length of the supervector was greater than the number of classes ($13 \times J > k$, where $J \geq 5, k = 45$), the between-class covariance matrix became close to singular or singular. This fact resulted in eigendecomposition with complex valued transformation matrix, which was undesirable.

Therefore, we used for these cases a modified computation of Σ_B according to [7] as follows:

$$\widetilde{\Sigma}_B = \frac{1}{n} \sum_{i=1}^{n} (\mathbf{x}_i - \boldsymbol{\mu})(\mathbf{x}_i - \boldsymbol{\mu})^T. \tag{9}$$

This way of computation can be interpreted as a finer estimation of Σ_B because each training supervector contributes to a final estimation of Σ_B (more data points are used) in comparison with the estimation represented by Equation 6.

The given covariance matrices are used to formulate the optimization criterion for LDA, which tries to maximize the between-class scatter (covariance) over the within-class scatter (covariance). It can be shown that the covariance matrices resulting from the linear transformation W (in the p-dimensional space) become $\widetilde{\Sigma}_B^p = W^T \Sigma_B W$ and $\widetilde{\Sigma}_W^p = W^T \Sigma_W W$. The objective function can be defined as

$$J(W) = \frac{|\widetilde{\Sigma}_B|}{|\widetilde{\Sigma}_W|} = \frac{|W^T \Sigma_B W|}{|W^T \Sigma_W W|}. \tag{10}$$

This optimization problem is equivalent to the generalized eigenvalue problem

$$\Sigma_B \mathbf{v} = \lambda \Sigma_W \mathbf{v}, \text{ for } \lambda \neq 0, \tag{11}$$

where $\mathbf{v}$ is a square matrix of eigenvectors and λ represents the eigenvalues. The solution can be obtained by applying an eigendecomposition to the matrix

$$\Sigma_W^{-1} \Sigma_B. \tag{12}$$

The reduced representation W_p of W is made by choosing p eigenvectors corresponding to p largest eigenvalues.

2.2. Class definition in LDA

Since LDA is a supervised method, it needs additional information about the class structure of the training data. In the past few years, several choices for LDA class definition in ASR were proposed and experimentally investigated. For small vocabulary phoneme-based ASR systems LDA yielded an improvement with phone level conventional class definition [4, 8]. In these cases the Viterbi-trained context independent phonemes are used as classes. For HMM-based recognizers the time-aligned HMM states can define the classes [14]. Another reasonable method is to use the subphone levels as LDA classes [15]. We showed in our work [17] that an alternative phonetic class definition based on phonetic segmentation can lead to improvement.

For large vocabulary phoneme-based ASR systems there exist several ways to define the classes. One might argue that the conventional phone-level definition is the appropriate one. For triphone-based recognizers the context-dependent or context-independent triphones can be used [13] or the tied states in context dependent acoustic models [6].

In this work we used the conventional phone-level classes for LDA and 2DLDA. The phonetic segmentation was obtained from embedded training and automatic phone alignment (see

Section 5.3). Thus, the number of classes in LDA-based experiments was identical with the number of phonemes and also with the number of trained monophone models. The disadvantage of the phone segmentation obtained from embedded training can be potentially the inaccuracy of the determined phone boundaries compared to the actual boundaries.

3. Two-Dimensional Linear Discriminant Analysis

Linear Discriminant Analysis used as a feature extraction or dimension reduction method in applications with high-dimensional data may not perform always optimally. Especially, when the dimension of the data exceeds the number of data points, the scatter matrices can become singular. This is known as the singularity or undersampled problem in LDA, which is its intrinsic limitation.

Two-Dimensional Linear Discriminant Analysis (hereinafter 2DLDA) [19] was primarily designed to overcome the singularity problem in classical LDA. 2DLDA overcomes the singularity problem implicitly. The key difference between LDA and 2DLDA is in the data representation model. While conventional LDA works with vectorized representation of data, the 2DLDA algorithm works with data in matrix representation. Therefore, the data collection is performed as a collection of matrices, instead of a single large data matrix. This concept has been used for example in [18] for PCA.

It is known that the optimal transformation matrix in LDA can be obtained by applying an eigendecomposition to the scatter matrices. Generally, these matrices can be singular because they are estimated from high-dimensional data. In recent years, several approaches have been developed to solve such problems related to high-dimensional computing [10]. One of these approaches is called PCA+LDA and it is a widely used two-stage algorithm especially in face recognition [3]. All mentioned methods require the computation of eigendecomposition of large matrices, which can lead to degradation of the efficiency.

2DLDA alleviates the difficult computation of the eigendecomposition in methods discussed above. Since it works with matrices instead of high-dimensional supervectors (as in classical LDA), the eigendecomposition in 2DLDA is computed on matrices with much smaller sizes than in LDA. This reduces the processing time and memory costs of 2DLDA compared to LDA.

3.1. Mathematical description

Let $A_i \in \mathbf{R}^{r \times c}$, $\langle 1; n \rangle$ be the n training speech signals in the corpus. Suppose there are k classes $\Pi_1, \ldots, \Pi_k$, where Π_i has n_i feature vectors. Let

$$M_i = \frac{1}{n_i} \sum_{X \in \Pi_i} X, \quad i \in \langle 1; k \rangle \tag{13}$$

be the mean of the i-th class and

$$M = \frac{1}{n} \sum_{i=1}^{k} \sum_{X \in \Pi_i} X \tag{14}$$

be the global mean. In [19], for face recognition, X originally represents a training image. For speech recognition, X represents the concatenated acoustic vectors (supervector) computed on successive speech frames [12]. In fact, X is a matrix composed by combination of acoustic vectors computed on successive speech frames. We can call this matrix analogously to supervector as supermatrix.

2DLDA considers an $(l_1 \times l_2)$-dimensional space $\mathcal{L} \otimes \mathcal{R}$, which is a tensor product of the spaces - $\mathcal{L}$ spanned by vectors $\{u_i\}_{i=1}^{l_1}$ and $\mathcal{R}$ spanned by vectors $\{v_i\}_{i=1}^{l_2}$. Since in 2DLDA, the speech is considered as a two-dimensional element, two transformation matrices, L and R are defined as $L = [u_1, \ldots, u_{l_1}], L \in \mathbf{R}^{r \times l_1}$ and matrix $R = [v_1, \ldots, v_{l_2}], R \in \mathbf{R}^{c \times l_2}$. These matrices map each $A_i \in \mathbf{R}^{r \times c}$ to a matrix $B_i \in \mathbf{R}^{l_1 \times l_2}$ as:

$$B_i = L^T A_i R, \quad i \in \langle 1; n \rangle. \tag{15}$$

Due to difficult computing of optimal L and R simultaneously, [19] derived an iterative algorithm, which for fixed R computes the optimal L. With computed L it can be updated R. The procedure is several times repeated. As in classical LDA, the scatter matrices are computed similarly, but in two-dimensional concept. Note that in 2DLDA are defined two within-class scatter matrices S_w^R and S_w^L and two between-class scatter matrices S_b^R and S_b^L concurrently. Scatter matrices coupled with R are defined as follows:

$$S_w^R = \sum_{i=1}^{k} \sum_{X \in \Pi_i} (X - M_i) R R^T (X - M_i)^T, \tag{16}$$

$$S_b^R = \sum_{i=1}^{k} n_i (M_i - M) R R^T (M_i - M)^T. \tag{17}$$

For fixed R, L can be then computed by solving an optimization problem:

$$max_L \; trace\left(\left(L^T S_w^R L\right)^{-1} \left(L^T S_b^R L\right) \right). \tag{18}$$

This problem can be solved as an eigenvalue problem:

$$S_w^R \mathbf{x} = \lambda S_b^R \mathbf{x}. \tag{19}$$

L can be then obtained in similar way as in LDA by applying an eigendecomposition to matrix resulting from:

$$\left(S_w^R\right)^{-1} S_b^R. \tag{20}$$

Scatter matrices coupled with L are defined as follows:

$$S_w^L = \sum_{i=1}^{k} \sum_{X \in \Pi_i} (X - M_i)^T L L^T (X - M_i), \tag{21}$$

$$S_b^L = \sum_{i=1}^{k} n_i (M_i - M)^T L L^T (M_i - M). \tag{22}$$

In this way, with obtained L it can be computed the optimal R by solving an optimization problem:

$$max_R \ trace\left((R^T S_w^L R)^{-1}(R^T S_b^L R)\right). \tag{23}$$

This problem can be solved as an eigenvalue problem:

$$S_w^L \mathbf{x} = \lambda S_b^L \mathbf{x}. \tag{24}$$

The optimal R can be then obtained by applying an eigendecomposition to matrix resulting from:

$$(S_w^L)^{-1} S_b^L. \tag{25}$$

It should be noted that the sizes of scatter matrices in 2DLDA are much smaller that those in LDA. Specifically, the size of S_w^R and S_b^R is $r \times r$ and the size of S_w^L and S_b^L is $c \times c$.

3.2. Pseudocode of 2DLDA algorithm

1. Compute the mean M_i of ith class for each i as $M_i = \frac{1}{n_i} \sum_{X \in \Pi_i} X$;
2. Compute the global mean as $M = \frac{1}{n} \sum_{i=1}^{k} \sum_{X \in \Pi_i} X$;
3. $R_0 \leftarrow$ identity matrix;
4. For j from 1 to I
5.

$$S_w^R \leftarrow \sum_{i=1}^{k} \sum_{X \in \Pi_i} (X - M_i) R_{j-1} R_{j-1}^T (X - M_i)^T, \tag{26}$$

$$S_b^R \leftarrow \sum_{i=1}^{k} n_i (M_i - M) R_{j-1} R_{j-1}^T (M_i - M)^T; \tag{27}$$

6. Compute the first l_1 eigenvectors $\{\phi_l^L\}_{l=1}^{l_1}$ of $(S_w^R)^{-1} S_b^R$;
7. $L_j \leftarrow [\phi_1^L, \ldots, \phi_{l_1}^L]$;
8.

$$S_w^L \leftarrow \sum_{i=1}^{k} \sum_{X \in \Pi_i} (X - M_i)^T L_j L_j^T (X - M_i), \tag{28}$$

$$S_b^L \leftarrow \sum_{i=1}^{k} n_i (M_i - M)^T L_j L_j^T (M_i - M); \tag{29}$$

9. Compute the first l_2 eigenvectors $\{\phi_l^R\}_{l=1}^{l_2}$ of $(S_w^L)^{-1} S_b^L$;
10. End for
11. $L \leftarrow L_I, R \leftarrow R_I$;
12. $B_l \leftarrow L^T A_l R$, for $l = 1, \ldots, n$;
13. return $(L, R, B_1, \ldots, B_n)$.

The most time consuming steps in 2DLDA computing are lines 5, 8 and 13. The algorithm depends on the initial choice of R_0. In [19] it was showed and recommended to choose an identity matrix as R_0.

4. Principal component analysis

Principal component analysis (PCA) [9] is a linear feature transformation and dimensionality reduction method, which maps the n-dimensional input possibly correlated data to K-dimensional $(K < n)$ linearly uncorrelated variables (mutually independent principal components) with respect to the variability. PCA converts the data by a linear orthogonal transformation using the first few principal components, which usually represent about 80% of the overall variance. The principal component basis minimizes the mean square error of approximating the data. This linear basis can be obtained by application of an eigendecomposition to the global covariance matrix estimated from the original data.

4.1. Mathematical description

The characteristic mathematical stages of PCA can be briefly described as follows [2, 9]. Firstly suppose that the training data are represented by M n-dimensional feature vectors $x_1, x_2, \ldots, x_M$. One of the integral parts of PCA is the centering of all vectors (subtracting the mean) as:

$$\Phi_i = x_i - \bar{x}, \quad i \in \langle 1; M \rangle, \tag{30}$$

where

$$\bar{x} = \frac{1}{M} \sum_{i=1}^{M} x_i \tag{31}$$

is the training mean vector. From the centered vectors Φ_i the centered data matrix with dimension $n \times M$ is created as:

$$A = [\Phi_1 \Phi_2 \ldots \Phi_M]. \tag{32}$$

To represent the variance of the data across different dimensions, the global covariance matrix is computed as:

$$C = \frac{1}{M-1} \sum_{i=1}^{M} \Phi_i \Phi_i^T = \frac{1}{M-1} \sum_{i=1}^{M} (x_i - \bar{x})(x_i - \bar{x})^T = \frac{1}{M-1} A A^T. \tag{33}$$

An eigendecomposition is applied to the covariance matrix in order to obtain its eigenvectors $u_1, u_2, \ldots, u_n$ and corresponding eigenvalues $\lambda_1, \lambda_2, \ldots, \lambda_n$ and it satisfies the linear equation:

$$C u_i = \lambda_i u_i, \quad i \in \langle 1; n \rangle. \tag{34}$$

The principal components are determined by K leading eigenvectors resulting from the decomposition. The dimensionality reduction step is performed by keeping only the eigenvectors corresponding to the K largest eigenvalues $(K < n)$. These eigenvectors form the transformation matrix U_K with dimension $n \times K$:

$$U_K = [u_1 u_2 \ldots u_K], \tag{35}$$

while $\lambda_1 > \lambda_2 > \ldots > \lambda_n$. Finally, the linear transformation $\mathbf{R}_n \to \mathbf{R}_K$ is computed according to Equation (1) as:

$$y_i = U_K^T \Phi_i = U_K^T (x_i - \bar{x}), \quad i \in \langle 1; M \rangle. \tag{36}$$

where y_i represents the transformed feature vector. The value of K can be chosen as needed or according to the following comparative criterion:

$$\frac{\sum_{i=1}^{K} \lambda_i}{\sum_{i=1}^{n} \lambda_i} > T, \qquad (37)$$

where the threshold $T \in \langle 0.9; 0.95 \rangle$. Since

$$\sum_{i=1}^{n} \lambda_i = trace(U), \qquad (38)$$

the comparative criterion can be rewritten as:

$$\frac{\sum_{i=1}^{K} \lambda_i}{trace(U)} > T. \qquad (39)$$

4.2. Classical PCA in ASR

In this section we describe PCA trained from the whole amount of training data (see Section 5.1). Two kinds of input data for PCA were used. The first kind was represented by 26-dimensional LMFE features and the second one by the 13-dimensional MFCCs. Each parametrized speech signal in the corpus is represented by a LMFE or MFCC matrix $X^{(i)}$, $i \in \langle 1; N \rangle$ with dimension $26 \times n_i$ (or $13 \times n_i$, see Section 5.2), where n_i represents the number of frames in i-th recording and N represents the number of training speech signals ($N=36917$).

At the first stage, the initial data preparation is performed, which requires the mathematical computations described by Equations 30-32. The global covariance matrix is computed according to Equation 33 and then decomposed to a set of eigenvector-eigenvalue pairs. According to the K largest eigenvalues the corresponding eigenvectors were chosen. These ones formed the transformation matrix U_K (see Equation 35), which was used to transform the train and test corpus into PCA feature space.

Note that the final dimension (K) of the feature vectors after PCA transformation was chosen independently from the criterion formula (Equation 37). Detailed reasons are given in Sections 5.2 and 6.3. However, for interest, the determined optimal dimensions for different PCA configurations computed by Equation 37 are listed in Section 6.3.

4.3. Partial-data trained PCA

In case of relatively small training corpus there is no problem to compute the covariance matrix. But, in case of large corpora (thousands of recordings) and high-dimensional data there may occur a problem related to processing time ($\approx$ several hours) consumption and memory requirements ($\approx 20GB$). We found that for PCA learning is not necessary to use the whole training data but it may be sufficient a part of them [16]. In other words, PCA can be trained from limited (reduced) amount of training data, while the performance is maintained, or even improved. We called this procedure as *Partial-data trained PCA*.

Partial-data PCA training can be viewed as a kind of feature selection process. The main idea is to select the statistically significant data (feature vectors) from the whole amount of training data. There are two major processing stages. The first stage is the data selection based on PCA separately applied to all training feature vectors. Suitable vectors are concatenated into one train matrix, which is treated as the input for the main PCA. The second stage is the main PCA (see Section 4.1).

Suppose now that apply the same conditions as in Section 4.1. Then the selection process based on PCA (without projecting phase) can be described as follows. Each 26-dimensional LMFE (or 13-dimensional MFCC) feature vector x_i, $i \in \langle 1; M \rangle$ (see Section 5.2) is reshaped to its matrix version X_i, $i \in \langle 1; M \rangle$ with dimension 2×13 (in case of MFCC vectors, the 13-dimensional vector was extended with zero coefficient in order to reshape to matrix with dimension 2×7). After mean subtraction the covariance matrix is computed as:

$$C_i = \frac{1}{k-1} X_i X_i^T, \quad i \in \langle 1; M \rangle; \ k = 13 \ (\text{for MFCC}, k = 7). \tag{40}$$

In the next step, the eigendecomposition is performed on the covariance matrix C_i, which results in i sets of eigenvectors w_{i1}, w_{i2} and eigenvalues α_{i1}, α_{i2}:

$$C_i w_{ij} = \alpha_{ij} w_{ij}, \quad i \in \langle 1; M \rangle, j \in \langle 1; 2 \rangle, \tag{41}$$

where

$$W_i = [w_{i1} w_{i2}]. \tag{42}$$

Note that the parameters w_{i1}, w_{i2} and α_{i1}, α_{i2} at each iteration i are updated with new parameters resulting from a new eigendecomposition. For PCA-based selection the eigenvectors w_{i1}, w_{i2} are not used. On the other hand, the eigenvalues α_{i1}, α_{i2} are the key elements because the selective criterion is based exactly on them. Using these eigenvalues, the percentage proportion P_i is computed as:

$$P_i = \frac{\alpha_{i1}}{\sum\limits_{j=1}^{2} \alpha_{ij}} = \frac{\alpha_{i1}}{\alpha_{i1} + \alpha_{i2}} = \frac{\alpha_{i1}}{trace(C_i)}, \tag{43}$$

which determines the percentage of the variance explained by the first eigenvalue in the eigenspectrum. Further, it is necessary to choose a threshold T. It can be chosen from two different intervals. The first one is defined as $T_1 \in \langle 50; \approx 65 \rangle$ and the second one as $T_2 \in \langle \approx 85; 99.9 \rangle$. Then the selective criterion can be based on the following logical expressions:

$$P_i \leq T_1 \tag{44}$$

for the first interval, or

$$P_i \geq T_2 \tag{45}$$

for the second interval. If the evaluation of the expression yields a logical true then the current feature vector is classified as statistically significant for PCA training. This vector is stored and the selection continues for the next vector. In this way, the whole training corpus is processed. From the selected vectors a training matrix is composed, which is treated as the input for the main PCA described in Section 4.1. As was mentioned in Section 4.1, there are M training vectors in the corpus. If the selected subset contains M' vectors $(M' \ll M)$ then the Equation 32 can be modified as:

$$A' = [\phi_1 \phi_2 \ldots \phi_{M'}], \tag{46}$$

where ϕ_i is the mean subtracted feature vector in the new train matrix. The next mathematical computations are identical with Equations 33-36. The partial-data training procedure for LMFE feature vectors is illustrated in the Figure 4.3. Note that for MFCC-based partial-data PCA the figure would be analogous with the Figure 4.3.

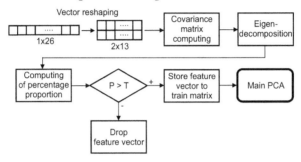

Figure 1. Block diagram of the partial-data PCA training procedure

The new train matrix can be viewed as a radically-reduced, more relevant representation of the training corpus. It has a nearly homoscedastic variance structure because it contains only those feature vectors, which have almost the same variance distribution. Feature vectors selected from the interval represented by threshold T_1 can be characterized as data clusters, which have very small variance distribution explained by the first eigenvalue among the direction of the corresponding first eigenvector. On the other hand, the feature vectors from the interval represented by threshold T_2 are clusters, which have large variance distribution among the first eigenvector. In both cases, the largeness of the variance is determined by the first eigenvalue. The size of the selected partial data set depends on the value of T_1 or T_2. The size of partial set can be expressed in percentage amount as:

$$subset\_size = \frac{M'}{M} \times 100. \tag{47}$$

We found that a practical importance has a ratio, when

$$\frac{M'}{M} \in \langle 0.001; 0.15 \rangle, \tag{48}$$

so the selected subset contains maximally 15% of data of the whole training data amount. For example, there are approximately 19 million training vectors in our corpus. According to Equation 48 it is sufficient to extract $\approx$ 19000 vectors for partial-data training. But, as it will be showed in Section 6.3.2 this argument does not apply to all cases. The time cunsumption and memory costs of the covariance matrix computation of the reduced data set are much smaller than the costs of the covariance matrix computation in case of the whole corpus. In case of partial-data training it is needed to allocate the memory only for one investigated feature vector and for the other data elements for mathematical computations. These memory requirements are of order of units of megabytes. In other words, the advantage of the partial-data training is that it does not require the loading of the whole data matrix in the main memory.

5. Speech corpus and experimental conditions

5.1. Speech corpus

All experiments were evaluated by using a Slovak speech corpus *ParDat1* [5], which contains approx. 100 hours spontaneous parliamentary speech recorded from 120 speakers (90% of men). For acoustic modeling 36917 training utterances were exactly used. For testing purposes 884 utterances were used.

5.2. Speech preprocessing

The speech signal was preemphasized and windowed using Hamming window. The window size was set to $25ms$ and the step size was $10ms$. Fast Fourier transform was applied to the windowed segments. Mel-filterbank analysis with 26 channels was followed by logarithm application to the linear filter outputs. This processing resulted in 26-dimensional LMFE features, which were used for PCA-based processing.

In case of MFCC baseline feature extraction, the LMFE vectors were further decorrelated by discrete cosine transform (DCT). The first 12 MFCCs were retained and augmented with the 0-th coefficient. During the acoustic modeling the first and second order derrivatives were computed and added to the basic vectors. Thus, the final MFCC vectors were 39-dimensional.

For LDA and 2DLDA-based processing the 13-dimensional MFCC vectors were used as the input for these methods. In order to regular comparison of recognition accuracy levels in the evaluation process all of LDA and 2DLDA models were trained using 39-dimensional LDA (2DLDA) vectors. In the evaluation, the 39-dimensional MFCC models were treated as reference models so the dimensions were identical. The number of classes k used in LDA and 2DLDA were identical with the number of phonetic classes in acoustic modeling ($k = 45$).

5.3. Acoustic modeling

Our recognition system used context independent monophones modeled using a three-state left-to-right HMMs. The number of Gaussian mixtures per state was a power of 2, starting from 1 to 256. The phone segmentation of 45 phones was obtained from embedded training and automatic phone alignment. The number of trained monophone models corresponded to the number of phonemes and basic classes for LDA and 2DLDA. For testing purposes a word lattice was created from a bigram language model. The language model was built from the test set. The vocabulary size was 125k. The feature extraction, HMM training and testing by using HTK (Hidden Markov Model) Toolkit [20] were performed.

5.4. Evaluation

In order to evaluate the experiments we chose the accuracy as the evaluation parameter. Accuracies were computed as the ratio of the number of all word matches (resulting from the recognizer) to the number of the reference words [20]. In all experiments the accuracy is given in percentage.

6. Experiments and results

This section is a major part of the whole chapter. It provides a detailed and extensive experimental evaluation of the performance of the mentioned linear transformation methods and their combinations. The section presents the results of the recognition accuracy levels resulting from different experimental configurations.

6.1. Conventional LDA-based processing

In this section, the conventional LDA is investigated. The LDA-based statistical computing was performed according to mathematical description of Equations 3–12 in Section2.1. Note that the class label of each supervector composed according to Equation 8 was assigned to it according to the class label of the current basic vector $\mathbf{x}[j]$ at the center position j. In our experiments we tried 5 lengths J of supervector; $J = 3,5,7,9$ and 11. This means that the dimensions of the covariance matrices in the statistical estimation were 39×39, 65×65, 91×91, 117×117 and 143×143. As it was mentioned in Section 2.1, in case when the length of supervector was greater than the number of classes, the between-class scatter (covariance) matrices were close to singular. From this reason we used for these cases the computation of Σ_B according to Equation 9.

6.1.1. Supervector compositions and the scatter matrices

It is known that the covariance (scatter) matrices are in general symmetric square positive-definite regular matrices. These arguments apply also for matrices in LDA. Since in LDA the covariance matrices are computed from supervectors, there may occur a problem with the symmetry of these matrices. We found that the symmetry depends on the way, in which the supervectors are constructed. The Figure 2 illustrates two types of supervector construction with example of vector length 4. The subfigure (a) illustrates the classical way of construction of supervector by using a simple concatenation. The subfigure (b) illustrates a construction, where the final structure of the supervector is preserved according to the structure of the basic vectors. Thus, if the first few coefficients of the basic vector preserve a higher energy than the coefficients with lower order, then the new supervector follows this tendency.

It should be noted that the arrangement of the coefficients in the supervector impacts the symmetry of the matrices and this can affect other properties. These facts are proven in Figure 3. From these figures it can be seen the influence of the supervector construction to the symmetry of the scatter matrices. Figures 3 (a) and (c) represent the within-class scatter matrices in case, when the supervectors are constructed according to Figure 2 (a). It can be seen that these matrices are multisymmetric. On the other hand, the matrices in Figures 3 (b) and (d) are purely symmetric. They were computed from supervectors constructed according to Figure 2 (b).

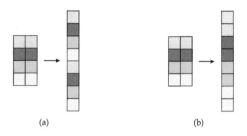

(a)   (b)

Figure 2. Different types of supervector composition; (a) composition with simple concatenating, (b) composition with retaining the structure of the basic vector

6.1.2. Between-class scatter matrix and the singularity

As was mentioned in Section 2.1, the between-class scatter matrices for context length greater than $J = 3$ were computed according to Equation 9 instead of the classical Equation 6. The Figure 4 (a) demonstrate that the between-class scatter matrix computed for context length $J = 5$ according to Equation 6 is not symmetric. In addition it is computed from supervectors constructed according to Figure 2 (a). The Figure 4 (b) illustrates a similar case as in Figure 4 (a). This matrix is computed from supervectors constructed according to Figure 2 (b). It can be seen that this matrix si only close to symmetric and in the statistical estimation this can result in singular between-class matrix and complex valued numbers in the transformation LDA matrix. Note that the symmetric between-class scatter matrices in Figure 3 were computed according to Equation 9.

6.1.3. Results

The experiments based on LDA can be divided into three categories related to dimension of the LDA transformation matrix. The first category is represented by LDA matrix with dimension 13×39. Thus, for transformation were retained only the first 13 eigenvectors corresponding to 13 leading eigenvalues. The final dimension of the features were expanded to 39 with Δ and $\Delta\Delta$ coefficients. The second category is represented by LDA matrix with dimension 19×39 so for transformations were used more LDA coefficients. Note that the final dimension of features was 38 ($19 + \Delta$). The third category is represented by LDA matrix with dimension 39×39 and in this case were not used the Δ and $\Delta\Delta$ coefficients. The difference between these three categories is that for acoustic modeling were used various numbers of dimensions and data-dependent and data-independent Δ and $\Delta\Delta$ coefficients. The LDA coefficients with lower order (14–39) can be viewed as Δ and $\Delta\Delta$ coefficients estimated in data-dependent manner. The experimental results for LDA are given in the Table 1. The results are analyzed separately for the mentioned categories.

1. The highest accuracies were achieved for 13 LDA coefficients expanded with Δ and $\Delta\Delta$ coefficients and for $J = 3$. The maximum improvement compared to MFCC model is $+2.05\%$ for 4 mixtures. Only for 1 mixture any improvement was achieved.

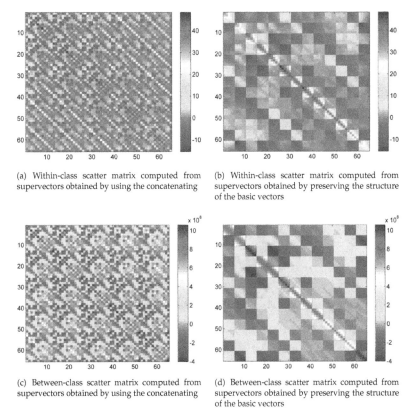

(a) Within-class scatter matrix computed from supervectors obtained by using the concatenating

(b) Within-class scatter matrix computed from supervectors obtained by preserving the structure of the basic vectors

(c) Between-class scatter matrix computed from supervectors obtained by using the concatenating

(d) Between-class scatter matrix computed from supervectors obtained by preserving the structure of the basic vectors

Figure 3. Within-class and between-class scatter matrices computed from supervectors with length 65 composed in different ways

2. In case of LDA matrix with dimension 19×39 the improvement is lower than in the previous case. The performance only for 2, 4, 8 and 256 mixtures was improved. It can be also seen that for 256 mixtures the improvement for higher context length was achieved. Note that acoustic models in this experiment have smaller dimension as the reference model ($38 < 39$).

3. The results in the last case, when the dimension of LDA matrix was 39×39 are not satisfactory. In all cases, the performance was decreased. But we can conclude that the longer lengths of context are suitable for higher dimensions of transformation matrix (without Δ and $\Delta\Delta$).

6.2. 2DLDA-based processing

In this section we extensively evaluate the performance of 2DLDA at different configurations and compare with the reference MFCC model and also with the performance of conventional

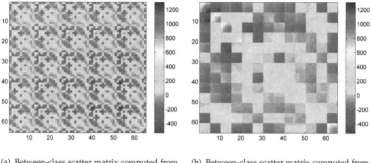

(a) Between-class scatter matrix computed from supervectors constructed according to Figure 2 (a)

(b) Between-class scatter matrix computed from supervectors constructed according to Figure 2 (b)

Figure 4. Close to symmetric between-class scatter matrices computed according to Equation 6 for context length $J = 5$

Number of mixtures	1	2	4	8	16	32	64	128	256
MFCC model (39-dim.)	82.32	83.26	85.06	87.77	89.53	90.83	91.48	92.37	92.50
13 LDA+Δ + $\Delta\Delta$ (39-dim.)	81.37	83.60	87.11	88.47	90.03	90.88	91.80	92.48	92.90
Abs. difference	−0.95	+0.34	+2.05	+0.70	+0.50	+0.05	+0.32	+0.11	+0.40
Context length J	J=3	J=3	J=3	J=3	J=3	J=3	J=3	J=3	J=3
Supervector length	39	39	39	39	39	39	39	39	39
19 LDA +Δ (38-dim.)	82.02	83.46	85.97	88.27	89.32	90.45	91.37	82.18	92.65
Abs. difference	−0.30	+0.20	+0.91	+0.50	−0.21	−0.38	−0.11	−0.19	+0.15
Context length J	J=3	J=3	J=3	J=3	J=5	J=7	J=5	J=5	J=5
Supervector length	39	39	39	39	65	91	65	65	65
39 LDA (39-dim.)	79.82	81.41	83.31	85.13	86.83	88.19	89.10	89.98	90.69
Abs. difference	−2.50	−1.85	−1.75	−2.64	−2.70	−2.64	−2.38	−2.39	−1.81
Context length J	J=3	J=3	J=5	J=7	J=7	J=5	J=5	J=7	J=7
Supervector length	39	39	65	91	91	65	65	91	91
Max. accuracy of LDA	82.02	83.60	87.11	88.47	90.03	90.88	91.80	92.48	92.90
Max. abs. difference	−0.30	+0.34	+2.05	+0.70	+0.50	+0.05	+0.32	+0.11	+0.40

Table 1. Accuracy levels (%) for conventional LDA with different number of retained dimensions (13, 19 and 39) compared to baseline MFCC model

LDA reported in Section 6.1.3. The whole mathematical 2DLDA computing was performed according to Equations 13–25. The statistical estimations are similar as in conventional LDA. The main difference is that it is necessary to compute two eigendecompositions and we have two transformation matrices; L and R. 2DLDA does not deal with supervectors as in LDA but with supermatrices, which are the basic data elements in 2DLDA (instead of vectors). These supermatrices were created from the basic cepstral vectors by coupling them together. Similarly as in LDA, we used 5 different sizes of supermatrices according to the number of contextual vectors (context size J). Thus, the sizes of supermatrices were $13 \times 3, 13 \times 5, 13 \times 7,$

13×9 and 13×11. Consequently, the class mean, global mean, within-class scatter matrix and between-class scatter matrix have corresponding sizes according to the current length of context. For example, when the context size J was set to 7, in statistical estimation 7 cepstral vectors were coupled together to form a supermatrix 13×7. Then, the statistical estimators have the following dimensions:

- class means M_i : 13×7,
- global mean M : 13×7,
- left within-class scatter matrix S_w^L : 7×7,
- left between-class scatter matrix S_b^L : 7×7,
- right within-class scatter matrix S_w^R : 13×13,
- right between-class scatter matrix S_b^R : 13×13,
- left transformation matrix L : 13×13,
- right transformation matrix R : 7×7.

The mathematical computations resulted in the transformations L and R. These matrices were then used to transform the whole speech corpus. In this way, each supermatrix created from the coupled vectors in the recording was transformed to its reduced version. The dimension reduction step was done by choosing the required size of L and R. In the next step, each transformed supermatrix was re-transformed to vector according to the matrix-to-vector alignment. The specific dimensions used in transformations are listed in the Table 2. Since the mathematical part of 2DLDA is an iteration algorithm it was necessary to set the number of iterations I. In [19] it is recommended to run the iteration loop only once ($I = 1$), which significantly reduces the total running time of the algorithm. In our 2DLDA experiments we run the for loop three times ($I = 3$).

The results of 2DLDA performance can be divided into three categories, similarly as in case of LDA and are given in the Table 2.

1. The first category is represented by vector of dimension 13, which resulted from transformation. The final dimension was 39 (13 2DLDA $+\Delta + \Delta\Delta$ coefficients). As it can be seen from the Table 2, this case resulted in the highest accuracies for 2DLDA with context length $J = 3$.

2. The second category is represented by vector of dimension 19. The final dimension was 38 (19 2DLDA $+\Delta$ coefficients). Note that for example in case of transformed supermatrix with dimension 10×2 to obtain a vector with dimension 19, the last coefficient in the matrix-to-vector alignment was ignored. From the Table 2 it can be seen that 2DLDA at this dimension does not perform successfully. The performance of the base MFCC model was not improved.

3. For the third category applies similar conclusions as in the previous case. In these experiments the feature vector dimension was 39 (without Δ and $\Delta\Delta$ coefficients).

The maximum improvement achieved by 2DLDA was $+2.01\%$ for context length $J = 3$ and for one iteration ($I = 1$).

Number of mixtures	1	2	4	8	16	32	64	128	256
MFCC model (39-dim.)	82.32	83.26	85.06	87.77	89.53	90.83	91.48	92.37	92.50
13 2DLDA+Δ + ΔΔ (39-dim.)	82.67	84.60	87.07	88.87	90.28	91.16	91.70	92.46	92.82
Abs. difference of 2DLDA	+0.35	+1.34	+2.01	+1.10	+0.75	+0.33	+0.22	+0.09	+0.32
Abs. difference of LDA	−0.95	+0.34	+2.05	+0.70	+0.50	+0.05	+0.32	+0.11	+0.40
Context length J of 2DLDA	J=3	J=3	J=3	J=3	J=3	J=3	J=3	J=3	J=3
Supermatrix full size	13×3	13×3	13×3	13×3	13×3	13×3	13×3	13×3	13×3
Retained matrix $(L \times R)$	13×1	13×1	13×1	13×1	13×1	13×1	13×1	13×1	13×1
Num. of iterations I	I=3	I=1	I=1	I=1	I=1	I=1	I=1	I=1	I=1
19 2DLDA +Δ (38-dim.)	79.35	81.90	84.03	86.42	88.31	89.63	90.77	91.41	92.19
Abs. difference of 2DLDA	−2.97	−1.36	−1.03	−1.35	−1.22	−1.20	−0.71	−0.96	−0.31
Abs. difference of LDA	−0.30	+0.20	+0.91	+0.50	−0.21	−0.38	−0.11	−0.19	+0.15
Context length J of 2DLDA	J=5	J=5	J=5	J=5	J=5	J=5	J=5	J=5	J=5
Supermatrix full size	13×5	13×5	13×5	13×5	13×5	13×5	13×5	13×5	13×5
Retained matrix $(L \times R)$	10×2	10×2	10×2	7×3	7×3	10×2	7×3	7×3	10×2
Num. of iterations I	I=3	I=1	I=1	I=3	I=1	I=1	I=2	I=1	I=1
39 2DLDA (39-dim.)	80.13	81.51	83.62	85.78	87.62	88.91	90.15	91.00	91.66
Abs. difference of 2DLDA	−2.19	−1.75	−1.44	−1.99	−1.91	−1.92	−1.33	−1.37	−0.84
Abs. difference of LDA	−2.50	−1.85	−1.75	−2.64	−2.70	−2.64	−2.38	−2.39	−1.81
Context length J of 2DLDA	J=3	J=5	J=3	J=5	J=5	J=5	J=5	J=5	J=7
Supermatrix full size	13×3	13×5	13×3	13×5	13×5	13×5	13×5	13×5	13×7
Retained matrix $(L \times R)$	13×3	13×3	13×3	13×3	13×3	13×3	13×3	13×3	10×4
Num. of iterations I	I=1	I=3	I=1	I=3	I=3	I=1	I=1	I=1	I=1
Max. accuracy of LDA	82.02	83.60	87.11	88.47	90.03	90.88	91.80	92.48	92.90
Max. abs. difference	−0.30	+0.34	+2.05	+0.70	+0.50	+0.05	+0.32	+0.11	+0.40
Max. accuracy of 2DLDA	82.67	84.60	87.07	88.87	90.28	91.16	91.70	92.46	92.82
Max. abs. difference	+0.35	+1.34	+2.01	+1.10	+0.75	+0.33	+0.22	+0.09	+0.32

Table 2. Accuracy levels (%) for 2DLDA with different number of retained dimensions compared to baseline MFCC model and conventional LDA

6.3. PCA-based processing

In this section, we experimentally evaluate the performance of the full-data trained PCA method by using the whole amount of training data for LMFE and MFCC features. In the next part of this section we present the results of partial-data trained PCA with various parameters. Note that all of the PCA-based models were transformed with PCA matrix with dimension 13×13 and the features were then expanded with Δ and ΔΔ coefficients. This resulted in final dimension 39.

6.3.1. Full-data trained PCA

As it was mentioned, PCA requires allocation of the whole data matrix in the memory. In addition, the covariance matrix is computed from this data matrix, which may be a computationally very difficult operation. In order to compare the partial-data trained models with the full-data trained model it was necessary to do the above mentioned computation.

The full-data trained PCA was performed on a Linux machine with 32GB memory. The training data were loaded in the memory sequentially by data blocks and then concatenated to one data matrix (see Equation 32). From this matrix the covariance matrix according to Equation 33 was computed. Then the integral parts of PCA according to Equations 34-36 were performed. In the next step, the acoustic modeling based on the PCA transformed features was done. The evaluation results of the full-data trained PCA for LMFE features are listed in the Table 5 and for MFCC features in the Table 6.

6.3.2. Partial-data trained PCA

The selective process for the feature vectors according to Fig. 1 was performed and M-times repeated. Overall, 10 partial-data trained models with LMFE features were learned. 5 models were learned for selection based on threshold T_1 and 5 ones for T_2. For MFCC features apply an identical scheme. The parameters for these models are listed in the Table 3 and Table 4. According to Equation 48, 5 subset models (0.1%, 1%, 5%, 10% and 15%) were composed.

Approx. DB size	0.1%	1%	5%	10%	15%
Num. of vectors M'	22229	187248	947804	1936764	2842838
Threshold T_1	51.40	54.05	59.10	63.00	65.75
Opt. dimension d	$d=8$	$d=8$	$d=8$	$d=8$	$d=9$
Approx. DB size	0.1%	1%	5%	10%	15%
Num. of vectors M'	23547	206624	962434	1899584	2849321
Threshold T_2	98.00	96.10	93.20	91.00	89.20
Opt. dimension d	$d=5$	$d=6$	$d=7$	$d=8$	$d=8$

Table 3. Parameters used for partial-data PCA models trained from LMFE

Approx. DB size	0.1%	1%	5%	10%	15%
Num. of vectors M'	21021	195034	952664	1900915	2857423
Threshold T_1	51.10	53.35	57.45	60.60	63.10
Opt. dimension d	$d=12$	$d=12$	$d=12$	$d=12$	$d=12$
Approx. DB size	0.1%	1%	5%	10%	15%
Num. of vectors M'	20697	194742	965972	1941011	2860557
Threshold T_2	98.60	96.40	92.62	89.70	87.50
Opt. dimension d	$d=11$	$d=12$	$d=12$	$d=12$	$d=12$

Table 4. Parameters used for partial-data PCA models trained from MFCC

One of the output parameters of the partial-data PCA is the optimal dimension d determined by Equation (37). It represents the number of principal components, which could be used to transform the input data with retaining 95% of global variance. Note that the threshold values T_1 and T_2 were determined on experimental basis. The results of the partial-data PCA models are listed in the Table 5 and Table 6 for LMFE and MFCC features, respectively. Note that the table contains only the highest accuracies chosen from all models.

From the Table 5 we can conclude that for LMFE features the selected subsets of size 0.1% and 5% are not suitable to partial-data PCA training. In addition, an improvement in comparison with full-data trained PCA was achieved only for 32–256 mixtures. The maximum absolute improvement +0.43% for 64 mixtures was achieved.

Mixtures	Acc. of full PCA	Acc. of partial-data PCA	Difference	Threshold	Part of DB
1	82.80%	82.06%	−0.74%	$T_2 = 89.2$	15%
2	84.10%	83.88%	−0.22%	$T_2 = 89.2$	15%
4	86.01%	85.93%	−0.08%	$T_1 = 63.0$	10%
8	88.88%	88.21%	−0.67%	$T_2 = 89.2$	15%
16	89.84%	89.82%	−0.02%	$T_2 = 91.0$	10%
32	90.31%	90.72%	+0.41%	$T_2 = 91.0$	10%
64	91.00%	91.43%	+0.43%	$T_2 = 91.0$	10%
128	91.72%	91.91%	+0.19%	$T_2 = 96.1$	1%
256	92.30%	92.60%	+0.30%	$T_2 = 89.2$	15%

Table 5. Accuracy levels for LMFE-based full-data and partial-data trained PCA

In case of MFCC features used as the input for partial-data PCA training, the results are more satisfactory. From the Table 6 it can be seen that for all mixtures an improvement was achieved. The maximum absolute improvement is +1.25% for 1 mixture. It could be also mentioned that for MFCC features the proposed method used the smaller selected subsets ($\approx$ 1%) in comparison with LMFE features.

Mixtures	Acc. of full PCA	Acc. of partial-data PCA	Difference	Threshold	Part of DB
1	82.35%	83.60%	+1.25%	$T_1 = 51.10$	0.1%
2	84.24%	84.79%	+0.55%	$T_1 = 53.35$	1%
4	85.94%	86.33%	+0.39%	$T_1 = 53.35$	1%
8	87.83%	88.08%	+0.25%	$T_2 = 92.62$	5%
16	89.14%	89.36%	+0.22%	$T_2 = 92.62$	5%
32	90.19%	90.32%	+0.13%	$T_2 = 89.70$	10%
64	90.90%	91.27%	+0.37%	$T_1 = 53.35$	1%
128	91.20%	91.78%	+0.58%	$T_1 = 57.45$	5%
256	91.76%	92.19%	+0.43%	$T_2 = 96.40$	1%

Table 6. Accuracy levels for MFCC-based full-data and partial-data trained PCA

6.4. PCA-based 2DLDA

As was mentioned in Section 1, one of the issues of this chapter is the interaction of two types of linear transformations in one experiment. More specifically, the aim of this section is to present an evaluation of the mentioned interaction of PCA and 2DLDA. In other words, in this experiment we used as the input for 2DLDA the PCA-based feature vectors instead of MFCC vectors. We wanted here to demonstrate that the PCA features have comparative properties as MFCC features and that 2DLDA trained from PCA features can achieve comparative performance as 2DLDA trained from MFCC features. The PCA training was done in two ways. The first one ist the classical full-data training and the second one is the partial-data training (see Table 7).

From the results of the experiment given in the Table 7 we can conclude the following arguments. For 4 of 9 cases the performance of 2DLDA was improved using PCA features as its input. But for 3 cases of 4 the improvement was achieved for full-data training.

Number of mixtures	1	2	4	8	16	32	64	128	256
13 2DLDA$+\Delta+\Delta\Delta$ (39-dim.)	82.67	84.60	87.07	88.87	90.28	91.16	91.70	92.46	92.82
13 PCA+2DLDA$+\Delta+\Delta\Delta$(39-dim.)	82.26	84.50	87.17	89.03	90.44	91.10	91.95	92.43	92.69
Part of DB	5%	5%	100%	100%	100%	100%	10%	10%	1%
Type of threshold	T_1	T_2	–	–	–	–	T_1	T_1	T_1
Abs. difference	-0.41	-0.10	$+0.10$	$+0.16$	$+0.16$	-0.06	$+0.25$	-0.03	-0.13

Table 7. Accuracy levels (%) of PCA-based 2DLDA

6.5. Global experimental evaluation of all methods

In the last section we conclude the experimental results presented in the whole chapter. Overall, we present seven types of experiments evaluating the performance of some kind of linear feature transformation applied in feature extraction in Slovak phoneme-based continuous speech recognition. Each result of the partial experiment is summarized and compared with the other results in the Table 8. The graphical comparison is given in Figure 5.

Number of mixtures	1	2	4	8	16	32	64	128	256
Conventional LDA	82.02	83.60	87.11	88.47	90.03	90.88	91.80	**92.48**	**92.90**
2DLDA	82.67	84.60	87.07	88.87	90.28	**91.16**	91.70	92.46	92.82
Full-data PCA (LMFE)	82.80	84.10	86.01	88.88	89.84	90.31	91.00	91.72	92.30
Full-data PCA (MFCC)	82.35	84.24	85.94	87.83	89.14	90.19	90.90	91.20	91.76
Partial-data PCA (LMFE)	82.06	83.88	85.93	88.21	89.82	90.72	91.43	91.91	92.60
Partial-data PCA (MFCC)	**83.60**	**84.79**	86.33	88.08	89.36	90.32	91.27	91.78	92.19
PCA+2DLDA	82.26	84.50	**87.17**	**89.03**	**90.44**	91.10	**91.95**	92.43	92.69
MFCC (reference)	82.32	83.26	85.06	87.77	89.53	90.83	91.48	92.37	92.50
Max. of transformed model	**83.60**	**84.79**	**87.17**	**89.03**	**90.44**	**91.16**	**91.95**	**92.48**	**92.90**
Abs. improvement	$+1.28$	$+1.53$	$+2.11$	$+1.26$	$+0.91$	$+0.33$	$+0.47$	$+0.11$	$+0.40$

Table 8. Global comparison of partial experiments for all types of linear transformations

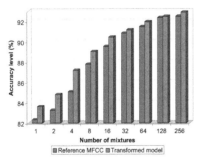

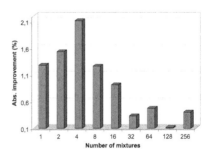

(a) Comparison of transformed and MFCC models   (b) Absolute improvement of transformed models

Figure 5. Graphical global evaluation of all experiments compared to reference MFCC model

7. Conclusions and discussions

The global conclusion of the experimental part of this chapter can be divided into few following deductions.

- Principal Component Analysis can improve the performance of the MFCC-based acoustic model. As the input for PCA can be used LMFE or MFCC features.

- The proposed partial-data trained PCA achieves better results compared to full-data trained PCA. Higher improvements can be achieved in case of MFCC features used as input for partial-data PCA.

- The conventional Linear Discriminant Analysis leads to improvements almost for all mixtures, but there may occur a problem related to singularity of between-class scatter matrix in case of larger lengths of context J.

- 2DLDA achieves comparable improvements as LDA (a little bit smaller). On the other hand, it is much more stable than LDA and there is no problem with the singularity, because 2DLDA overcomes it implicitly (much smaller dimensions of scatter matrices).

- In the last step, we clearly demonstrated that the combination of PCA and 2DLDA (subspace learning) leads to further refinement and improvement compared to performance of 2DLDA.

8. Future research intentions

Based on the presented knowledge and our research intentions in the near future we would like to develop an algorithm to elimination of using the class label information (class definition) in the LDA-based experiments. In other words, we want to train the LDA and its similar supervised modifications in unsupervised way without using the labeling of speech corpus.

Acknowledgments

The research presented in this paper was supported by the Ministry of Education under the research projects VEGA 1/0386/12 and MŠ SR 3928/2010–11 and by the Slovak Research and Development Agency under the research project APVV–0369–07.

Author details

Jozef Juhár and Peter Viszlay
Technical University of Košice, Slovakia

9. References

[1] Abbasian, H., Nasersharif, B., Akbari, A., Rahmani, M. & Moin, M. S. [2008]. Optimized linear discriminant analysis for extracting robust speech features, *Proc. of the 3rd Intl. Symposium on Communications, Control and Signal Processing*, St. Julians, pp. 819–824.

[2] Bebis, G. [2003]. *Principal Components Analysis*, Department of Computer Science, University of Nevada, Reno.

[3] Belhumeur, P., Hespanha, J. & Kriegman, D. [1997]. Eigenfaces vs. Fisherfaces: recognition using class specific linear projection, *IEEE Pattern Analysis and Machine Intelligence* 19: 711–720.

[4] Beulen, K., Welling, L. & Ney, H. [1995]. Experiments with linear feature extraction in speech recognition, *Proc. of European Conf. on Speech Communication and Technology*, pp. 1415–1418.

[5] Darjaa, S., Cerňak, M., Š. Beňuš, Rusko, M., Sabo, R. & Trnka, M. [2011]. *Rule-based triphone mapping for acoustic modeling in automatic speech recognition*, Vol. 6836 LNAI of *Lecture Notes in Computer Science (including subseries Lecture Notes in Artificial Intelligence and Lecture Notes in Bioinformatics)*.

[6] Duchateau, J., Demuynck, K., Compernolle, D. V. & Wambacq, P. [2001]. Class definition in discriminant feature analysis, *Proc. of European Conf. on Speech Communication and Technology, EUROSPEECH'01*, Aalborg, Denmark, pp. 1621–1624.

[7] Geirhofer, S. [2004]. Feature reduction with linear discriminant analysis and its performance on phoneme recognition, *Technical Report ECE272*, Dept. of Electrical and Computer Engineering, University of Illinois at Urbana-Champaign.

[8] Haeb-Umbach, R. & Ney, H. [1992]. Linear discriminant analysis for improved large vocabulary continuous speech recognition, *Proc. of the IEEE Intl. Conf. on Acoustics, Speech, and Signal Processing, ICASSP'92*, San Francisco, CA, pp. 13–16.

[9] Jolliffe, I. T. [1986]. *Principal Component Analysis*, Springer-Verlag, New York, USA.

[10] Krzanowski, W. J., Jonathan, P., Mccarthy, W. V. & Thomas, M. R. [1995]. Discriminant analysis with singular covariance matrices: methods and applications to spectroscopic data, *Applied Statistics* 44: 101–115.

[11] Kumar, N. [1997]. *Investigation of Silicon Auditory Models and Generalization of Linear Discriminant Analysis for Improved Speech Recognition*, PhD thesis, Johns Hopkins Universtiy, Baltimore, Maryland.

[12] Li, X. B. & O'Shaughnessy, D. [2007]. Clustering-based Two-Dimensional Linear Discriminant Analysis for Speech Recognition, *Proc. of the 8th Annual Conference of the International Speech Communication Association*, pp. 1126–1129.

[13] Pylkkönen, J. [2006]. LDA based feature estimation methods for LVCSR, *Proc. of the 9th Intl. Conf. on Spoken Language Processing, INTERSPEECH'06*, Pittsburgh, PA, USA, pp. 389–392.

[14] Schafföner, M., Katz, M., Krüger, S. E. & Wendemuth, A. [2003]. Improved robustness of automatic speech recognition using a new class definition in linear discriminant analysis, *Proc. of the 8th European Conf. on Speech Communication and Technology, EUROSPEECH'03*, Geneva, Switzerland, pp. 2841–2844.

[15] Song, H. J. & Kim, H. S. [2002]. Improving phone-level discrimination in LDA with subphone-level classes, *Proc. of the 7th Intl. Conf. on Spoken Language Processing, ICSLP'02*, Denver, Colorado, USA, pp. 2625–2628.

[16] Viszlay, P. & Juhár, J. [2011]. Feature selection for partial training of transformation matrix in PCA, *Proc. of the 13th Intl. Conf. on Research in Telecommunication Technologies, RTT'11*, Techov, Brno, Czech Republic, pp. 233–236.

[17] Viszlay, P., Juhár, J. & Pleva, M. [2012]. Alternative phonetic class definition in linear discriminant analysis of speech, *Proc. of the 19th International Conference on Systems, Signals and Image Processing, IWSSIP'12*, Vienna, Austria. Accepted, to be published.

[18] Yang, J., Zhang, D., Frangi, A. F. & Yang, J.-Y. [2004]. Two–Dimensional PCA: A New Approach to Appearance–Based Face Representation and Recognition, *IEEE Transactions on Pattern Analysis and Machine Intelligence* 26: 131–137.

[19] Ye, J., Janardan, R. & Li, Q. [2005]. Two-dimensional linear discriminant analysis, *L. K. Saul, Y. Weiss and L. Bottou (Eds.): Advances in Neural Information Processing Systems* 17: 1569–1576.

[20] Young, S., Evermann, G., Gales, M., Hain, T., Kershaw, D., Liu, X. A., Moore, G., Odell, J., Ollason, D., Povey, D., Valtchev, V. & Woodland, P. [2006]. *The HTK Book (for HTK Version 3.4)*. First Published Dec. 1995.

Speech Enhancement

Esophageal Speech Enhancement Using a Feature Extraction Method Based on Wavelet Transform

Alfredo Victor Mantilla Caeiros and Hector Manuel Pérez Meana

Additional information is available at the end of the chapter

1. Introduction

People that suffer from diseases such as throat cancer require that their larynx and vocal cords be extracted by surgery, requiring then rehabilitation in order to be able to reintegrate to their individual, social, familiar and work activities. To accomplish this, different methods have been suggested, such as: The esophageal speech, the use of tracheoesophageal prosthetics and the Artificial Larynx Transducer (ALT), also known as "electronic larynx" [1, 2].

The ALT, which has the shape of a handheld device, introduces an excitation in the vocal tract by applying a vibration against the external walls of the neck. The excitation is then modulated by the movement of the oral cavity to produce the speech sound. This transducer is attached to the speaker's neck, and in some cases to the speaker's cheeks. The ALT is widely recommended by voice rehabilitation physicians because it is very easy to use even for new patients, although the voice produced by these transducers is unnatural and with low quality, besides that it is distorted by the ALT produced background noise. Thus, ALT results in a considerably degradation of the quality and intelligibility of speech, problem for which an optimal solution has not yet been found [2].

The esophageal speech, on the other hand, is produced by the compression of the contained air in the vocal tract, from the stomach to the mouth through the esophagus. This air is swallowed and it produces a vibration of the esophageal upper muscle as it passes through the esophageal-larynx segment, producing the speech. The generated sound is similar to a burp, the tone is commonly very low, and the timbre is generally harsh. As in the ALT produced speech, the voiced segments of esophageal speech are the most affected parts of the speech within a word or phrase resulting an unnatural speech. Thus many efforts have been carried out to improve its quality and intelligibility.

Several approaches have been proposed to improve the quality and intelligibility of alaryngeal speech, esophageal as well as ALT produced speech [2, 3].

This chapter presents an alaryngeal speech enhancement system, which uses several methods for speech recognition such as voiced and unvoiced segment detection, feature extraction method and pattern recognition algorithms.

The content of this chapter is a follows:

1. Acquisition and preprocessing of esophageal speech: This section explains the acquisition and preprocessing of speech signal including filtering, segmentation and windowing.

2. Voiced/unvoiced segment detection: This section discusses several methods for classifying voiced and unvoiced segments such as:
    -   Pitch detection
    -   Zero crossing
    -   Formant Analysis

3. Feature extraction: The performance of any speech recognition algorithm strongly depends on the accuracy of the feature extraction method. This section exposes some important feature extraction methods such as the Linear Predictive Coding (LPC), the Cepstral Coefficients, as well as a feature extraction method based on an inner ear model, which takes into account the fundamental concepts of critical bands using a wavelet function. The later method emulates the basilar membrane operation, through a multiresolution analysis similar to that performed by a wavelet transform.

4. Clasiffier: The parameter vector obtained in the feature extraction stage is supplied to a classifier. The classification stage consists of neural networks, which identifies the voiced segments present in segment under analysis.

5. Voice synthesis: The voiced segments detected are replaced by voiced segments of a normal speaker and concatenated with unvoiced and silent segments to produce the restored speech.

6. Results: Finally, using objective and subjective evaluation methods, it shows that the proposed system provides a fairly good improvement of the quality and intelligibility of alaryngeal speech signals.

2. Methods

Figure 1 shows a block diagram of the proposed system. It is based on the replacement of voiced segments of alaryngeal speech by their equivalent normal speech voiced segments, while keeping the unvoiced and silence segments without change. The main reason is that the voiced segments have a more significant impact on the speech quality and intelligibility than the unvoiced segments.

The following explains the stages of the system.

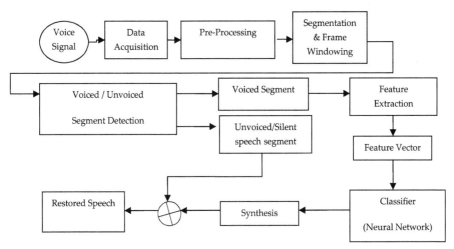

Figure 1. Block Diagram

2.1. Data acquisition

The first stage consists of recording a speech file, from an esophageal speaker. The audio data is kept as a WAV file. All files are monaural and they are digitalized in PCM (Pulse Code Modulation) format using a sampling rate of 8000Hz with a resolution of 8bits.

2.2. Preprocessing

The digital signal is low-pass filtered to reduce the background noise. This stage is implemented by a 200 order digital FIR filter with a cut-off frequency of 900Hz. A common practice for speech recognition is the use of pre-emphasis filter in order to amplify the higher frequency components of the signal with the purpose of emulating the additional sensibility of the human ear to high frequencies. Generally a high pass filter characterized by a slope of 20 dB per decade is used [4].

2.3. Segmentation and frame windowing

The filtered signal is divided into 100ms segments (800 samples) and at the same time each segment is subdivided into 10ms blocks, on which the later processing is going to be realized. The size of these blocks is determined by the quasi-periodic and quasi-stationary character of speech in such interval.

A Hamming window is applied to the segmented signal so that the extreme samples of the segments had less weight that the central samples. The window's length is chosen to be larger than the frame interval, preventing a loss of information which could take place during the transitions from one frame to the next.

2.4. Voiced/unvoiced segment detection

A voiced (sonorous) segment is characterized by a periodic or quasiperiodic behavior in time, a fine harmonic frequency structure produced by the vibration of the vocal chords, as well as a high energy concentration due to the little obstruction that the air meets in its way through the vocal tract. The vowels and some consonants present such behavior.

Several approaches have been proposed to detect the voiced segments of speech signals. However the use of a single criterion of decision to determine if a speech segment is voiced or unvoiced is not enough. Thus most algorithms in the speech processing area use the combination of more than one criterion. The proposed speech restoration method uses the combination of energy average, zero crossing and formant analysis of speech signal for voiced/unvoiced segment classification

2.4.1. Energy average

A first criterion ponders the average power of each frame by comparing it to that of its surroundings. An interval of 100 milliseconds in the neighborhood of the actual frame was selected. As part of the system's initial configuration, two thresholds are fixed. If the quotient between the frame's average power and that of the frame's surrounding is smaller than the lower threshold, the frame is labeled as unvoiced. Otherwise, if the quotient is larger than the higher threshold, the frame would be taken as voiced. For those cases in which the rate of average power lies between both thresholds, the energy criterion is not enough to determine the signal's nature.

2.4.2. Zero crossing

The second criterion is based on the signal periodicity using the number of zero crossings in each frame. Here two thresholds are used to establish that in a noise free speech segment of 10ms a voiced segment has about 12 zero crossings, while in an unvoiced segment has about 50 zero crossings [5, 6]. These values are not fixed and must be adjusted according to the sampling frequency used. In the proposed algorithm, for a sampling frequency of 8 kHz the maximum value of zero crossings that could be detected in 10ms is approximately 40. Thus an upper threshold of 30 was chosen for voiced/unvoiced classification.

2.4.3. Formant analysis

The third criterion is based on the amplitude of formants which, represents the resonance frequency of the vocal tract. Formants are the envelope peaks of the speech signal power spectrum density. The frequencies in which the first formants are produced are of great importance in speech recognition [4].

The formants are obtained from the polynomial roots generated by the linear prediction coefficients (LPC) that represent the vocal tract filter. Once the formants, whose frequency is defined by the angle of the roots closer to the unitary circle, are obtained, they are ordered in an ascending form and the first three formants are chosen as parameters of the speech segment. These formants are then stored in the system so that they can be employed to take the voiced/invoiced decision. Using the normalized Fast Fourier Transform (FFT) the amplitude of the formant frequency can be obtained.

To take the decision whether the segment is voiced or not, the value of the formants amplitude is normalized each 100 millisecond segment. Then the algorithm finds the maximum value of each formant among the 10 values stored for each fragment. Then each value is divided between the estimated maximum values as shown in (1).

$$AF_1 = \left[\frac{AF_{1-1}}{AF_{1Max}} \quad \frac{AF_{1-2}}{AF_{1Max}} \quad ..... \quad \frac{AF_{1-10}}{AF_{1Max}} \right]$$

$$AF_2 = \left[\frac{AF_{2-1}}{AF_{2Max}} \quad \frac{AF_{2-2}}{AF_{2Max}} \quad ... \quad \frac{AF_{2-10}}{AF_{2Max}} \right] \quad (1)$$

$$AF_3 = \left[\frac{AF_{3-1}}{AF_{3Max}} \quad \frac{AF_{3-2}}{AF_{3Max}} \quad .... \quad \frac{AF_{3-10}}{AF_{3Max}} \right]$$

The local normalization process is justified for esophageal speakers due to the loss of energy as they speak. Once the normalized values are obtained, the decision is made using an experimental threshold value which is equal to 0.25. It can be seen as a logic mask in the algorithm if the normalized values greater than 0.25 are set to one, otherwise are set to zero, as shown in (2).

$$\frac{AFx - N}{AFx\ max} = \begin{cases} 0 & \dfrac{AFx - N}{AFx\ max} < 0.25 \\ 1 & \dfrac{AFx - N}{AFx\ max} > 0.25 \end{cases} \quad (2)$$

Next an 'and' logic operation is applied with the three formant array using the values obtained after the threshold operation. Here only the segments in which the three formants have values over the 0.25 are considered to be voiced segments.

Finally, using the three criterions mentioned above, a window is applied to the original signal which is equal to one if the segment is classified as voiced by the three methods; and it is equal to zero otherwise, such that only the voiced segments of the original signal are obtained.

2.5. Feature vector extraction

The performance of any speech recognition algorithm strongly depends on the accuracy of the feature extraction method. This fact has motivated the development of several efficient algorithms to estimate a set of parameters that allow a robust characterization of the speech signal. Some of these methods are: The Linear Prediction Coefficients (LPCs), Formants

Frequencies Analysis, Mel Frequency Cepstral Coefficients (MFCC) among others [5,6]. This section discusses these methods and proposes one based on Wavelet Transform.

2.5.1. Linear Prediction Coefficients (LPCs)

The LPCs methods are based on the fact that the signal can be approximated from a weighted sum of precedent samples [7]. This approximation is given by:

$$s'_n = \sum_{k=1}^{p} a_k s_{n-k} \tag{3}$$

where a_k (1<k<p) is a set of real constants known as predictor coefficients, that must be calculated, and p is the predictor order. The problem of linear prediction resides on finding the predictor coefficients a_k that minimize the error between the real value of the function and the approximated function.

To minimize the total quadratic error is necessary to calculate the autocorrelation coefficients. This is a matrix equation with different recursive solutions, the commonly used is the Levinson recursion.

The developed algorithm takes each segment of 10 milliseconds and calculates its linear prediction coefficients. The number of predictor coefficients is obtained by substituting the sampling frequency value (f_s) in (4).

$$p = 4 + \frac{f_s}{1000} = 4 + \frac{8000}{1000} = 12 \tag{4}$$

The sequence of the minimal error could be interpreted as the output of the H(z) filter when it is excited by the S_n signal. H(z) is usually known as an inverted filter. The approximated transfer function could be obtained if it is assumed that the transfer function S(z) of the signal is modeled as an only pole filter with the form of (5).

$$\hat{S}(z) = \frac{A}{H(z)} = \frac{A}{1 - \sum_{k=1}^{p} a_k z^{-k}} \tag{5}$$

The LPC coefficients correspond to $\hat{S}(z)$ poles. Therefore, the LPC analysis aims to calculate the filter properties of the vocal tract that produces the sonorous signal.

2.5.2. Formant frequencies analysis

Formants are the envelope peaks of the speech signal spectrum that represent the resonance frequency of the vocal tract.

If the spectrum of a speech signal can be approximated only by its poles, then the formants could be obtained from the $\hat{S}(z)$ poles. The poles of $\hat{S}(z)$ can be calculated making the denominator of (5) to zero and solving it to find its roots. The S plane conversion is done by substituting z by e^{skT}, where sk is the pole in the s plane. The resultant roots are generally conjugated complex pairs.

Formants frequencies are obtained from the polynomial roots generated by the linear prediction coefficients. The formant frequency is defined by the angle of the roots closer to the unitary circle. A root, with an angle close to zero, indicates the existence of a formant near the origin. A root whose angle is in close proximity to π indicates that the formant is located near the maximum frequency, in this case 4000Hz. Since the frequency dominion is symmetric with respect to the vertical axis, the roots located in the inferior semi plane of z plane can be ignored.

Let r_p as a linear prediction coefficient root with real part ϕ_p and imaginary part θ_p.

$$r_p = \phi_p + j\theta_p \tag{6}$$

The roots (r) which are located in the superior semi plane near the unitary circle can be obtained using (7).

$$r_p = \begin{cases} 0 & for \quad \theta_p \leq 0.01 \\ r_p & for \quad \theta_p > 0.01 \end{cases} \tag{7}$$

By using the arctangent function is possible to obtain the roots angle. Doing this, the roots are mapped into the frequency dominion by using (8) to get the formants.

$$for_p = \vartheta_p \frac{f_s}{2\pi} \tag{8}$$

Once the formants are obtained, they are organized in ascending order, and the first three are chosen as parameters of the speech segment.

2.5.3. Mel Frequency Cepstral Coefficients (MFCC)

The cepstral coefficients estimation is another widely used feature extraction method in speech recognition problems. These coefficients form a very good features vector for the development of speech recognition algorithms, sometimes better than the LPC ones.

Cepstrum is defined as the inverse Fourier transform of spectrum module logarithm (9)

$$c(t) = F^{-1}\left[\log\left(S(\omega)\right)\right] \tag{9}$$

Developing de above equation it obtains:

$$c(t) = F^{-1}\left\{\left[\log E(\omega)\right] + \left[\log H(\omega)\right]\right\} \tag{10}$$

The above equation indicates that Cepstrum of a signal is the sum of Cepstrum excitation source and the vocal tract filter. The vocal tract information is of slow variation, and it appears in the first cepstrum coefficients. For speech recognition application the vocal tract information is more important than excitation source. The cepstral coefficients can be estimated from the LPC coefficients applying the following recursion:

$$c_0 = \ln \sigma^2$$

$$c_m = a_m + \sum_{k=1}^{m-1} \left(\frac{k}{m} \right) c_k a_{m-k} \qquad 1 \le m \le p \qquad (11)$$

$$c_m \sum_{k=1}^{m-1} \left(\frac{k}{m} \right) c_k a_{m-k} \qquad m > p$$

where Cm is the n-th LPC-Cepstral coefficients, a is the i-th LPC coefficients and m is the Cepstral index.

Usually the number of cepstral coefficients is equal to the number of LPC ones to avoid noise. A representation derived from the coefficients cepstrum are the Mel Frequency Cepstral Coefficients (MFCC) whose fundamental difference with Cepstrum coefficients is that the frequency bands are positioned according to a logarithmic scale known as MEL scale, which approximates the frequency response of the human auditory system more efficiently than Fast Fourier Transform(FFT).

2.5.4. Feature extraction method based on Wavelet Transform

Most widely used feature extraction methods, such as those described above, are based on modeling the form in which the speech signal is produced. However if the speech signals are processed taking into account the form in which they are perceived by the human ear, similar or even better results may be obtained. Thus using an ear model-based feature extraction method might represent an attractive alternative, since this approach allows characterizing the speech signal in the form that it is perceived [8]. This section proposes a feature extraction method based on an inner ear model, which takes into account the fundamentals concepts of critical bands.

In the inner ear, the basilar membrane carries out a time-frequency decomposition of the audible signal through a multiresolution analysis similar to that performed by a wavelet transform. Thus to develop a feature extraction method that emulates the basilar membrane operation, it should be able to carry out a similar frequency decomposition, as proposed in the inner ear model developed by Zhang et. al [9]. In this model the dynamics of basilar membrane, which has a characteristic frequency equal to f_c, can be modeled by using a gamma-tone filter which consists of a gamma distribution multiplied by a pure tone of frequency f_c. The shape of the gamma distribution α, is related to the filter order while the scale θ, is related to period of occurrence of the events under analysis, when they have a Poisson distribution. Thus the gamma-tone filter representing the impulse response of the basilar membrane is given by (12)

$$\psi_\theta^\alpha(t) = \frac{1}{(\alpha-1)!\,\theta^\alpha} t^{\alpha-1} e^{\frac{-t}{\theta}} \cos(2\pi t/\theta) \quad t>0 \tag{12}$$

Equation (12) defines a family of gamma-tone filters characterized by θ and α. Thus to emulate the basilar membrane behavior, it is necessary to look for the more suitable filter bank which, according to the basilar membrane model given by Zhang [9], can be obtained if we set $\theta=1$ and $\alpha=3$, *since* such values (12) result in the best approximation to the inner ear dynamics. From (12) we have:

$$\psi(t) = \frac{1}{2} t^2 e^{-t} \cos(2\pi t) \quad t>0 \tag{13}$$

Taking the Fourier transform of (13)

$$\Psi(\omega) = -\frac{(\omega-2\pi)^2}{\left[1+j(\omega-2\pi)\right]^3} + \frac{(\omega+2\pi)^2}{\left[1+j(\omega+2\pi)\right]^3} \tag{14}$$

It can be shown that ψ (t) presents the expected attributes of a mother wavelet since it satisfies the admissibility condition given by (15)

$$\int_{-\infty}^{\infty} \frac{|\Psi(\omega)|^2}{|\omega|} d\omega < \infty \tag{15}$$

This means that ψ (t) can be used to analyze and then reconstruct a signal without loss of information [10]. That is the functions given by (13) constitute an unconditional basis in $L^2(\mathbf{R})$ and then we can estimate the expansion coefficients of an audio signal $f(t)$ by using the scalar product between $f(t)$ and the function $\psi(t)$ with translation τ and scaling factor s as follows:

$$C(\tau,s) = \frac{1}{\sqrt{s}} \int_0^\infty f(t)\psi\left(\frac{t-\tau}{s}\right) dt \tag{16}$$

A sampled version of (16) must be specified because we require characterizing discrete time speech signals. To this end, a sampling of the scale parameter, s, involving the psychoacoustical phenomenon known as critical bandwidths will be used [11].

The critical bands theory models the basilar membrane operation as a filter bank in which the bandwidth of each filter increases as its central frequency also increases. This requirement can be satisfied using the Bark frequency scale that is a logarithmic scale in which the frequency resolution of any section of the basilar membrane is exactly equal to one Bark, regardless of its characteristic frequency. Because the Bark scale is characterized by a biological parameter, there is not an exact expression for it given as a result several different proposals available in the literature. Among them, the statistical fitting provided by Schroeder et al [11], appears to be a suitable choice. Thus using the approach provided, the relation between the linear frequency, f in Hz and the Bark frequency Z, is given by

$$Z = 7\ln\left(\frac{f}{650} + \sqrt{\left(\frac{f}{650}\right)^2 + 1}\right) \tag{17}$$

Using (17) the j-th scaling factor s_j given by the inverse of the j-th central frequency in Hz, f_c, corresponding to the j-th band in the Bark frequency scale becomes

$$s_j = \frac{e^{j/7}}{325\left(e^{2/7} - 1\right)}, \quad j = 1, 2, 3, \dots \tag{18}$$

The inclusion of bark frequency in the scaling factor estimation, as well as the relation between (17) and the dynamics of basilar membrane, allows frequency decomposition similar to that carried out by the human ear. Since the scaling factor given by (18) satisfies the Littlewood-Paley theorem (19)

$$\lim_{j \to +\infty} \frac{s_{j+1}}{s_j} = \lim_{j \to +\infty} \frac{e^{(j+1)/7}\left(e^{2j/7} - 1\right)}{e^{j/7}\left(e^{2(j+1)/7} - 1\right)} = e^{-1/7} \neq 1 \tag{19}$$

there is not information loss during the sampling process. Finally the number of subbands is related to the sampling frequency as follows

$$j_{max} = \mathrm{int}\left(7\ln\left(\frac{f_s}{1300} + \sqrt{\left(\frac{f_s}{1300}\right)^2 + 1}\right)\right) \tag{20}$$

Therefore, for a sampling frequency equal to 8 KHz the number of subbands becomes 17. Finally, the translation axis is naturally sampled because the input data is a discrete time signal and then the j-th decomposition signal can be estimated as follows

$$C_j(m) = \sum_{-\infty}^{\infty} f(n)\psi_j(n - m) \tag{21}$$

where

$$\psi_j(n) = \frac{1}{2}\left(\frac{nT}{s_j}\right)^2 e^{-\left(\frac{nT}{s_j}\right)} \cos\left(\frac{2\pi nT}{s_j}\right) \quad n > 0 \tag{22}$$

In (22) T denotes the sampling period. The expansion coefficients C_j obtained for each subband are used to estimate the feature vector to be used during the training and recognition tasks.

Using (21), the feature vector used for voiced segment identification consists of the following parameters:

a. The energy of the *m-th,* speech signal frame $\overline{x^2}(n)$, where $1 \le n \le N$ and N is number of samples in the *m-th* frame.

b. The energy contained in each one of the 17 wavelet decomposition levels of *m-th* speech frame $C_j^2(m)$, where $1 \le j \le 17$

c. The difference between the energy of the previous and actual frames given by (23)

$$d_x(m) = \overline{x^2}(n - mN) - \overline{x^2}(n - (m-1)N) \tag{23}$$

d. The difference between the energy contained in each one of the 17 wavelet decomposition levels of current and previous frames given by (24)

$$\overline{v}_j = \overline{c_j^2}(m) - \overline{c_j^2}(m-1) \tag{24}$$

where m is the number frame. Then the feature vector derived using the proposed approach becomes

$$\mathbf{X}(m) = \left[\overline{x^2}(n - mN), \overline{c_1^2}(m), \overline{c_2^2}(m), .., \overline{c_{17}^2}(m), d_x(m), \overline{v}_1(m), \overline{v}_2(m), .., \overline{v}_{17}(m) \right] \tag{25}$$

The last eighteen members of the feature vector include the spectral dynamics of speech signal concatenating the variation from the past feature vector to the current one.

2.6. Classification stage

The classification stage consists of one neural network, which identifies the vowel, in cascade with a parallel array of 5 neural networks, which are used to identify the alaryngeal speech segment to be changed by its equivalent normal speech segment, as shown in Figure 2. At this point, the estimated feature vector, given by (25), is feed into the first ANN (Figure 2) to estimate vowel present in the segment under analysis. Once the vowel is identified, the same feature vector is feed into the five ANN structures of the second stage, along with the output of first ANN, to identify the vowel-consonant combination contained in the voiced segment under analysis. The output of enabled ANN corresponds to the codebook index of identified segment. Thus the first ANN output is used to enable the ANN corresponding to the detected vowel, disabling the other four while the second ANN is used to identify the vowel-consonant or vowel-vowel combination. The ANN in the first stage has 10 hidden neurons while the ANNs in the second stage have 25.

The ANN training process is carried out in two steps. First the ANN used to identify the vowel contained in the speech segment is trained in a supervised manner using the backpropagation algorithm. After convergence is achieved, the enabled ANN in the second stage is used to identify the vowel-consonant or vowel-vowel combination and is also trained in a supervised manner using the backpropagation algorithm , while the coefficients vectors of the other 4 ANN are kept constant. In all cases 650 different alaryngeal voiced segments with a convergence factor equal to 0.009 are used, achieving a global mean square error of 0.1 after 400,000 iterations.

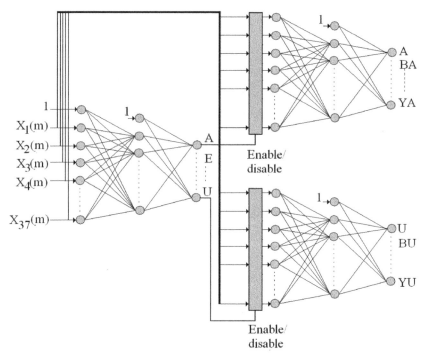

Figure 2. Pattern recognition stage. The first ANN indentifies the vowel present in the segment and the other 5 ANN identify the consonant-vowel combination.

2.7. Synthesis stage

This stage provides the restored speech signal. According to Figure 1, if a silence or unvoiced segment is detected, the switch is enabled and the segment is concatenated with the previous one to produce the output signal. If voice activity is detected, the speech segment is analyzed using the energy analysis, the zero crossings number and the formant analysis explained in section 2.4. If a voiced segment is detected, it is identified using pattern recognition techniques (ANN). Then the alaryngeal voiced segment is replaced by the equivalent normal speech voiced segment, contained in the codebook, which is finally concatenated with the previous segments to synthesize the restored speech signal.

3. Results

Figure 3 shows the plot of mono-aural recordings of Spanish words "abeja" (a), "adicto" (b) and "cupo" (c), pronounced by an esophageal speaker with a sample frequency of 8 kHz, respectively, including the detected voiced segments. Figure 3 shows that a correct detection is achieved using the combination of several features, in this case zero crossing, formants analysis and energy average.

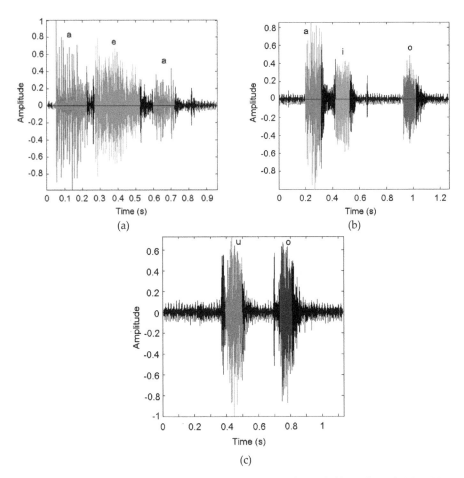

Figure 3. Detected voiced/unvoiced segments of esophageal speech signal of Spanish words "abeja" (a), "adicto" (b) and "cupo" (c).

Figure 4 shows the produced esophageal speech signal corresponding to the Spanish word "cachucha" (cap) together with the restored signal obtained using the proposed system. The corresponding spectrograms of both signals are shown in Figure 5.

To evaluate the actual performance of the proposed system, two different criteria were used: the bark spectral distortion (MBSD) and the mean opinion scoring (MOS). The bark spectrum $L(f)$ reflects the ear's nonlinear transformation of frequency and amplitude, together with the important aspects of its frequency and spectral integration properties in response to complex sounds. Using the Bark spectrum, an objective measure of the distortion can be defined using the overall distortion as the mean Euclidian distance between the spectral vectors of the normal speech, $L_n(k,i)$, and the processed ones, $L_p(k,i)$, taken over successive frames as follows.

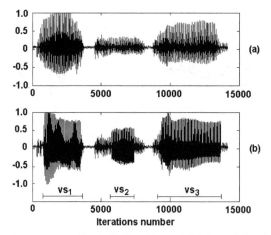

Figure 4. Waveforms trace corresponding to the Spanish word, "Cachucha", (Cap). a) produced Esophageal speech, b) restored speech.

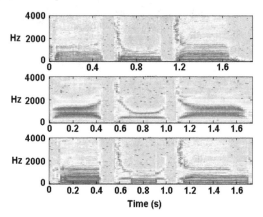

Figure 5. Spectrograms trace corresponding to the Spanish word, "Cachucha" (Cap). a) Normal speech, b) Produced Esophageal Speech, c) Restored speech.

$$MBSD = \frac{\sum_{k=1}^{N}\sum_{i=1}^{M}\left[L_n(k,i)-L_p(k,i)\right]^2}{\sum_{k=1}^{N}\sum_{i=1}^{M}L_n^2(k,i)} \tag{26}$$

where $L_n(k,i)$ is the Bark spectrum of the kth segment of the original signal, $L_p(k,i)$ is the Bark spectrum of the processed signal and M is the number of critical bands. Figures 6 and 7 show the Bark spectral trace of both, the esophageal speech produced and enhanced signals, respectively corresponding to the Spanish words "hola" (hello) and "mochila" (bag). Here the MBSD during voiced segments was equal 0.2954 and 0.4213 for "hola" and "mochila", respectively, while during unvoiced segments the MBSD was 0.6815 and 0.7829 for "hola" and "mochila" respectively. The distortion decreases during the voiced periods as suggested by (26). Evaluation results using the Bark spectral distortion measures show that a good enhancement can be achieved using the proposed method.

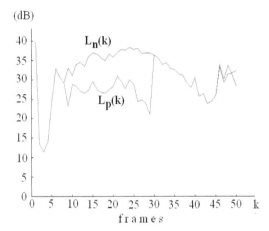

Figure 6. Bark spectral trace of normal, $L_n(k)$, and enhanced, $L_p(k)$, speech signals of the Spanish word "hola".

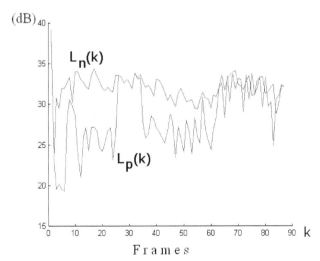

Figure 7. Bark spectral trace of normal, $L_n(k)$, and enhanced, $L_p(k)$, speech signals of the Spanish word "mochila".

A subjective evaluation was also performed using the Mean Opinion Scoring (MOS) in which the proposed system was evaluated by 200 normal speaking persons and 200 alaryngeal ones (Table 1 and Table 2), from the point of view of intelligibility and speech quality where 5 is the highest score and 1 is the lowest one. In both cases the speech intelligibility and quality evaluation without enhancement are shown for comparison. These evaluation results show that the proposed system improves the performance of [2] which reports a MOS of 2.91 when the enhancement system is used and 2.3 without enhancement. These results also show that, although the improvement is perceived by the alaryngeal and normal speakers, the improvement is larger in the opinion of alaryngeal speakers. Thus the proposed system is expected to have a quite good acceptance among the alaryngeal speakers, because the proposed system allows synthesizing several kinds of male and female speech signals.

Finally, about 95% of alaryngeal persons participating in the subjective evaluation preferred the use of the proposed system during conversation. Subjective evaluation shows that quite a good performance enhancement can be obtained using the proposed system.

	Normal listener		Alaryngeal listener	
	Quality	Intelligibility	Quality	Intelligibility
MOS	2.30	2.61	2.46	2.80
Var	0.086	0.12	0.085	0.11

Table 1. Subjective evaluation of esophageal speech without enhancement.

	Normal listener		Alaryngeal listener	
	Quality	Intelligibility	Quality	Intelligibility
MOS	2.91	2.74	3.42	3.01
Var	0.17	0.102	0.16	0.103

Table 2. Subjective evaluation of proposed alaryngeal speech enhancement system

The performance of the voiced segments classification stage was evaluated using 450 different alaryngeal voiced segments. The system failed to classify correctly 22 segments, which represents a misclassification rate of about 5% using a network as identification method, while a misclassification of about 7% was obtained using the Hidden Markov Models (HMM). The comparison results are given in Table 3.

Identification Method	Normal Speech	Alaryngeal Speech
ANN	98%	95%
HMM	97%	93%

Table 3. Recognition performance using two different identification methods using the feature extraction method based on wavelet transform.

The behavior of proposed feature extraction method was compared with the performance of several other wavelet functions for evaluation purposes. Comparison results are shown in Table 4 which show that proposed method has better performance than other wavelet based feature extraction methods.

	Proposed method	Daub 4 wavelet	Haar wavelet	Mexican hat wavelet	Morlet wavelet
Recognition rate	95%	75%	40%	79%	89%

Table 4. Performance of different wavelet based feature enhanced methods when an ANN is used as identification method.

4. Conclusions

This chapter proposed an alaryngeal speech restoration system, suitable for esophageal and ALT produced speech, based on a pattern recognition approach where the voiced segments are replaced by equivalent segments of normal speech contained in a codebook. Evaluation results show a correct detection of voiced segment by comparison between their spectrograms to those spectrograms of normal speech signal. Objective and subjective evaluation results show that the proposed system provides a good improvement in the intelligibility and quality of esophageal produced speech signals. These results show that proposed system is an attractive alternative to enhance the alaryngeal speech signals. This chapter also presents a flexible structure that allows the use of the proposed system to enhance esophageal and artificial laryinx produced speech signals without further modifications. The proposed system could be used to enhance alaryngeal speech in several practical situations such as telephone and teleconference systems, thus improving the voice and quality life of alaryngeal people.

Author details

Alfredo Victor Mantilla Caeiros
Tecnológico de Monterrey, Campus Ciudad de Mexico, México

Hector Manuel Pérez Meana
Instituto Politécnico Nacional, México

5. References

[1] H. K. Barney, H. L. Hawork, F. E., and Dunn, (1959), "An experimental transitorized artifcial larynx",. Bell System Technical Journal, 38, 1337-1356..

[2] G. Aguilar, M. Nakano-Miyatake and H. Perez-Meana, (2005), Alaryngeal Speech Enhancement Using Pattern Recognition Techniques", IEICE Trans. Inf. & Syst. Vol. E88-D, No. 7, pp. 1618-1622.

[3] D. Cole, S. Sridharan and M. Geva, (1997), "Application of noise reduction techniques for alaryngeal speech enhancement", IEEE TECON, Speech and Image Processing for Computing and Telecommunications, pp. 491-494.

[4] H. David, et.al. (2001) "Acoustics and psychoacoustics", Ed: Focal Press. Second Edition.

[5] L. Rabiner, B. Juang, (1993), "Fundamentals of Speech Recognition", Prentice Hall, Piscataway, USA.

[6] L. R. Rabiner, B. H. Juang and C. H. Lee, (1996), An Overview of Automatic Speech Recognition", in Automatic Speech and Speaker Recognition: Advanced Topics, C. H. Lee, F. K. Soong and K. K. Paliwal editors, Kluwer Academic Publisher, pp. 1-30, Norwell MA.

[7] D.G. Childers, (2000), "Speech Processing and syntesis toolboxes", Wiley & Sons, inc.

[8] A. Mantilla-Caeiros, M. Nakano-Miyatake, H. Perez-Meana, (2007), "A New Wavelet Function for Audio and Speech Processing", 50th MWSCAS, pp. 101-104.

[9] X. Zhang, M. Heinz, I. Bruce and L. Carney, (2001), "A phenomenological model for the responses of auditory-nerve fibers: I. Nonlinear tuning with compression and suppression", Acoustical Society of America, vol. 109, No.2, pp 648-670.

[10] R. M. Rao, A. S. Bopardikar (1998) ,"Wavelets Transforms, Introduction to Theory and Applications", Addison Wesley, New York.

[11] M. R. Schroeder, (1979) "Objective measure of certain speech signal degradations based on masking properties of the human auditory perception", Frontiers of Speech Communication Research, Academic Press, New York.

## Chapter 9

Improvement on Sound Quality of the Body Conducted Speech from Optical Fiber Bragg Grating Microphone

Masashi Nakayama, Shunsuke Ishimitsu and Seiji Nakagawa

Additional information is available at the end of the chapter

1. Introduction

Speech communication can be impaired by the wide range of noise conditions present in air. Researchers in the field of speech applications have been investigating how to improve the performances of signal extraction and its recognition in the conditions. However, it is not yet possible to measure clear speech in environments where there are low Signal-to-Noise Ratios (SNR) of about 0 dB or less (H. Hirsch and D. Pearce, 2000). Standard rate scales, such as CENSREC (N. Kitaoka et al., 2006) and AURORA (H. Hirsch and D. Pearce, 2000), are typically discussed for evaluating performances of speech recognition in noisy environments and have shown that speech recognition rates are approximately 50–80% when under the influence of noise, demonstrating the difficulty of achieving high percentages. With these backgrounds, many signal extraction and retrieval methods have been proposed in previous research. There is one of approaches in signal extractions, body-conducted speech (BCS) which is little influence from noise in air however it does not measure 2 kHz above in frequency characteristics. However, these need normal speech or parameters measured simultaneously with body-conducted speech. Because these parameters are not measured in noisy environments, the authors have been investigating the use of body-conducted speech which is generally called bone-conducted speech, where the signal is also conducted through the skin and bone in a human body (S. Ishimitsu, 2008) (M. Nakayama et al., 2011). Conventional retrieval methods for sound quality of body-conducted speech are the Modulation Transfer Function (MTF), Linear Predictive Coefficients (LPC), direct filtering and the use of a throat microphone (T. Tamiya, and T. Shimamura, 2006) (T. T. Vu et al., 2006) (Z. Liu et al., 2004) (S. Dupont, et al., 2004). As a research in state-of-the art, the research fields is expanded to speech communications between a patient and an operator in a Magnetic Resonance Imaging (MRI) room which has a noisy sound environment with a strong magnetic field (A. Moelker et al., 2005). Conventional microphone such as an accelerometer composed of magnetic materials are not allowed in this environment, which requires a special microphone made of non-magnetic material.

For this environment the authors proposed a speech communication system that uses a BCS microphone with an optical fiber bragg grating (OFBG microphone) (M. Nakayama et al., 2011). It is composed of only non-magnetic materials, is suitable for the environment and should provide clear signals using our retrieval method. Previous research using an OFBG microphone demonstrated the effectiveness and performance of signal extraction in an MRI room. Its performance of speech recognition was evaluated using an acoustic model constructed with unspecified normal speech (M. Nakayama et al., 2011). It is concluded that an OFBG microphone can produce a clear signal with an improved performance compared to an acoustic model made by unspecified speeches. The original signal of an OFBG microphone enabled conversation however some stress was felt because its signal was low in sound quality. Therefore one of the research aims is to improve the quality with our retrieval method which used differential acceleration and noise reduction methods.

In this chapter, it will be shown in experiments and discussions for the body-conducted speeches with the method which is measured with an accelerometer and an OFBG microphone, as one of topics is a state-of-the-art in the research field of signal extraction under noisy environment. Especially, it is mainly investigated in evaluations of the microphones, signal retrievals with the method and applying the method to a signal in sentence unit long for estimating and recovering of sound qualities.

2. Speech and body-conducted speech

2.1. Conventional body-conducted speech microphone

Speech as air-conducted sound is easily affected by surrounding noise. In contrast, body-conducted speech is solid-propagated sound and thus less affected by noise. A word is uttered by a 20-year-old male in a quiet room. Table 1 details the recording environments for microphone and acclerometer emploied in this research. Speech is measured 30 cm from the mouth using a microphone, and body-conducted speech is extracted from the upper lip using the accelerometer as conventional microphone which is shown in Figure 1. This microphone position is that commonly used for the speech input of a car navigation system. The upper lip, as a signal-extraction position, provides the best cepstral coefficients as feature parameters for speech recognition (S. Ishimitsu et al., 2004). Figures 2 and 3 show uttered words "Asahi" in quiet room, taken from the JEIDA database, which contains 100 local place names (S. Itahashi, 1991). Speech is measured a cleary signal in frequency characteristics however body-conducted speech lacks high-frequency components above 2 kHz. So the performance is reduced when the signal is used for the recognition directory.

Recorder	TEAC RD-200T
Microphone	Ono Sokki MI-1431
Microphone amplifier	Ono Sokki SR-2200
Microphone position	30cm (Between mouth and microphone)
Accelerometer	Ono Sokki NP-2110
Accelerometer amplifier	Ono Sokki PS-602
Accelerometer position	Upper lip

Table 1. Recording environments for microphone and accelerometer

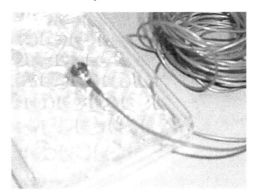

Figure 1. Accelerometer

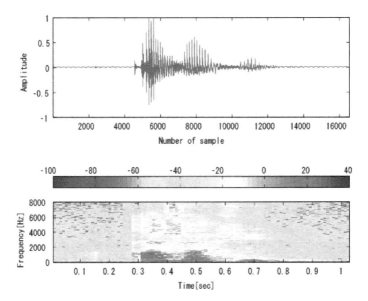

Figure 2. Speech from microphone in quiet

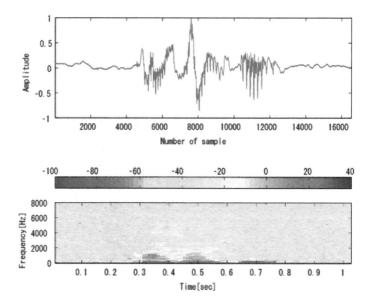

Figure 3. BCS from accelerometer in quiet

2.2. Optical Fiber Bragg Grating microphone

To extend testing to scenarios such as that in which noise sound is generated with strong magnetic field, in communications between a patient and an operator in an MRI room, an OFBG microphone is employed to record body-conducted speech there because it can measure a clearer signal than an accelerometer and be used in an environment with a strong magnetic field. It is examined the effectiveness of the microphone in an MRI room in which a magnetic field is produced by an open-type magnetic resonance imaging system. Tables 2 and 3 detail the recording environments for OFBG microphone which is shown in Figure 4. Noise levels in the room did not measure at the recording point such as the mouth of the speaker because a sound-level meter did not permit into the room since it composed from magnetic materials. Therefore, the noise level is measured at the entrance of the room, and consequently may be higher than the noise level at the signal recording point; the noise level is given in Table 2. Owing to patient discomfort during the recordings, only 20 words and 5 sentences were recorded in the room where a scene is shown in Figure 5. Figure 6 shows the body-conducted speech recorded from the OFBG microphone in the room when activated a MRI. Compared the signal with conventional BCS, it is clearer than that for body-conducted speech measured by accelerometer because characteristics of frequencies above 2 kHz can be found.

Figure 4. OFBG microphone

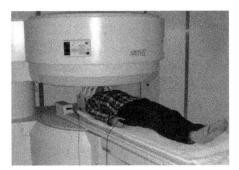

Figure 5. Signal recording in an MRI room

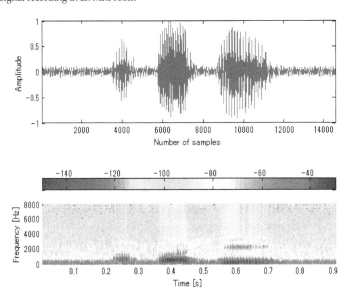

Figure 6. BCS from OFBG microphone

MRI model	HITACH AIRIS II
Environment	MRI (OFF): 61.6 dB SPL
	MRI (ON): 81.1 dB SPL
Speakers	two males (22 and 23 years old)
	two females (23 and 24 years old)
Vocabulary	twenty words × two sets: JEIDA 100 local place names
	five sentences × three sets: ATR database sentences

Table 2. Recording environment 1 for OFBG microphone

Device name	Type name
Pickup	Optoacoustics Optimic4130
Optical-electronic conversion device	Optoacoustics EOU200
Recorder	TEAC LX-10

Table 3. Recording environment 2 for OFBG microphone

3. Speech recognition with OFBG microphone

The quality of the signal recorded with the OFBG microphone, is higher than the quality of BCS recorded with accelerometer. Generally, the quality of speech sound is evaluated by the mean opinion score from 1 to 5 however this requires much evaluation data to achieve adequate significance levels. For the reason, it is evaluated the sound quality through speech recognition using acoustic models estimated with the speech of unspecified speakers as results of recognition performances. In speech recognition, the best candidate is chosen and decided by likelihoods derived from acoustic models and feature parameters such as cepstral parameters, which are calculated from the recorded speech (D. Li, and D. O'Shaughnessy, 2003) (L. Rabiner, 1993). As a result, the recognition performances and likelihoods are statistical results since human errors and other factors are not considered.

3.1. Experimental conditions

Table 4 shows the experimental conditions for isolated word recognition in speech recognition. The experiment employs the Julius, speech recognition decoder, which is a large-vocabulary continuous-speech recognition system for Japanese language (T. Kawahara et al., 1999) (A. Lee et al., 2001). The decoder requires a dictionary, acoustic models and language models. The dictionary describes connections of sub-words in each word, such as phonemes and syllables, which are the acoustic models. Language models give the probability for a present word given a former word in corpora. The purpose of the experiment is only the evaluation of the clarity or the similarity of signals and acoustic models. Since language models are not required in this experiment, Julian version 3.4.2 is used for isolated-word recognition especially. Thus, the experiments are used the same acoustic models estimated by HTK with JNAS to evaluate closeness of signals when highest recognition performance is achieved (S. Young et al., 2000) (K. Itou et al, 1999).

3.2. Experimental results

Table 5 shows recognition results of isolated word recognition in each data set, and Table 6 gives averages of recognition results in each speaker. The recognition results for the OFGB microphone are found to be superior to the recognition results for the conventional BCS microphone. The differences in isolated-word recognition rates are about 15% to 35% respectively. These results show the effectiveness of the OFBG microphone when is measured clearly signals with it.

Speaker	two males (22 and 23 years old) two female (23 and 24 years old)
Number of datasets	20 words × three sets/person
Vocabulary	JEIDA 100 local place names
Recognition system	Julian 3.4.2
Acoustic model	gender-dependent triphone model
Model conditions	16 mixture Gaussian, clustered 3000 states
Feature vectors	MFCC(12)+ΔMFCC(12)+ΔPow(1)=25 dim.
Training condition	more than 20,000 samples JANS with HTK 2.0

Table 4. Experimental conditions for isolated word recognition

Speaker	MRI off			MRI on		
	set 1	set 2	set 3	set 1	set 2	set 3
Male 1	85%	80%	90%	30%	40%	50%
Male 2	90%	75%	85%	50%	60%	60%
Female 1	35%	35%	35%	20%	20%	20%
Female 2	80%	70%	70%	75%	70%	75%

Table 5. Recognition results of isolated word recognition in each data set

Speaker	MRI off	MRI on
Male 1	85.0%	40.0%
Male 2	83.3%	56.7%
Female 1	35.0%	20.0%
Female 2	73.3%	73.3%

Table 6. Averages of recognition results

4. Improvement on sound quality of body-conducted speech in word unit

The OFBG microphone can measure a high quality signal compared to a BCS of an accelerometer. To realize conversations without stress, signals with improved in sound qualities are required. Consequently, one of aims in the research is to invent and examine a method for improving sound quality. Many researchers and researches which are already introduced in the chapter of introduction, are unaware that a BCS does not have frequency components 2 kHz and higher. Mindful of this condition, conventional retrieval methods for BCS that need the speech and its parameters are proposed and investigated, however speech is not measured easily in noisy environments. Therefore a signal retrieval method for a BCS only performs well with itself. In realizing this progressive idea, the method is invented a signal retrieval method without speech and the other parameters because effective frequency components in signals over 2 kHz are found however there contains very low gains.

4.1. Differential acceleration

Formula (1) shows an equation for estimating using the differential acceleration from the original BCS.

$$x_{differential}(i) = x(i+1) - x(i) \tag{1}$$

$x_{differential}(i)$ is the differential acceleration signal that is calculated from each frame of a BCS. Because of low gains in its amplitude, it requires adjusting to a suitable level for hearing or processing. Figure 7 shows a differential acceleration estimated from Figure 6 using Formula (1), with the adjusted gain. It seems that the differential acceleration signal is composed of speech mixed with stationary noise, so we expected to be able to remove it completely with the noise reduction method because the signal has a high SNR compared to the original signal. Consequently, it is proposed the signal estimation method using differential acceleration and a conventional noise reduction method (M. Nakayama et al., 2011).

4.2. Noise reduction method

As a first approach to noise reduction, it is examined the effectiveness of a spectral subtraction method for the reduction of stationary noise. However, improvements in performances for the frequency components is inadequated with this approach. The noise spectrum is simply subtracted by a spectral subtraction method, so a Wiener-filtering method is expected to estimate the spectrum envelope of speech using linear prediction coefficients. Therefore, it is tried to extract a clear signal using the Wiener-filtering method, which could estimate and obtain the effective frequency components from noisy speech. Formula (2) shows the equation used for the Wiener-filtering method.

$$H_{Estimate}(\omega) = \frac{H_{Speech}(\omega)}{H_{Speech}(\omega) + H_{Noise}(\omega)} \qquad (2)$$

An estimated spectrum $H_{Estimate}(\omega)$ can be converted to a retrieval signal from the differential acceleration signal. It can be calculated from the speech spectrum $H_{Speech}(\omega)$ and noise spectrum $H_{Noise}(\omega)$. In particular, $H_{Speech}(\omega)$ is calculated with autocorrelation functions and linear prediction coefficients using a Levinson-Durbin algorithm (J. Durbin, 1960), and $H_{Noise}(\omega)$ is then estimated using autocorrelation functions.

4.3. Evaluations

Signal retrieval for a signal measured by an OFBG microphone is performed using the same parameters in the method because a propagation path of body-conducted speech in a human body is not affected by either quiet or noisy environments. Figure 8 shows a retrieval signal from Figure 7 using a Wiener-filtering method where the linear prediction coefficients and autocorrelation functions are 1 and the frame width is 764 samples. These procedures were repeated five times on a signal to remove a stationary noise. From a retrieval signal, high frequency components from 2 kHz and above were recovered with these settings. This proposed method could also be applied to obtain a clear signal from body-conducted speech measured with OFBG microphone in noisy sound and high magnetic field environment.

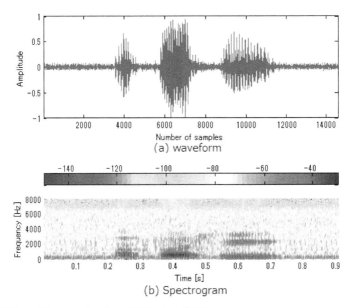

Figure 7. Differential acceleration from OFBG microphone

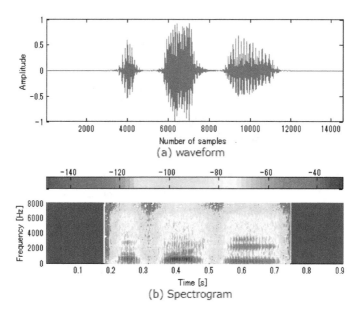

Figure 8. Retrieval signal from OFBG microphone

5. Improvement on sound quality of body-conducted speech in sentence unit

The effectiveness of signal retrieval for body-conducted speech in word unit measured by an accelerometer and an OFBG microphone has been demonstrated at former sections. However the effectiveness of body-conducted speech in word unit is proven, signals in sentence unit need to be examined for practical use such as conversations in the noisy environment. Though the investigation for the sentence unit is an important evaluation, so it could revolutionize speech communications in the environment. As a first step in signal retrieval for sentence unit, the method adopts the method to signals in word unit because the transfer function between the microphone and sound source seems to change little whether word or sentence unit, and is examined a body-conducted speech in sentence unit directly measured by an accelerometer and an OFBG microphone.

5.1. Body-conducted speech from an accelerometer

In experiments on signal retrieval using an accelerometer, speech and body-conducted speech were measured in a quiet room of our laboratory and engine room of the training ship at the Oshima National College of Maritime Technology, where there is noisy environments with working a main engine and two generator, are shown Figures 9 (a) and (b). The recording environment is also used Table 1, however the speaker who uttered a word differs from a speaker in a former section. Noise within the engine room, under the two conditions of anchorage and cruising, were 93 and 98 dB SPL, respectively, and the SNR measurements from microphone. There was –20 and –25 dB SNR, respectively. In this research, the signal is experimented under cruising condition to estimate retrieval signals.

A 22-year-old male uttered A01 sentence from the ATR503 sentence database, and the sentence is a commonly used sentence in speech recognition and application (M. Abe et al., 1991). And the sentence is composed of the followings in sub-word of mora.

*   /a/ /ra/ /yu/ /ru/ /ge/ /N/ /ji/ /tsu/ /wo/ /su/ /be/ /te/ /ji/ /bu/ /N/ /no/ /ho/ /u/ /he/ /ne/ /ji/ /ma/ /ge/ /ta/ /no/ /da/

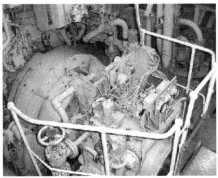 

(a) Main engine of Oshima-maru   (b) Signal recording in the engine room

Figure 9. The engine room in Oshima-maru

Figures 10 and 11 show a speech and a body-conducted speech in sentence unit measured by a conventional microphone and accelerometer in a quiet room when a 22 years-old male uttered the sentence. Although the accelerometer is held with fingers, sounds are measured clearly because it was firmly held to the upper lip with a suitable pressure. Figure 12 shows a differential acceleration from Figure 11, becomes clearly signal with little noise because the BCS is high SNR.

Figures 13 and 14 show a speech and a body-conducted speech in sentence unit in the noisy environment. Speech is completely swamped by the intense noise from the engine and generators. On the other hand, body-conducted speech in Figure 14 is affected a little by the noise but can be measured. Because SNR in Figure 14 has low gain, differential acceleration in Figure 15 is considered that the performance of signal retrieval is reduced. Figure 16 shows the signal retrieval from the differential acceleration works well when the treated four times since the performance is sufficient to recover the frequency characteristics. As a result, it is concluded that body-conducted speech is as clear as possible without noise disturbance.

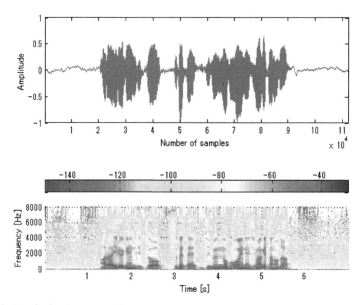

Figure 10. Speech of sentence in quiet

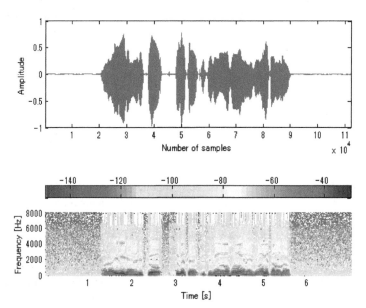

Figure 11. BCS of sentence in quiet

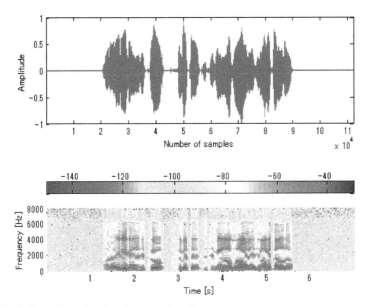

Figure 12. Differential acceleration of sentence in quiet

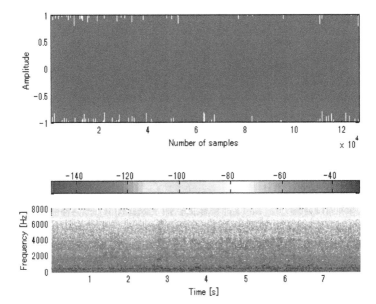

Figure 13. Speech of sentence in noise environment

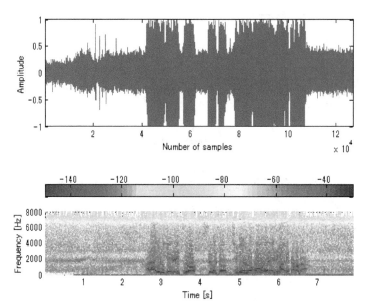

Figure 14. BCS of sentence in noise environment

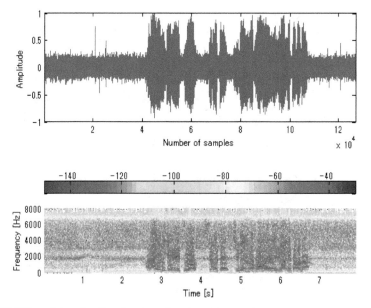

Figure 15. Differential acceleration of sentence in noise environment

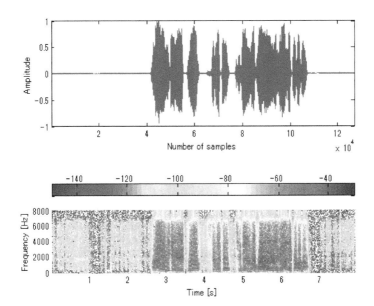

Figure 16. Retrieval BCS of sentence in noise environment

5.2. Body-conducted speech from OFBG microphone

The quality of the signal measured by the OFBG microphone in the noisy environment of an
MRI room was investigated here. A speaker uttered the sentence A01 during the operation
of MRI devices, such that there was an 81 dB SPL-noise environment. Although a sound
level meter was not permitted in the room, so it is measured in front of the gate door in the
room. Figure 17 shows the signal of the uttered sentence recorded by the OFBG microphone
in the MRI room when MRI equipment was in operation. Since the signal is clear, it is
expected that the frequency characteristics of the signal can be recovered employing the
signal retrieval method. Figures 18 and 19 show the differential acceleration and retrieved
signal from the OFBG microphone in the MRI room when the MRI equipment was in
operation and the method treated three times. These figures confirm to improve in the
sound quality of BCS in sentence, and it also concluded that the SNR in BCS is best when it
has high level.

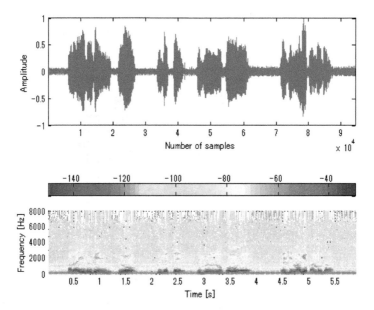

Figure 17. BCS of sentence in MRI room

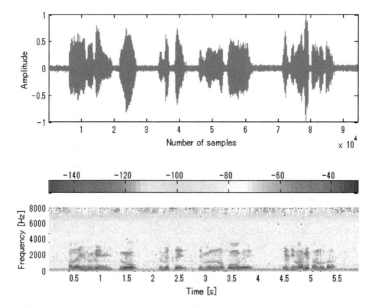

Figure 18. Differential acceleration of sentence in MRI room

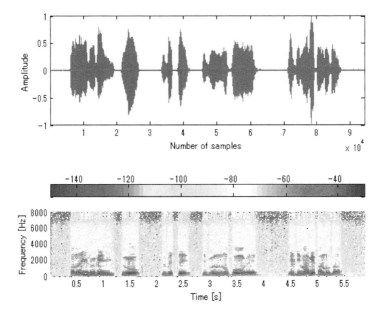

Figure 19. Retrieval signal of sentence in MRI room

6. Conclusions and future works

This section presents improvements on sound quality of body-conducted speeches measured with an accelerometer and an OFBG microphone. Especially, an MRI room has heavy noisy sound and high magnetic field environment. The environment does not allow bringing accelerometer such as a conventional body-conducted speech microphone which is made from magnetic materials. For conversations and communications between a patient and an operator in the room, an OFBG microphone is proposed, which can measure clear signals compared to accelerometer.

And then, the performances of signal retrieval method in sentence with the microphones that are an accelerometer and an OFBG microphone were evaluated, and the effectiveness is confirmed with time–frequency analysis and speech recognition. From this background, it is investigated estimating clear body-conducted speech in sentence unit from an OFBG microphone with our signal retrieval method that used combined differential acceleration and noise reduction. Applying the method to the signal measured recovered which in sound quality that was evaluated using time-frequency analysis. Thus, its retrieval method can also be applied to a signal measured by an OFBG microphone with the same settings because its conduction path is not affected by the noise in the air. The signals were measured in quiet and noisy rooms, specifically an engine room and MRI room. The signals were clearly obtained employing the signal retrieval method and the same settings used for the word unit as a first step. To obtain a clearer signal with the signal retrieval method, the pressure at which the microphone is held is important, and the sounds have high SNR in original BCS.

As future works, it needs to extend the signal retrieval method for practical use and improvement of algorithm for advance.

Author details

Masashi Nakayama
Kagawa National College of Technology, Japan
National Institute of Advanced Industrial Science and Technology (AIST), Japan

Shunsuke Ishimitsu
Hiroshima City University, Japan

Seiji Nakagawa
National Institute of Advanced Industrial Science and Technology (AIST), Japan

Acknowledgement

The authors thank Mr. K. Oda, Mr. H. Nagoshi and his colleagues in Ishimitsu laboratory of Hiroshima City University, members of the Living Informatics Research Group, Health Research Institute, National Institute of Advanced Industrial Science and Technology (AIST) for their support in the signal recording, and crew members of the training ship, Oshima-maru, Oshima National College of Maritime Technology.

7. References

A. Lee, T. Kawahara, and K. Shikano (2001). Julius - an open source real-time large vocabulary recognition engine, in Proceedings of European Conference on Speech Communication and Technology (EUROSPEECH), pp. 1691-1694

A. Moelker, R. A. J. J. Maas, M. W. Vogel, M. Ouhlous, and P. M. T. Pattynama (2005). Importance of bone-conducted sound transmission on patient hearing in the MR scanner, Journal of Magnetic Resonance Imaging, Volume 22, Issue 1, pp.163-169

D. Li, and D. O'Shaughnessy (2003). Speech Processing: A Dynamic and Optimization-Oriented Approach, Marcel Dekker Inc.

H. Hirsch, and D. Pearce (2000). The AURORA experimental framework for the performance evaluation of speech recognition systems under noisy conditions, in proceedings of ISCA ITRW ASR2000, pp.181-188

J. Durbin (1960). The Fitting of Time-Series Models, Review of the International Statistical Institute, Vol.28 No.3, pp. 233-244

K. Itou, M. Yamamoto, K. Takeda, T. Takezawa, T. Matsuoka, T. Kobayashi, K. Shikano, and S. Itahashi (1999). JNAS : Japanese speech corpus for large vocabulary continuous speech recognition research, Journal of the Acoustical Society of Japan (E), 20(3), pp.199-206

L. Rabiner (1993). Fundamentals of Speech Recognition, Prentice Hall

M. Abe, Y. Sagisaka, T. Umeda, and H. Kuwabara (1990). Manual of Japanese Speech Database, ATR

M. Nakayama, S. Ishimitsu, and S. Nakagawa (2011). A study of making clear body-conducted speech using differential acceleration, IEEJ Transactions on Electrical and Electronic Engineering, Vol.6 Issue 2, pp.144-150

M. Nakayama, S. Ishimitsu, H. Nagoshi, S. Nakagawa, and K. Fukui (2011). Body-conducted speech microphone using an Optical Fiber Bragg Grating for high magnetic field and noisy environments, in proceedings of Forum Acusticum 2011

N. Kitaoka, T. Yamada, S. Tsuge, C. Miyajima, T. Nishiura, M. Nakayama, Y. Denda, M. Fujimoto, K. Yamamoto, T. Takiguchi, S. Kuroiwa, K. Takeda, and S. Nakamura (2006). CENSREC-1-C: development of evaluation framework for voice activity detection under noisy environment, IPSJ SIG Technical Report, 2006-SLP-63, pp.1–6

S. Dupont, C. Ris, and D. Bachelart (2004). Combined use of closetalk and throat microphones for improved speech recognition under non-stationary background noise, in proceedings of COST278 and ISCA Tutorial and Research Workshop (ITRW) on Robustness Issues in Conversational Interaction, paper31

S. Ishimitsu (2008). Construction of a Noise-Robust Body-Conducted Speech Recognition System, in Chapter of Speech Recognition, IN-TECH

S. Ishimitsu, H. Kitakaze, Y. Tsuchibushi, H. Yanagawa, and M. Fukushima (2004). A noise-robust speech recognition system making use of body-conducted signals, Acoustical Science and Technology, Vol. 25 No. 2, pp.166-169

S. Ishimitsu, M. Nakayama, and Y. Murakami (2004). Study of Body-Conducted Speech Recognition for Support of Maritime Engine Operation, in Journal of the JIME, Vol.39 No.4, pp.35-40 (in Japanese)

S. Itahashi (1991). A noise database and Japanese common speech data corpus, Journal of ASJ, Vol.47 No.12, pp. 951-953

S. Young, J. Jansen, J. Odell, and P. Woodland (2000). The HTK Book for V2.0, Cambridge University

T. Kawahara, A. Lee, T. Kobayashi, K. Takeda, N. Minematsu, K. Itou , A. Ito, M. Yamamoto, A. Yamada, T. Utsuro, and K. Shikano (1999). Japanese dictation toolkit – 1997 version, Journal of ASJ, Vol. 20, No. 3, pp.233–239

T. T. Vu, M. Unoki, and M. Akagi (2006). A Study on Restoration of Boneconducted Speech With LPC Based Model, IEICE Technical Report, SP2005-174, pp.67-78

T. Tamiya, and T. Shimamura (2006). Improvement of Body-Conducted Speech Quality by Adaptive Filters, IEICE Technical Report, SP2006-191, pp.41-46

Z. Liu, Z. Zhang, A. Acero, J. Droppo, and X. Huang (2004). Direct Filtering for Air- and Bone-Conductive Microphones, in proceedings of IEEE International Workshop on Multimedia Signal Processing (MMSP'04), pp.363-366

## Chapter 10

Cochlear Implant Stimulation Rates and Speech Perception

Komal Arora, Richard Dowell and Pam Dawson

Additional information is available at the end of the chapter

1. Introduction

1.1. Cochlear implant system

For individuals with severe to profound hearing losses, due to disease or damage to the inner ear, acoustic stimulation (via hearing aids) may not provide sufficient information for adequate speech perception. In such cases direct electrical stimulation of the auditory nerve by surgically implanted electrodes has been beneficial in restoring useful hearing. This chapter will provide a general overview regarding sound perception through electrical stimulation using multi channel cochlear implants.

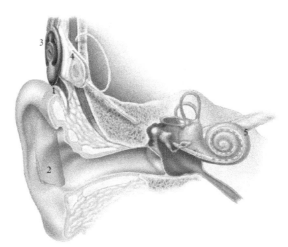

Figure 1. Cochlear implant system (Cowan, 2007)

The multiple channel cochlear implants consist of 1) a microphone which picks up sounds from the environment, 2) a sound processor which converts the analog sounds into a digitally coded signal, 3) a transmitting coil which transmits this information to the 4) receiver stimulator which decodes the radio frequency signals transmitted from the sound processor into the electrical stimuli responsible for auditory nerve stimulation via 5) an electrode array which provides multiple sites of stimulation within the cochlea (figure 1).

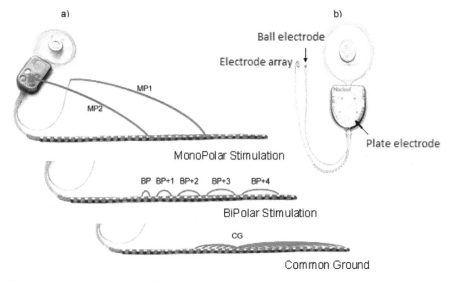

Figure 2. a) Stimulation modes. b) Extracochlear electrodes (Seligman, 2007).

Most of the current cochlear implant systems use *intracochlear* and *extracochlear* electrodes. Three different modes of current stimulation have been used in cochlear implant systems – Monopolar, bipolar and common ground (figure 2a). In monopolar stimulation, current is passed between one active intracochlear electrode and the extracochlear electrodes (which provide the return current path) placed either as a ball electrode under the temporalis muscle (MP1) or a plate electrode on the receiver casing (MP2) (figure 2b). When both of these extracochlear electrodes act as return electrodes in parallel, it is called MP1+2 configuration. In bipolar stimulation, current flows between an active and a return electrode within the cochlea; whereas in common ground stimulation, current flows from one electrode within the cochlea to all other intracochlear electrodes.

1.2. Speech processing in cochlear implants

The basic function of speech processing is to extract the speech information present in the acoustic signals and process it to produce a decoded version of the electrical stimulation signals that are transmitted as radio frequency (RF) signals to the receiver stimulator. The receiver stimulator converts this information into electrical stimulation patterns. A number of speech processing strategies are available in current CI systems. This presents a choice of fitting parameters when setting up a system for individual patients. These parameters include the rate of stimulation, number of channels to be activated, mode of stimulation, electrical pulse width etc. These parameters along with the amplitude mapping of all available electrodes define a "map" for an individual cochlear implantee. Amplitude mapping involves measuring for each active electrode, the user's threshold (T) level that is the level at which he/ she can just hear the stimulus and the maximum comfortable (C) level, that is, the level which produces a loud but comfortable sensation. These maps are loaded in the client's sound processor. An individual cochlear implantee's speech perception outcomes may differ based on the type of strategy he/she is using (Pasanisi et al., 2002; Psarros et al., 2002; Skinner et al., 2002a, b; Plant et al., 2002)

The current Nucleus® cochlear implants employ filter bank strategies which analyse the incoming signal using a bank or band-pass filters. The earliest filter bank strategy implemented in Nucleus cochlear implants called Spectral Maxima Sound processor (SMSP) (McDermott et al., 1992) did not extract features from the speech waveform. Instead, the incoming speech signal was sent to 16 band pass filters with centre frequencies from 250 Hz to 5400 Hz. The output from the six channels with the greatest amplitude (maxima) was compressed to fit the patient's electrical dynamic range. The resultant output was then sent to the six selected electrodes at a rate of 250 pulses per channel (pps/ch). It is beyond the scope of this chapter to provide detailed information on all available speech coding strategies. A more comprehensive review of speech processing strategies is provided in Loizou (1998). A brief review of the most commonly currently used speech processing strategy in Nucleus devices is provided in section 1.2.3. Figure 3 shows the overall signal flow in the most commonly used filterbank strategies: Continuous Interleaved Sampling (CIS), Spectral Peak (SPEAK) and Advanced combination Encoders (ACE™).

Figure 3. Audio signal path used in current filterbank strategies (Swanson, 2007).

1.2.1. Front end

The input signal is at first picked up by the microphone and undergoes front end processing. The front end includes a *preamplifier, pre- emphasis, automatic gain control* and *sensitivity control*. The preamplifier amplifies the weak signals so that they can be easily handled by the rest of the signal processing. After that a pre- emphasis of 6dB/octave in frequency is applied to the signal. This again increases the gain for high frequency speech sounds. The automatic gain control helps reduce distortion or overloading. In Nucleus systems, the AGC has infinite compression, that is, the signal is at first amplified linearly to a certain level and compressed if it reaches beyond that fixed point. This type of compression controls only the amplitude without distorting the temporal pattern of the speech waveform. The last part of the front end processing is automatic sensitivity control (ASC). Sensitivity refers to the effective gain of the sound processor and affects the minimum acoustic signal strength required to produce stimulation. At a higher sensitivity setting less signal strength is needed. On the other hand, at very low sensitivity settings, higher sound pressure levels are needed to stimulate threshold or comfortable levels. The sensitivity setting determines when the AGC will start acting and is aligned to C-level stimulation. This is automated in the current Nucleus cochlear implant devices and is called as ASC. The front end processing discussed so far is similar in SPEAK, CIS or ACE.

1.2.2. Filterbank

After the front end processing, the signal passes through a series of partially overlapping band pass filters (each passing a different frequency range) where the signal is analyzed in terms of frequency and amplitude. The filterbank splits the audio signal into number of frequency bands simulating the auditory filter mechanism in normal hearing. The filter bands in the ACE strategy in current Nucleus processors are spaced linearly from 188 to 1312 Hz and thereafter logarithmically up to 7938 Hz. Each filter band is allocated to one intracochlear electrode in the implant system according to the tonotopic relationship between frequency and place in the cochlea.

Different speech coding strategies differ in the number of filter bands they use. For example the Nucleus implementation of CIS strategy has a small number (4 to 12) of wide bands, and SPEAK and ACE strategies have a large number (20 to 22) of narrow bands. The maximum number of bands is determined by the number of electrodes that are available in the particular implant system.

1.2.3. Sampling and selection

To produce a satisfactory digital representation of a signal, the acoustic signal needs to be sampled sufficiently rapidly. According to the Nyquist theorem, the sampling rate should be twice the frequency to be represented. Aliasing errors can occur at lower rates. In the SPrint™ and Freedom™ processors, the filterbank uses a mathematical algorithm known as Fast Fourier Transform (FFT). This technique splits the spectrum into discrete lines or "bins" spaced at regular intervals in frequency. The sound is sampled at a regular rate in blocks, typically of 128 samples. The sampling rate for the Nucleus processors (SPrint™ and Freedom™ BTE) that use FFT is 16 kHz.

On the other hand, the ESPrit™ processors use analog switched capacitor filters. For smaller behind the ear units such as ESPrit™ and ESPrit™ 3G processors (used in the experiments discussed in this chapter, sections 3 and 4) switched capacitor filters were used because they were most power efficient at that time. These switched capacitor filters sample low frequencies at a rate of 19 kHz and high frequencies at a rate of 78 kHz. This filtered signal is further rectified to extract the envelopes. In the ESPrit™ series of processors filter outputs are measured using peak detectors. These peak detectors in ESPrit™ processors are matched to the time response of the filters as each filter in the filterbank has different time response. The Med-El implants use Hilbert transform for measuring filter outputs. Hilbert transform gives amplitude response equal to bandpass filter response.

After the low pass filtering in SPrint™ / Freedom™ and peak detection in ESPrit™ processors, the outputs are further analyzed for the amplitude maxima. Each analysis window selects N maxima amplitudes (depending on the strategy) from filterbank outputs. The rate at which a set of N amplitude maxima are selected is referred to as the update rate. In Freedom™/ SPrint™ processors this rate is fixed at 760 Hz. However, in the ESPrit™ series of processors, it varies. For the high level sounds, the update rate is 4 kHz and for low level sounds, it is 1 kHz. This is also the rate at which new information is generated by the sound processor. In Med-El sound processors, using CIS strategy, new data is available from the sound processor at the stimulation rate.

The following sections describe how sampling and selection is done for each strategy.

1.2.3.1. Spectral Peak (SPEAK) strategy

The Spectral Peak (SPEAK) strategy is a derivative of the SMSP strategy (McDermott,et al.,1992) where the number of channels was increased from 16 to 20 with the center frequencies ranging from 250-10,000Hz. The frequency boundaries of the filters could be varied. It also provided flexibility to choose the number of maxima from one to ten with an average of six. The selected electrodes were stimulated at a fixed rate that varied between 180 and 300 pps/ch. The stimulation rate was varied depending upon the number of maxima selected. In case of limited spectral content, lesser maxima were selected and the stimulation rate increased which provided more temporal information and hence may have compensated for reduced spectral cues. Similarly when more maxima were selected, the stimulation rate was reduced (Loizou, 1998). This strategy was implemented in the Spectra sound processor (Seligman and Mc Dermott, 1995) and was next incorporated in the Nucleus 24™ series of sound processors. However, the SPrint™ and Freedom™ systems (in Nucleus 24 series) used a fixed analysis rate of 250 Hz. Nucleus 24 also allowed for higher rates which are covered in the description of ACE strategy (section 1.2.3.3). A typical SPEAK strategy in the Nucleus devices consists of 250 pps/ch stimulation rate with the selection of six or eight maxima out of 20 channels.

1.2.3.2. Continuous Interleaved Sampling (CIS) strategy

The CIS strategy (Wilson et al., 1991) was developed for the Ineraid implant. In this strategy, the filterbank has six frequency bands. The envelope of the waveform is estimated at the output of each filter. These envelope signals are sampled at a fixed rate. The envelope outputs are finally compressed to fit the dynamic range of electric hearing and then used to modulate biphasic pulses. The filter output in terms of electrical pulses is delivered to six fixed intracochlear electrodes. The key feature of the CIS strategy is the use of higher stimulation rates to provide better representation of temporal information. The variations in the pulse amplitude can track the rapid changes in the speech signal. This is possible due to the shorter pulses with minimal delays/inter-pulse interval (Wilson et al., 1993). The possible benefits of using high stimulation rates are discussed further in the Section 2. The stimulation rate used in the CIS strategy is generally 800 pps/ch or higher. A modified version (CIS+) of the CIS strategy is used these days, more typically in Med- El implants. CIS+ uses a Hilbert Transformation (Stark and Tuteur, 1979) to represent the amplitude envelope of the filter outputs. This transformation tracks the acoustic signal more closely for a more accurate representation of its temporal dynamics compared to the other techniques used to represent the amplitude envelope in other implant systems like "wave rectification", "low-pass filtering" or "fast Fourier transform" (Med-El, 2008).

1.2.3.3. Advanced combination encoder (ACE™) strategy

The ACE™ strategy (Vandali et al., 2000) is similar to the SPEAK strategy except that it combines the higher stimulation rate feature of the CIS strategy. Selection of electrodes is similar to the SPEAK strategy; however it can also be programmed to stimulate fixed electrode sites as in CIS. Thus this strategy attempts to provide the combined benefits of good spectral and temporal information for speech. Figure 4 depicts the schematic diagram of the ACE strategy. The filter bands in the ACE strategy are spaced linearly from 188 to 1312 Hz and thereafter logarithmically up to 7938 Hz.

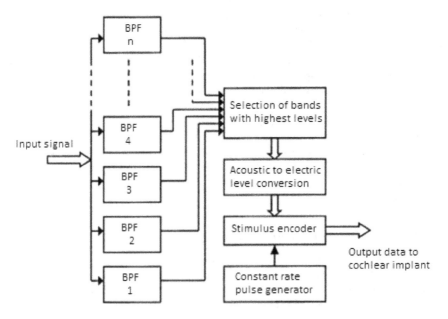

Figure 4. Schematic diagram of the ACE strategy (McDermott, 2004).

The output of the filters is low pass filtered with an envelope cut off frequency between 200 and 400 Hz (In SPrint™ and Freedom™ processors). The ESPrit™ series of processors use peak detectors (discussed in section 1.2.3) rather than low pass filtering. After the envelopes from each of the band pass filters are extracted, a subset of filters with the highest amplitudes is selected. These are called maxima which can number from 1 to 20. The range of stimulation rates in ACE can be selected from a range of 250 to 3500 pps/ch.

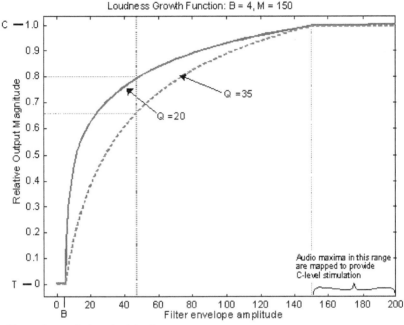

Figure 5. Loudness growth function in a Nucleus cochlear implant system. The x-axis shows the input level (dB SPL) and the y-axis shows the current level. The steeper loudness curve has smaller Q (Swanson, 2007).

1.3. Amplitude mapping

The next stage is amplitude mapping where energy in each filter band decides the amplitude of the pulses delivered to the corresponding electrodes. An amplitude conversion function is applied to convert acoustic levels into electrical levels. This function is described in terms of T-SPL and C-SPL. T-SPL refers to the sound pressure level (SPL) required to stimulate at threshold level (around 25 dB) and C-SPL refers to the sound pressure level required to stimulate at maximum comfortable level (65 dB). For speech at normal conversational levels, there are hardly any speech sounds below 25 dB SPL. A standard 40 dB input dynamic range (IDR) that is the difference between the T-SPL and C-SPL is mapped on to an electrical or output dynamic range which depends on the threshold and maximum comfortable electrical levels (typically about 8 dB). Thus, the output from the filters is compressed to fit the electrical dynamic range. The compression is described by the loudness growth function. The parameter Q (steepness factor) controls the steepness of the loudness growth curve (figure 5). Nucleus ESPrit™ processors operate on the input DR of 30 dB. IDR can be increased up to 50 dB in current Nucleus sound processors.

1.4. Radio frequency (RF) encoder

The data from the sound processor is transmitted to the receiver stimulator. The transmitted code is made up of a digital data stream and transmitted by pulsing the RF carrier. The receiver-stimulator decodes the current specific information (e.g. electrode selection, current level, mode of stimulation etc.) and converts this information into electrical stimulus pulses.

The biphasic electrical current pulses are then delivered non-simultaneously to the corresponding electrodes at a fixed rate. The non-simultaneous presentation (one electrode is stimulated at one time) of current pulses is used to avoid channel interaction (Wilson et al., 1998). The range of stimulation rates available in current Nucleus devices range from 250 pps/ch to 3500 pps/ch. In the current study the Nucleus ESPrit™ 3G processor was used which has a maximum stimulation rate of 2400 pps/ch. However, it is unlikely that these higher stimulation rates provide any additional temporal information unless the processor update rate is at least equivalent (760 Hz in SPrint™ and Freedom™ processors and 1000 - 4000 Hz in ESPrit™ processors). From the signal processing point of view, the ESPrit™ series of processors have the potential to add new temporal information with high rates because of their higher update rate (1-4 kHz).

2. Electrical hearing

As discussed in the sections above, various speech coding strategies and choice of fitting parameters are available in current CI systems. Studies have demonstrated that different strategies and/or parameter choices can provide benefits to individual patients but there is no clear method for determining these for a particular individual. The current literature in this area shows a lack of consistency in outcomes, particularly, when the electrical stimulation rate is varied. There could be some underlying physiological or psychological correlates behind it. For example the outcomes may be related to the temporal processing abilities of CI users. This section will review some of the existing literature pertaining to the stimulation rate effects on the performance of the cochlear implant subjects.

2.1. Stimulation rate effects on speech perception

The stimulus signals delivered in existing CI systems are generally derived by sampling the temporal envelope of each channel at some constant (analysis) rate and using its intensity to control the stimulation current level delivered to the corresponding electrode site (again at a constant stimulation rate which is typically equal to the analysis rate). The range of stimulation rates employed in devices varies extensively amongst systems from low (<500 pps/ch), to moderate (500-1000 pps/ch), through to high (>1000 pps/ch). Figure 6 shows the effect of stimulation rate in processing the syllable /ti/. The bottom most waveform is the original speech envelope of channel 5 for the syllable /ti/. As seen in the 200 pps/ch stimulation rate condition, pulses are spaced relatively far apart, so this sort of processing may not be able to extract all of the important temporal fine structure of the original waveform. When a higher pulse rate is used, the pulses are placed more closely and they can carry the temporal fine structure more precisely (Loizou et al., 2000). From a signal processing point of view this seems reasonable, however in practice, perceptual performance of CI users is often not improved when using higher rates.

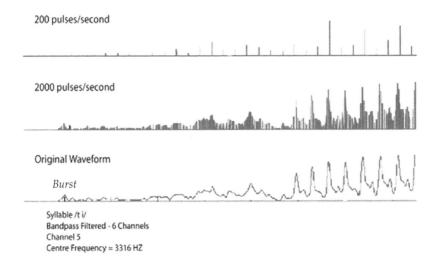

Figure 6. The pulsatile waveforms for channel 5 of the syllable /ti/ with stimulation rates of 200 pps/ ch and 2000 pps/ch. The syllable /ti/ was band pass filtered into six channels and the output was rectified and sampled at the rates indicated in this figure. The bottom panel shows the speech envelope of channel 5 for syllable /ti/ (modified from Loizou et al., 2000).

When considering the appropriate rate to employ for coding of F0 temporal information, Nyquist's theorem states that the rate must be at least twice the highest frequency to be represented. However, according to McKay et al (1994), the stimulation rate for CI systems should be at least four times the highest frequency to be represented. This suggests that rates of >1200 pps per channel are needed to effectively code the voice pitch range up to 300 Hz. On the other hand studies examining neural responses to electrical stimulation in animals have shown that at rates above >800 pps/ch, there is poorer phase locking and less effective entrainment of neurons due to refractory effects being more dominant (Parkins, 1989; Dynes &Delgutte, 1992). It is therefore simplistic to assume that a higher stimulation rate alone will necessarily result in more effective transfer of temporal information in the auditory system.

A number of studies explored the effect of stimulation rate on speech perception in CI users. Results for some of the previous studies using the continuous interleaved sampling (CIS) speech coding strategy and the MED-El implant showed benefits for moderate and high stimulation rates (Loizou et al, 2000; Keifer et al, 2000; Verchuur, 2005; Nie et al, 2006). However, other studies using the CIS strategy did not show a benefit for high rates (Plant et al, 2002; Friesen et al, 2005). The comparison of these studies is complicated by the use of different implant systems. Studies using the Nucleus devices with 22 intracochlear electrodes and the ACE strategy did not show a conclusive benefit for higher rates (Vandali et al, 2000; Holden et al, 2002; Weber et al, 2007; Plant et al, 2007). Again, there are some limitations in these studies due to the specific hardware used. The higher stimulation rates tested by Vandali et al (2000) and Holden et al (2002) probably did not add any extra temporal information due to the limited analysis rate of 760 Hz employed in the SPrint™ processor used in those studies. Many of these studies reported large individual variability among subjects. Although the recent study by Plant et al (2007) found no significant group mean differences between higher rate and lower rate programs, five of the 15 subjects obtained significantly better scores with higher rates (2400 pps/ch & 10 maxima, or 3500 pps/ch & 9 maxima) compared to lower rates (1200 pps/ch & 10 maxima, or 1200 pps/ch & 12 maxima) for speech tests conducted in quiet or noise. Only two subjects obtained significant benefits in both tests using the higher set of rates, and the results were not conclusive because significant learning effects were observed in the study. Likewise, in the study by Weber et al (2007), group speech perception scores in quiet and noise did not demonstrate a significant difference between stimulation rates of 500, 1200, and 3500 pps/ch using the ACE strategy. However, some variability in individual scores was observed for six of the 12 subjects for the sentences in noise test.

Reports on subjects' preferences for particular stimulation rates with Nucleus devices have shown results in favor of low to moderate stimulation rates. In the study done by Vandali et al (2000), 250 and 807 pps/ch rates were preferred over 1615 pps/ch. Similarly, Balkany et al (2007) reported preferences for slower set of rates (500 to 1200 pps/ch, ACE strategy) for 37 of the 55 subjects, compared to faster set of rates (1800 to 3500 pps/ ch, ACE RE strategy). Authors also reported that the rate preference by individual subjects tended towards the slower rates within each of the two sets of stimulation rates. Similarly, in a clinical trial conducted in North America and Europe by Cochlear Ltd (2007) on subject selection of stimulation rate with the Nucleus Freedom system, there was a preference for stimulation rates of 1200 pps/ch or lower. Speech perception test results also showed improved performance with stimulation rates of 1200 pps/ch or lower compared to a higher set of rates (1800, 2400, and 3500 pps/ch).

2.2. Perception of complex sounds in electric hearing

Both spectral and temporal information in acoustic signals encoded by the auditory system are important for speech perception in normal hearing. Spectral and temporal information are coded by the site (or place) and timing of neural activity along the basilar membrane respectively. For speech sounds, (broad) spectral information such as, the frequency and bandwidth of vowel formants, is encoded via place along the tonotopic axis of the cochlea. Fine spectral structure is also encoded, such as the frequency of the fundamental (F0) and lower-order harmonics of the fundamental for voiced sounds (Plomp, 1967; Houtsma, 1990).

Temporal properties of speech encoded in the auditory system comprise low frequency envelope cues (<50 Hz) which provide information about phonetic features of speech, higher frequency envelope information (>50 Hz), such as F0 periodicity information in auditory filters in which vowel harmonics are not resolved, and most importantly fine temporal structure (Rosen, 1992). The perceived quality or timbre of complex sounds is mostly attributable to the spectral shape. For example, each vowel has specific formant frequencies and patterning of these formant frequencies helps in determining the vowel quality and vowel identity (Moore, 2003b).

The frequency coding in cochlear implants takes place in two ways: a) spectral information presented via the distribution of energy on multiple electrodes along the cochlea, b) temporal information which is mainly presented via the amplitude envelopes of the electrical stimulation pulses. These two ways of coding and the spectral shape coding are described in the following sub sections.

2.2.1. Spectral/ Place pitch coding

In current multichannel cochlear implants, the pitch sensations produced at various electrodes vary depending on the position of electrodes at different sites in the cochlea (Simmons, 1966; Pialoux et al., 1976; Clark et al., 1978; Tong et al., 1979, 1982; Burian et al., 1979). An important finding of some of these studies was that the subjects' description of pitch being sharp or dull depended on whether the higher or lower frequency regions excited according to the tonotopic organization of the cochlea (Clark et al., 1978; Tong et al., 1979, 1982; Donaldson and Nelson, 2000; Busby and Clark, 2000). However, place coding is relatively crude due to the limited numbers of electrodes (up to 22) in current cochlear implant systems compared to approximately 15,000 receptor hair cells in the normal cochlea, degeneration of auditory nerve fibres innervating the cochlea, and the fact that electrode arrays do not access the full length of the cochlea (Ketten et al., 1998; Baskent and Shannon, 2004). That is, the most apical electrodes do not stimulate the most apical site in the cochlea. In addition, the tonotopicity seen in the CI is not perfect in all subjects. Some subjects cannot discriminate between the pitches across different electrodes and/or a more basal electrode may sound lower in pitch than a more apical one (so called pitch reversal) (Busby et al., 1994; Cohen et al., 1996; Nelson et al., 1995; Donaldson and Nelson, 2000). Spatial separation between electrodes has also been found to affect CI users' pitch perception ability. Increased separation improved pitch ranking performance of CI subjects (Nelson et al., 1995; Tong and Clark, 1985). In addition, most CI listeners cannot make full use of the spectral information available through their implants. Friesen et al. (2001) reported no significant improvement in speech perception (in quiet and noise) as the number of electrodes was increased beyond eight. The above mentioned place anomalies could affect the speech perception of cochlear implantees as spectral pitch is an important attribute in speech. Therefore, the use of temporal information to assist speech perception for cochlear implant users may be quite important.

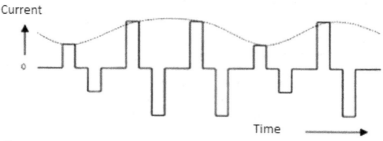

Figure 7. An amplitude modulated current pulse train (McDermott, 2004).

2.2.2. Temporal pitch coding

In current fixed rate speech processing strategies, the amplitude of the pulse trains on each electrode is modulated by the amplitude envelope of the acoustic signal (figure 7). The amplitude of pulse trains on each electrode depends on their corresponding amplitudes estimated from the filter bank. These amplitude variations over time are responsible for the subjective temporal pitch in cochlear implant users. In these filter bank strategies, the speech information is low pass filtered within each frequency band using a filter frequency between 200- 400 Hz with the elimination of most of the fine temporal structure. Thus, temporal information is mainly presented via the amplitude envelopes of the electrical stimulation pulses. The slower overall variations in amplitude over time modulating high-frequency carrier refer to the envelope of a waveform. The rapid variations in amplitude over time with average rate close to the carrier signal are described as the fine structure portion of a waveform. An example of a filtered speech waveform with its envelope and fine structure composition is depicted in figure 8.

As mentioned earlier, temporal information provides envelope, periodicity and fine structure information in speech (Rosen, 1992). Low frequency temporal envelope information is sufficient for segmental speech information (Fu and Shannon, 2000; Shannon et al., 1995; Xu et al., 2002). These studies show that 16-20 Hz temporal information is sufficient when adequate spectral cues are available and in case of poor spectral cues subjects may be forced to use envelope frequencies up to 50 Hz. On the other hand, higher frequency temporal cues may assist CI listeners to perceive the finer fundamental frequency (F0) temporal cues. Fu et al. (2004) found that for normal hearing subjects and cochlear implantees, voice gender recognition improved when the speech envelope low pass filter frequency was increased from 20- 320 Hz. It is possible that if a listener can attend to the voice pitch of the target speaker, he can separate the speech from competing noise thereby improving the overall speech perception (Brokx and Nooteboom, 1982; Assmann and Summerfield, 1990). A need for higher resolution spectral information (for instance, an increased number of channels) is likely to be needed for improving speech perception in noise (Fu et al., 1998; Dorman et al., 1998). If this increased spectral resolution can not be obtained with current electrode technology, better coding of periodicity cues may provide another avenue for improving performance for CI users.

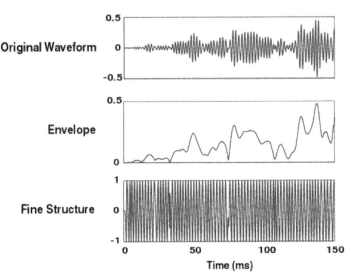

Figure 8. The envelope and fine structure components of a filtered speech signal (http://research.meei.harvard.edu/chimera/motivation.html).

Psychophysical studies of electrical stimulation in the human auditory system indicate that temporal pitch information up to 300 Hz is probably available to CI users (Eddington et al., 1978; Tong et al., 1979; Shannon, 1983; Moore & Carlyon, 2005).These studies used steady pulse trains (with varied rate of stimulation) delivered to single electrode sites. For very low pulse rates (<50 Hz), the signal is reported to be perceived as buzz-like sound and for rates above 300 Hz, a little change in perceived pitch is reported. This ability of CI users varies with a few being able to discriminate rate increases up to 1000 Hz (Fearn and Wolfe, 2000; Townshend et al., 1987).

2.2.3. Coding of spectral shape/timbre

Spectral shape is important in the perception of complex sounds, including dynamic characteristics; however, in cochlear implant users it is particularly important. Spectral shape discrimination can help in identifying vowels in the speech and many other types of sound even when other acoustic cues are absent (McDermott, 2004). In the normal auditory system spectral shape is represented by the relative response across filters. There are different ways to code the relative level across filters such as relative firing rates of neurons as a function of characteristic frequency (place coding); relative amount of phase locking between neurons and the different frequency components (temporal coding); and by the level dependent phase changes on the basilar membrane. In implant systems, spectral shape, like frequency coding is coded by filtering the signal into several frequency bands and the relative magnitude of the electric signal across electrode channels. The coding of spectral shape cannot be as precise as that in the normal ear due to the relatively small number of effective channels in current cochlear implant systems. In addition, the detailed temporal information relating to formant frequencies is not conveyed due to the inability to effectively code temporal information above about 300 Hz. One approach to improving the representation of the temporal envelope and higher frequency periodicity cues is to increase the low pass filter frequency applied to the amplitude envelope and/or to use higher stimulation rates. However, results so far do not conclusively show benefit for higher rates (section 2.1). Furthermore, it is also not clear how effectively CI listeners can resolve these temporal modulations.

In normal hearing and hearing impaired subjects, temporal resolution can be characterized by the temporal modulation transfer function (TMTF) which relates the threshold for detecting changes in the amplitude of a sound to the rapidity of changes/modulation frequency (Bacon and Viemeister, 1985; Burns and Viemeister, 1976; Moore and Glasberg, 2001). In this task, modulation detection can be measured for a series of modulation frequencies. The stimuli used in these experiments are either amplitude modulated noise or complex tones. To study temporal modulation independent from spectral resolution, spectral cues are removed by using broadband noise as a carrier. This type of stimulus has waveform envelope variations but no spectral cues. Complex tones are the combination of two or more pure tones. This type of sinusoidal amplitude modulated (SAM) signal has components at $fc-fm$, fc, $fc+fm$ where fc is the carrier frequency and fm is the modulation frequency (figure 9b).

The components above and below the centre frequency are called sidebands. If fc (e.g.1200, 1400, 1600 Hz) is an integer multiple of fm (200 Hz), it forms a harmonic structure otherwise, it is called an inharmonic waveform. In signal theory and acoustic literature, amplitude modulated signals are described by the formula:

$$\left(1 + m \sin 2\pi . fm. t\right) \sin 2\pi fc\ t \tag{1}$$

where t is time and m is the modulation index ($m= 1$ means 100% modulation). Figure 9(a) shows an example of an amplitude modulated signal. The pink color waveform shows the depth of modulation. In acoustic hearing, m = MD (modulation depth) which is defined as:

$$m = \left(peak - trough\right) / \ \left(peak + trough\right) \tag{2}$$

where peak and trough refer to the peak and trough (Sound Pressure Level, SPL) levels of the modulation envelope.

However, in cochlear implant stimulation, the loudness of signals is governed more-so by peaks in the stimulus envelope rather than average stimulus level. Thus, when presenting AM signals to CI users, the peak level of the AM signal is held fixed and only the trough of the modulation envelope is reduced. Eq. 3 describes the SAM formula used in study 2.

$$\sin(2\pi \times fc \times t) \times \left[1 + 0.5m \times \left(\sin(2\pi \times fm \times t) - 1\right)\right] \qquad (3)$$

where fc is the carrier frequency, fm is the modulation frequency, t is time, m is the modulation index which controls the modulation depth (MD), where

$$m = 1 - 1/MD \qquad (4)$$

and where modulation depth (in cochlear implant stimulation) is defined by the peak over trough (peak/trough) level in the envelope. The psychophysical measure tested in study 2 was modulation detection threshold (MDT) which refers to the depth of modulation necessary to just allow discrimination between a modulated and unmodulated waveform. In this study stimuli were presented through the cochlear implant sound processor. Modulation depth (MD) was converted into modulation index (m) using Eq. (3) for all analysis. This was because most of the studies which measured modulation detection in CI recipients have used modulation index (m) for analysis purposes.

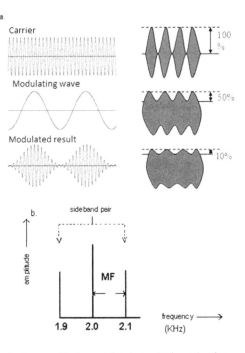

Figure 9. a) An example of an amplitude modulated signal. The pink color waveforms show the depth of modulation. b) The sinusoidally amplitude modulated signal with 2000 Hz carrier frequency (fc), 100 Hz modulation frequency (MF).

The limitation with the sinusoidal carriers is that the modulation introduces sidebands which can be heard as separate signals. Also the results of modulation detection may be influenced by the "off frequency listening". That is if the carrier and the modulated frequency are separated quite apart the sounds can be heard from the auditory filters centered at the carrier frequency or the sideband frequency depending on the intensity of modulation (Moore and Glasberg, 2001). However, in study 2 a sinusoidal carrier was used instead of noise as the carrier because subjects with cochlear hearing loss have reduced frequency selectivity (Glasberg and Moore, 1986; Moore, 2003) leading to poor spectral resolution of the sidebands. Thus, TMTF in such cases is mainly influenced by temporal resolution over a wide range of modulation frequencies (Moore and Glasberg, 2001). It is also difficult for the CI users to spectrally resolve the components of complex tones (Shannon, 1983). In addition; the noise signal would have its own temporal envelope which can confound the results of modulation detection (Moore and Glasberg, 2001).

3. Study 1: Effect of stimulation rate on speech perception

This section provides the details of the study by Arora et al (2009), which examined the effect of low to moderate stimulation rates on speech perception in Nucleus CI users with addition of two more subjects.

3.1. Rationale

If low to moderate stimulation rates do indeed provide equivalent or better speech perception, then recipients may also benefit from reductions in system power consumption and processor/device size and complexity. So far, low to moderate rates have not been explored well in Nucleus™ 24 implants with the ACE strategy, especially in the range of 250-900 pps/ch in spite of the fact that this range of rates is often used clinically[1] with Nucleus devices, (which worldwide are the most used devices so far among CI recipients). The authors thus chose to examine rates of 275, 350, 500, and 900 pps/ch in this study.

This study was specifically designed to determine:

- Whether rates of stimulation (between 275 and 900 pps/ch) have an effect on the speech perception in quiet and noise for the group of adult CI subjects.
- Whether optimal rate varies among various subjects.
- Whether there is a relation between the subjective preference measured with comparative questionnaire and the speech perception scores.

3.2. Method

Ten postlingually deaf adult subjects using the Nucleus™ 24 Contour™ implant and ESPrit™ 3G sound processor participated in the study. Table 1 shows the demographic data for the subjects. Low to moderate stimulation rates of 275, 350, 500 and 900 pulses-per-second/channel (pps/ch) were evaluated.

---

[1] As per the information available from Melbourne Cochlear Implant Clinic (RVEEH, University of Melbourne) and Sydney Cochlear implant Center (The University of Sydney).

Test material comprised CNC open set monosyllabic words (Peterson, & Lehiste, 1962) presented in quiet and Speech Intelligibility test (SIT) open set sentences (Magner, 1972) presented in four talker babble noise. Four lists of CNC words were presented in each session at a level of 60 dB SPL RMS. An adaptive procedure (similar to the procedure used by Henshall and McKay, 2001) was used to measure speech reception threshold (SRT) for the sentence test in noise. Four such SRT estimates were recorded in each session. All four stimulation rate programs were balanced for loudness. A repeated ABCD experimental design was employed.

Take home practice was provided with each stimulation rate. A comparative questionnaire was provided to the CI subjects at the end of the repeated ABCD protocol. Subjects were asked to compare all four rate programs for similar lengths of time over a period of two weeks with a constant sensitivity setting for all stimulation rates.

Subject	Age	Cause of deafness	Duration of implant use (yr)	Everyday stimulation rate* and strategy.
1	58	Hereditary	4	900 pps/ch, ACE
2	67	Otosclerosis	5	720 pps/ch, ACE
3	64	Unknown	5	900 pps/ch, ACE
4	64	Unknown	5	250 pps/ch, SPEAK
5	74	Unknown	4	1200 pps/ch, ACE
6	75	Otosclerosis	8	250 pps/ch, SPEAK
7	62	Unknown	8	250 pps/ch, SPEAK
8	68	Unknown	6	250 pps/ch, ACE
9	69	Unknown	4	900 pps/ch, ACE
10	72	Unknown	5	500 pps/ch, ACE

*Prior to commencement of the study

Table 1. Subject details.

The ACE strategy was used for all stimulation rates. For the 275 pps/ch case, the stimulation rate was jittered in time by approximately 10%, which tends to lower the rate to approximately 250 pps/ch. This was done to minimize the audibility of the constant stimulation rate. It may have been beneficial if all other stimulation rates tested in this study were also jittered (i.e., to avoid a possible confound). The number of maxima was eight for all the conditions. Clinical default settings for pulse width, mode (MP1+2) and frequency to electrode mapping were employed. The pulse width was increased in cases where current level needed to exceed 255 CL units to achieve comfortable levels. The sound processor was set at the client's preferred sensitivity and held constant throughout the study.

Thresholds (T-levels) and Comfortable listening levels (C-levels) were measured for all mapped electrodes and for each rate condition. T-levels were measured using a modified Hughson-Westlake procedure with an ascending step size of 2 current levels (CLs) and a descending step size of 4 CLs. C-levels were measured with an ascending technique that slowly increases the levels from the baseline T-levels until the client reported that the sound was loud but still comfortable. Loudness balancing was performed at C-levels as well as at 50% level of the dynamic range, using a sweep across four consecutive electrodes at a time. Subjects were asked whether stimulation of all four electrodes sounded equally loud and if not, T- and C-levels were adjusted as necessary. Speech like noise "ICRA" (International Collegium of Rehabilitative Audiology) (Dreschler et al., 2001) was presented at 60 dB SPL RMS for all programs to ensure that each were similar in loudness for conversational speech. The comparison was conducted using a paired-comparison procedure, in which all possible pairings of conditions were compared twice. Adjustments were made to C-levels if necessary to achieve similar loudness across all rate programs.

3.3. Results

3.3.1. CNC words

Figure 10 shows percentage correct CNC word scores for the ten subjects for the four stimulation rate programs. The scores were averaged across the two evaluation sessions. Repeated measures two-way analysis of variance (ANOVA) for the group revealed no significant differences across the four rate programs (F [3, 27] = 2.14; p= 0.118). Furthermore, there was no significant main effect for session (F [3, 27] = 2.05; p= 0.186). The interaction effect between rate and session was not significant (F [3, 27] = 2.30; p= 0.099).

In the individual analyses, subject 1 showed significantly better scores for the 500 and 900 pps/ch programs compared to the 350 pps/ch program. There was no significant difference between the 500 and 900 pps/ch programs. Subject 8 showed best CNC scores with the 500 pps/ch program but the 900 pps/ch program showed poorer performance compared to all other programs. Subject 10 showed significantly better scores with 500 pps/ch compared to the 350 pps/ch program.

3.3.2. Sentence test results

Figure 11 shows average SRTs obtained for each subject and the group SRT on the SIT sentences for each stimulation rate program. Lower SRT values indicate better speech perception in noise. Repeated measures two-way analysis of variance revealed a significant main effect for stimulation rate (F [3, 27] = 7.79; p<0.001). Group analysis showed significantly better SRT with the 500 pps/ch program compared to 275 pps/ch (p= 0.002) and 350 pps/ch (p = 0.034). Also 900 pps/ch program showed significantly better SRT compared to 275 pps/ch (p = 0.005). Eight out of ten subjects showed improved performance with the 500 or 900 pps/ch rate programs. Small but significant learning effects were observed for sentences in noise scores for all four stimulation rate programs (F [3, 27] = 9.39; p= 0.013). Mean SRT decreased by 0.6 dB during the second session. There was no significant interaction effect between stimulation rate and the evaluation stage (F [3, 27] = 2.04; p= 0.13).

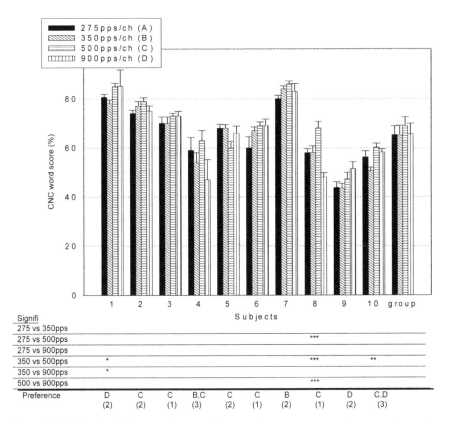

Figure 10. Individual patient's percentage correct scores and group mean percentage correct scores for CNC words in quiet. Statistically significant differences (post hoc Tukey test) are shown in the tables presented below each bar graph (*p ≤ 0.05, **p ≤ 0.01, ***p ≤ 0.001). Each subject's subjective preference in quiet along with the degree of preference (1 - very similar, 2 - slightly better, 3 - moderately better, 4 - much better) are shown below the chart.

Individual data analysis revealed a significant rate effect for the sentence test (p<0.001) in eight out of ten subjects. All of these eight subjects showed improved performance with the 500 and/or 900 pps/ch rate programs. Subject 1 performed equally well with the 500 and 900 pps/ch stimulation rate programs. The performance was significantly better with both these programs compared to the 275 and 350 pps/ch rate programs (p<0.05). Subject 2 showed improved performance with the 900 pps/ch program. Pair wise multiple comparison with the Tukey test indicated significant differences between the mean SRT obtained with 275 pps/ch program versus all other rate programs (p< 0.05), and also between the mean SRT obtained with the 350 and 900 pps/ch programs (p= 0.025). No significant differences were observed between the SRTs for the 350 and 500 pps/ch programs and the SRTs for the 500 and 900 pps/ch programs.

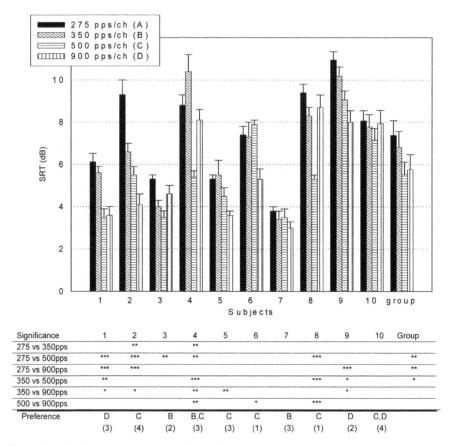

Significance	1	2	3	4	5	6	7	8	9	10	Group
275 vs 350pps		**		**							
275 vs 500pps	***	***	**	**				***			**
275 vs 900pps	***	***							***		**
350 vs 500pps	**			***				***	*		*
350 vs 900pps	*	*		**	**				*		
500 vs 900pps				**		*		***			
Preference	D	C	B	B,C	C	C	B	C	D	C,D	
	(3)	(4)	(2)	(3)	(3)	(1)	(3)	(1)	(2)	(4)	

Figure 11. Individual patient's mean speech reception threshold (SRT) and group mean SRT for SIT sentences in competing noise. Statistically significant differences (post hoc Tukey test) are shown in the tables presented below each bar graph (*p ≤ 0.05, **p ≤ 0.01, ***p ≤ 0.001). Each subject's subjective preference in noise along with the degree of preference (1 - very similar, 2 - slightly better, 3 - moderately better, 4 - much better) are shown below the chart.

Subjects 5 and 6 also obtained their best SRTs with the 900 pps/ch compared to 350 and 500 pps/ch stimulation rates (p <0.05). Subject 9 showed improved performance with 900 pps/ch compared to 275 pps/ch (p<0.001) and 350 pps/ch (p= 0.01) programs. This subject also showed better SRT for 500 pps/ch compared to 275 pps/ch rate program (p= 0.032). Subjects 3, 4 and 8 performed best with the 500 pps/ch stimulation rate. For subject 3, the results for 500 pps/ch condition were significantly better than 275 pps/ch stimulation rate (p=0.001). For subject 4 and subject 8, mean SRTs with 500 pps/ch stimulation rate were significantly better than all other stimulation rates. Subjects 7 and 10 did not show any significant difference in performance when tested for sentences in noise for all four stimulation rates.

3.3.3. Comparative performance questionnaire

Figure 12 shows group mean ratings of helpfulness for the stimulation rate programs for the four questionnaire subcategories and averaged across these subcategories. Friedman repeated measures ANOVA on ranks revealed no significant effect of stimulation rate on subjects' average helpfulness ratings across 18 listening situations (X^2 [3] = 7.58, p= 0.056). Furthermore, there was no significant effect of rate for the listening categories: listening in quiet (X^2[3] =1.70, p= 0.63) and listening media devices (X^2 [3] = 7.56, p= 0.056). Helpfulness ratings for listening in noise (X^2[3] = 9.16, p= 0.027) and listening to soft speech (X^2[3] = 7.83, p= 0.05) showed a significant effect of stimulation rate, however, pair wise multiple comparisons using Dunn's method revealed no significant differences between any pairs of rate programs for these two categories.

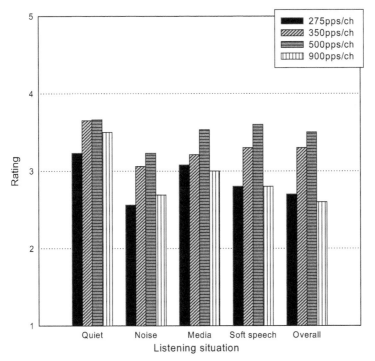

Figure 12. Group mean preference ratings of helpfulness for the four rate programs averaged across four categories (listening in quiet, listening in noise, listening media devices & listening to soft speech) and across 18 listening situations (overall). A rating of 1 represented "no help" and a rating of 5 represented "extremely helpful.

After providing helpfulness ratings, subjects were asked to indicate their first preferences in quiet, noise and overall. Table 2 shows the number of subjects reporting their first preferences in quiet, noise and overall for the four rate programs. Chi-square analysis revealed no significant differences between the distribution of preferences in quiet ($X^2[5]$ = 9.24, p= 0.099), noise ($X^2[5]$ =5.62, p= 0.344) and overall ($X^2[5]$ =5.62, p= 0.344). Figures 10 and 11 indicate individual subjects' preferred programs in quiet and in noise respectively.

Subjects were asked to describe if their preferred rate program sounded "very similar", "slightly better", "moderately better" or "much better" than the other programs. As shown in figure 10, five subjects reported their preferred program in quiet to be slightly better than other programs, two reported them moderately better and the remaining three subjects reported them as very similar to other programs. For speech in noise (figure 11), four subjects rated their preferred program in noise as moderately better than other programs; two subjects rated them much better than other programs; two subjects rated them slightly better and the remaining two reported them as very similar to other programs.

3.3.4. Relationship between questionnaire results and speech perception outcomes

The questionnaire results were described in terms of average ratings of helpfulness and the subject's first preferences in quiet, noise and overall. For nine out of the ten subjects there was consistency in the average helpfulness ratings in noise and the subjects' first preferences in noise. There was no close relation between the helpfulness ratings and the first preferences in quiet.

There does not appear to be a close relationship between each subject's subjective preference and the rate program that provided best speech perception. Only two subjects (subject 1 and 8), who scored consistently better on a particular rate program in quiet and noise, chose that program as the most preferred. However, only subject 1 showed consistency between speech test outcomes and helpfulness ratings in quiet and noise. One subject showed consistency between the rate program that provided best speech perception in noise and the most preferred program in noise. Subject 9 scored best with 900 pps/ch rate in noise and preferred this rate in noise. This subject rated 350, 500 and 900 pps/ch equally on helpfulness rating.

For two subjects (subjects 2 and 3) there was a partial agreement between the speech perception scores in noise and the subjective preference. Subject 2 performed best with 900 pps/ch for speech perception in noise, but there was no significant difference in speech performance in noise for 500 and 900 pps/ch. This subject preferred 500 pps/ch stimulation rate in quiet and noise and the average rating of helpfulness in noise was also highest for 500 pps/ch rate. Subject 3 performed best with 500 pps/ch for sentence perception in noise and preferred this program when listening in quiet. This subject preferred 350 pps/ch rate in noise and overall and the average helpfulness rating in noise was highest with this rate program.

Five subjects' (subjects 4, 5, 6, 7 and 10) speech test outcomes did not agree with their subjective preferences. However, the average helpfulness ratings were more or less similar to the first preferences for these five subjects.

At the conclusion of the study, six of the ten subjects (subjects 2, 3, 4, 6, 7 and 10) continued to use a different rate program compared to their everyday rate program (used prior to the commencement of the study). One of these six subjects (subject 6) preferred to continue with the rate program with the best sentence in noise perception score and the remaining five subjects continued with the most preferred program (overall) based on the questionnaire results.

	275 pps/ch	350 pps/ch	500 pps/ch	900 pps/ch	350 = 500 pps/ch	500 = 900 pps/ch
Quiet	0	1	5	2	1	1
Noise	0	2	4	2	1	1
Overall	0	2	4	2	1	1

Table 2. The table shows the number of subjects reporting their first preferences in quiet, noise and overall for the four rate programs.

3.4. Discussion

3.4.1. Speech perception in quiet and noise

The group averaged scores for monosyllables in quiet showed no significant effect of rate. However, significantly better group results for sentence perception in noise were observed for 500 and 900 pps/ch rates compared to 275 pps/ch stimulation rate and for 500 pps/ch compared to 350 pps/ch rate. Individual data analysis showed improvements with stimulation rates of 500 pps/ch or higher in eight out of ten subjects for sentence perception in noise. Three out of these eight subjects showed benefit with 500 pps/ch and four subjects showed benefit with 900 pps/ch rate. One subject showed improvement with both 500 and 900 pps/ch stimulation rates.

Four out of ten subjects were using 250 pps/ch stimulation rate in their clinical fitted processor before the commencement of the study. Two out of these four subjects showed improved performance with 500 pps/ch, one improved with 900 pps/ch, and the remaining subject showed no effect of rate on speech perception. This suggests that subjects had enough time to become familiar with the higher rate conditions. The remaining six subjects in the study had been using stimulation rates ranging between 500-1200 pps/ch prior to commencement of the study. Four out of these six subjects (including the subject who performed equally with 500 and 900 pps/ch) showed improvement with 900 pps/ch stimulation rate. Better speech perception with 900 pps/ch rate could have been due to the prolonged use of higher stimulation rates prior to commencement of the study.

The CNC test results are somewhat consistent with previous studies that used Nucleus devices with the ACE strategy (Vandali et al., 2000; Holden et al., 2002; Plant et al., 2007 and Weber et al., 2007). In these studies, monosyllabic word or consonant perception was not affected by the increasing stimulation rates. Results in this study are also somewhat consistent with a recent clinical trial by Cochlear Ltd. (2007) (Reference Note 1), which showed no significant difference in the lower (500-1200 pps/ch) or higher set of rates (1800-3500 pps/ch) for the subjects tested with CNC words.

Most of the previous studies that used Nucleus devices have reported variable rate effects for CI individuals. Some of the subjects in these studies have shown improvement with increased stimulation rates for some of the speech material. Therefore, these studies emphasize the importance of optimizing stimulation rates for individual cochlear implantees. Their results suggest that increasing stimulation rates could provide clinical benefit to some of the cochlear implantees (Vandali et al., 2000; Holden et al., 2002; Plant et al., 2002; Plant et al., 2007). The variable effect of increasing stimulation rates in these studies is consistent with the results of this study, in that not all subjects preferred or showed improved performance with the highest rate (900 pps/ch) tested. For instance, subject 4 and subject 8 performed significantly better with the 500 pps/ch compared to the 900 pps/ch rate. However, in the studies by Vandali et al. (2000) and Holden et al. (2002) the higher stimulation rates probably did not add any extra temporal information due to the limited update rate in SPrint™ processor (760 Hz). In the SPrint™ processor, stimulation rates below 760 Hz provide new information in every cycle because filter analysis rate is set to equal the stimulation rate; however, stimulation rates above 760 Hz are obtained by repeating stimulus frames. Similarly the results of the study by Holden et al. (2002) may have been compromised by the limited analysis rate in the SPrint™ processor. In contrast to these studies, the current study did not use SPrint™ processors. The current study used ESPrit™ 3G processors which have an update rate of 1 kHz for low level sounds and an update rate of 4 kHz for high level sounds.

Analysis of speech perception results across sessions in this study revealed no significant effect of session for the group CNC scores in quiet. However, a significant effect of session was observed for sentence perception in noise scores. Whilst a session effect was observed (which may well have been due to task/rate program learning), scores for all four rate programs showed similar effects of session. Thus given that a balanced design for evaluation of rate was employed in this study, no one rate condition was advantaged by learning within the study.

3.4.2. Subjective preferences and speech perception

Some individual variability was also observed in subjective preference results, although the majority of subjects chose 500 or 350 pps/ch rates as their first preferences in quiet, noise and overall.

The individual subjective preference findings in this study initially appear at odds with the results of speech perception outcomes in quiet, in which results for seven of the ten subjects showed no significant effect of rate for monosyllables in quiet. However, six of these seven subjects indicated that there was little difference between their preferred rate program and the other rate programs (see figure 10). On the other hand, three of the five subjects (subjects 1, 2, 4, 8 and 9) who showed some consistencies between the speech perception and the subjective preferences in noise indicated that their preferences were reasonably strong and that their preferred programs were moderately/much better than the other rate programs (see figure 11). Two of the five subjects, in which inconsistencies between the speech perception in noise and the subjective preference in noise were observed, indicated a weak preference for their preferred rates. The other three, however indicated a strong preference for their preferred rate.

3.4.3. Clinical ramifications

The present study's findings support previous research, suggesting that optimization of stimulation rate is useful and can lead to better CI recipient outcomes. However, optimization becomes difficult when speech testing outcomes are incompatible with the subject's questionnaire responses. The present study did not reveal a close relation between speech perception outcomes and questionnaire responses. It is possible that the questionnaire data in this study is less likely to be as reliable as the speech perception data. Self reported data in questionnaires is often affected by factors such as how well the subject interprets questions, and compares different rate programs. For example, a recipient may not compare the different rate programs under similar listening conditions. In this study, there was the added difficulty of not being able to toggle between the four rate programs. The recipient instead had to swap processors to compare all four programs. However, all recipients were diligent in taking the two ESPrit™ 3G processors to compare the four rate programs in the 18 listening situations.

Although optimization of stimulation rate appears to be beneficial, time restraints will often prevent clinicians from comparing speech perception outcomes with different stimulation rates. An adaptive procedure called genetic algorithm (Holland, 1975) may offer potential in optimizing stimulation rate along with other parameters. This procedure, based on the genetic "survival of the fittest", guides the recipient through hundreds of processor MAPs towards preferred programs in quiet and in noise. The MAPs vary in terms of speech coding parameters such as, stimulation rate, number of channels, and number of maxima. To date, genetic algorithm (GA) research in experienced CI recipients has not shown better outcomes compared to standard MAPs programmed using default parameters (Wakefield et al., 2005; Lineaweaver et al., 2006). It remains to be seen whether or not the GA algorithm provides significant benefits for newly implanted subjects who are not biased by prolonged use of default parameters such as a particular stimulation rate.

Preference of the majority of subjects in this study for 500 pps/ch rate in quiet, noise and overall is somewhat consistent with the results of Balkany et al. (2007), where 67% of the subjects preferred the slower strategy (ACE) over the faster rate strategy (ACE RE) with the majority of subjects preferring the slowest rate in each strategy (500 pps/ch in ACE and 1800 pps/ch in ACE RE). However, in contrast to the present study, there was no significant effect of rate on the speech perception outcomes in their study.

Subjects who had been using 250 pps/ch stimulation rate for their everyday use prior to commencement of the present study showed improved performance with 500 or 900 pps/ch. In light of this finding, it is recommended that CI recipients who have been using very low stimulation rates should be mapped with either 500 or 900 pps/ch and given an opportunity to trial the higher rate MAP in different listening environments over a number of weeks.

The findings of previous research (Weber et al., 2007; Cochlear Ltd. 2007, Reference Note 1; Balkany et al., 2007) suggest that for majority of the subjects using Nucleus implants, stimulation rates between 500 pps/ch and 1200 pps/ch should be tried. The present investigation's findings are compatible, suggesting that clinicians should program Nucleus recipients with the rates 500 pps/ch or 900 pps/ch. However, it needs to be remembered that the present study's conclusions are based on a limited number of subjects. Clinicians could consider providing the 500 pps/ch rate as an initial option with the ACE strategy. This rate has the advantage of offering increased battery life compared to the 900 pps/ch rate. Then, if time permits, recipients could compare the 500 pps/ch rate to the 900 pps/ch rate. If for example, the recipient prefers 900 pps/ch and test results in noise show better performance for 900 pps/ch compared to 500 pps/ch, he/she could then be given the opportunity to try 1200 pps/ch.

4. Study 2: Effect of stimulation rate on modulation detection

This section provides the details of the study by Arora et al (2010) which determined whether modulation detection at different stimulation rates predicts speech perception at these rates.

4.1. Rationale

Modulation detection thresholds (MDTs) measured electrically have been found to be closely related to the subjects' speech perception ability with CI and auditory brainstem implant (Cazals et al, 1994, Fu, 2002; Colletti and Shannon, 2005). In addition, studies investigating the effect of relatively high and low stimulation rates on MDTs have shown that MDTs are poorer at high stimulation rates (Galvin and Fu, 2005; Pfingst et al., 2007). The study by Galvin and Fu (2005) showed that rate had a significant effect on the MDTs with lower rates (250 pps/ch) having lower thresholds than the higher rates (2000 pps/ch). Similarly, lower MDTs for 250 pps/ch compared to 4000 pps/ch stimulation rate were observed in the study by Pfingst et al. (2007). These studies suggest that the response properties of auditory neurons to electrical stimulation along with limitation imposed by their refractory behavior must be considered in CI systems (Wilson et al., 1997; Rubinstein et al., 1998). Pfingst et al. (2007) also reported that the average MDTs for 250 pps/ch and 4000 pps/ch were lowest at the apical and the basal end of the electrode array respectively.

Across site variations in modulation detection found by Pfingst et al. (2007, 2008) suggest that testing modulation detection only at one or two sites (as in the studies by Shannon, 1992; Busby et al., 1993; Cazals et al, 1994; Fu, 2002; Galvin and Fu, 2005) may not provide a complete assessment of a CI recipient's modulation sensitivity. In addition, in modern CI sound processors, speech is not coded at one or two specific electrode sites. In current filter bank strategies, many electrode sites are stimulated sequentially based on the amplitude spectrum of the input waveform. In a typical ACE strategy, up to 8 to 10 electrodes are selected based on the channels with the greatest amplitude. Thus, when measuring MDTs, it may be more realistic to measure them with speech-like signals, which will measure modulation detection across multiple electrodes.

In the current study, modulation sensitivity for low to moderate stimulation rates was measured using acoustic stimuli. Electrode place and intensity coding of the stimuli was representative of vowel-like signals. The vowel-like stimulus stimulated multiple electrodes as in the ACE strategy. It can be argued that MDTs measured across multiple electrodes may be dominated by a few electrodes due to across electrode variations in stimulus levels. However, in the current study all subjects used MP1+2 mode of stimulation and thus the across electrode variations in stimulation levels were small for all subjects. The depth and frequency of sinusoidal amplitude modulation in the stimulus envelope of each channel was controlled in the experiment. Given that it has been found that CI subjects are most sensitive to the modulations between 50-100 Hz (Shannon, 1992; Busby et al., 1993), modulation frequencies of 50 and 100 Hz were examined. Speech recognition has been found to correlate well with MDTs averaged across various stimulation levels of the electrical dynamic range (Fu, 2002). Therefore, this study presented stimuli at an acoustic level that produced electrical levels close to the subjects' most comfortable loudness (MCL) level of stimulation and at a softer acoustic level of 20 dB below this. In previous CI literature, MDTs have been measured using modulated electrical pulse trains; however, in the present study MDTs were measured using acoustic vowel-like stimuli (referred to as Acoustic MDTs in this chapter). Thus for comparison to previous literature, the Acoustic MDTs were transformed to their equivalent current MDTs (referred to as Electric MDTs in this chapter). Acoustic MDTs were of interest because when stimuli are presented acoustically, the differences among different stimulation rate maps are taken into account as in real-life situations for CI users. It is likely that Acoustic MDTs are affected by the subjects' electrical dynamic ranges which can vary with rate of stimulation. This study examined the influence of electrical dynamic range on Acoustic MDTs.

This study was specifically designed to determine:

- Whether rates of stimulation (between 275 and 900 pps/ch) affect modulation detection for vowel-like signals stimulating multiple electrodes.
- Whether modulation detection at different stimulation rates predicts speech perception at these rates.

4.2. Method

Modulation detection thresholds were measured for the same 10 subjects who had previously participated in study 1. A repeated ABCD experimental design for the four rate conditions was employed. Evaluation order for rate conditions was balanced across subjects. Four MDT data points were recorded for each rate condition at two modulation frequencies and two stimulation levels (4 data points X 4 rates X 2 modulation frequencies X 2 levels) in each phase of the repeated experimental design.

A sinusoidally amplitude modulated acoustic signal with a carrier frequency of 2 kHz was presented to the audio input of a research processor. The research processor maps were based on the map parameters used in study 1. Most strategy parameters (e.g. number of maxima, pulse width, mode) were kept the same as those used in study 1. However, the maps differed from conventional maps in that only one band-pass filter with a bandwidth of 1.5 to 2.5 kHz (center frequency = 2 kHz) was mapped to all the active electrodes in the map. This was done so that all electrodes received the same temporal information for the test stimuli. The electrical threshold and comfortable levels of stimulation for each electrode were taken from the maps used in study 1.

The signal was used to modulate the envelope of electrical pulse trains interleaved across eight electrode sites. The choice of which 8 electrodes were activated in the maps was based on which electrodes were on average activated in conventional maps for the vowels /a/ and /i/ spoken by a male Australian speaker. This was done by analyzing the spectrograms of each vowel (four different tokens per vowel) and measuring the spectral magnitude at frequencies which coincided with the center frequencies of the bands used in the conventional maps. Two separate vowel maps, one for each vowel, with different sets of fixed electrodes were created. The SAM acoustic stimuli when presented through the experimental map thus provided vowel-like place coding and a SAM temporal envelope code on each channel activated. In addition, the modulation frequency and depth could be controlled systematically via the input SAM signal. For convenience this stimulus will be referred to as a vowel-like SAM stimulus throughout this study.

Modulation frequencies of 50 and100 Hz were presented at an acoustic level that produced electrical levels close to the subjects' most comfortable level (MCL) of stimulation and at an acoustic level 20 dB below this. Modulation depth was varied in the 3AFC task to obtain a threshold level where the subject could discriminate between the modulated and unmodulated waveform for a particular modulation frequency. A jitter of +/- 3 dB was applied to minimize any loudness effects on measurement of MDTs.

4.3. Results

4.3.1. Stimulation rate effect on electrical dynamic range

As stimulation rate increased from 250 to 900 pps/ch, mean DR (averaged across the eight most active electrodes that were selected as maxima when coding vowels /a/ and /i/) increased from 40.5 to 51.7 CL (or from ~6.9 dB to 8.9 dB in current) for the vowel /a/ map and from 37.6 to 47.8 CL (or from ~6.5 dB to 8.2 dB in current) for the vowel /i/ map. These levels were obtained after all four rate programs were balanced for loudness.

4.3.2. Effects of stimulation rate, modulation frequency and presentation level on MDTs

4.3.2.1. Acoustic MDTs

Figure 13 shows Acoustic MDTs for the two modulation frequencies and four stimulation rate conditions measured at MCL in the left most panels (a, c, and e) and at MCL-20 dB in the right most panels (b, d, and f). MDTs are shown separately for each vowel in the top and middle panels (a and b for vowel /a/, c and d for vowel /i/) and averaged across both vowels in the bottom panels (e and f).

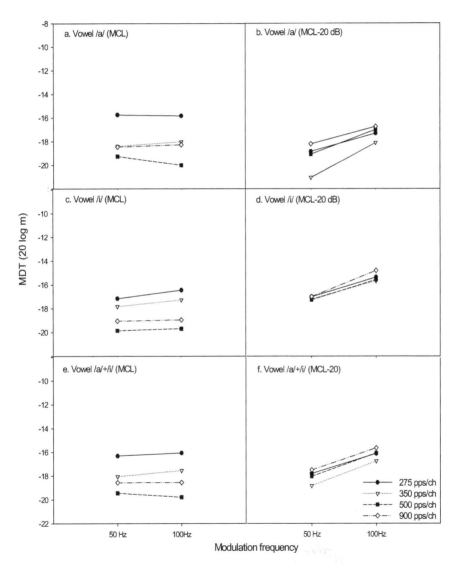

Figure 13. Acoustic MDTs, averaged across the subject group, measured at MCL and MCL-20 dB for two modulation frequencies and four stimulation rates.

Repeated measures analysis of variance for Acoustic MDTs averaged across the two vowels revealed a significant effect of rate (F [3, 27] = 3.6, p = 0.026). The Mauchley test of Sphericity showed that sphericity was violated for the rate effect. However, the effect remained significant after the G-G (Greenhouse and Geisser, 1959) correction was applied to the degrees of freedom and the p values.

Post-hoc comparisons for the effect of rate revealed significantly lower MDTs for 500 pps/ch compared to 275 pps/ch rate. There were no significant effects of the other main factors, "modulation frequency" and "level", on MDTs. The interaction between rate and modulation frequency was not significant, but there was a significant interaction between rate and level. Post-hoc comparisons revealed significantly lower MDTs for 500 and 900 pps/ch rates compared to 275 pps/ch rate at MCL, but no significant effect of rate at MCL-20 dB. MDTs at MCL were significantly lower than those at MCL-20 dB for the rate of 500 pps/ch. The interaction between modulation frequency and level was significant. MDTs for 50 Hz were significantly lower than those for 100 Hz modulation at MCL-20 dB and MDTs at MCL were significantly lower compared to those at MCL-20 dB for the modulation frequency of 100 Hz. A similar pattern of results to those above were observed for separate analyses of each vowel.

4.3.2.2. Electric MDTs

Figure 14 shows Electric MDTs, averaged across the subject group, for the two modulation frequencies and four stimulation rate programs measured at MCL and MCL-20 dB level. Repeated measures three-way analysis of variance for Electric MDTs averaged across the two vowels revealed a significant effect of rate (F [3, 27] = 3.54, p = 0.028), modulation frequency (F [1, 27] = 6.66, p = 0.030), and level (F [1,27] = 78.88, p < 0.001). The sphericity assumption was violated for the effect of rate; however, the effect remained significant after the G-G correction was applied.

Post-hoc comparisons for the rate effect revealed no significant comparisons between pairs of stimulation rates. Post-hoc comparisons for the effect of modulation frequency revealed significantly lower MDTs for 50 Hz compared to those for 100 Hz modulation frequency and the post-hoc comparisons for the effect of level revealed significantly lower MDTs at MCL compared to those at MCL-20 dB.

The interaction between rate and modulation frequency was not significant. Interaction between rate and level was significant. At MCL-20 dB, MDTs for 900 pps/ch rate were significantly poorer than all other stimulation rates whereas there was no significant effect of rate at MCL. MDTs at MCL were significantly lower than those at MCL-20 dB for all stimulation rates. The interaction effect between modulation frequency and level was also significant. At MCL, there was no significant effect of modulation frequency on MDTs whereas at MCL-20 dB, MDTs for 50 Hz were significantly lower than those at 100 Hz modulation frequency. MDTs at MCL were significantly lower compared to those at MCL-20 dB for both modulation frequencies (50 and 100 Hz) Again, similar patterns of results to those above at MCL and MCL-20 dB were observed for separate analyses of each vowel.

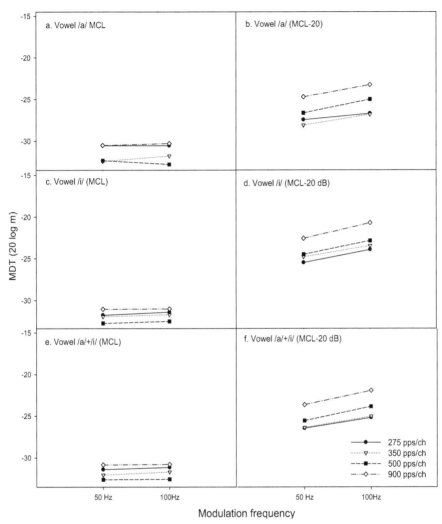

Figure 14. Electric MDTs, averaged across the subject group, measured at MCL and MCL-20 dB for two modulation frequencies and four stimulation rates.

4.3.2.3. Relationship between the speech perception outcomes and MDTs

Analysis of covariance (ANCOVA) to assess the effect of MDTs averaged across both stimulation levels (MCL and MCL-20 dB) on speech perception results (study 1) showed no significant relationships between Acoustic or Electric MDTs and speech perception in quiet and noise. Similar results were obtained on a separate analysis for the Acoustic and Electric MDTs measured at MCL-20 dB.

Results of the ANCOVA showed that MDTs (averaged across 50 and 100 Hz modulation frequencies) at different simulation rates at MCL predicted sentences in noise outcomes (SRTs) at these stimulation rates (F [1, 29] = 9.26, p = 0.005). Lower MDTs were associated with lower SRTs. The ANCOVA results also revealed that the estimate for the average slope for subjects was 0.35 (se = 0.11). There were no significant effects of Acoustic or Electric MDTs measured at MCL on speech perception in quiet (CNC scores).

ANCOVA results to assess the effect of electrical dynamic range on SRTs showed a significant relationship between electrical dynamic range and SRTs (F [1, 29] = 5.52, p = 0.026). The estimate for the average slope for subjects was -0.084 (se = 0.035).

4.4. Discussion

4.4.1. Effects of modulation frequency and presentation level on MDTs

Both Acoustic and Electric MDTs were significantly lower for 50 Hz compared to 100 Hz modulation frequency at the lower presentation level (MCL-20 dB). These results are somewhat consistent with the findings of previous studies in which a progressive increase in modulation thresholds for modulation frequencies above approximately 100 Hz has been reported (Shannon, 1992; and Busby et al., 1993). The Electric MDTs (averaged across 50 and 100 Hz modulation frequencies) presented at MCL were either equivalent to, or better than, those at MCL-20 dB for all rates examined. The Acoustic MDTs at MCL were significantly better than those at MCL-20 dB for 500 pps/ch for MDTs averaged across 50 and 100 Hz. These findings are compatible with those of previous studies (Shannon, 1992; Fu, 2002; Galvin and Fu, 2005; Pfingst et al., 2007).

4.4.2. Effects of stimulation rate on MDTs

Significant effects of stimulation rate were found for MDTs; however the effects varied between presentation levels and between how MDTs were defined. For Electric MDTs, which were derived from the modulation depth of current levels (in μA) averaged across the stimulated electrodes, best MDTs were observed for rates of 500 pps/ch or lower, and poorest MDTs were obtained at 900 pps/ch. This trend was significant at the lower presentation level (MCL-20 dB).In contrast, for Acoustic MDTs derived directly from the modulation depth in the SAM stimulus; the effect of rate was somewhat different and varied across level. At the high presentation level (MCL), best MDTs were observed for rates of 500 pps/ch or higher, and poorest thresholds were observed at the lower stimulation rates. No significant effect of rate was observed at MCL-20 dB.

The differences across rates between the Acoustic and Electric MDTs can be partially attributed to differences in the range of electrical current levels employed across each rate map. Because the electrical dynamic range employed in maps increased with increasing stimulation rate, a smaller depth of modulation in the acoustic input signal is required for higher rate maps in order to produce the same range of modulation in electrical current levels coded for each rate map. Thus, the effects observed for MDTs expressed in acoustic levels in which modulation sensitivity was better at 900 pps/ch compared to 350 and 275 pps/ch, can be partly accounted for by the increase in electrical dynamic range that was coded in the higher rate maps, at least for MDTs measured at the higher presentation level. At the lower presentation level, it is likely that the increased dynamic range at 900 pps/ch rate could not compensate for the poorer Electric MDTs obtained at that rate.

It can be argued that differences in the absolute current levels at each rate examined (due to different T and C levels for each rate program) might have affected the MDT results. This effect could be more pronounced at MCL-20 dB level, because the effects of stimulation rate on loudness summation are larger at lower stimulation levels (McKay and McDermott, 1998; McKay et al., 2001) which is consistent with the reduction in T levels with increasing rate noted in the current study. However, care was taken to loudness balance all rate programs and thus absolute differences in current levels coded for each rate condition are unlikely to have translated to substantial differences in loudness across rates.

There is some psychophysical evidence (Galvin and Fu, 2005 and Pfingst et al., 2007) to support the findings of the current study, although these studies explored a different range of stimulation rates and modulation frequencies. They did report better MDTs for lower stimulation rates (250 pps/ch) compared to the higher stimulation rates (≥ 2000 pps/ch) which is consistent with the poorer Electric MDTs found at 900 pps/ch compared to the lower rates in the present study.

4.4.3. Relationship between modulation detection and speech perception

This study did not observe significant relationship between speech perception and Acoustic or Electric MDTs averaged across MCL and MCL-20 dB. This finding is inconsistent with the previous findings which reported a significant correlation between speech perception scores and average modulation detection thresholds at various stimulation levels across the dynamic range (Fu, 2002; Luo et al., 2008).This difference may be in part attributed to the fact that the mean MDTs which were measured through direct electrical stimulation in these previous studies across the various levels of dynamic range are not comparable to the mean MDTs measured at only two stimulation levels in the present study. These studies did not report relationships between speech perception and MDTs at specific stimulation levels. In addition, stimulation rate was not examined in these studies.

For modulation detection measured at MCL, significant effects of Acoustic MDTs and electrical dynamic range (DR) on speech recognition in noise were found in the present study. Acoustic MDTs were of interest, because for both speech and modulation tests, the stimuli were presented through sound processor maps and thus the effects of electrical stimulation level differences between maps with different dynamic ranges were taken into account. Furthermore, a positive correlation between electrical DR and speech test results in noise suggests that the increase in electrical DR with rate contributed to the increase in speech test scores in noise with rate, at least for rates up to 500 pps/ch. These results were somewhat consistent with the previous findings by Pfingst and Xu (2005) which showed that subjects with larger mean dynamic range had better speech recognition in quiet and noise.

At the highest rate (900 pps/ch), speech perception results were equal to, or worse, than those at 500 pps/ch, particularly for the speech in noise test. In addition, Electric MDTs were poorest at 900 pps/ch compared to 500 pps/ch, which is consistent with findings of other studies where poorer MDTs were observed for higher rates of stimulation (e.g., Galvin and Fu, 2005 and Pfingst et al., 2007). Thus, the benefits to speech perception obtained with an increase in electrical DR may be offset by a reduction in modulation detection sensitivity with increasing rate. The rate for which the effect of increased electrical DR is counteracted by a decrease in modulation detection sensitivity is likely to vary between subjects, speech material, and presentation levels. For the subjects in the current study, although a rate of 500 pps/ch was found to provide the best speech perception results, it is possible that some other rate between 500 and 900 pps/ch, or perhaps even higher, may have provided better speech perception results and/or a better correlation with the electrical DR and modulation detection sensitivity.

At the lower presentation levels (MCL-20 dB), MDTs (Acoustic and Electric) did not correlate with speech perception outcomes. Similar findings were observed by Chatterjee and Peng (2008). In their study no significant correlation was obtained between MDTs measured at soft levels (i.e., at 50% of the dynamic range) and speech intonation recognition presented at comfortable levels.

4.4.4. Clinical ramifications

An interesting observation of the current study was that the effect of rate on MDTs and speech perception was not monotonic and that lowest (best) MDTs were obtained at a rate of 500 pps/ch. Furthermore, no significant benefit in speech perception was obtained using the higher rate of 900 pps/ch. Thus, clinicians could consider providing the 500 pps/ch rate as an initial option with the ACE strategy, which also has the advantage of offering increased battery life compared to the higher stimulation rates. However, it needs to be remembered that the present study's conclusions are based on a limited number of subjects and that rates between 500 and 900 pps/ch, or even higher, were not examined. Such rates may have provided benefits to speech perception above those obtained at a rate of 500 pps/ch.

5. Conclusion

The above studies investigated the effect of slow and moderate stimulation rates on speech perception and modulation detection in recipients of the Nucleus cochlear implant. Group results for sentence perception in noise showed improved performance for 500 and/or 900 pps/ch stimulation rates but no significant rate effect was observed for monosyllabic perception in quiet. Most subjects preferred the 500 pps/ch stimulation rate in noise. However, a close relationship between each subject's subjective preference and the rate program that provided best speech perception was not observed.

The variable outcomes obtained in the reported studies on stimulation rate could be influenced by factors such as audiological history, length of implant use, and duration of hearing loss, speech processing strategy employed or the implant system used by the implantee. Given the variability of these factors across subjects, it may be important to optimize the stimulation rate for an individual cochlear implantee.

In study 2, cochlear implant subjects' speech perception was compared with their psychoacoustic temporal processing abilities. The aim was to find an objective method for optimizing stimulation rates for cochlear implantees. This study uniquely used multi-channel stimuli to measure modulation detection. Best Acoustic MDTs at MCL were obtained at a rate of 500 pps/ch. MDTs at 900 pps/ch rate were slightly worse and poorest results were observed at the lower rates. No significant effect of rate was observed for Acoustic MDTs at MCL-20 dB. For Electric MDTs at MCL-20 dB, best MDTs were obtained for rates of 500 pps/ch or lower, and poorest MDTs were obtained at 900 pps/ch. Acoustic MDTs are a realistic measure of MDTs since they take into account the map differences in dynamic range across stimulation rates. Acoustic MDTs at MCL at different stimulation rates predicted sentence perception in noise at these rates.

5.1. Future research

The ESPrit™ 3G processor offers an option to use a stimulation rate of 720 pps/ch, which was not evaluated in the current study. It would have been interesting to investigate sentence perception in noise with 720 pps/ch for subjects 4 and 8 who showed benefit with 500 pps/ch but showed deterioration with 900 pps/ch. The future work could explore the relationship between speech perception and modulation detection across higher rates of stimulation (>900 pps/ch). In addition, speech perception tests could also be carried out at softer levels to examine possible correlations with MDTs measured at softer levels.

Author details

Komal Arora and Richard Dowell
Department of Otolaryngology, The University of Melbourne, Australia

Pam Dawson
The HEARing CRC, Australia

Acknowledgement

The author would like to express appreciation to the research subjects who participated in studies one and two. The studies were supported by University of Melbourne

Notes

1. Cochlear Ltd. 2007. Selecting stimulation rate with the Nucleus freedom system. White paper prepared by Cochlear Ltd.

6. References

Arora, K., Dawson, P., Dowell, R. C., Vandali A. E. (2009). Electrical stimulation rate effects on speech perception in cochlear implants. International Journal of Audiology, Vol 48 (8).

Arora, K., Vandali A. E., Dawson, P., Dowell, R. C. (2010). Effects of electrical stimulation rate on modulation detection and speech recognition by cochlear implant users. International Journal of Audiology Vol 50 (2).

Assmann, P. F., & Summerfield, Q. (1990). Modeling the perception of concurrent vowels: vowels with different fundamental frequencies. *J Acoust Soc Am, 88*(2), 680-697.

Bacon, S. P., & Viemeister, N. F. (1985). Temporal modulation transfer functions in normal-hearing and hearing-impaired listeners. *Audiology, 24*(2), 117-134.

Balkany, T., Hodges, A., Menapace, C., Hazard, L., Driscoll, C., Gantz, B., et al. (2007). Nucleus Freedom North American clinical trial. *Otolaryngol Head Neck Surg, 136*(5), 757-762.

Baskent, D., & Shannon, R. V. (2004). Frequency-place compression and expansion in cochlear implant listeners. *J Acoust Soc Am, 116*(5), 3130-3140.

Brokx, J. P. L., & Nooteboom, S. G. (1982). Intonation and perceptual seperation of simultaneous voices. *Journal of Phonetics, 10*, 23- 36.

Burian, K. (1979). [Clinical observations in electric stimulation of the ear (author's transl)]. *Arch Otorhinolaryngol, 223*(1), 139-166.

Burns, E. M., & Viemeister, N. F. (1976). Nonspectral pitch. *J Acoust Soc Am, 60*(4), 863-869.

Busby, P. A., & Clark, G. M. (2000). Pitch estimation by early-deafened subjects using a multiple-electrode cochlear implant. *J Acoust Soc Am, 107*(1), 547-558.

Busby, P. A., Tong, Y. C., & Clark, G. M. (1993). The perception of temporal modulations by cochlear implant patients. *J Acoust Soc Am, 94*(1), 124-131.

Busby, P. A., Whitford, L. A., Blamey, P. J., Richardson, L. M., & Clark, G. M. (1994). Pitch perception for different modes of stimulation using the cochlear multiple-electrode prosthesis. *J Acoust Soc Am, 95*(5 Pt 1), 2658-2669.

Cazals, Y., Pelizzone, M., Saudan, O., & Boex, C. (1994). Low-pass filtering in amplitude modulation detection associated with vowel and consonant identification in subjects with cochlear implants. *J Acoust Soc Am, 96*(4), 2048-2054.

Chatterjee, M., & Peng, S. C. (2008). Processing F0 with cochlear implants: Modulation frequency discrimination and speech intonation recognition. *Hear Res, 235*(1-2), 143-156.

Clark, G. M., Black, R., Forster, I. C., Patrick, J. F., & Tong, Y. C. (1978). Design criteria of a multiple-electrode cochlear implant hearing prosthesis [43.66.Ts, 43.66.Sr]. *J Acoust Soc Am, 63*(2), 631-633.

Cohen, L. T., Busby, P. A., Whitford, L. A., & Clark, G. M. (1996). Cochlear implant place psychophysics 1. Pitch estimation with deeply inserted electrodes. *Audiol Neurootol, 1*(5), 265-277.

Cohen, N. L., and Waltzman, S. B. (1993). Partial insertion of the Nucleus multichannel cochlear implant: Technique and results, Am. J. Otol, 14(4), 357–361.

Colletti, V., & Shannon, R. V. (2005). Open set speech perception with auditory brainstem implant? *Laryngoscope, 115*(11), 1974-1978.

Cowan, B. (March, 2007). *Historical and BioSafety Overview*. Paper presented at the Cochlear Implant Training Workshop, Bionic Ear Institute, Melbourne.

Donaldson, G. S., & Nelson, D. A. (2000). Place-pitch sensitivity and its relation to consonant recognition by cochlear implant listeners using the MPEAK and SPEAK speech processing strategies. *J Acoust Soc Am, 107*(3), 1645-1658.

Dorman, M. F., Loizou, P. C., Fitzke, J., & Tu, Z. (1998). The recognition of sentences in noise by normal-hearing listeners using simulations of cochlear-implant signal processors with 6-20 channels. *J Acoust Soc Am, 104*(6), 3583-3585.

Dynes, S. B., & Delgutte, B. (1992). Phase-locking of auditory-nerve discharges to sinusoidal electric stimulation of the cochlea. *Hear Res, 58*(1), 79-90.

Eddington, D. K., Dobelle, W. H., Brackmann, D. E., Mladejovsky, M. G., & Parkin, J. L. (1978). Auditory prostheses research with multiple channel intracochlear stimulation in man. *Ann Otol Rhinol Laryngol, 87*(6 Pt 2), 1-39.

Fearn, R., & Wolfe, J. (2000). Relative importance of rate and place: experiments using pitch scaling techniques with cochlear implants recipients. *Ann Otol Rhinol Laryngol Suppl, 185*, 51-53.

Fletcher, H. (1940). Auditory Patterns. *Reviews of Modern Physics, 12*, 47-65.

Friesen, L. M., Shannon, R. V., Baskent, D., & Wang, X. (2001). Speech recognition in noise as a function of the number of spectral channels: comparison of acoustic hearing and cochlear implants. *J Acoust Soc Am, 110*(2), 1150-1163.

Fu, Q. J. (2002). Temporal processing and speech recognition in cochlear implant users. *Neuroreport, 13*(13), 1635-1639.

Fu, Q. J., Chinchilla, S., & Galvin, J. J. (2004). The role of spectral and temporal cues in voice gender discrimination by normal-hearing listeners and cochlear implant users. *J Assoc Res Otolaryngol, 5*(3), 253-260.

Fu, Q. J., & Shannon, R. V. (2000). Effect of stimulation rate on phoneme recognition by nucleus-22 cochlear implant listeners. *J Acoust Soc Am, 107*(1), 589-597.

Fu, Q. J., Shannon, R. V., & Wang, X. (1998). Effects of noise and spectral resolution on vowel and consonant recognition: acoustic and electric hearing. *J Acoust Soc Am, 104*(6), 3586-3596.

Galvin, J. J., 3rd, & Fu, Q. J. (2005). Effects of stimulation rate, mode and level on modulation detection by cochlear implant users. *J Assoc Res Otolaryngol, 6*(3), 269-279.

Glasberg, B. R., & Moore, B. C. (1986). Auditory filter shapes in subjects with unilateral and bilateral cochlear impairments. *J Acoust Soc Am, 79*(4), 1020-1033.

Holden, L. K., Skinner, M. W., Holden, T. A., & Demorest, M. E. (2002). Effects of stimulation rate with the Nucleus 24 ACE speech coding strategy. *Ear Hear, 23*(5), 463-476.

Holland, J. H. (1975). *Adaptation in Natural and Artificial Systems: An Introductory Analysis with Applications to Biology, Control, and Artificial Intelligence:* Arbor, MI: University of Michigan Press.

Ketten, D. R., Skinner, M. W., Wang, G., Vannier, M. W., Gates, G. A., & Neely, J. G. (1998). In vivo measures of cochlear length and insertion depth of nucleus cochlear implant electrode arrays. *Ann Otol Rhinol Laryngol Suppl, 175*, 1-16.

Kiefer, J., Hohl, S., Sturzebecher, E., Pfennigdorff, T., & Gstoettner, W. (2001). Comparison of speech recognition with different speech coding strategies (SPEAK, CIS, and ACE) and their relationship to telemetric measures of compound action potentials in the nucleus CI 24M cochlear implant system. *Audiology, 40*(1), 32-42.

Kiefer, J., von Ilberg, C., Rupprecht, V., Hubner-Egner, J., & Knecht, R. (2000). Optimized speech understanding with the continuous interleaved sampling speech coding strategy in patients with cochlear implants: effect of variations in stimulation rate and number of channels. *Ann Otol Rhinol Laryngol, 109*(11), 1009-1020.

Loizou, P. C. (1998). Mimicking the human ear. *IEEE Signal Processing Magazine, 15*, 101-130.

Loizou, P. C., Poroy, O., & Dorman, M. (2000). The effect of parametric variations of cochlear implant processors on speech understanding. *J Acoust Soc Am, 108*(2), 790-802.

Luo, X., Fu, Q. J., Wei, C. G., & Cao, K. L. (2008). Speech recognition and temporal amplitude modulation processing by Mandarin-speaking cochlear implant users. *Ear Hear, 29*(6), 957-970.

Magner, M. E. (1972). A speech intelligibility test for Deaf Children (Clark School for the Deaf, Northhampton, MA).

McDermott, H. J., McKay, C. M., & Vandali, A. E. (1992). A new portable sound processor for the University of Melbourne/Nucleus Limited multielectrode cochlear implant. *J Acoust Soc Am, 91*(6), 3367-3371.

McDermott, H. J. (2004). Music perception with cochlear implants: a review. *Trends Amplif, 8*(2), 49-82.

McKay, C. M., & McDermott, H. J. (1998). Loudness perception with pulsatile electrical stimulation: the effect of interpulse intervals. *J Acoust Soc Am, 104*(2 Pt 1), 1061-1074.

McKay, C. M., Remine, M. D., & McDermott, H. J. (2001). Loudness summation for pulsatile electrical stimulation of the cochlea: effects of rate, electrode separation, level, and mode of stimulation. *J Acoust Soc Am, 110*(3 Pt 1), 1514-1524.

Meddis, R., & Hewitt, M. J. (1991). Virtual pitch and phase sensitivity of a computer model of the auditory periphery. I: Pitch identification. *J Acoust Soc Am, 89*(6), 2866-2882.

Middlebrooks, J. C. (2008). Cochlear-implant high pulse rate and narrow electrode configuration impair transmission of temporal information to the auditory cortex. *J Neurophysiol, 100*(1), 92-107.

Moore, B. C., & Glasberg, B. R. (2001). Temporal modulation transfer functions obtained using sinusoidal carriers with normally hearing and hearing-impaired listeners. *J Acoust Soc Am, 110*(2), 1067-1073.

Moore, B. C. J., & Carlyon, R. P. (2005). Perception of pitch by people with cochlear hearing loss and by cochlear implant users. In C. J. Plack, A. J. Oxenham, R. R. Fay & A. N. Popper (Eds.), *Pitch: Neural Coding and Perception* (Vol. 24, pp. 234-277): New York: Springer-Verlag.

Moore, B. (2008). Basic auditory processes involved in the analysis of speech sounds. *Philo Trans Roy Soc B-Bio Sc, 363*(1493), 947-963.

Nelson, D. A., Van Tasell, D. J., Schroder, A. C., Soli, S., & Levine, S. (1995). Electrode ranking of "place pitch" and speech recognition in electrical hearing. *J Acoust Soc Am, 98*(4), 1987-1999.

Nie, K., Barco, A., & Zeng, F. G. (2006). Spectral and temporal cues in cochlear implant speech perception. *Ear Hear, 27*(2), 208-217.

Parkins, C. W. (1989). Temporal response patterns of auditory nerve fibers to electrical stimulation in deafened squirrel monkeys. *Hear Res, 41*(2-3), 137-168.

Pasanisi, E., Bacciu, A., Vincenti, V., Guida, M., Berghenti, M. T., Barbot, A., et al. (2002). Comparison of speech perception benefits with SPEAK and ACE coding strategies in pediatric Nucleus CI24M cochlear implant recipients. *Int J Pediatr Otorhinolaryngol, 64*(2), 159-163.

Pfingst, B. E., Zwolan, T. A., & Holloway, L. A. (1997). Effects of stimulus configuration on psychophysical operating levels and on speech recognition with cochlear implants. *Hear Res, 112*(1-2), 247-260.

Pfingst, B. E., Xu, L., & Thompson, C. S. (2007). Effects of carrier pulse rate and stimulation site on modulation detection by subjects with cochlear implants. *J Acoust Soc Am, 121*(4), 2236-2246.

Pialoux, P. (1976). [Cochlear implants]. *Acta Otorhinolaryngol Belg, 30*(6), 567-568.

Plant, K., Holden, L., Skinner, M., Arcaroli, J., Whitford, L., Law, M. A., et al. (2007). Clinical evaluation of higher stimulation rates in the nucleus research platform 8 system. *Ear Hear, 28*(3), 381-393.

Psarros, C. E., Plant, K. L., Lee, K., Decker, J. A., Whitford, L. A., & Cowan, R. S. (2002). Conversion from the SPEAK to the ACE strategy in children using the nucleus 24 cochlear implant system: speech perception and speech production outcomes. *Ear Hear, 23*(1 Suppl), 18S-27S.

Rosen, S. (1992). Temporal information in speech: acoustic, auditory and linguistic aspects. *Philos Trans R Soc Lond B Biol Sci, 336*(1278), 367-373.

Rubinstein, J. T., Abbas, P.J., & Miller, C. A. (1998). *The neurophysiological effects of simulated audtitory prostheses stimulation.* Paper presented at the Eighth Quarterly Progress Report N01- DC- 6 2111.

Rubinstein, J. T., Wilson, B. S., Finley, C. C., & Abbas, P. J. (1999). Pseudospontaneous activity: stochastic independence of auditory nerve fibers with electrical stimulation. *Hear Res, 127*(1-2), 108-118.

Seligman, P., & McDermott, H. (1995). Architecture of the Spectra 22 speech processor. *Ann Otol Rhinol Laryngol Suppl, 166*, 139-141.

Seligman, P. (March, 2007). Behind-The-Ear Speech Processors. Paper presented at Cochlear Implant Training Workshop, Bionic Ear Institute, Melbourne.

Shannon, R. V. (1983). Multichannel electrical stimulation of the auditory nerve in man. I. Basic psychophysics. *Hear Res, 11*(2), 157-189.

Shannon, R. V. (1992). Temporal modulation transfer functions in patients with cochlear implants. *J Acoust Soc Am, 91*(4 Pt 1), 2156-2164.

Shannon, R. V., Zeng, F. G., Kamath, V., Wygonski, J., & Ekelid, M. (1995). Speech recognition with primarily temporal cues. *Science, 270*(5234), 303-304.

Simmons, F. B. (1966). Electrical stimulation of the auditory nerve in man. *Arch Otolaryngol, 84*(1), 2-54.

Skinner, M. W., Arndt, P. L., & Staller, S. J. (2002a). Nucleus 24 advanced encoder conversion study: performance versus preference. *Ear Hear, 23*(1 Suppl), 2S-17S.

Skinner, M. W., Holden, L. K., Whitford, L. A., Plant, K. L., Psarros, C., & Holden, T. A. (2002b). Speech recognition with the nucleus 24 SPEAK, ACE, and CIS speech coding strategies in newly implanted adults. Ear Hear, 23(3), 207-223.

Skinner, M. W., Ketten, D. R., Holden, L. K., Harding, G. W., Smith, P. G.,Gates, G. A., Neely, J. G., Kletzker, G. R., Brunsden, B., and Blocker, B. (2002c). CT-Derived estimation of cochlear morphology and electrode array position in relation to word recognition in Nucleus 22 recipients. J.Assoc. Res. Otolaryngol, 3(3), 332–350.

Stark, H., & Tuteur, F. B. (1979). *Modern Electrical Communications*: Englewood Cliffs, NJ: Prentice-Hall.

Tong, Y. C., Black, R. C., Clark, G. M., Forster, I. C., Millar, J. B., O'Loughlin, B. J., et al. (1979). A preliminary report on a multiple-channel cochlear implant operation. *J Laryngol Otol, 93*(7), 679-695.

Tong, Y. C., Clark, G. M., Blamey, P. J., Busby, P. A., & Dowell, R. C. (1982). Psychophysical studies for two multiple-channel cochlear implant patients. *J Acoust Soc Am, 71*(1), 153-160.

Townshend, B., Cotter, N., Van Compernolle, D., & White, R. L. (1987). Pitch perception by cochlear implant subjects. *J Acoust Soc Am, 82*(1), 106-115.

Vandali, A. E., Sucher, C., Tsang, D. J., McKay, C. M., Chew, J. W. D., & McDermott, H. J. (2005). Pitch ranking ability of cochlear implant recipients: A comparison of sound-processing strategies. *J Acoust Soc Am, 117*(5), 3126.

Vandali, A. E., Whitford, L. A., Plant, K. L., & Clark, G. M. (2000). Speech perception as a function of electrical stimulation rate: using the Nucleus 24 cochlear implant system. *Ear Hear, 21*(6), 608-624.

Verschuur, C. A. (2005). Effect of stimulation rate on speech perception in adult users of the Med-El CIS speech processing strategy. *Int J Audiol, 44*(1), 58-63.

Viemeister, N. F. (1979). Temporal modulation transfer functions based upon modulation thresholds. *J Acoust Soc Am, 66*(5), 1364-1380.

Weber, B. P., Lai, W. K., Dillier, N., von Wallenberg, E. L., Killian, M. J., Pesch, J., et al. (2007). Performance and preference for ACE stimulation rates obtained with nucleus RP 8 and freedom system. *Ear Hear, 28*(2 Suppl), 46S-48S.

Wilson, B. S. (1991). Better speech recognition with cochlear implants. *Nature, 352*(6332), 236-238.

Wilson, B. S., Finley, C. C., Lawson, D. T., Wolford, R. D., & Zerbi, M. (1993). Design and evaluation of a continuous interleaved sampling (CIS) processing strategy for multichannel cochlear implants. *J Rehabil Res Dev, 30*(1), 110-116.

Wilson, B. S., Finley, C. C., Lawson, D. T., & Zerbi, M. (1997). Temporal representations with cochlear implants. *Am J Otol, 18*(6 Suppl), S30-34.

Wilson, B. S., Rebscher, S., Zeng, F. G., Shannon, R. V., Loeb, G. E., Lawson, D. T., et al. (1998). Design for an inexpensive but effective cochlear implant. *Otolaryngol Head Neck Surg, 118*(2), 235-241.

Xu, L., Thompson, C. S., & Pfingst, B. E. (2005). Relative contributions of spectral and temporal cues for phoneme recognition. *J Acoust Soc Am, 117*(5), 3255-3267.

Xu, L., Tsai, Y., & Pfingst, B. E. (2002). Features of stimulation affecting tonal-speech perception: implications for cochlear prostheses. *J Acoust Soc Am, 112*(1), 247-258.

Speech Modelling

## Chapter 11

Cross-Word Arabic Pronunciation Variation Modeling Using Part of Speech Tagging

Dia AbuZeina, Husni Al-Muhtaseb and Moustafa Elshafei

Additional information is available at the end of the chapter

1. Introduction

Speech recognition is often used as the front-end for many natural language processing (NLP) applications. Some of these applications include machine translation, information retrieval and extraction, voice dialing, call routing, speech synthesis/recognition, data entry, dictation, control, etc. Thus, much research work has been done to improve the speech recognition and the related NLP applications. However, speech recognition has some obstacles that should be considered. Pronunciation variations and small words misrecognition are two major problems that lead to performance reduction. Pronunciation variations problem can be divided into two parts: within-word variations and cross-word variations. These two types of pronunciation variations have been tackled by many researchers using different approaches. For example, cross-word problem can be solved using phonological rules and/or small-word merging. (AbuZeina et al., 2011a) used the phonological rules to model cross-word variations for Arabic. For English, (Saon & Padmanabhan, 2001) demonstrated that short words are more frequently misrecognized, they also had achieved a statistically significant enhancement using small-word merging approach.

An automatic speech recognition (ASR) system uses a decoder to perform the actual recognition task. The decoder finds the most likely words sequence for the given utterance using Viterbi algorithm. The ASR decoder task might be seen as an alignment process between the observed phonemes and the reference phonemes (dictionary phonemic transcription). Intuitively, to have a better accuracy in any alignment process, long sequences are highly favorable instead of short ones. As such, we expect enhancement if we merge words (short or long). Hence fore, a thorough investigation was performed on Arabic speech to discover a suitable merging cases. We found that Arabic speakers usually augment two consecutive words; a noun that is followed by an adjective and a preposition that is followed by a word. Even though we believe that other cases are found in Arabic speech, we chose two cases to validate our proposed method. Among the ASR components, the pronunciation dictionary and the language model were used to model our above mentioned objective. This means that the acoustic models for the baseline and the enhanced method are the same.

This research work is conducted for Modern Standard Arabic (MSA). So, the work will necessarily contain many examples in Arabic. Therefore, it would be appropriate for the reader if we start first by providing a Romanization (Ryding, 2005) of the Arabic letters and diacritical marks. Table 1 shows the Arabic–Roman letters mapping table. The diacritics Fatha, Damma, and Kasra are represented using a, u, and i, respectively.

Arabic	Roman	Arabic	Roman	Arabic	Roman	Arabic	Roman
ء (hamza)	’	د (daal)	d	ض (Daad)	D	ك (kaaf)	k
ب (baa')	b	ذ (dhaal)	dh	ط (Taa')	T	ل (laam)	l
ت (taa')	t	ر (raa')	r	ظ (Zaa')	Z	م (miim)	m
ث (thaa')	th	ز (zaay)	z	ع ('ayn)	'	ن (nuun)	n
ج (jiim)	j	س (siin)	s	غ (ghayn)	gh	ه (haa')	h
ح (Haa')	H	ش (shiin)	sh	ف (faa')	f	و (waaw)	w or u
خ (khaa')	kh	ص (Saad)	S	ق (qaaf)	q	ي (yaa')	y or ii

Table 1. Arabic–Roman letters mapping table

To validate the proposed method, we used Carnegie Mellon University (CMU) Sphinx speech recognition engine. Our baseline system contains a pronunciation dictionary of 14,234 words from a 5.4 hours pronunciation corpus of MSA broadcast news. For tagging, we used the Arabic module of Stanford tagger. Our results show that part of speech (PoS) tagging is considered a promising track to enhance Arabic speech recognition systems.

The rest of this chapter is organized as follows. Section 2 presents the problem statement. Section 3 demonstrates the speech recognition components. In Section 4, we differentiate between within-word and cross-word pronunciation variations followed by the Arabic speech recognition in Section 5. The proposed method is presented in Section 6 and the results in Section 7. The discussion is provided in Section 8. In Section 9, we highlight some of the future directions. We conclude the work in Section 10.

2. Problem statement

Continuous speech is characterized by augmenting adjacent words, which do not occur in isolated speech. Therefore, handling this phenomenon is a major requirement in continuous speech recognition systems. Even though Hidden Markov Models (HMMs) based ASR decoder uses triphones to alleviate the negative effects of cross-word phenomenon, more effort is still needed to model some cross-word cases that could not be avoided using triphones. In continuous ASR systems, the dictionary is usually initiated using corpus transcription words, i.e. each word is considered as an independent entity. In this case, speech cross-word merging will reduce the performance. Two main methods are usually used to model the cross-word problem, phonological rules and small-word merging. Even though the phonological rules and small-word merging methods enhance the performance, we believe that generating compound words is also possible using PoS tagging.

Initially, there are two reasons why cross-word modeling is an effective method in speech recognition system: First, the speech recognition problem appears as an alignment process, hence for, having long sequences is better than short ones as demonstrated by (Saon and Padmanabhan, 2001). To illustrate the effect of co-articulation phenomenon (merging of words in continuous speech), let us examine Figure 1 and Figure 2. Figure 1 shows the words to be considered with no compound words, while Figure 2 shows the words with compound words. In both figures we represented the hypotheses words using bold black lines. During decoding, the ASR decoder will investigate many words and hypotheses. Intuitively, the ASR decoder will choose the long words instead of two short words. The difference between the two figures is the total number of words that will be considered during the decoding process. Figure 2 shows that the total number of words for the hypotheses is less than the total words in Figure 1 (Figure 1 contains 34 words while Figure 2 contains 18 words). Having less number of total words during decoding process means having less decoding options (i.e. less ambiguity), which is expected to enhance the performance.

Second, compounding words will lead to more robust language model. the compound words which are represented in the language model will provide better representations of words relations. Therefore, enhancement is expected as correct choice of a word will increase the probability of choosing a correct neighbor words. The effect of compounding words was investigated by (Saon & Padmanabhan, 2001). They mathematically demonstrated that compound words enhance the language model performance, therefore, enhancing the overall recognition output. They showed that the compound words have the effect of incorporating a trigram dependency in a bigram language model. In general, the compound words are most likely to be correctly recognized more than two separated words. Consequently, correct recognition of a word might lead to another correct word through the enhanced N-grams language model. In contrast, misrecognition of a word may lead to another misrecognition in the adjacent words and so on.

For more clarification, we present some cases to show the short word misrecognition, and how is the long word is much likely to be recognized correctly. Table 2 shows three speech files that were tested in the baseline and the enhanced system. Of course, it is early to show some results, but we see that it is worthy to support our motivation claim. In Table 2, it is clear that the misrecognitions were mainly occurred in the short words (the highlighted short words were misrecognized in the baseline system).

In this chapter, the most noticeable Arabic ASRs performance reduction factor, the cross-word pronunciation variations, is investigated. To enhance speech recognition accuracy, a knowledge-based technique was utilized to model the cross-word pronunciation variation at two ASR components: the pronunciation dictionary and the language model. The proposed knowledge-based approach method utilizes the PoS tagging to compound consecutive words according to their tags. We investigated two pronunciation cases, a noun that is followed by an adjective, and a preposition that is followed by a word. the proposed method showed a significant enhancement.

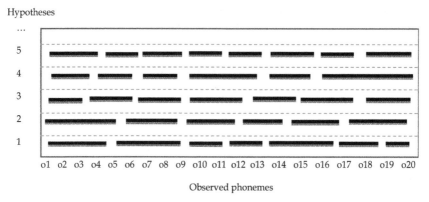

Figure 1. A list of hypotheses without compounding words

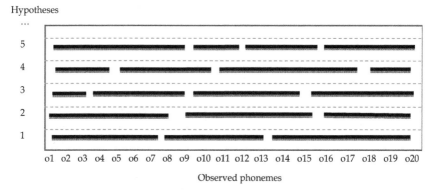

Figure 2. A list of hypotheses with compounding words

3. Speech recognition

Modern large vocabulary, speaker-independent, continuous speech recognition systems have three knowledge sources, also called linguistic databases: acoustic models, language model, and pronunciation dictionary (also called lexicon). Acoustic models are the HMMs of the phonemes and triphones (Hwang, 1993). The language model is the module that provides the statistical representations of the words sequences based on the transcription of the text corpus. The dictionary is the module that serves as an intermediary between the acoustic model and the language model. The dictionary contains the words available in the language and the pronunciation of each word in terms of the phonemes available in the acoustic models.

Figure 3 illustrates the sub-systems that are usually found in a typical ASR system. In addition to the knowledge sources, an ASR system contains a Front-End module which is used to convert the input sound into feature vectors to be usable by the rest of the system. Speech recognition systems usually use feature vectors that are based on Mel Frequency Cepstral Coefficients (MFCCs), (Rabiner and Juang, 2004).

The speech files to be tested	سَيَتَقَابَلَانِ وَجهًا لِوَجه فِي المُبَارَاةِ النِّهَائِيَّة sayataqabalani wajhan liwajh fy 'lmubarah 'lniha'iya وَمُمَثِّلِينَ عَن عَدَدٍ مِن الدُّوَلِ الأُورُوبِيَّة wamumathilyna 'an 'adadin mina 'lduwali 'l'wrubiya
The baseline system results	سَيَتَقَابَلَانِ وَجهًا لِوَجه المُبَارَاةِ النِّهَائِيَّة sayataqabalani wajhan liwajh 'lmubarah 'lniha'iya وَمُمَثِّلِينَ عَن إنَّ الدُّوَلِ الأُورُوبِيَّة wamumathilyna 'an 'inna 'lduwali 'l'wrubiya
The enhance system results	سَيَتَقَابَلَانِ وَجهًا لِوَجه فِي المُبَارَاةِ النِّهَائِيَّة sayataqabalani wajhan liwajh fy 'lmubarah 'lniha'iya وَمُمَثِّلِينَ عَن عَدَدٍ مِن الدُّوَلِ الأُورُوبِيَّة wamumathilyna 'an 'adadin mina 'lduwali 'l'wrubiya

Table 2. Illustrative cross-word misrecognition results

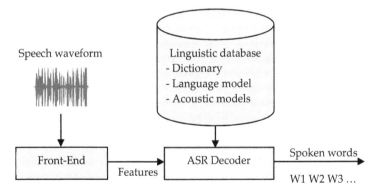

Figure 3. An ASR architecture

The following is a brief introduction to typical ASR system components. The reader can find more elaborate discussion in (Jurafsky and Martin, 2009).

3.1. Front-end

The purpose of this sub-system is to extract speech features which play a crucial role in speech recognition performance. Speech features includes Linear Predictive Cepstral Coefficients (LPCC), MFCCs and Perceptual Linear Predictive (PLP) coefficients. The Sphinx engine used in this work is based on MFCCs.

The feature extraction stage aims to produce the spectral properties (features vectors) of speech signals. The feature vector consists of 39 coefficients. A speech signal is divided into overlapping short segments that are represented using MFCCs. Figure 4 shows the steps to extract the MFCCs of a speech signal (Rabiner & Juang, 2004). These steps are summarized below.

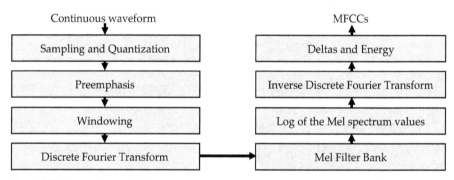

Figure 4. Feature vectors extraction

Sampling and Quantization: Sampling and quantization are the two steps for analog-to-digital conversion. The sampling rate is the number of samples taken per second, the sampling rate used in this study is 16 k samples per seconds. The quantization is the process of representing real-valued numbers as integers. The analysis window is about 25.6 msec (410 samples), and consecutive frames overlap by 10 msec.

Preemphasis: This stage is to boost the high frequency part that was suppressed during the sound production mechanism, so making the information more available to the acoustic model.

Windowing: Each analysis window is multiplied by a Hamming window.

Discrete Fourier Transform: The goal of this step is to obtain the magnitude frequency response of each frame. The output is a complex number representing the magnitude and phase of the frequency component in the original signal.

Mel Filter Bank: A set of triangular filter banks is used to approximate the frequency resolution of the human ear. The Mel frequency scale is linear up to 1000 Hz and logarithmic thereafter. For 16 KHz sampling rate, Sphinx engine uses a set of 40 Mel filters.

Log of the Mel spectrum values: The range of the values generated by the Mel filter bank is reduced by replacing each value by its natural logarithm. This is done to make the statistical distribution of spectrum approximately Gaussian.

Inverse Discrete Fourier Transform: This transform is used to compress the spectral information into a set of low order coefficients which is called the Mel-cepstrum. Thirteen MFCC coefficients are used as a basic feature vector, $x_t(k)$ $0 \le k \le 12$.

Deltas and Energy: For continuous models, the 13 MFCC parameters along with computed delta and delta-deltas parameters are used as a single stream 39 parameters feature vector. For semi-continuous models, x(0) represents the log Mel spectrum energy, and is used separately to derive other feature parameters, in addition to the delta and double delta parameters. Figure 5 shows part of the feature vector of a speech file after completing the feature extraction process. Each column represents the basic 13 features of a 25.6 milliseconds frame.

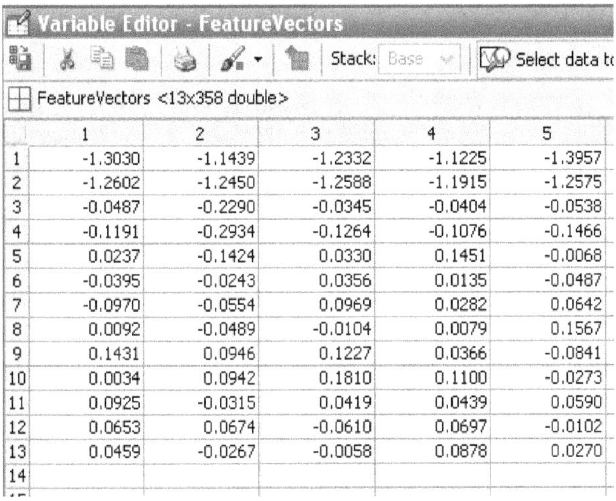

Variable Editor - FeatureVectors				
FeatureVectors <13x358 double>				
	1	2	3	4	5
1	-1.3030	-1.1439	-1.2332	-1.1225	-1.3957
2	-1.2602	-1.2450	-1.2588	-1.1915	-1.2575
3	-0.0487	-0.2290	-0.0345	-0.0404	-0.0538
4	-0.1191	-0.2934	-0.1264	-0.1076	-0.1466
5	0.0237	-0.1424	0.0330	0.1451	-0.0068
6	-0.0395	-0.0243	0.0356	0.0135	-0.0487
7	-0.0970	-0.0554	0.0969	0.0282	0.0642
8	0.0092	-0.0489	-0.0104	0.0079	0.1567
9	0.1431	0.0946	0.1227	0.0366	-0.0841
10	0.0034	0.0942	0.1810	0.1100	-0.0273
11	0.0925	-0.0315	0.0419	0.0439	0.0590
12	0.0653	0.0674	-0.0610	0.0697	-0.0102
13	0.0459	-0.0267	-0.0058	0.0878	0.0270
14					

Figure 5. snapshot of the MFCCs of a speech file

3.2. Linguistic database

This part contains the modifications required for a particular language. It contains three parts: acoustic models, language model, and pronunciation dictionary. Acoustic models contain the HMMs used in recognition process. The language model contains language's words and their combinations, each combination has two or three words. A pronunciation dictionary contains the words and their pronunciation phonemes.

3.2.1. Acoustic models

Acoustic models are statistical representations of the speech phones. Precise acoustic model is a key factor to improve recognition accuracy as it characterizes the HMMs of each phone. Sphinx uses 39 English phonemes (The CMU Pronunciation Dictionary, 2011). The acoustic models use a 3- to 5-state Markov chain to represent the speech phone (Lee, 1988). Figure 6 shows a representation of a 3-state phone's acoustic model. In Figure 6, S1 is the representation of phone at the beginning, while S2 and S3 represent of the phone at the middle and the end states, respectively. Associated with S1, S2, and S3 are state emission probabilities, $b_j(x_t) = P(o = x_t \mid S_t = j)$, representing the probability of observing the feature vector in the state j. The emission probabilities are usually modeled by Gaussian mixture densities.

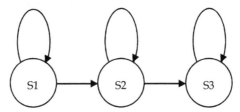

Figure 6. 3-state phone acoustic model

In continuous speech, each phoneme is influenced in different degrees by its neighboring phonemes. Therefore, for better acoustic modeling, Sphinx uses triphones. Triphones are context dependent models of phonemes; each triphone represents a phoneme surrounded by specific left and right phonemes (Hwang, 1993).

3.2.2. Language model

The N-gram language model is trained by counting N-gram occurrences in a large transcription corpus to be then smoothed and normalized. In general, an N-gram language model is used to calculate the probability of a given sequence of words as follows:

$$P(w_1^n) = \prod_{k=1}^{n} p(w_k \mid w_1^{k-1})$$

Where n is limited to include the words' history as bigram (two consequent words), trigram (three consequent words), 4-gram (four consequent words), etc. for example, by assigning n=2, the probability of a three word sequence using bigram is calculated as follows: $P(w_1 w_2 w_3) = p(w_3 \mid w_2) p(w_2 \mid w_1) p(w_1)$

The CMU statistical language tool is described in (Clarkson & Rosenfeld, 1997). The CMU statistical language tool kit has been used to generate our Arabic statistical language model. Figure 7 shows the steps for creation and testing the language model, the steps are:

- Compute the word unigram counts.
- Convert the word unigram counts into a vocabulary list.
- Generate bigram and trigram tables based on this vocabulary.

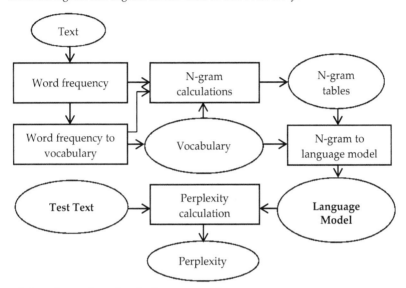

Figure 7. Steps for creating and testing language model

The CMU language modeling tool comes with a tool for evaluating the language model. The evaluation measures the perplexity as indication of the convenient (goodness) of the language model. For more information of the perplexity, please refer to Section 7.

3.2.3. Pronunciation dictionary

Both training and recognition stages require a pronunciation dictionary which is a mapping table that maps words into sequences of phonemes. A pronunciation dictionary is basically designed to be used with a particular set of words. It provides the pronunciation of the vocabulary for the transcription corpus using the defined phoneme set. Like acoustic models and language model, the performance of a speech recognition system depends critically on the dictionary and the phoneme set used to build the dictionary. In decoding stage, the dictionary serves as intermediary between the acoustic model and the language model.

There are two types of dictionaries: closed vocabulary dictionary and open vocabulary dictionary. In closed vocabulary dictionary, all corpus transcription words are listed in the dictionary. In contrast, it is possible to have non-corpus transcription words in the open vocabulary dictionary. Typically, the phoneme set, that is used to represent dictionary words, is manually designed by language experts. However, when human expertise is not available, the phoneme set is possible to be selected using data-driven approach as demonstrated by (Singh et al. 2002). In addition to providing phonemic transcriptions of the words of the target vocabulary, the dictionary is the place where alternative pronunciation variants are added such as in (Ali et al., 2009) for Arabic.

3.3. Decoder (Recognizer)

With help from the linguistic part, the decoder is the module where the recognition process takes place. The decoder uses the speech features presented by the Front-End to search for the most probable words and, then, sentences that correspond to the observed speech features. The recognition process starts by finding the likelihood of a given sequence of speech features based on the phonemes HMMs.

The speech recognition problem is to transcribe the most likely spoken words given the acoustic observations. If $O = o_1, o_2, ... o_n$ is the acoustic observation, and $W = w_1, w_2, ... w_n$ is a word sequence, then:

$$\widehat{W} = \underbrace{arg\ max}_{for\ all\ words}\ P(W)P(O \mid W)$$

Where $\widehat{W}$ is the most probable word sequence of the spoken words, which is also called maximum posteriori probability. $P(W)$ is the prior probability computed in the language model, and $P(O \mid W)$ is the probability of observation computed using the acoustic model.

4. Pronunciation variation

The main goal of ASRs is to enable people to communicate more naturally and effectively. But this ultimate dream faces many obstacles such as different speaking styles which lead to "pronunciation variation" phenomenon. This phenomenon appears in the form of insertions, deletions, or substitutions of phoneme(s) relative to the phonemic transcription in the pronunciation dictionary. (Benzeghiba et al., 2007) presented the speech variability sources: foreign and regional accents, speaker physiology, spontaneous speech, rate of speech, children speech, emotional state, noises, new words, and more. Accordingly, handling these obstacles is a major requirement to have better ASR performance.

There are two types of pronunciation variations: cross-word variations and within-word variations. A within-word variation causes alternative pronunciation(s) of the same word. In contrast, a cross-word variation occurs in continuous speech in which a sequence of words forms a compound word that should be treated as a one entity. The pronunciation variation can be modeled in two approaches: knowledge-based and data-driven. Knowledge-based depends on linguistic studies that lead to the phonological rules which are called to find the possible alternative variants. On the other hand, data-driven methods depend solely on the pronunciation corpus to find the pronunciation variants (direct data-driven) or transformation rules (indirect data-driven). In this chapter, we will use the knowledge-based approach to model the cross-word pronunciation variation problem.

As pros and cons of both approaches, the knowledge-based approach is not exhaustive; not all of the variations that occur in continuous speech have been described. Whereas obtaining reliable information using data-driven is difficult. However, (Amdal & Fossler-Lussier 2003) mentioned that there is a growing interest in data-driven methods over the knowledge-based methods due to lack of domains expertise. Figure 8 displays these two techniques. Figure 8 also distinguishes between the types of variations and the modeling techniques by a dashed line. The pronunciation variation types are above the dashed line whereas the modeling techniques are under the dashed line.

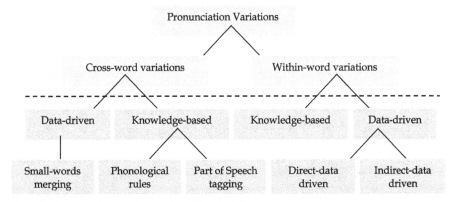

Figure 8. Pronunciation variations and modeling techniques

5. Arabic speech recognition

This work focuses on Arabic speech recognition, which has gained increasing importance in the last few years. Arabic is a Semitic language spoken by more than 330 million people as a native language (Farghaly & Shaalan, 2009). While Arabic language has many spoken dialects, it has a standard written language. As a result, more challenges are introduced to speech recognition systems as the spoken dialects are not officially written. The same country could contain different dialects and a dialect itself can vary from region to another according to different factors such as religion, gender, urban/rural, etc. Speakers with different dialects usually use modern standard Arabic (MSA) to communicate.

5.1. Modern standard Arabic

In this chapter, we consider the modern standard Arabic (MSA) which is currently used in writing and in most formal speech. MSA is also the major medium of communication for public speaking and news broadcasting (Ryding, 2005) and is considered to be the official language in most Arabic-speaking countries (Lamel et al., 2009). Arabic language challenges will be presented in the next section. Followed by the literature review and recent results efforts in Arabic speech recognition. For more information about modern standard Arabic, (Ryding, 2005) is a rich reference.

5.2. Arabic speech recognition challenges

Arabic speech recognition faces many challenges. First, Arabic has many dialects where same words are pronounced differently. In addition, the spoken dialects are not officially written, it is very costly to obtain adequate corpora, which present a training problem for the Arabic ASR researchers (Owen et al., 2006). Second, Arabic has short vowels (diacritics), which are usually ignored in text. The lack of diacritical marks introduces another serious problem to Arabic speech recognition. Consequently, more hypotheses' words will be considered during decoding process which may reduce the accuracy. (Elmahdy et al., 2009) summarized some of the problems raised in Arabic speech recognition. They highlighted the following problems: Arabic phonetics, diacritization problem, grapheme-to-phoneme, and morphological complexity. Although foreign phoneme sounds as /v/ and /p/ are used in Arabic speech in foreign names, the standard Arabic letters do not have standard letter assigned for foreign sounds. Second, the absence of the diacritical marks in modern Arabic text creates ambiguities for pronunciations and meanings. For example, the non-diacritized Arabic word (كتب) could be read as one of several choices, some of which are: (كَتَبَ,he wrote), (كُتِبَ, it was written), and (كُتُب, books). Even though, an Arabic reader can interpret and utter the correct choice, it is hard to embed this cognitive process in current speech recognition and speech synthesis systems. The majority of Arabic corpora available for the task of acoustic modeling have non-diacritized transcription. (Elmahdy et al., 2009) also showed that grapheme-to-phoneme relation is only true for diacritized Arabic script. Hence fore, Arabic speech recognition has an obstacle because the lack of diacritized corpora. Arabic morphological complexity is demonstrated by the large number of affixes (prefixes, infixes, and suffixes) that can be added to the three consonant radicals to form patterns. (Farghaly& Shaalan, 2009) provided a comprehensive study of Arabic language challenges and solutions. The mentioned challenges include: the nonconcatenative nature of Arabic morphology, the absence of the orthographic representation of Arabic diacritics from contemporary Arabic text, and the need for an explicit grammar of MSA that defines linguistic constituency in the absence of case marking. (Lamel et al., 2009) presented a number of challenges for Arabic speech recognition such as no diacritics, dialectal variants, and very large lexical variety. (Alotaibi et al., 2008) introduced foreign-accented Arabic speech as a challenging task in speech recognition. (Billa et al., 2002) discussed a number of research issues for Arabic speech recognition, e.g., absence of diacritics in written text and the presence of compound words that are formed by the concatenation of certain conjunctions, prepositions, articles, and pronouns, as prefixes and suffixes to the word stem.

5.3. Literature and recent work

A number of researchers have recently addressed development of Arabic speech recognition systems. (Abushariah et al., 2012) proposed a framework for the design and development of a speaker-independent continuous automatic Arabic speech recognition system based on a phonetically rich and balanced speech corpus. Their method reduced the WER to 9.81% for a diacritized transcription corpus, as they have reported. (Hyassat & Abu Zitar, 2008) described an Arabic speech recognition system based on Sphinx 4. Three corpora were developed, namely, the Holy Qura'an corpus of about 18.5 hours, the command and control corpus of about 1.5 hours, and the Arabic digits corpus of less than 1 hour of speech. They also proposed an automatic toolkit for building pronunciation dictionaries for the Holy Qur'an and standard Arabic language. (Al-Otaibi, 2001)] provided a single-speaker speech dataset for MSA. He proposed a technique for labeling Arabic speech. using the Hidden Markov Model Toolkit (HTK), he reported a recognition rate for speaker dependent ASR of 93.78%. (Afify et al. , 2005) compared grapheme-based recognition system with explicitly modeling diacritics (short vowels). They found that a diacritic modeling improves recognition performance. (Satori et al. , 2007) used CMU Sphinx tools for Arabic speech recognition. They demonstrated the use of the tools for recognition of isolated Arabic digits. They achieved a digits recognition accuracy of 86.66% for data recorded from six speakers. (Alghamdi et al., 2009) developed an Arabic broadcast news transcription system. They used a corpus of 7.0 h for training and 0.5 h for testing. The WER they obtained was 14.9%. (Lamel et al., 2009) described the incremental improvements to a system for the automatic transcription of broadcast data in Arabic, highlighting techniques developed to deal with specificities (no diacritics, dialectal variants, and lexical variety) of the Arabic language. (Billa et al., 2002) described the development of audio indexing system for broadcast news in Arabic. Key issues addressed in their work revolve around the three major components of the audio indexing system: automatic speech recognition, speaker identification, and named entity identification. (Soltau et al., 2007) reported advancements in the IBM system for Arabic speech recognition as part of the continuous effort for the Global Autonomous Language Exploitation (GALE) project. The system consisted of multiple stages that incorporate both diacritized and non-diacritized Arabic speech model. The system also incorporated a training corpus of 1,800 hours of unsupervised Arabic speech. (Azmi et al., 2008) investigated using Arabic syllables for speaker-independent speech recognition system for Arabic spoken digits. The pronunciation corpus used for both training and testing consisted of 44 Egyptian speakers. In a clean environment, experiments showed that the recognition rate obtained using syllables outperformed the rate obtained using monophones, triphones, and words by 2.68%, 1.19%, and 1.79%, respectively. Also in noisy telephone channel, syllables outperformed the rate obtained using monophones, triphones, and words by 2.09%, 1.5%, and 0.9%, respectively. (Elmahdy et al., 2009) used acoustic models trained with large MSA news broadcast speech corpus to work as multilingual or multi-accent models to decode colloquial Arabic. (Khasawneh et al., 2004) compared the polynomial classifier that was applied to isolated-word speaker-independent Arabic speech and dynamic time warping (DTW) recognizer. They concluded that the polynomial classifier produced better recognition performance and much faster testing response than the DTW recognizer. (Shoaib et al., 2003) presented an approach to develop a robust Arabic speech recognition system based on a hybrid set of speech features. The hybrid set consisted of intensity contours and formant frequencies. (Alotaibi, 2004) reported achieving high-performance Arabic digits recognition using recurrent networks. (Choi et al., 2008) presented recent improvements to their English/Iraqi Arabic speech-to-speech translation system. The presented system-wide improvements included user interface, dialog manager, ASR, and machine translation components. (Nofal et al., 2004) demonstrated a design and implementation of stochastic-based new acoustic models for use with a command and control system speech recognition system for the Arabic. (Mokhtar & El-Abddin, 1996) represented the techniques and algorithms used to model the acoustic-phonetic structure of Arabic speech recognition using HMMs. (Park et al. , 2009) explored the training and adaptation of multilayer perceptron (MLP) features in Arabic ASRs. They used MLP features to incorporate short-vowel information into the graphemic system. They also used linear input networks (LIN) adaptation as an alternative to the usual HMM-based linear adaptation. (Imai et al.,1995) presented a new method for automatic generation of speaker-dependent phonological rules in order to decrease recognition errors caused by pronunciation variability dependent on speakers. (Muhammad et al., 2011) evaluated conventional ASR system for six different types of voice disorder patients speaking Arabic digits. MFCC and Gaussian mixture models (GMM)/HMM were used as features and classifier, respectively. Recognition result was analyzed for recognition for types of diseases. (Bourouba et al., 2006) presented a HMM/support vectors machine (SVM) (k-nearest neighbor) for recognition of isolated spoken Arabic words. (Sagheer et al., 2005) presented a visual speech features representation system. They used it to comprise a complete lip-reading system. (Taha et al. , 2007) demonstrated an agent-based design for Arabic speech recognition. They defined the Arabic speech recognition as a multi-agent system where each agent had a specific goal and deals with that goal only. (Elmisery et al., 2003) implemented a pattern matching algorithm based on HMM using field programmable gate array (FPGA). The proposed approach was used for isolated Arabic word recognition. (Gales et al., 2007) described the development of a phonetic system for Arabic speech recognition. (Bahi & Sellami, 2001) presented experiments performed to recognize isolated Arabic words. Their recognition system was based on a combination of the vector quantization technique at the acoustic level and markovian modeling. (Essa et al., 2008) proposed a combined classifier architectures based on Neural Networks by varying the initial weights, architecture, type, and training data to recognize Arabic isolated words. (Emami & Mangu, 2007) studied the use of neural network language models (NNLMs) for Arabic broadcast news and broadcast conversations speech recognition. (Messaoudi et al., 2006) demonstrated that by building a very large vocalized vocabulary and by using a language model including a vocalized component, the WER could be significantly reduced. (Vergyri et al., 2004) showed that the use of morphology-based language models at different stages in a large vocabulary continuous speech recognition (LVCSR) system for Arabic leads to WER reductions. To deal with the huge lexical variety, (Xiang et al., 2006) concentrated on the transcription of Arabic broadcast news by utilizing morphological decomposition in both acoustic and language modeling in their system. (Selouani & Alotaibi, 2011) presented genetic algorithms to adapt HMMs for non-native speech in a large vocabulary speech recognition system of MSA. (Saon et al., 2010) described the Arabic broadcast transcription system fielded by IBM in the

GALE project. they reported improved discriminative training, the use of subspace Gaussian mixture models (SGMM), the use of neural network acoustic features, variable frame rate decoding, training data partitioning experiments, unpruned n-gram language models, and neural network based language modeling (NNLMs) . The achieved WER was 8.9% on the evaluation test set. (Kuo et al., 2010) studied various syntactic and morphological context features incorporated in an NNLM for Arabic speech recognition.

6. The proposed method

Since the ASR decoder works better with long words, our method focuses on finding a way to merge transcription words to increase the number of long words. For this purpose, we consider to merge words according to their tags. That is, merge a noun that is followed by an adjective, and merge a preposition that is followed by a word. we utilizes PoS tagging approach to tag the transcription corpus. the tagged transcription is then used to find the new merged words.

A tag is a word property such as noun, pronoun, verb, adjective, adverb, preposition, conjunction, interjection, etc. Each language has its own tags. Tags may be different from language to language. In our method, we used the Arabic module of Stanford tagger (Stanford Log-linear Part-Of-Speech Tagger, 2011). The total number of tags of this tagger is 29 tags, only 13 tags were used in our method as listed in Table 3. As we mentioned, we focused on three kinds of tags: noun, adjectives, and preposition. In Table 3, DT is a shorthand for the determiner article (ال التعريف) that corresponds to "the" in English.

#	Tag	Meaning	Example
1	ADJ_NUM	Adjective, Numeric	الرابعة السابع،
2	DTJJ	DT + Adjective	الجديد النفطية،
3	DTJJR	Adjective, comparative	العليا الكبرى،
4	DTNN	DT + Noun, singular or mass	المنظمة، العاصمة
5	DTNNP	DT + Proper noun, singular	القاهرة العراق،
6	DTNNS	DT + Noun, plural	السيارات، الولايات
7	IN	Preposition subordinating conjunction	حرف جر مثل : في حرف مصدري مثل :أن
8	JJ	Adjective	قيادية جديدة،
9	JJR	Adjective, comparative	كبرى أدنى،
10	NN	Noun, singular or mass	إنتاج، نجم
11	NNP	Proper noun, singular	لبنان أوبك،
12	NNS	Noun, plural	طلبات توقعات،
13	NOUN_QUANT	Noun, quantity	الربع، ثلثي

Table 3. A partial list of Stanford Tagger's tag with examples

In this work, we used the Noun-Adjective as shorthand for a compound word generated by merging a noun and an adjective. We also used Preposition-Word as shorthand for a compound word generated by merging a preposition with a subsequent word. The prepositions used in our method include:

(منذ ، حتى ، في ، على ، عن ، الى ، من) ➔ (mundhu, Hata, fy, 'ala, 'an, 'ila, min), Other prepositions were not included as they are rarely used in MSA. Table 4 shows the tagger output for a simple non-diacritized sentence.

An input sentence to the tagger	وأوضح عضو لجنة المقاولين في غرفة الرياض بشير العظم wa 'wdaHa 'udwu lajnata 'lmuqawilyna fy ghurfitu 'lriyaD bashyru 'l' aZm
Tagger output (read from left to right)	غرفة/NN في/IN DTNNS/المقاولين NN/لجنة NN/عضو VBD/وأوضح DTNN/العظم NNP/بشير DTNNP/الرياض

Table 4. An Arabic sentence and its tags

Thus, the tagger output is used to generate compound words by searching for Noun-Adjective and Preposition-Word sequences. Figure 9 shows two possible compound words: (بَرنَامِجِضَنْخم) and (فِيالأُردُن) for Noun-Adjective case and for Preposition-Word case, respectively. These two compound words are, then, represented in new sentences as illustrated in Figure 9. Therefore, the three sentences (the original and the new ones) will be used, with all other cases, to produce the enhanced language model and the enhanced pronunciation dictionary.

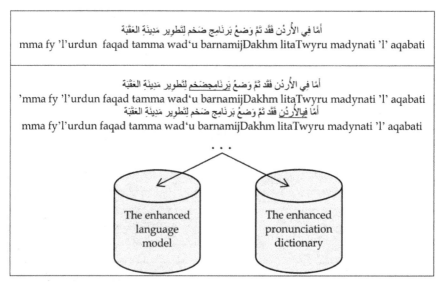

Figure 9. The compound words representations

Figure 10 shows the process of generating a compound word. It demonstrates that a noun followed by an adjective will be merged to produce a one compound word. similarly , the preposition followed by a word will be merged to perform a one compound word. It is noteworthy to mention that our method is independent from handling pronunciation variations that may occur at words junctures. That is, our method does not consider the phonological rules that could be implemented between certain words.

The steps for modeling cross-word phenomenon can be described by the algorithm (pseudocode) shown in Figure 11. In the figure, the Offline stage means that the stage is implemented once before decoding, while Online stage means that this stage needs to be repeatedly implemented after each decoding process.

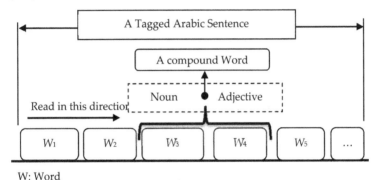

Figure 10. A Noun-Adjective compound word generation

Offline Stage
Using a PoS tagger, have the transcription corpus tagged
For all tagged sentences in the transcription file
  For each two adjacent tags of each tagged sentence
    If the adjacent tags are adjective/noun or word/preposition
      Generate the compound word
      Represent the compound word in the transcription
    End if
  End for
End for
Based on the new transcription, build the enhanced dictionary
Based on the new transcription, build the enhanced language model
Online Stage
Switching the variants back to its original separated words

Figure 11. Cross-word modeling algorithm using PoS tagging

7. The results

The proposed method was investigated on a speaker-independent modern standard Arabic speech recognition system using Carnegie Mellon University Sphinx speech recognition engine. Three performance metrics were used to measure the performance enhancement: the word error rate (WER), out of vocabulary (OOV), and perplexity (PP).

WER is a common metric to measure performance of ASRs. WER is computed using the following formula:

$$WER = \frac{S + D + I}{N}$$

Where:

- S is the number of substituted words,
- D is the number of deleted words,
- I is the number of inserted words,
- N is the total number of words in the testing set.

The word accuracy can also be measured using WER as the following formula:

Word Accuracy = 1 − WER

OOV is a metric to measure the performance of ASRs. OOV is known as a source of recognition errors, which in turn could lead to additional errors in the words that follow (Gallwitz et al., 1996). Hence fore, increasing OOVs plays a significant role in increasing WER and deteriorating performance. In this research work, the baseline system is based on a closed vocabulary. The closed vocabulary assumes that all words of the testing set are already included in the dictionary. (Jurafsky & Martin, 2009) explored the differences between open and closed vocabulary. In our method, we calculate OOV as the percentage of recognized words that are not belonging to the testing set, but to the training set. The following formula is used to find OOV:

$$OOV \text{ (baseline system)} = \frac{\text{none testing set words}}{\text{total words in the testing set}} * 100$$

The perplexity of the language model is defined in terms of the inverse of the average log likelihood per word (Jelinek, 1999). It is an indication of the average number of words that can follow a given word, a measure of the predictive power of the language model, (Saon & Padmanabhan ,2001). Measuring the perplexity is a common way to evaluate N-gram language model. It is a way to measure the quality of a model independent of any ASR system. Of course, The measurement is performed on the testing set. A lower perplexity system is considered better than one of higher perplexity. The perplexity formula is:

$$PP(W) = \sqrt[N]{\frac{1}{P(w_1, w_2, ..., w_N)}}$$

Where PP is the perplexity, P is the probability of the word set to be tested W=w₁, w₂, ... , wN, and N is the total number of words in the testing set.

The performance detection method proposed by Plötz in (Plötz,2005) is used to investigate the achieved recognition results. A 95% is used as a level of confidence. The WER of the baseline system (12.21 %) and the total number of words in the testing set (9288 words) are used to find the confidence interval [εl , εh]. The boundaries of the confidence interval are found to be [12.21 – 0.68 , 12.21 + 0.68] ➔ [11.53,12.89]. If the changed classification error rate is outside this interval, this change can be interpreted as statistically significant. Otherwise, It is most likely caused by chance.

Table 5 shows the enhancements for different experiments. Since the enhanced method (in Noun-Adjective case) achieved a WER of (9.82%) which is out of the above mentioned confidence interval [11.53,12.89], it is concluded that the achieved enhancement is statistically significant. The other cases are similar, i.e. (Preposition-Word, and Hybrid cases also achieved a significant improvement).

#	Experiment	Accuracy (%)	WER (%)	Enhancement (%)
	Baseline system	87.79	12.21	----------
1	Noun-Adjective	90.18	9.82	2.39
2	Preposition-Word	90.04	9.96	2.25
3	Hybrid (1 & 2)	90.07	9.93	2.28

Table 5. Accuracy achieved and WERs for different cases

Table 5 shows that the highest accuracy achieved is in Noun-Adjective case. The reduction in accuracy in the hybrid case is due to the ambiguity introduced in the language model. For more clarification, our method depends on adding new sentences to the transcription corpus that is used to build the language model. Therefore, adding many sentences will finally cause the language model to be biased to some n-grams (1-grams, 2-grams, and 3-grams) on the account of others.

The common way to evaluate the N-gram language model is using perplexity. The perplexity for the baseline is 34.08. For the proposed cases, the language models' perplexities are displayed in Table 6. The measurements were taken based on the testing set, which contains 9288 words. The enhanced cases are clearly better as their perplexities are lower. The reason for the low perplexities is the specific domains that we used in our corpus, i.e. economics and sports.

#	Experiment	Perplexity	OOV (%)
	Baseline System	34.08	328/9288 = 3.53%
1	Noun-Adjective	3.00	287/9288 = 3.09%
2	Preposition-Word	3.22	299/9288 = 3.21%
3	Hybrid (1 & 2)	2.92	316/9288 = 3.40%

Table 6. Perplexities and OOV for different experiments

The OOV was also measured for the performed experiments. Our ASR system is based on a closed vocabulary, so we assume that there are no unknown words. The OOV was calculated as the percentage of recognized words that do not belong to the testing set, but to the training set. Hence,

$$\text{OOV (baseline system)} = \frac{\text{none testing set words}}{\text{total words in the testing set}} * 100$$

which is equal to 328/9288*100= 3.53%. For the enhanced cases, Table 6 shows the resulting OOVs. Clearly, the lower the OOV the better the performance is, which was achieved in all three cases.

Table 7 shows some statistical information collected during experiments. The "Total compound words" is the total number of Noun-Adjective cases found in the corpus transcription. The "unique compound words" indicates the total number of Noun-Adjective cases after removing duplicates. The last column, "compound words replaced" is the total number of compound words that were replaced back to their original two disjoint words after the decoding process and prior to the evaluation stage.

#	Experiment	Total compound words	unique compound words	compound words replaced
1	Noun-Adjective	3328	2672	377
2	Preposition-Word	3883	2297	409
3	Hybrid (1 & 2)	7211	4969	477

Table 7. Statistical information for compound words

Despite the claim that the Stanford Arabic tagger accuracy is more than 96%, a comprehensive manual verification and correction were made on the tagger output. It was reasonable to review the collected compound words as our transcription corpus is small (39217 words). For large corpora, the accuracy of the tagger is crucial for the results. Table 8 shows an error that occurred in the tagger output. The word, for example, "وقال"(waqala) should be VBD instead of NN.

Sentence to be tagged	هذا وقال رئيس لجنة الطاقة بمجلس النواب ورئيس الرابطة الروسية للغاز إن الاحتكارات الأوروبية hadha waqala ra'ysu lajnati 'lTaqa bimajlisi 'lnuwab wa ra'ysu 'lrabiTa 'lrwsiya llghaz 'ina 'l'iHtikarati 'liwrobiya
Stanford Tagger output (read from left to right)	هذا/DT وقال/NN رئيس/NN لجنة/NN الطاقة/NN بمجلس/DTNN النواب/DTNN ورئيس/NN الرابطة/DTNN الروسية/DTJJ للغاز/NNP إن/NNP الاحتكارات/DTNNS الأوروبية/DTJJ

Table 8. Example of Stanford Arabic Tagger Errors

Table 9 shows an illustrative example of the enhancement that was achieved in the enhanced system. It shows that the baseline system missed one word "من"(min) while it appears in the enhanced system. Introducing a compound word in this sentence avoided the misrecognition that occurred in the baseline system.

The text of a speech file to be tested	في المَرحَلَةِ السَّابِعَةِ وَالثَّلاثْين من الدَّوريِّ الإسْبَانِيِّ لِكُرَةِ القَدَم fy 'lmarHalati 'lsabi' a wa 'lthalathyn mina 'ldawry 'l'sbany likurati 'lqadam
As recognized by the baseline system	في المَرحَلَةِ السَّابِعَةِ وَالثَّلاثْين الدَّوريِّ الإسْبَانِيِّ لِكُرَةِ القَدَم fy 'lmarHalati 'lsabi' a wa 'lthalathyn mina 'ldawry 'l'sbany likurati 'lqadam
As recognized by the enhanced system	في المَرحَلَةِ السَّابِعَةِ وَالثَّلاثْين مِن الدَّوريِّالإسْبَانِيِّ لِكُرَةِ القَدَم fy 'lmarHalati 'lsabi' a wa 'lthalathyn mina 'ldawry 'l'sbany likurati 'lqadam
Final output after decomposing the merging	في المَرحَلَةِ السَّابِعَةِ وَالثَّلاثْين مِن الدَّوريِّ الإسْبَانِيِّ لِكُرَةِ القَدَم fy 'lmarHalati 'lsabi' a wa 'lthalathyn mina 'ldawry 'l'sbany likurati 'lqadam

Table 9. An example of enhancement in the enhanced system

According to the proposed algorithm, each sentence in the enhanced transcription corpus can have a maximum of one compound word, since sentences are added to the enhanced corpus once a compound word is formed. Finally, After the decoding process, the results are scanned in order to decompose the compound words back to their original form (two separate words). This process is performed using a lookup table such as:

الكُوَيتالدُّوَلِيٌّ← الكُوَيت الدُّوَلِيٌّ ('lkuwaytldawly ➔ 'lkuwayt 'ldawly)

فيمَطَارٍ ➔ في مَطَارٍ (fymatari ➔ fy matari)

8. Discussion

Table 10 shows comparison results of the suggested methods for cross-word modeling. It shows that PoS tagging approach outperform the other methods (i.e. the phonological rules and small word merging) which were investigated on the same pronunciation corpus. The use of phonological rules was demonstrated in (AbuZeina et al. 2011a) while merging of small-words method was presented in (AbuZeina et al. 2011b). even though PoS tagging seems to be better than the other methods, more research should be carried out for more confidence. So, the comparison demonstrated in Table 10 is subject to change as more cases need to be investigated for both techniques. That is, cross-word was modeled using only two Arabic phonological rules, while only two compounding schemes were applied in PoS tagging approach.

The recognition time is compared with the baseline system. The comparison includes the testing set which includes 1144 speech files. The specifications of the machine where we conducted the experiments were as follows: a desktop computer which contains a single processing chip of 3.2GHz and 2.0 GB of RAM. We found that the recognition time for the enhanced method is almost the same as the recognition time of the baseline system. This means that the proposed method is almost equal to the baseline system in term of time complexity.

#	System	Accuracy (%)	Execution Time (minutes)
	Baseline system	87.79	34.14
1	phonological rules	90.09	33.49
2	PoS tagging	90.18	33.05
3	small word merging	89.95	34.31
4	Combined system (1,2,and3)	88.48	30.31

Table 10. Comparison between cross-word modeling techniques

9. Further research

As future work, we propose investigating more word-combination cases. In particular, we expect that the construct phrases *Idafa* (الإضافة) make a good candidate. Examples include: (مدينة القدس , madynatu 'lquds). (مطار بيروت , maTaru bayrwt) , (سلسلة جبال, silsilt jibal), Another suggested candidate is the Arabic "and" connective (واو العطف), such as: (مواد أدبية, mawad 'dabiyah wa lughawiyah), (yata'allaqu biqaDaya 'l' iraqi wa 'lsudan يتعلق بقضايا العراق والسودان). A hybrid system could also be investigated. It is possible to use the different cross-word modeling approaches in a one ASR system. It is also worthy to investigate how to model the compound words in the language model. In our method, we create a new sentence for each compound word. we suggest to investigate representing the compound word exclusively with its neighbors. for example, instead of having two complete sentences to represent the compound words (بَرنَامِجضَخم , barnamijDakhm) and (فِيالأَردُن , fy'l'urdun) as what we proposed in our method:

أَمَّا فِي الأَردُن فَقَد تَمَّ وَضعُ بَرنَامِجضَخم لِتَطويِر مَدِينَةِ العَقَبَة

'mma fy 'l'urdun faqad tamma wad'u barnamijDakhm litaTwyru madynati 'l' aqabati

أَمَّا فِيالأَردُن فَقَد تَمَّ وَضعُ بَرنَامِج ضَخم لِتَطويِر مَدِينَةِ العَقَبَة

' mma fy'l'urdun faqad tamma wad'u barnamijDakhm litaTwyru madynati 'l' aqabati

We propose to add the compound words only with their adjacent words like:

وَضعُ بَرنَامِجضَخم لِتَطويِر

waD'u barnamijDakhm litaTwyr

أَمَّا فِيالأَردُن فَقَد

' mma fy 'l'urdun faqad

A comprehensive research work should be made to find how to effectively represent the compound words in the language model. In addition, we highly recommend further research in PoS tagging for Arabic.

10. Conclusion

The proposed knowledge-based approach to model cross-word pronunciation variations problem achieved a feasible improvement. Mainly, PoS tagging approach was used to form compound words. The experimental results clearly showed that forming compound words using a noun and an adjective achieved a better accuracy than merging of a preposition and its next word. The significant enhancement we achieved has not only come from the cross-word pronunciation modeling in the dictionary, but also indirectly from the recalculated n-grams probabilities in the language model. We also conclude that Viterbi algorithm works better with long words. Speech recognition research should consider this fact when designing dictionaries. We found that merging words based on their types (tags) leads to significant improvement in Arabic ASRs. We also found that the proposed method outperforms the other cross-word methods such as phonological rules and small-words merging.

Author details

Dia AbuZeina, Husni Al-Muhtaseb and Moustafa Elshafei
King Fahd University of Petroleum and Minerals, Dhahran, Saudi Arabia

Acknowledgement

The authors would like to thank King Fahd University of Petroleum and Minerals for providing the facilities to write this chapter. We also thank King Abdulaziz City for Science and Technology (KACST) for partially supporting this research work under Saudi Arabia Government research grant NSTP # (08-INF100-4).

11. References

Abushariah, M. A.-A. M.; Ainon, R. N.; Zainuddin, R.; Elshafei, M. & Khalifa, O. O. Arabic speaker-independent continuous automatic speech recognition based on a phonetically rich and balanced speech corpus. Int. Arab J. Inf. Technol., 2012, 9, 84-93

AbuZeina D., Al-Khatib W., Elshafei M., "Small-Word Pronunciation Modeling for Arabic Speech Recognition: A Data-Driven Approach", Seventh Asian Information Retrieval Societies Conference, Dubai, 2011b.

AbuZeina D., Al-Khatib W., Elshafei M., Al-Muhtaseb H., "Cross-word Arabic pronunciation variation modeling for speech recognition" , International Journal of Speech Technology , 2011a.

Afify M, Nguyen L, Xiang B, Abdou S, Makhoul J. Recent progress in Arabic broadcast news transcription at BBN. In: Proceedings of INTERSPEECH. 2005, pp 1637–1640

Alghamdi M, Elshafei M, Almuhtasib H (2009) Arabic broadcast news transcription system. Int J Speech Tech 10:183–195

Ali, M., Elshafei, M., Alghamdi M. , Almuhtaseb, H. , and Alnajjar, A., "Arabic Phonetic Dictionaries for Speech Recognition". Journal of Information Technology Research, Volume 2, Issue 4, 2009, pp. 67-80.

Alotaibi YA (2004) Spoken Arabic digits recognizer using recurrent neural networks. In: Proceedings of the fourth IEEE international symposium on signal processing and information technology, pp 195–199

Al-Otaibi F (2001) speaker-dependant continuous Arabic speech recognition. M.Sc. thesis, King Saud University

Amdal I, Fosler-Lussier E (2003) Pronunciation variation modeling in automatic speech recognition. Telektronikk, 2.2003, pp 70–82.

Azmi M, Tolba H,Mahdy S, Fashal M(2008) Syllable-based automatic Arabic speech recognition in noisy-telephone channel. In: WSEAS transactions on signal processing proceedings, World Scientific and Engineering Academy and Society (WSEAS), vol 4, issue 4, pp 211–220

Bahi H, Sellami M (2001) Combination of vector quantization and hidden Markov models for Arabic speech recognition. ACS/IEEE international conference on computer systems and applications, 2001

Benzeghiba M, De Mori R et al (2007) Automatic speech recognition and speech variability: a review. Speech Commun 49(10–11):763–786.

Billa J, Noamany M et al (2002) Audio indexing of Arabic broadcast news. 2002 IEEE international conference on acoustics, speech, and signal processing (ICASSP)

Bourouba H, Djemili R et al (2006) New hybrid system (supervised classifier/HMM) for isolated Arabic speech recognition. 2nd Information and Communication Technologies, 2006. ICTTA'06

Choi F, Tsakalidis S et al (2008) Recent improvements in BBN's English/Iraqi speech-to-speech translation system. IEEE Spoken language technology workshop, 2008. SLT 2008

Clarkson P, Rosenfeld R (1997) Statistical language modeling using the CMU-Cambridge toolkit. In: Proceedings of the 5th European conference on speech communication and technology, Rhodes, Greece.

Elmahdy M, Gruhn R et al (2009) Modern standard Arabic based multilingual approach for dialectal Arabic speech recognition. In: Eighth international symposium on natural language processing, 2009. SNLP'09

Elmisery FA, Khalil AH et al (2003) A FPGA-based HMM for a discrete Arabic speech recognition system. In: Proceedings of the 15th international conference on microelectronics, 2003. ICM 2003

Emami A, Mangu L (2007) Empirical study of neural network language models for Arabic speech recognition. IEEE workshop on automatic speech recognition and understanding, 2007. ASRU

Essa EM, Tolba AS et al (2008) A comparison of combined classifier architectures for Arabic speech recognition. International conference on computer engineering and systems, 2008. ICCES 2008

Farghaly A, Shaalan K (2009) Arabic natural language processing: challenges and solutions. ACM Trans Asian Lang Inform Process 8(4):1–22.

Gales MJF, Diehl F et al (2007) Development of a phonetic system for large vocabulary Arabic speech recognition. IEEE workshop on automatic speech recognition and understanding, 2007. ASRU

Gallwitz F, Noth E, et al (1996) A category based approach for recognition of out-of-vocabulary words. In: Proceedings of fourth international conference on spoken language, 1996. ICSLP 96

Hwang M-H (1993) Subphonetic acoustic modeling for speaker-independent continuous speech recognition, Ph.D. thesis, School of Computer Science, Carnegie Mellon University.

Hyassat H, Abu Zitar R (2008) Arabic speech recognition using Sphinx engine. Int J Speech Tech 9(3–4):133–150

Imai T, Ando A et al (1995) A new method for automatic generation of speaker-dependent phonological rules. 1995 international conference on acoustics, speech, and signal processing, 1995. ICASSP-95

Jelinek F (1999) Statistical methods for speech recognition, Language, speech and communication series. MIT, Cambridge, MA

Jurafsky D, Martin J (2009) Speech and language processing, 2nd edn. Pearson, NJ

Khasawneh M, Assaleh K et al (2004) The application of polynomial discriminant function classifiers to isolated Arabic speech recognition. In: Proceedings of the IEEE international joint conference on neural networks, 2004

Kirchhofl K, Bilmes J, Das S, Duta N, Egan M, Ji G, He F, Henderson J, Liu D, Noamany M, Schoner P, Schwartz R, Vergyri D (2003) Novel approaches to Arabic speech recognition: report from the 2002 John-Hopkins summer workshop, ICASSP 2003, pp I344–I347

Kuo HJ, Mangu L et al (2010) Morphological and syntactic features for Arabic speech recognition. 2010 IEEE international conference on acoustics speech and signal processing (ICASSP)

Lamel L, Messaoudi A et al (2009) Automatic speech-to-text transcription in Arabic. ACM Trans Asian Lang Inform Process 8(4):1–1822 2 Arabic Speech Recognition Systems

Lee KF (1988) Large vocabulary speaker independent continuous speech recognition: the Sphinx system. Doctoral dissertation, Carnegie Mellon University.

Messaoudi A, Gauvain JL et al (2006) Arabic broadcast news transcription using a one million word vocalized vocabulary. 2006 IEEE international conference on acoustics, speech and signal processing, 2006. ICASSP 2006 proceedings

Mokhtar MA, El-Abddin AZ (1996) A model for the acoustic phonetic structure of Arabic language using a single ergodic hidden Markov model. In: Proceedings of the fourth international conference on spoken language, 1996. ICSLP 96

Muhammad G, AlMalki K et al (2011) Automatic Arabic digit speech recognition and formant analysis for voicing disordered people. 2011 IEEE symposium on computers and informatics (ISCI)

Nofal M, Abdel Reheem E et al (2004) The development of acoustic models for command and control Arabic speech recognition system. 2004 international conference on electrical, electronic and computer engineering, 2004. ICEEC'04

Owen Rambow, David Chiang, et al., Parsing Arabic Dialects, Final Report – Version 1, January 18, 2006
http://old-site.clsp.jhu.edu/ws05/groups/arabic/documents/finalreport.pdf

Park J, Diehl F et al (2009) Training and adapting MLP features for Arabic speech recognition.IEEE international conference on acoustics, speech and signal processing, 2009. ICASSP 2009

Plötz T (2005) Advanced stochastic protein sequence analysis, Ph.D. thesis, Bielefeld University

Rabiner, L. R. and Juang, B. H., Statistical Methods for the Recognition and Understanding of Speech, Encyclopedia of Language and Linguistics, 2004.

Ryding KC (2005) A reference grammar of modern standard Arabic (reference grammars). Cambridge University Press, Cambridge.

Sagheer A, Tsuruta N et al (2005) Hyper column model vs. fast DCT for feature extraction in visual Arabic speech recognition. In: Proceedings of the fifth IEEE international symposium on signal processing and information technology, 2005

Saon G, Padmanabhan M (2001) Data-driven approach to designing compound words for continuous speech recognition. IEEE Trans Speech Audio Process 9(4):327–332.

Saon G, Soltau H et al (2010) The IBM 2008 GALE Arabic speech transcription system. 2010 IEEE international conference on acoustics speech and signal processing (ICASSP)

Satori H, Harti M, Chenfour N (2007) Introduction to Arabic speech recognition using CMU Sphinx system. Information and communication technologies international symposium proceeding ICTIS07, 2007

Selouani S-A, Alotaibi YA (2011) Adaptation of foreign accented speakers in native Arabic ASR systems. Appl Comput Informat 9(1):1–10

Shoaib M, Rasheed F, Akhtar J, Awais M, Masud S, Shamail S (2003) A novel approach to increase the robustness of speaker independent Arabic speech recognition. 7th international multi topic conference, 2003. INMIC 2003. 8–9 Dec 2003, pp 371–376

Singh, R., B. Raj, et al. (2002). "Automatic generation of subword units for speech recognition systems." Speech and Audio Processing, IEEE Transactions on 10(2): 89-99.

Soltau H, Saon G et al (2007) The IBM 2006 Gale Arabic ASR system. IEEE international conference on acoustics, speech and signal processing, 2007. ICASSP 2007

Stanford Log-linear Part-Of-Speech Tagger, 2011.
http://nlp.stanford.edu/software/tagger.shtml

Taha M, Helmy T et al (2007) Multi-agent based Arabic speech recognition. 2007 IEEE/WIC/ACM international conferences on web intelligence and intelligent agent technology workshops

The CMU Pronunciation Dictionary (2011), http://www.speech.cs.cmu.edu/cgi-bin/cmudict, Accessed 1 September 2011.

Vergyri D, Kirchhoff K, Duh K, Stolcke A (2004) Morphology-based language modeling for Arabic speech recognition. International conference on speech and language processing. Jeju Island, pp 1252–1255

Xiang B, Nguyen K, Nguyen L, Schwartz R, Makhoul J (2006) Morphological ecomposition for Arabic broadcast news transcription. In: Proceedings of ICASSP, vol I. Toulouse, pp 1089–1092

Incorporating Grammatical Features in the Modeling of the Slovak Language for Continuous Speech Recognition

Ján Staš, Daniel Hládek and Jozef Juhár

Additional information is available at the end of the chapter

1. Introduction

The task of creation of a language model consists of the creation of the large-enough training corpus containing typical documents and phrases from the target domain, collecting statistical data, such as counts of word n-tuples (called n-grams) from the a collection of prepared text data (training corpus), further processing of the raw counts and deducing conditional probabilities of words, based on word history in the sentence. Resulting word tuples and corresponding probabilities form the language model.

The major space for improvement of the precision of the language model is in the *language model smoothing*. Basic method of the probability estimation, called *maximum likelihood* that utilizes n-gram counts directly obtained from the training corpus is often insufficient, because it results zero probability to those word n-grams not seen in the training corpus.

One of the possible ways to update n-gram probabilities lies in the incorporation of the grammatical features, obtained from the training corpus. Basic methods of the language modeling work just with sequences of words and does not take any language grammar into account. Current language modeling techniques are based on the statistics of the sequences of words in the sentences, obtained from a training corpora. If the information about the language grammar have to be included in the final language model, it had to be done in a way that is compatible with the statistical character of the basic language model. More precisely, this means to propose a method of extraction of the grammatical features from the text, compile a statistical model based on these grammatical features and finally, make use of these probabilities in refining probabilities of the basic, word-based language model.

The process of extraction of the grammatical information from the text means assigning one of the list possible features for each word in the sentence of the training corpus, forming up several word classes, where one word class consists of each word in the vocabulary of the speech recognition system that can have the same grammatical feature assigned. Statistics collected from these word classes then represent a general grammatical features of the training text, that can be then used to improve original word-based probabilities.

1.1. Data sparsity in highly inflectional languages

Language modeling is an open problem for a long time and still cannot be considered as solved. Most of the research has been performed in the domain of English - as a consequence, most of the proposed methods work well with languages similar to English. Processing languages different from English, such as Slavic languages still have to deal with specific problems.

As it is stated in [25], common aspects of highly inflectional languages with non mandatory word order is inflective nature of Slavic languages, where: "...majority of lexical items modify its basic form according to grammatical, morphological and contextual relations. Nouns, pronouns, adjectives and numerals change their orthographic and phonetic forms with respect to grammatical case, number and gender."

This property, together with rich morphology brings extremely large lexicons. Slavic languages are also characterized by free word order in the sentence. The same meaning can be expressed by more possible word orders in the sentence and grammatical correctness still stays valid.

The main problems of forming a language model of Slavic languages can be summarized as:

- vocabulary size is very high, one word has many inflections and forms;
- size of necessary training text is very large – it is hard to catch all events;
- number of necessary n-grams is very large.

Solutions presented in [25] are mostly based on utilization of grammatical features and manipulation of the dictionary:

- dictionary based on most frequent lemmas;
- dictionary based on most frequent word-forms;
- dictionary based on morphemes.

Each of these methods require a special method of preprocessing of the training corpus and producing a language model. Every word in the training corpus is replaced by the corresponding item (lemma, word-form or a sequence of morphemes) and a language model is constructed using the processed corpus. For a highly inflectional language, where thanks to the large dictionary the estimation of the probabilities is very difficult, language modeling using a extraction of the grammatical features of words seems to be a beneficial way how to improve general accuracy of the speech recognition .

2. Language modeling with sparse training corpus

The biggest issue of building a language model is data sparsity. To get a correct maximum likelihood estimate, all possible trigram combinations should be in the training corpus. This is very problematic, if a bigger dictionary is taken into account. Just in the case of usual, 100k word dictionary that will sufficiently cover the most of the commonly used communication, there are 10^{15} possible combinations. This amount of text that will contain all combinations that are possible with this dictionary is just impossible to gather and process. In the most cases, training corpora are much smaller, and as a consequence, number of extracted n-grams is also smaller. Then it is possible that if a trigram does not exist in a training corpus, it will have zero probability, even if the trigram combination is perfectly possible in the target language.

To deal with this problem, process of adjusting calculated probabilities called *smoothing* is necessary. This operation will move part of the probability mass from the n-grams that is present in the training corpus to the n-grams that are not present in the training corpus and has to be calculated from data that is available.

Usually, in the case of missing n-gram in the language model, required probability is calculated by using available n-grams of lower order using *back-off scheme* [19]. For example, if the trigram is not available, bigram probabilities are used to estimate probability of the trigram. Using the same principle, if the bigram probability is not present, unigram probabilities are used for calculation of the bigram probability. This principle for bigram language model is depicted in the Fig. 1.

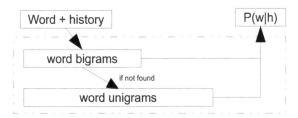

Figure 1. Backoff scheme in a bigram language model

Often, the back-off scheme is not enough by itself for efficient smoothing of the language model, and n-gram probabilities have to be adjusted even more. Common additional techniques are methods based on adjusting of n-gram counts, such as *Laplace smoothing*, *Good-Touring method*, *Witten-Bell* [5] or *modified Knesser-Ney* [21] algorithms. The problem of this approach is that these methods are designed for languages that are not very morphologically rich. As it is showed in [17, 24], is that this kind of smoothing does not bring expected positive effect for highly inflectional languages with large vocabulary.

Another common approach for estimating a language model from sparse data is *linear interpolation*, also called *Jelinek-Mercer smoothing* [16]. This method allows a combination of multiple independent sources of knowledge into one, that is then used for compose the final language model. In the case of trigram language model, this approach can calculate the final probability as a linear combination of unigram, bigram and trigram *maximum likelihood estimates*. Linear interpolation is not the only method of combining of multiple knowledge sources, other possible approaches are *maximum entropy* [1], *log-linear interpolation* [20] or *generalized linear interpolation* [15].

For a bigram model, a linear interpolation scheme of utilizing bigrams and unigrams is depicted in the Fig. 2. In this case, the final probability is calculated as a linear combination of both sources according to the equation:

$$P = \lambda P_1 + (1 - \lambda)P_2. \tag{1}$$

Interpolation parameter λ can be set empirically, or can be calculated by one of the optimization methods, e.g. by using *expectation-maximization* algorithm. The coefficient λ have to be chosen, such that the final language model composed from the training corpus fits best the target domain, represented by the testing corpus.

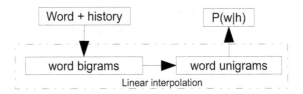

Figure 2. Bigram model with linear combination

3. Class based language models

The presented basic language modeling methods are usually not sufficient for successful real-world automatic speech recognition system. To overcome a data-sparsity problem, *class-based language models* were proposed in [4]. This approach offers ability to group words into classes and work with a class as it was a single word in the language model. This feature means that the class-based language model can considerably reduce sparsity of the training data. Also, an advantage is that the class-based models take into the account dependencies of words, not included in the training corpus.

Probability of a word, conditioned on its history $P(w_i|w_{i-1} \ldots w_{i-n+1})$ in the class-based language model can be described using equation [4]:

$$P(w_i|w_{i-1} \ldots w_{i-n+1}) = P(c_i|c_{i-1} \ldots c_{i-n+1})P(w_i|c_i), \tag{2}$$

where $P(c_i|c_{i-1} \ldots c_{i-n+1})$ is probability of a class c_i, where word w_i belongs, based on the class history. In this equation, probability of a word w according to its history of $n - 1$ words $h = \{w_{i-1} \ldots w_{i-n+1}\}$ is calculated as a product of class-history probability $P(c_i|c_{i-1})$ and word-class probability $P(w_i|c_i)$.

3.1. Estimation of the class-based language models

As it is described in [18], if using *maximum likelihood estimation*, n-gram probability can be calculated in the same way as in the word-based language models:

$$P(c_i|c_{i-1} \ldots c_{i-N+1}) = \frac{C(c_{i-n+1} \ldots c_i)}{C(c_{i-n+1} \ldots c_{i-1})}, \tag{3}$$

where $C(c_{i-N+1} \ldots c_i)$ is a count of sequence of classes in the training corpus and $C(c_{i-n+1} \ldots c_{i-1})$ is count of the history of the class c_i in the training corpus.

The word-class probability can be estimated as a fraction of a word count $C(w)$ and class total count $C(c)$:

$$P(w|c) = \frac{C(w)}{C(c)}. \qquad (4)$$

Basic feature of the class-based models is lowering number of independent parameters [4] of the resulting language model. For word-based n-gram language model, there is a probability value for each n-gram, as well as back-off weight for lower order n-grams. For class-based model, a whole set of words is reduced to a single class and class-based model describes statistical properties of that class. Another advantage is that the same classical smoothing methods that were presented above can be used for a class-based language model as well.

3.2. Word clustering function

Classes in the class-based model bring bigger level of generalization, rather than manipulating with words, model deals with whole classes of words. Advantage of this approach is significantly lower number of n-grams, where resulting number of n-grams depends on a number of classes.

Generalization of words to classes using the clustering function can reduce data sparsity problem. Each class substitutes whole group of words in the class-based language model, therefore a much larger number of word sequences that are possible in the language can be covered by the language model - there is a much higher probability that a certain word sequence will have a non-zero probability. From this reason, it is possible to see class-based language model as a certain type of language model smoothing - partitioning of the dictionary.

The basic idea of the class-based language model is to take additional dependencies between words into account by grouping words into classes and finding dependencies between these classes. Each word in the given training corpus can be clustered to the corresponding classes, where each class can contain words with similar semantic or grammatical meaning. Words in the classes then share common statistical properties according to their context. In general, one word can belong to multiple classes and one class can contain more words.

In the context of a class-based language model, a class can be seen as a group of words. Each this kind of group can be defined using a function. This word clustering function g that can map any word w from the dictionary V and its context h to one of the possible classes c from the set of all classes C can be described as:

$$g(w,h) \to c, \qquad (5)$$

where class c is from the set of all possible classes G, word w is from vocabulary V and h is surrounding context of the word w. This function can be defined in multiple ways - utilizing expert knowledge, or using data-driven approaches for word-classes induction and can have various features.

If the word clustering function is generalized to include every possible word, class-based language model equation then can it can be written as:

$$P(w|h) = P_g(g(w,h)|g(h))P(w|g(w,h)). \qquad (6)$$

4. A method for utilizing grammatical features in the language modeling

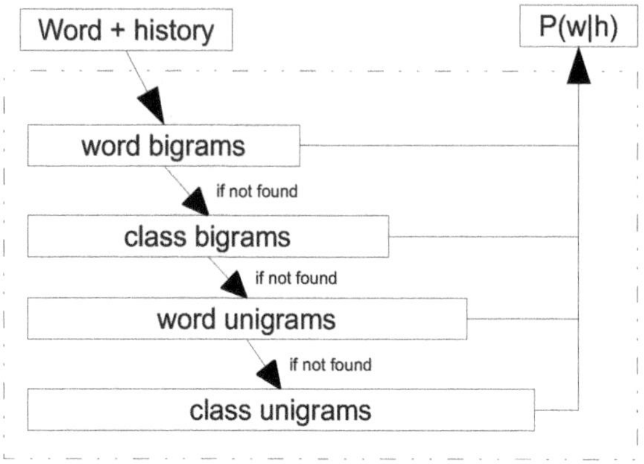

Figure 3. Back-off scheme for the language model

The main problem with class-based language models is how to optimally design a word clustering function g. The word clustering function can be induced in a purely uncontrolled way, based on heuristics "words with the same context belongs to the same class", or some knowledge about the grammatical features of the target language can be used. Inspired by the algorithm proposed in [4] and [32] proposes an automatically induced word classes for building a class-based language model. On the other hand, it seems to be feasible to include some information about the grammar of the language. *Stem-based morphological language model* are proposed in [8, 33].

There is extensive research performed in the task of utilizing grammatical features in a class-based models. The work presented in [23] states that a combination of a plain word-based models with a class-based models can bring improvement in the accuracy of the speech recognition. [22] evaluates a linear combination of the classical word-based language models and grammar-based class models for several languages (English, French, Spanish, Greek).

As it was presented in the previous text, class-based models have some features that are desirable, such as reducing training data sparsity. On the other hand, the main feature of the class-based language model, generalization of the words, can be disadvantage for the most common n-grams. If word-based n-gram exist in the training corpus, it is very possible that it will have more accurate probability than the corresponding class-based n-gram. For less frequent n-grams, class-based language model might be more precise.

It seems that class-based language models using grammatical features might be useful in the automatic speech recognition. Advantage of the class-based model is mainly in the estimation of the probability of events that are rare in the training corpus. On the other hand, events that are relatively frequent, are better estimated by the word-based language model. The ideal solution will be to connect both models, so they can cooperate - frequent cases would be evaluated by the word-based n-grams, less frequent events would be evaluated by the class-based n-grams. Example schematics for this solution would be in the Fig. 3.

From this reason a linear combination of a class-based with word-based language model is proposed. It should be performed in a way that the resulting language model will mostly take into account word-based n-grams if they are available and in the case that here is no word-based n-gram it will fall back to the class-based n-gram that uses grammatical features, as it is showed in the Fig. 3.

4.1. Linear interpolation of the grammatical information

This framework can be implemented using linear interpolation method, where the final probability of the event is calculated as a weighted sum of two components - class-based and word-based model. As it is known that the word based-model almost always give better precision, coefficient of the word-based component should be much higher than the class-based component. Probability of the event will be affected by the class-based component mainly in the case, when the word-based component $P_w(w|h)$ will give zero probability, because it was not seen in the training corpus. On the other hand, the class-based components $P_g(g(w)|g(h))$ might be still able to provide non-zero probability, because rare event can be estimated from words that are similar in the means of the word clustering function g.

Class-based language model utilizing grammatical features, then consists of two basic parts: word-based and class-based language model that was constructed using word clustering function (as it is in the Fig. 2).

Probability of a word, according to its history $P(w|h)$ then can be calculated using equation:

$$P(w|h) = \lambda P_w(w|h) + (1 - \lambda)P_g(g(w)|g(h))P(w|g(w)), \tag{7}$$

where P_w is probability returned by the word-based model and P_g is probability returned by the class-based model with the word-clustering function g that utilizes information about grammar of the language.

This kind of language model consists of the following components:

- vocabulary V that contains a list of known word of the language model;
- word-based language model constructed from the training corpus that can return word-history probability $P_w(w|h)$;
- word clustering function $g(w, h)$ that maps words into classes;
- class-based language model $P_g(g(w)|g(h))$ created from a training corpus and processed by the word clustering function $g(w, h)$;
- word-class probability function that assigns a probability of occurrence of a word in the given class $P(w|g(w))$;
- interpolation constant λ from interval $(0, 1)$ that expresses weight of the word-based language model.

The first part of this language model can be created using classical language modeling methods from the training corpus. To create a class-based model, the training corpus has to be processed by the word clustering function and every word has to be replaced by its corresponding class. From this processed training corpus, a class-based model can be built. During this process, a word-class probability function has to be estimated. This function expresses probability distribution of words in the class. The last step is to determine the interpolation parameter λ, should be set to values close (but lower) to 1.

4.2. Extracting grammatical features

The hardest part of this process seems to be processing of the training corpus by the grammatical feature extraction function. Description of the sentence by its grammatical features is basically a classification task, where each word and its context has assigned one feature from a list of all possible features. This conforms to the Eq. 5, that puts words into classes.

Common grammatical features (usable for a highly inflective languages with non-mandatory word order in the sentence):

- part-of-speech, a label that expresses grammatical categories of the word in a sentence, such as number, case or grammatical gender;
- lemma, a basic form of the word;
- word suffix, a part of the word that inflects according to the grammatical form of the word;
- word stem, a part of the word that does not inflect and usually carries meaning of the word.

There are more possible methods of segmentation of words into such features. Basically, they can be divided into two groups - *rule-based* and *statistics-based methods*. In the following text, a rule-based method for identifying a stem or a suffix of the word will be presented and a statistic-based method for finding the word lemma or part-of-speech will be introduced.

4.2.1. Suffix and stem identification method

Suffix or stem identification method belongs to the field of the morphological analysis of the language. There is a number of specialized methods and tools, such as *Morfessor* [6] using uncontrolled learning methods. More methods of the morphological analysis are provided in [9]. Disadvantage of the majority of proposed methods is that they are not very suitable for Slavic languages. From this reason, a specialized method is necessary.

Because Slovak language is characterized by a very rich morphology, mainly on the suffix side, a simple method, taking specifics of the language is presented. The method is based on suffix identification, based on a list, obtained by counting suffixes in the list of all words (from [29]) and taking suffixes with high occurence.

First necessary thing is a list of suffixes. This list can be obtained by studying a dictionary of words, or some simple count-based analysis can be used.

1. a dictionary of the most common words in the language has been obtained;
2. from each word longer than 6 characters, a suffix of length 2, 3 or 4 characters has been extracted;
3. number of occurrences of each extracted suffix has been calculated;
4. a threshold has been chosen and suffixes with count higher than the threshold has been added to the list of all suffixes.

If the list of the most common suffixes is created, it is possible to easily identify the stem and suffix and stem of the word.

1. if the word is shorted than 5 characters, suffix cannot be extracted;
2. if word is longer than 5 characters, word ending of length $n = 5$ is examined. If it is in the list of the most common suffixes, it is the result. If the ending of length n is not in the list, algorithm continues with $n - 1$;
3. if no suffix has been identified, word is considered as a class by itself.

Disadvantage of this method is that it is statistically based and it is not always precise and some suffixes found might not be grammatically correct.

This suffix or stem assignment function then can be used as a word clustering function that can assign certainly one class to every word. Words with the same suffix or stem will then belong to the same class and according to the properties of the language, they will share similar statistical features.

4.2.2. Part-of-speech or lemma identification using statistical methods

Suffix extraction task is not too complicated and a simple algorithm can be used to achieve plausible results. It is straight-forward and one word will always the same suffix, because no additional information, such as context is considered. On the other hand, the process of identification of the part-of-speech is much more difficult and context-dependent. In the case of the Slovak language, the same word can have many different tags assigned, depending on the surrounding context of the word.

Part-of-speech (POS) tag, assigned to a word expresses grammatical categories of a word in a sentence. The same word can have multiple POS tags and surrounding context of the word has to be used to specify correct grammatical category. This task is difficult also for trained human annotator and requires sufficient knowledge about the grammar of the language.

Using a set of hand-crafted rules to assign a POS tag to a word did not show up to be useful. In a morphologically rich language, the number of possible POS tags is very high and covering every case by a rule seems to be exceptionally complex. Even if there are some approaches using uncontrolled learning techniques [10], useful in the cases, when no a priori knowledge is available the most commonly used approach is in statistical methods that make use of the hand-annotated corpora.

The most commonly used classification methods are based on a *hidden Markov models*, e.g. *HunPOS* [11], based on *TnT* [2] that is a statistical model is trained on a set of manually annotated data. In some approaches, an expert knowledge can be directly inserted to the statistical system, e.g. *rule-based tagger* [13].

Common statistical approaches include:

- Brill tagger (transformation learning) [3];
- hidden Markov model classifier [11];
- maximum entropy (log-linear regression) classifier [27];
- averaged perceptron methods [30, 34].

Lemma assignment task is very similar to the part-of-speech assignment task, and very similar methods can be used. The part-of-speech or lemma assignment function can be used as a word clustering function, when forming a class-based language model. The problem with this approach is that it is possible that one word can belong to more classes at once that can bring a lower precision of the language model.

4.2.3. Hidden Markov model based on word clustering

Hidden Markov models is a commonly used method for a sequential classification of the text. This kind of classifier can be used for various tasks, where a disambiguation is necessary, such as part-of-speech tagging, lemmatization or named entity recognition. Also, it is essential for other tasks in the automatic speech recognition, such as acoustic modeling. The reason for a high popularity of this method is very good performance, both in precision and speed and well-described mathematical background.

The problem of assigning the best sequence of tags or classes $g_{best}(W) = \{c_1, \ldots c_n\}$ to a sequence of words $W = \{w_1, w_2 \ldots w_n\}$ can be described by the equation:

$$g_{best}(W) = arg \max_i P(g_i(W)|W), \tag{8}$$

where the best sequence of classes $g_{best}(W)$ is assigned from all class sequences that are possible for the word sequence W, according to the probability of occurrence of the class sequence in the case of the given word sequence W.

There are several problems with this equation. First, the number of possible sequences $g_i(W)$ is very high and it is not computationally feasible to verify them individually. Second, there has to be a framework for expressing probability of the sequence $P(g_i(W)|W)$ and calculating its maximum.

The hidden Markov model is defined as a quintuple:

- G_0 - a priori probability distribution of all classes;
- G - set of possible states (classes);
- W - set of possible observations (words);
- A - state transition matrix, that expresses probability $P(c_i|c_{i-1})$ of occurrence of the class c_i, if class c_{i-i} preceded in the sequence;
- B - observation probability matrix, that gives probability $P(w_i|c_i)$ of word w_i for the class c_i.

For construction of the hidden Markov model for the task of POS tagging, all of these components should be calculated, as precisely as it is possible. The most important part of the whole process is manually prepared training corpus, where each word has a class assigned by hand. This process is very difficult and requires a lot of work of human annotators.

When annotated corpus is available, estimation of the main components of the hidden Markov model, matrices A and B is relatively easy. Again, the maximum likelihood method can be used, together with some smoothing techniques:

$$A = P(c_i|c_{i-1}) = \frac{C(c_{i-1}, c_i)}{C(c_{i-1})} \tag{9}$$

and

$$B = P(w_i|c_i) = \frac{C(w_i, c_i)}{C(c_i)}, \tag{10}$$

where $C(c_{i-1}, c_i)$ is count of the pair of succeeding classes c_{i-1}, c_i, $C(c_i)$ is count of the class c_i in the training corpus. After matrices A and B are prepared, the best sequence of classes for the given sequence of words can be calculated using a method of dynamic programming - the Viterbi algorithm.

As it was stated above, the Slovak language is characterized by its rich morphology and large vocabulary and this fact makes the task of the POS tagging more difficult. During experiments, it has shown up that these basic methods are not sufficient, and additional modification of the matrices A and B is required.

For this purpose, a *suffix-based smoothing method* has been designed, similar but not the same as in [2]. Here, an accuracy improvement can be achieved by calculation of the suffix-based probability $P(g_{suff}(w_i)|c_i)$. This probability estimate uses the same word-clustering function for assigning words into classed as is presented above. Again, the observation probability matrix is adjusted using a linear combination:

$$B = \lambda P(w_i|c_i) + (1 - \lambda)P(g_{suff}(w_i)|c_i). \tag{11}$$

This operation helps to better estimate probability of the word w_i in for the class c_i, even if a pair w_i, c_i does not exist in the training corpus. The second component of the expression improves the probability estimate with counts of words, that are similar to the word w_i.

5. Experimental evaluation

Basically, language models can be evaluated in two possible ways. In the extrinsic evaluation is language model tested in simulated real-life environment and performance of the whole automatic speech recognition system is observed. The result of the recognition is compared to the annotation of the testing set. Standard measure for extrinsic evaluation is *word error rate* (*WER*) that is calculated as:

$$WER(W) = \frac{C_{INS} + C_{DEL} + C_{SUB}}{C(W)}, \tag{12}$$

where C_{INS} is number of false inserted words, C_{DEL} is number of unrecognized words and C_{SUB} is number of words that were confused (substituted), when the result of the recognition is compared to the word sequence W.

WER is evaluation of the real output of the whole automatic speech recognition system. It evaluates user experience and is affected by all components of the speech recognition system.

On the other hand, intrinsic evaluation is the one "that measures the quality of the model, independent on any application" [18]. For *n*-gram language models, the most common evaluation metric is *perplexity* (*PPL*). "The perplexity can be also viewed as a weighted averaged branching factor of the language model. The branching factor for the language is the number of possible next words that can follow any word" [18]. Similarly to the extrinsic method of evaluation, a testing corpus is required. The resulting perplexity value is always connected with the training corpus. According to the previous definition, perplexity can be expressed by the equation:

$$PPL(W) = \sqrt[N]{\prod_{i=1}^{N} \frac{1}{P(w|h)}}, \tag{13}$$

where $P(w|h)$ is a probability, returned by the tested language model and expresses probability of all words conditioned by its histories from the testing corpus of the length N.

Compared to the extrinsic methods of evaluation, it offers several advantages. Usually, evaluation using perplexity is much faster and simpler, because only testing corpus and language model evaluation tool is necessary. Also, this method eliminates unwanted effects of other components of the automatic speech recognition system, such as acoustic model of phonetic transcription system.

5.1. Training corpus

The most important thing that is necessary for building good language model is correctly prepared training data in a sufficient amount. For this purpose, a text database [12] has been used. As it was mentioned in the introduction section, the training corpus should be large enough to cover the majority of the most common *n*-grams. Also, training data must be as similar as possible to the target domain.

The basic corpus of the adjudgements from the Slovak ministry of Justice has been prepared. The problem is that this corpus is not large enough and have to be complemented with texts from other domains. To enlarge this corpus with more general data, web-based newspaper oriented corpus of the text data from major Slovak newspaper web-sites has been collected. For the vocabulary, 381 313 the most common words has been selected. Contents of the training corpus is summarized in the Table 1.

Corpus	Words	Sentences	Size
Judicature	148 228 795	7 580 892	1.10 GB
Web	410 479 727	19 493 740	2.86 GB
Total	570 110 732	27 074 640	3.96 GB

Table 1. Training corpus

For training a class-based model utilizing grammatical features, further processing of the training corpus is required.

One of the goals of this study is to evaluate usefulness of the grammatical features for the language modeling. The tests are focused on following grammatical features that were mentioned in the previous text:

- part-of-speech;
- word lemma;
- word suffix;
- word stem.

For this purpose, a set of tools, implementing a word clustering function has been prepared. For the POS and lemma, a statistical classifier based on the hidden Markov model has been designed. This classifier has been trained on a data from the [29] (presented in [14]). Method of the statistical classifier is similar to the [2], but uses additional back-off method, based on a suffix extraction described in the previous section.

For identification of the suffix or the stem of the word, just simple suffix subtraction method presented above has been used. When compared to the statistical classifier, this method is much simpler and faster. Also, this kind of word clustering function is more uniform, because one word can belong to just one class. Disadvantage of this approach is that it does not allow to identify a suffix or stem to the words that are short. In this case, for those words that cannot be split, word is considered as a class by itself.

Word clustering by the suffix identification is performed in two versions. Version 1 is using 625 suffixes compiled by hand. Version 2 is using 7 578 statistically identified suffixes (as it was described above). For each grammatical feature, the whole training corpus has been processed and every word in the corpus had a class assigned, according to the used word clustering function.

To summarize, 7 training corpora has been created, one for each grammatical feature examined. First training corpus was the baseline, and other 6 corpora were created by processing of the baseline corpus:

- part-of-speech corpus, marked as POS1 has been created using our POS tagger, based on hiden Markov models;
- lemma-based corpus, marked as LEM1, has been created using our lemma tagger, based on hidden Markov models;
- suffix-based corpus 1, marked as SUFF1, has been created using suffix extraction method with 625 hand compiled suffixes;
- stem-based corpus 1, marked as STEM1, has been created using suffix extraction method with the same suffixes;
- suffix-based corpus 2, marked an SUFF2, has been created using suffix extraction method using statistically obtained 7 578 suffixes;
- stem-based corpus 2, marked as STEM2, obtained by the same method.

5.2. Basic language model preparation

These seven corpora then were able to enter the process of language model creation. For every prepared corpus, a language model has been built.

First necessary step is creation of the dictionary. For the baseline corpus, a dictionary of 381 313 the most frequented words has been selected.

For the class-based models, according to the Eq. 2, besides class-based language model probability $P(c|h_c)$, also word-class probability $P(w|c)$ is required. Again, using maximum likelihood, this probability has been calculated as:

$$P(w|c) = \frac{C(w, g(w))}{C(g(w))},\qquad(14)$$

where $C(w, gw)$ is number of occurrences of word W with class $c = g(w)$ and $C(g(w))$ is number of words in class $g(w)$. The processed corpora will be used for creation of the class-based language model.

Taking prepared training corpus, SRILM Toolkit [31] has been used to build trigram model with baseline smoothing method.

5.3. Basic language model evaluation

	SUFF1	SUFF2	POS1	LEM1	STEM1	STEM2	Baseline
Classes (unigram count)	924	37 704	1 255	122 141	115 318	81 780	329 690
Size (MB)	72	450	489	555	595	522	854
PPL basic	266.41	61.64	355.11	75.3	80.42	89.31	39.76
PPL ($\lambda = 0.98$)	37.32	29.56	38.87	38.87	35.74	34.73	n/a

Table 2. Evaluation of the language model perplexity

Result of this step is 7 language models, one classical word-based models and 6 class-based models, one for each word clustering function.

For quick evaluation, a perplexity measure has been chosen. As an evaluation corpus, 500 000 sentences of held-out data from the court of law adjudgements has been used. Results of the perplexity evaluation and characterization of the resulting language models are in the Table 2.

The results have shown that despite expectations. Perplexity of the class-based models constructed from the processed training corpora is always higher than the perplexity of the word-based models. Higher perplexity means, that the language model does not fit testing data so good. Word-based language model seems to be always better than the class-based model, even if there are some advantages of the class-based language model. But, class-based language models could be useful. Thanks to the word clustering function, they still provide extra information that is not included in the baseline model. The hypothesis say, that in some special cases, the class-based language model can give better result than the word-based model. The way, how this extra information can be utilized is linear interpolation with the baseline model, so it contains both word-based and class-based n-grams.

5.4. Creating class-based models utilizing grammatical features

A new set of the interpolated language models have been compiled using methodology described in the previous section. Each class-based model has been taken and together with the baseline word-based model, they were composed together using *linear interpolation*.

Weight of the word based model has been set to $\lambda = 0.98$ and also word class probability calculated in the previous step has been used.

The result of this process is again a class-based model. This new class-based model utilizing grammatical features contains two types of classes. Word-based class, where class contains only one member, the word. The second type of class is grammar-based class, where class contains all words, that are mapped by the word clustering function.

This new set of the interpolated language models have been evaluated for perplexity. Results are in the Table 2. It is visible that after the interpolation, perplexity of the interpolated models has decreased very much. This fact confirms the hypothesis about usability of the grammar-based language models.

5.5. Automatic speech recognition with class-based models utilizing grammatical features

The main reason for improvement of the language model is the improvement of the automatic speech recognition system. The correct evaluation of the language models in the task of the automatic speech recognition would not be complete without extrinsic test in the simulated real-world tasks of the recognition of the pre-recorded notes for adjudgements. Therefore, the main tool for evaluation is an automatic speech recognition system, originally designed for the judicature [28] with acoustic model [7].

For this purpose, two testing sets named APD1 and APD2 were used. Both test sets are focused on the task of transcription of the dictation for use at the Ministry of Justice. Each test set contain over 3 000 sentences that were recorded and annotated. After recognition of the recording, WER has been calculated by comparing the annotation with the result of the recognition using target language model.

To evaluate robustness of the language model, out-of-domain test has also been constructed. Purpose of this test is to find out, how the system will perform in a conditions that are different than the planned. For this test, a set of recordings from broadcast-news database [26] has been used.

Each test is summarized in the Table 3, where name, number of words, number of sentences and size can be found. Results of extrinsic tests can be shown in the Table 4.

Test Set	Sentences	Words
APD1	3 010	41 111
APD2	3 493	41 725
BN	4 361	40 823
Eval Corpus	500 000	15 777 035

Table 3. Test set

Test set	SUFF1	SUFF2	POS1	LEM1	STEM1	STEM2	Baseline
APD1	12.53	12.09	12.38	12.40	12.44	12.50	12.28
APD2	11.37	11.14	11.23	11.25	11.47	11.36	11.32
BN	21.91	21.40	21.87	21.84	21.70	21.63	21.23

Table 4. Language model WER [%] evaluation

5.6. Results of experiments and discussion

To summarize, the whole process of creating and evaluating a class-based language model that utilizes grammatical information can be described as:

1. train set and test set has been prepared;
2. baseline dictionary has been selected;
3. baseline language model has been prepared;
4. for each method of feature extraction, a class-based training corpus has been set-up. Each word in the train set and test set had a grammatical class assigned;
5. from each class-based training corpus, a class-expansion dictionary has been calculated. The dictionary contains information as a triplet $(c, P(w|c), w)$;
6. for each class-based training corpus, a class-based model has been prepared;
7. perplexity of the obtained class-based model has been evaluated;
8. for each class-based model, a linear interpolation with has been performed;
9. for every resulting class-based interpolated model perplexity has been calculated.

First conclusion from these experiments (see Table 2) is that the classic word based language models generally give better precision than the class-based grammar models. Their main advantage is the smoothing ability - estimating probability of the less frequent events using words that are grammatically similar. This advantage can be utilized using linear interpolation, where final probability is calculated as a weighted sum of the word-based component and class-based component. That will help in better distribution of the probability mass in the language model - thanks to the grammar component, more probability will be assigned to the events (word sequences) not seen in the training corpus. Effect of the grammar component is visible in the Table 2, where using simple suffix extraction method and linear interpolation helped to decrease perplexity of baseline language model by 25%.

Effect of the decreased perplexity has been evaluated in extrinsic tests - recognition of dictation of the legal texts. From this these tests, summarized in the Table 4 can be seen, how decreased perplexity affects final precision of the recognition process. In the case of the suffix extraction method, 2% relative WER reduction has been achieved. Interesting fact is that change of the perplexity not always led to decreasing of the WER. From this fact it is possible to say that perplexity of the language model is not always expressing quality of the language model in the task of the automatic speech recognition, where final performance is affected by more factors, and can be used just as a kind of clue in next necessary steps.

Next conclusion is that not every grammatical feature can be useful for increasing precision of the speech recognition. Each test shows notable differences in the perplexities and word error rates for each created language model. After a closer look at the results, it can be seen that those features that are based more on the morphology of the word, such as suffix or part-of-speech perform better than those that are more based on the semantics of the word, such as stem or lemma-based features (compare to [23]). Also, when comparing suffix extraction method 1 and 2, we can see that statistically obtained high number of classes yield better results, than the handcrafted list of suffixes.

6. Conclusion

This presented approach has shown that using suffix-based extraction method, together with interpolated class-based model can bring much smaller perplexity of the language model and considerably lower WER in the automatic speech recognition system. Even if a class-based models do not bring important improvement of the recognition accuracy, they can be used as a back-off schema in the connection with the classical word-based language models, using linear interpolation.

Class-based language models with utilization of the grammatical features allow:

- optimize search network of the speech recognition system by putting some words into classes;
- have ability to incorporate new words into the speech recognition system without the need of re-training the language model;
- better estimate probabilities of those n-grams that did not occur in the training corpus.

Disadvantages of the class-based language models:

- relatively larger search network (it includes both words and word-classes);
- more difficult process of the training language models.

The future work in this field should be focused on even better usability of this type of language model. First area that have not been mentioned in this work is the size of the language model. Size of the language model influences loading times, recognition speed and used disk space of the real-word speech recognition system. Effectively pruned language model should also bring better precision, because it removes n-grams that can be calculated from lower-order n-grams.

The second area that deserves more attention is the problem of language model adaptation. Thanks to the class-based nature of this type of language model, new words and new phrases can be inserted into the dictionary by the user and this feature should be inspected precisely.

This word has introduced a methodology for building a language model for highly inflective language such as Slovak. It can be also usable for similar languages with rich morphology, Polish or Czech. It brings a better precision and ability to include new words into the language model by the user without the need of re-training of the language model.

Acknowledgement

The research presented in this paper was supported by the Ministry of Education under the research project MŠ SR 3928/2010-11 (50%) and Research and Development Operational Program funded by the ERDF under the project ITMS-26220220141 (50%).

Author details

Ján Staš, Daniel Hládek and Jozef Juhár
Department of Electronics and Multimedia Communications
Technical University of Košice, Slovakia

7. References

[1] Berger, A., Pietra, V. & Pietra, S. [1996]. A maximum entropy approach to natural language processing, *Computational Linguistics* **22**(1): 71.

[2] Brants, T. [2000]. TnT: A statistical part-of-speech tagger, *Proc. of the 6th Conference on Applied Natural Language Processing*, ANLC'00, Stroudsburg, PA, USA, pp. 224–231.

[3] Brill, E. [1995]. Transformation-based error-driven learning and natural language processing: A case study in part-of-speech tagging, *Computational Linguistics* **21**: 543–565.

[4] Brown, P., Pietra, V., deSouza, P., Lai, J. & Mercer, R. [1992]. Class-based n-gram models of natural language, *Computational Linguistics* **18**(4): 467–479.

[5] Chen, S. F. & Goodman, J. [1999]. An empirical study of smoothing techniques for language modeling, *Computer Speech & Language* **13**(4): 359–393.

[6] Creutz, M. & Lagus, K. [2007]. Unsupervised models for morpheme segmentation and morphology learning, *ACM Transactions on Speech and Language Processing* **4**(1).

[7] Darjaa, S., Cerňak, M., Beňuš, v., Rusko, M.and Sabo, R. & Trnka, M. [2011]. Rule-based triphone mapping for acoustic modeling in automatic speech recognition, *Springer-Verlag, LNAI 6836* pp. 268–275.

[8] Ghaoui, A., Yvon, F., Mokbel, C. & Chollet, G. [2005]. On the use of morphological constraints in n-gram statistical language model, *Proc. of the 9th European Conference on Speech Communication and Technology*.

[9] Goldsmith, J. [2001]. Unsupervised learning of the morphology of a natural language, *Computational Linguistics* **27**(2): 153–198.

[10] Graça, J. V., Ganchev, K., Coheur, L., Pereira, F. & Taskar, B. [2011]. Controlling complexity in part-of-speech induction, *Journal of Artificial Intelligence Research* **41**(1): 527–551.

[11] Halácsy, P., Kornai, A. & Oravecz, C. [2007]. HunPos - An open source trigram tagger, *Proc. of the 45th Annual Meeting of the ACL on Interactive Poster and Demonstration Sessions*, Stroudsburg, PA, USA, pp. 209–212.

[12] Hládek, D. & Staš, J. [2010]. Text mining and processing for corpora creation in Slovak language, *Journal of Computer Science and Control Systems* **3**(1): 65–68.

[13] Hládek, D., Staš, J. & Juhár, J. [2011]. A morphological tagger based on a learning classifier system, *Journal of Electrical and Electronics Engineering* **4**(1): 65–70.

[14] Horák, A., Gianitsová, L., Šimková, M., Šmotlák, M. & Garabík, R. [2004]. Slovak national corpus, *P. Sojka et al. (Eds.): Text, Speech and Dialogue, TSD'04*, pp. 115–162.

[15] Hsu, B. J. [2007]. Generalized linear interpolation of language models, *IEEE Workshop on Automatic Speech Recognition Understanding, ASRU'2007*, pp. 136–140.

[16] Jelinek, F. & Mercer, M. [1980]. Interpolated estimation of Markov source parameters from sparse data, *Pattern recognition in practice* pp. 381–397.

[17] Juhár, J., Staš, J. & Hládek, D. [2012]. Recent progress in development of language model for Slovak large vocabulary continuous speech recognition, *Volosencu, C. (Ed.): New Technologies - Trends, Innovations and Research* . (to be published).

[18] Jurafsky, D. & Martin, J. H. [2009]. *Speech and Language Processing: An Introduction to Natural Language Processing, Computational Linguistics, and Speech Recognition (2nd Edition)*, Prentice Hall, Pearson Education, New Jersey.

[19] Katz, S. [1987]. Estimation of probabilities from sparse data for the language model component of a speech recognizer, *IEEE Transactions on Acoustics, Speech and Signal Processing* **35**(3): 400–401.

[20] Klakow, D. [1998]. Log-linear interpolation of language models, *Proc. of the 5th International Conference on Spoken Language Processing*.

[21] Kneser, R. & Ney, H. [1995]. Improved backing-off for m-gram language modeling, *Proc. of ICASSP* pp. 181–184.

[22] Maltese, G., Bravetti, P., Crépy, H., Grainger, B. J., Herzog, M. & Palou, F. [2001]. Combining word-and class-based language models: A comparative study in several languages using automatic and manual word-clustering techniques, *Proc. of EUROSPEECH*, pp. 21–24.

[23] Nouza, J. & Drabkova, J. [2002]. Combining lexical and morphological knowledge in language model for inflectional (czech) language, pp. 705–708.

[24] Nouza, J. & Nouza, T. [2004]. A voice dictation system for a million-word Czech vocabulary, *Proc. of ICCCT* pp. 149–152.

[25] Nouza, J., Zdansky, J., Cerva, P. & Silovsky, J. [2010]. Challenges in speech processing of Slavic languages (Case studies in speech recognition of Czech and Slovak), *in* A. E. et al. (ed.), *Development of Multimodal Interfaces: Active Listening and Synchrony*, LNCS 5967, Springer Verlag, Heidelberg, pp. 225–241.

[26] Pleva, M., Juhár, J. & Čižmár, A. [2007]. Slovak broadcast news speech corpus for automatic speech recognition, *Proc. of the 8th Intl. Conf. on Research in Telecomunication Technology, RTT'07*, Liptovský Ján, Slovak Republic, p. 4.

[27] Ratnaparkhi, A. [1996]. A maximum entropy model for part-of-speech tagging, *Proc. of Empirical Methods in Natural Language Processing*, Philadelphia, USA, pp. 133–142.

[28] Rusko, M., Juhár, J., Trnka, M., Staš, J., Darjaa, S., Hládek, D., Cerňák, M., Papco, M., Sabo, R., Pleva, M., Ritomský, M. & Lojka, M. [2011]. Slovak automatic transcription and dictation system for the judicial domain, *Human Language Technologies as a Challenge for Computer Science and Linguistics: 5th Language & Technology Conference* pp. 365–369.

[29] SNK [2007]. Slovak national corpus.
URL: *http://korpus.juls.savba.sk/*

[30] Spoustová, D., Hajič, J., Votrubec, J., Krbec, P. & Květoň, P. [2007]. The best of two worlds: Cooperation of statistical and rule-based taggers for Czech, *Proc. of the Workshop on Balto-Slavonic Natural Language Processing: Information Extraction and Enabling Technologies*, pp. 67–74.

[31] Stolcke, A. [2002]. SRILM – an extensible language modeling toolkit, *Proc. of ICSLP*, Denver, Colorado, pp. 901–904.

[32] Su, Y. [2011]. Bayesian class-based language models, *Proc. of ICASSP*, pp. 5564–5567.

[33] Vergyri, D., Kirchhoff, K., Duh, K. & Stolcke, A. [2004]. Morphology-based language modeling for arabic speech recognition, *Proc. of ICSLP*, pp. 2245–2248.

[34] Votrubec, J. [2006]. Morphological tagging based on averaged perceptron, *Proc. of Contributed Papers, WDS'06*, Prague, Czech Republic, pp. 191–195.

## Chapter 13

VOICECONET: A Collaborative Framework for Speech-Based Computer Accessibility with a Case Study for Brazilian Portuguese

Nelson Neto, Pedro Batista and Aldebaro Klautau

Additional information is available at the end of the chapter

1. Introduction

In recent years, the performance of personal computers has evolved with the production of ever faster processors, a fact that enables the adoption of speech processing in computer-assisted education. There are several speech technologies that are effective in education, among which text-to-speech (TTS) and automatic speech recognition (ASR) are the most prominent. TTS systems [45] are software modules that convert natural language text into synthesized speech. ASR [18] can be seen as the TTS inverse process, in which the digitized speech signal, captured for example via a microphone, is converted into text.

There is a large body of work on using ASR and TTS in educational tasks [14, 37]. All these speech-enabled applications rely on *engines*, which are the software modules that execute ASR or TTS. This work proposes a collaborative framework and associated techniques for constructing speech engines and adopts accessibility as the major application. The network has an important social impact in decreasing the recent digital divide among speakers of commercially attractive and underrepresented languages.

The incorporation of computer technology in learning generated multimedia systems that provide powerful "training tools", explored in computer-assisted learning [34]. Also, Web-based learning has become an important teaching and learning media [52]. However, the financial cost of both computer and software is one of the main obstacle for computer-based learning, especially in developing countries like Brazil [16].

The situation is further complicated when it comes to people with special needs, including visual, auditory, physical, speech, cognitive, and neurological disabilities. They encounter serious difficulties in having access to this technology and hence to knowledge. For example, according to the Brazilian Institute of Geography and Statistics (IBGE), 14.5% of the Brazilian population has some type of disability as detailed in Table 1. It is important then to understand how speech technologies can help educating people with disabilities [37].

Disability	Description	Number of people
Visual	including blindness, low vision, and reduced color perception	16,644,842
Auditory	including total or parcial hearing impairments	5,735,099
Physical	motor disabilities can include weakness, limitations of muscular control (such as involuntary movements, lack of coordination, or paralysis), limitations of sensation, joint problems, or missing limbs	9,355,844
Mental	including cognitive and neurological disabilities	2,844,936

Table 1. Profile of Brazilian people with disabilities based on data provided by IBG [20] (the total population is 190,732,694).

For the effective use of speech-enabled applications in education and assistive systems, reasonably good engines must be available [30, 43]. Besides, the cost of softwares and equipments cannot be prohibitive.

This work presents some results of an ambitious project, which aims at using the Internet as a collaborative network and help the academy and software industry in the development of speech science and technology for any language, including Brazilian Portuguese (BP). The goal is to collect, develop, and deploy resources and softwares for speech processing using a collaborative framework called VOICECONET. The public data and scripts (or software *recipes*) allow to establish baseline systems and reproduce results across different sites [48]. The final products of this research are a large-vocabulary continuous speech recognition (LVCSR) system and a TTS system for BP.

The remainder of the chapter is organized as follows. Section 2 presents a description of ASR and TTS systems. Section 3 describes the proposed collaborative framework, which aims at easing the task of developing ASR and TTS engines to any language. Section 4 presents the developed resources for BP such as speech databases and phonetic dictionary. The baseline results are presented in Section 5. Finally, Section 6 summarizes our conclusions and addresses future works.

2. Background on speech recognition and synthesis

First, this section provides a brief introduction to ASR and TTS systems. The last two topics present evaluation methods and development tools.

2.1. Automatic speech recognition (ASR)

The typical ASR system adopts a statistical approach based on *hidden Markov models* (HMMs) [22], and is composed by five main blocks: front end, phonetic dictionary, acoustic model, language model and decoder, as indicated in Figure 1. The two main ASR applications are *command and control* and *dictation* [18]. The former is relatively simpler, because the language model is composed by a grammar that restricts the acceptable sequences of words. The latter typically supports a vocabulary of more than 60 thousand words and demands more computation.

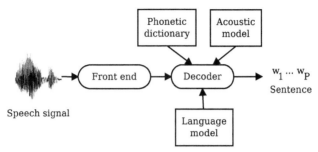

Figure 1. The main constituent blocks of a typical ASR system.

The conventional front end extracts segments (or *frames*) from the speech signal and converts, at a constant *frame rate* (typically, 100 Hz), each segment to a vector $\mathbf{x}$ of dimension L (typically, $L = 39$). It is assumed here that T frames are organized into a $L \times T$ matrix $\mathbf{X}$, which represents a complete sentence. There are several alternatives to parameterize the speech waveforms. In spite of the mel-frequency cepstral coefficients (MFCCs) analysis being relatively old [10], it has been proven to be effective and is used pervasively as the input to the ASR back end [18].

The language model of a dictation system provides the probability $p(\mathcal{T})$ of observing a sentence $\mathcal{T} = [w_1, \ldots, w_P]$ of P words. Conceptually, the decoder aims at finding the sentence $\mathcal{T}^*$ that maximizes a posterior probability as given by

$$\mathcal{T}^* = \arg\max_{\mathcal{T}} p(\mathcal{T}|\mathbf{X}) = \arg\max_{\mathcal{T}} \frac{p(\mathbf{X}|\mathcal{T})p(\mathcal{T})}{p(\mathbf{X})}, \tag{1}$$

where $p(\mathbf{X}|\mathcal{T})$ is given by the acoustic model. Because $p(\mathbf{X})$ does not depend on $\mathcal{T}$, the previous equation is equivalent to

$$\mathcal{T}^* = \arg\max_{\mathcal{T}} p(\mathbf{X}|\mathcal{T})p(\mathcal{T}). \tag{2}$$

In practice, an empirical constant is used to weight the language model probability $p(\mathcal{T})$ before combining it with the acoustic model probability $p(\mathbf{X}|\mathcal{T})$.

Due to the large number of possible sentences, Equation (2) cannot be calculated independently for each candidate sentence. Therefore, ASR systems use data structures such as lexical trees that are hierarchical, breaking sentences into words, and words into *basic units* as phones or triphones [18].

A phonetic dictionary (also known as lexical model) provides the mapping from words to basic units and vice-versa. For improved performance, continuous HMMs are adopted, where the output distribution of each state is modeled by a mixture of Gaussians, as depicted in Figure 2. The typical HMM topology is "left-right", in which the only valid transitions are staying at the same state and moving to the next.

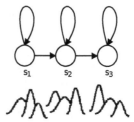

Figure 2. Pictorial representation of a left-right continuous HMM with three states $s_i, i = 1, 2, 3$ and a mixture of three Gaussians per state.

To reduce the computational cost of searching for $\mathcal{T}^*$ (decoding), hypotheses are pruned, i.e., some sentences are discarded and Equation (2) is not calculated for them [11]. In summary, after having all models trained, an ASR at the test stage uses the front end to convert the input signal to parameters and the decoder to search for the best sentence $\mathcal{T}$.

The acoustic and language models can be fixed during the test stage but adapting one or both can lead to improved performance. For example, the topic can be estimated and a specific language model used. This is crucial for applications with a technical vocabulary such as X-ray reporting by physicians [2]. The adaptation of the acoustic model is also important [25].

The ASR systems that use speaker independent models are convenient but must be able to recognize with a good accuracy any speaker. At the expense of requesting the user to read aloud some sentences, speaker adaptation techniques can tune the HMM models to the target speaker. The adaptation techniques can also be used to perform environmental compensation by reducing the mismatch due to channel or additive noise effects.

In this work, an ASR engine is considered to be composed by the decoder and all the required resources for its execution (language model, etc.). Similarly, a TTS engine consists of all software modules and associated resources, which will be briefly discussed in the sequel.

2.2. Text-to-speech (TTS)

A typical TTS system is composed by two parts: the front end and the back end [9]. Figure 3 depicts a simple functional diagram of a TTS system.

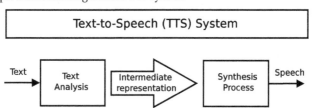

Figure 3. Functional diagram of a TTS system showing the front and back ends, responsible by the text analysis and speech synthesis, respectively.

The front end is language dependent and performs text analysis to output information coded in a way that is convenient to the back end. For example, the front end performs text normalization, converting text containing symbols like numbers and abbreviations into the equivalent written-out words. It also implements grapheme-to-phone conversion, syllabification and syllable stress determination, which assign phonetic transcriptions to each word and marks the text with prosodic information. Phonetic transcriptions and prosody information together compose the (intermediate) symbolic linguistic representation that is output by the front end.

The back end is typically language independent and includes the synthesizer, which is the block that effectively generates sound. With respect to the technique adopted for the back end, the main categories are the formant-based, concatenative and, more recently, HMM-based [45]. Historically, TTS systems evolved from a knowledge-based paradigm to a pragmatic data-driven approach.

2.3. Evaluation metrics

In most ASR applications the figure of merit of an ASR system is the word error rate (WER). In this work, the WER is defined as

$$\text{WER} = \frac{D + R}{W} \times 100\%, \tag{3}$$

where W is the number of words in the input sequence, R and D are the number of replacement and deletion errors on the recognized word sequence, respectively, when compared with the correct transcription.

Another metric for evaluating an ASR system is the real-time factor (xRT). The xRT is obtained by dividing the time that the system spends to recognize a sentence by its time duration. A lower xRT indicates a faster recognition.

The most common metric for evaluating a language model is the probability $p(\mathbf{T})$ that the model assigns to some test data $\mathbf{T} = \{\mathcal{T}_1, \mathcal{T}_2, \ldots, \mathcal{T}_S\}$ composed of S sentences. Independence among the sentences is assumed, which leads to $p(\mathbf{T}) = p(\mathcal{T}_1)p(\mathcal{T}_2) \ldots p(\mathcal{T}_S)$. Two measures are derived from this probability: perplexity and cross-entropy [18]. The cross-entropy $H_p(\mathbf{T})$ is defined as

$$H_p(\mathbf{T}) = -\frac{1}{W_{\mathbf{T}}} \log_2 p(\mathbf{T}), \tag{4}$$

where $W_{\mathbf{T}}$ is the number of words in $\mathbf{T}$.

The perplexity (PP) is the inverse of the average conditional probability of a next word, and is related to the cross-entropy $H_p(\mathbf{T})$ by

$$\text{PP} = 2^{H_p(\mathbf{T})}. \tag{5}$$

Lower cross-entropies and perplexities indicate less uncertainty in predicting the next word and, for a given task (vocabulary size, etc.), typically indicate a better language model.

With respect to TTS, the quality of speech outputs can be measured via two factors: intelligibility and pleasantness. Intelligibility can be divided into segmental intelligibility, which indicates how accurately spoken sentences have been received by the user, and comprehension, which measures how well the spoken sentences are understood. Segmental intelligibility can be measured in a similar way to WER by comparing transcriptions and reference messages. Comprehension can be measured by using questions or tasks which require listeners to understand the meaning of the messages.

Pleasantness of speech can be measured by collecting a large number of user opinions and using, for example, the mean opinion score (MOS) protocol [27]. The MOS is generated by averaging the results of a set of subjective tests where a number of listeners rate the heard audio quality of sentences read aloud by TTS softwares. It should be noted that intelligibility and pleasantness are related but not directly correlated. They also have a significant effect on user's acceptance: unpleasant speech output can lead to poor satisfaction with an otherwise sophisticated system.

2.4. Engines and tools for writing speech-enabled applications

The starting point to deploy a speech-enabled application is to count with an engine (ASR, TTS or both). There are commercial solutions from Microsoft [28], Nuance [29], and other companies. Currently, not all languages are supported, especially the so-called underrepresented ones. Therefore, a key aspect is to have available engines for the target language.

With respect to free engines, the MBROLA project [13] offers a set of TTS engines for 34 languages, including BP. Julius [24] and Sphinx-4 [51] are examples of open source decoders that can be used in association with the required resources to build ASR engines. For embedded (e.g., smartphones) applications, Julius and PocketSphinx [19] are the most popular engines. Research groups have made available engines for English, Japanese and other languages based on open source decoders Silva et al. [40].

Having an engine available, an *application programming interface* (API) eases the task of developing softwares for the final users, i.e., speech-enabled applications. The APIs specify a cross-platform interface to support command and control recognizers, dictation systems and speech synthesizers. As such, they contain not only the required TTS and ASR functionality but also numerous methods and events that allow programmers to query the characteristics of the underlying engine. An engine typically has its own API but there are at least two APIs that were designed for general use: the speech API from Microsoft [33] and the Java Speech API [21].

It should be noted the APIs for user interface accessibility, such as the Microsoft Active Accessibility platform and the AT-SPI toolkit on Linux. These softwares are designed to help developing assistive technology products, like screen readers and keyboards, interact with standard and custom user interface elements of an application (or the operating system), in order to provide better access for individuals who have physical or cognitive difficulties, impairments, or disabilities.

2.5. Tools for developing engines

Besides the research interest, two reasons for investing on the development of an engine is the lack of support to a given language and the need to minimize cost.

VOICECONET: A Collaborative Framework for Speech-Based Computer Accessibility with a
Case Study for Brazilian Portuguese

309

There are some free and mature software tools for building speech recognition and synthesis engines. HTK [55] is the most widespread toolkit used to build and adapt acoustic models, as well as HTS [54] (modified version of HTK) for building speech synthesis system. Statistical language models can be created with SRILM [44] or HTK.

Festival [4] offers a general multi-lingual (currently English and Spanish) framework for building speech synthesis systems. Another open source framework for TTS is the MARY platform [36]. Currently, MARY supports the German, English and Tibetan languages.

3. A collaborative framework for improved ASR and TTS

Having briefly discussed how the industry and academy are positioned to promote the development and adoption of speech-enabled applications, this section focuses on a key aspect for adopting this technology in education: using a collaborative network to increase the availability of engines.

3.1. The challenge of developing speech-enabled educational softwares

As mentioned, minimizing the cost of the application deployment can be the main reason to use a free engine or develop one. But, initially, this work has been motivated by circumventing the lack of an ASR engine for BP. For instance, when this work originated, the only desktop software for ASR dictation in BP was the IBM ViaVoice, which had been discontinued. Therefore, the intention of creating software for educating physically-impaired people was unfeasible unless engines were developed.

However, the task of designing a speech engine is not trivial and the existence of a collaborative environment, as proposed in this work, can be a decisive aspect. The availability of corpora ("databases") is a conditioning factor for the development of engines, and while there are many public resources for some languages (e.g., English and Japanese), the resources for underrepresented languages are still limited. A typical corpus for training and testing speech recognition and synthesis systems has speech files with their associated transcriptions, large amount of written texts and a phonetic dictionary.

The phonetic dictionary is an essential building block that does the correspondence between the orthography and the pronunciation(s). In practice, building a pronunciation dictionary for ASR is very similar to developing a grapheme-to-phone (G2P) module for TTS systems. In fact, a dictionary can be constructed by invoking a pre-existent G2P module. The task of designing a G2P module is difficult to perform and several techniques have been adopted over the last decade [6, 46].

As discussed, speech recognition and synthesis are data-driven technologies that require a relatively large amount of labeled data in order to achieve acceptable accuracy rates. The state-of-art HMM-based ASR and TTS methods also require a database, with multiple speakers in the case of ASR. In response to these needs, the next section suggests using the Internet as a collaborative network.

3.2. The proposed VOICECONET platform

The proposed collaborative framework aims at collecting desktop speech and text data at negligible costs for any language, in order to provide larger training data for ASR and TTS systems. Softwares for training and test statistical models are also made available. In the end, the whole community benefits with better ASR and TTS engines.

It is well-known that collaborative networks will be critically important to business and organizations by helping to establish a culture of innovation and by delivering operational excellence. Collaborative networks have been achieved on the base of academic partnership, including several universities and some companies specialized in developing and implementing software in the university domain [31]. The collaborative networks offer the possibility to reduce the duration and the costs of development and implementation of hard to automate, vast and expensive systems [1], such as developing a ASR or TTS engine.

There are already successful multi-language audio collaborative networks like the Microsoft's YourSpeech project and the Voxforge free speech corpus and acoustic model repository. The YourSpeech platform [5] is based on crowd sourcing approaches that aims at collecting speech data and provides means that allow users to donate their speech: a quiz game and a personalized TTS system. The VoxForge project [50] was set up to collect transcribed speech to create a free speech corpus for use with open source speech recognition engines. The speech audio files are compiled into acoustic models for use with open source speech recognition engines. This work complements these previous initiatives by focusing on documenting and releasing softwares and procedures for developing engines.

The proposed VOICECONET platform is comprehensive and based on the open source concept. It aims at easing the task of developing ASR and TTS engines to any language, including the underrepresented. In summary, the framework has the following features:

- Rely on a Web-based platform that was organized for collecting resources and improving the engines accuracy. Through this platform anyone can contribute with waveform files and the system rewards them with a speaker dependent acoustic model. The users can also create a custom language model depends on the tasks where the model is going to be used.

- The adopted softwares for building and evaluating engines (HTK, Julius, MARY, etc.) are freely available. A considerable amount of time is spent to learn how to use them, and the network shares scripts to facilitate.

- The shared reports and academic papers use the concept of reproducible research [48], and the results can be replicated in different sites.

In order to collect desktop labeled data, the system architecture is based on the client/server paradigm (see Figure 4). The client accesses the platform through a website [49] and is identified by an user ID. Once there, the user is invited to record random sentences, taken from a phonetically rich set [8], in order to guarantee complete phoneme coverage. The Java Applet used for recording control was based on the VoxForge related application. This control enables the system to access the user's computer and record audio using any of the installed devices. If the user selects the submit option, the recordings automatically stop and the wave files are streamed to the server. The user can submit the recorded sentences anytime.

When enough sentences are recorded, at least 3 minutes of audio, the user may choose to generate his/her speaker dependent acoustic model. At that moment, in the server, a script is used to process the audio and build an adapted acoustic model using the HTK tools. Then, the user may choose to download a file containing his/her speaker dependent acoustic model. Note that the quality of the model is increased by the number of recorded sentences.

Another feature allows context-dependent language model to be created. To create the language model it is necessary to input a small caps without punctuation text corpus in a simplified standard generalized markup language format. In this format, there can be only one sentence per line and each sentence is delimited by the tags $< s >$ and $< /s >$. In the sequel, a script is used to process the text and build a trigram ARPA format language model using the SRILM tools. To improve the model it is recommended that the user previously converts the input texts so that every number, date, money amount, time, ordinal number, websites and some abbreviations should be written in full.

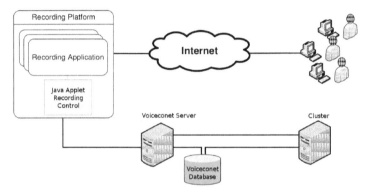

Figure 4. High level system architecture diagram.

At the time of writing of this chapter, VOICECONET is online for 1 month for the BP language. We have been receiving extremely positive feedback from the users. It was collected more than 60 minutes of audio from 15 speakers, and 5 language models were made available, adding up 10 thousand sentences. Figure 5 shows the VOICECONET platform website.

It is pedagogical to use an underrepresented language to illustrate how the global community can build and keep improving resources to all languages. Using the VOICECONET platform, the following speech-related resources for BP are currently shared: two multiple speakers audio corpora corresponding together to approximately 17 hours of audio, a phonetic dictionary with over 65 thousand words, a speaker independent HTK format acoustic model, and a trigram ARPA format language model. All these BP resources are publicly available [15] and the next section describes how they were developed.

4. Development of ASR and TTS engines: A case study

Taking again BP as an example, the most widely used corpus seems to be the Spoltech, distributed by the Linguistic Data Consortium (LDC). The LDC catalog also released the West Point Brazilian Portuguese Speech, a *read* speech database of microphone digital recordings from native and non-native speakers. These two corpora are not enough for fully developing

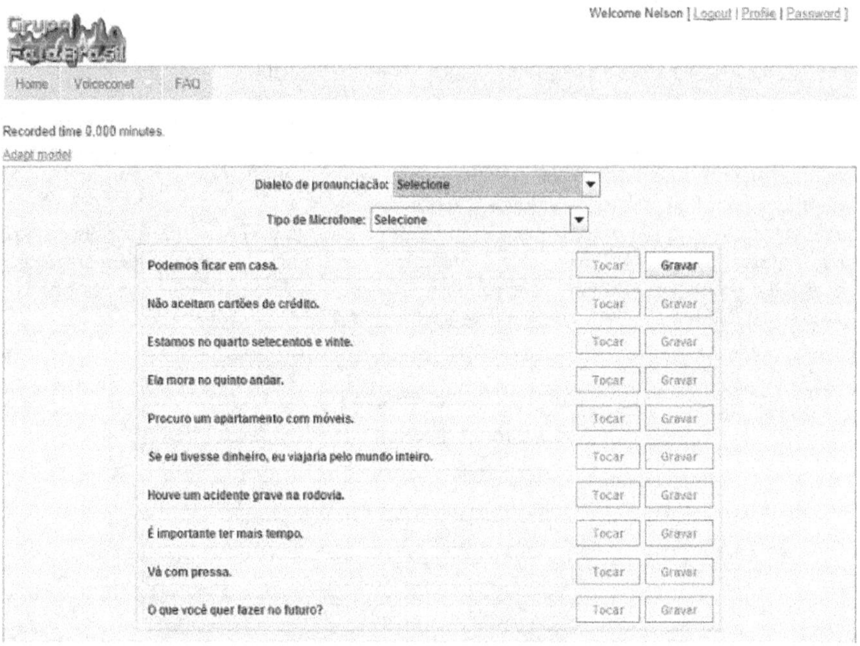

Figure 5. The VOICECONET platform website.

a state of art LVCSR systems, since they have together approximately dozen hours. For example, only the Switchboard telephone conservations corpus for English has 240 hours of recorded speech [17]. There were initiatives [35, 53] in the academy for developing corpora, but they have not established a sustainable collaboration among researchers.

Regarding end-users applications, there are important freely available systems. For instance, in Brazil, Dosvox and Motrix [47] are very popular among blind and physically-impaired people, respectively. Dosvox includes its own speech synthesizer, besides offering the possibility of using other engines. Dosvox does not provide ASR support. The current version of Motrix supports ASR only in English, which makes use of a ASR engine distributed for free by Microsoft.

There are advantages on adopting a proprietary software development model, but this work advocates the open source model. The next sections describe the resources developed in order to design speech engines for BP.

4.1. UFPAdic: A phonetic dictionary for BP

The phonetic dictionary used in this work was automatically generated using a phonetic transcription with stress determination algorithm for BP language described in Silva et al. [39]. The improvements proposed in Siravenha et al. [42] were also considered.

The proposed software (G2P converter) is based on phonological pre-established criteria and its architecture does not rely on intermediate stages, i.e., other algorithms such as syllabic division or plural identification. There is a set of rules not focus in any BP dialect for each grapheme and a specific order of application is assumed. First, the more specific rules are considered until a general case rule is reached, which ends the process. Therefore the developed G2P converter deals only with single words and does not implement co-articulation analysis between words.

The rules are specified in a set of regular expressions using the C# programming language. Regular expressions are also allowed in the definition of non-terminals symbols (e.g. #abacaxi#). The rules of the G2P converter are organized in three phases. Each phase has the following function:

- a simple procedure that inserts the non-terminal symbol # before and after each word.

- the stress phase that mark the stressed vowel of the word.

- the bulk of the system that convert the graphemes (including the stressed vowel brand) to 38 phones represented using the SAMPA phonetic alphabet [32].

Using the described G2P converter, a phonetic dictionary was created. It has 65,532 words and is called UFPAdic. These words were selected by choosing the most frequent ones in the CETENFolha corpus [7], which is a corpus based on the texts of the newspaper *Folha de S. Paulo* and compiled by NILC/*São Carlos*, Brazil. The G2P converter (executable file) and the UFPAdic are publicly available [15].

4.2. Syllabification

The developed G2P converter does not perform syllabification nor stress syllable identification. So these two tasks were implemented in a Java software publicly available at Fal [15]. The algorithm used for syllabification is described in Silva et al. [38]. The main idea of this algorithm is that all syllables have a vowel as a nucleus, and it can be surrounded by consonants or other (semi-vowels). Hence, one should locate the vowels that composes the syllable nuclei and isolate consonants and semivowels.

The original syllabification rules [38], as previously mentioned, consider the kind and the arrangement of graphemes to separate the syllables of a given word. However, there are some words whose syllabification is very difficult to perform correctly with only these two criteria, especially when such words have diphthongs, because they will require a number of very specific and well elaborated rules, in which each one will deal with just a few examples.

To overcome this difficulty, new linguistic rules, shown in Table 2, were proposed, each one not just considering the graphemes themselves, but also their stress. The first group deals with the falling diphthongs (the "vowel + glide" combination), while the second one deals with diphthongs that varies with hiatus (the "glide + vowel" combination). Due to the fact that diphthongs need this special treatment in their syllabification, it was defined that these rules must be evaluated before the 20 original ones.

The main motivation for analyzing the previously mentioned diphthongs comes from the perception of existing divergences between the scholars on such subject (like the position of a glide, inside a syllable, in the falling diphthongs, that was explained in Bisol [3]). Another point that ratifies the focus adopted in this analysis is the fact that vocalic segments, especially the ones with rising sonority, have presented many errors in the separations performed by the syllabification algorithm (in a previous analysis).

Sequence for the algorithm	Action	Example
...(a,e,o)(i(V_ton),u(V_ton))...	must be separated	sa-í-da, gra-ú-do
...(a,e,o)(i,u)...	stay in the same syllable	cãi-bra, mai-se-na
...(i,u)(a(V_ton),e(V_ton),o(V_ton))<Pont>...	must be separated	ta-man-du-á
...(i(V_ton),u(V_ton))(a,e,o)<Pont>...	must be separated	de-mo-cra-ci-a
...(i,u)(a,e,o)<Pont>...	stay in the same syllable	só-cio, cí-lio
...(i,u)(a,e,o)...	must be separated	bi-o-ma

Table 2. New syllabification rules.

In addition to that, the original rule 19 was updated to fix some errors that occurred when it was previously proposed. If the analyzed vowel is not the first grapheme in the next syllable to be formed and is followed by another vowel that precedes a consonant, then the analyzed vowel must be separated from the following graphemes. This new version of the rule 19 fixes some errors that were occurring in the syllabification of words like "teólogo", for example (the correct is "te-ó-logo", instead of "teó-lo-go", as shown in Silva et al. [38]).

Identifying the stress syllable proved to be an easier task that benefited from the fact that the developed G2P converter, in spite of not separating in syllable, was already able to identify the stressed vowel. After getting the result of the syllabification, it was then trivial to identify the syllable corresponding to the stress vowel.

4.3. LapsStory

The LapsStory corpus is based on spoken books or audiobooks. Having the audio files and their respective transcriptions (the books themselves), a considerable reduction in human resources can be achieved.

The original audio files were manually segmented to create smaller files, that were re-sampled from 44,100 Hz to 22,050 Hz with 16 bits. Currently, the LapsStory corpus consists of 8 speakers, which corresponds to 16 hours and 17 minutes of audio. Unfortunately, the LapsStory corpus cannot be completely released in order to protect the copyright of some audiobooks. Therefore, only part of the LapsStory corpus is publicly available, which corresponds to 9 hours of audio [15].

It should be noted that the acoustic environment of audiobooks is very controlled, so the audio files have no audible noise and high signal to noise ratio. Thus, when such files are used to train a system that will operate in a noisy environment, there is a problem with the acoustic mismatch. This difficulty was circumvented by the technique proposed in Silva et al.

[41], which showed that speaker adaptation techniques can be used to combat such acoustic mismatch.

4.4. LapsBenchmark

Another developed corpus is the LapsBenchmark, which aims to be a benchmark reference for testing BP systems. The LapsBenchmark's recordings were performed on computers using common (cheap) desktop microphones and the acoustic environment was not controlled.

Currently, the LapsBenchmark corpus has data from 35 speakers with 20 sentences each, which corresponds to 54 minutes of audio. It was used the phrases described in Cirigliano et al. [8]. The used sampling rate was 22,050 Hz and each sample was represented with 16 bits. The LapsBenchmark speech database is publicly available [15].

4.5. Resources required for TTS

In order to create a complete TTS system for BP, some specific resources had to be developed and procedures were executed, following the tutorials in Schröder & Trouvain [36]. The motivation for using the open-source MARY platform in this work was that it is completely written in Java and supports both concatenative and HMM-based synthesis.

Using the nomenclature adopted in the MARY framework, the task of supporting a new language can be split into the creation of a text processing module and the voice. The former enables the software to process BP text and, for example, perform the G2P conversion. The creation of a voice in this case corresponds to training HMMs using the HTS toolkit.

MARY requires a set of files for each language that it supports. This work adopted the recipe suggested by MARY for training finite state transducers (FST) [23]. The FST training procedure requires the definition of a phonetic alphabet and a list with the most frequent words in the target language. These two built files, specific for BP, are briefly described below:

- allophones.pt_BR.xml: is the phonetic alphabet, which must describe the distinctive features of each phone such as voiced/unvoiced, vowel/consonant, and others. A preliminary version of this file was developed by the authors using the SAMPA phonetic alphabet [32].

- pt_BR.dic: is a list that contains all the planned words with their corresponding phonetic transcriptions based on the phonetic alphabet previously described. These transcriptions are required to be separated into syllables and the stress syllable indicated.

After having a valid BP front end, the HTS toolkit was used to create an HMM-based back end. In order to facilitate the procedure, MARY provides the *VoiceImport* tool, illustrated in Figure 6, which is an automatic HMM training routine. For HMM training, one needs a labeled corpus with transcribed speech. It was used the speech data available with the BP demo for HTS [26], which has a total of 221 files, corresponding to approximately 20 minutes of audio. The word level transcriptions were not found at the HTS site and, for convenience to other users, were made available in electronic format at Fal [15].

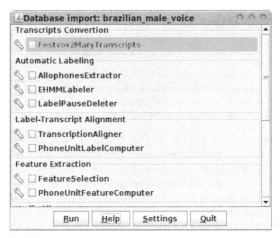

Figure 6. The GUI of the VoiceImport tool.

After this stage, the TTS system for BP is already supported by the MARY platform. All the developed resources and adopted procedures are publicly available [15].

5. Experimental results

This section presents the baseline results obtained with all the developed ASR and TTS resources for BP. The scripts and developed models were made publicly available [15]. All the experiments were executed on a computer with Core 2 Duo Intel processor (E6420 2.13 GHz) and 1 GB of RAM.

The target for the first tests presented was to understand, in practice, how the main components of a LVCSR system behave: the phonetic dictionary, acoustic model, language model and the decoder. The existing correlation between these components and the performance presented by the system are analyzed in respect of the xRT factor, as well as the WER. Finally, the quality of speech produced by the developed TTS system was compared with other synthesizers, including a commercial software.

5.1. Evaluation of the proposed syllabification rules

This experiment used 170 words in total that, aiming to delimitate the encountered problems, were divided in four contexts: falling diphthongs, rising diphthongs, diphthongs that varies with hiatus and false diphthongs. For each word, three syllabifications were analyzed and extracted from the following sources: a Portuguese web dictionary [12], the old version of the syllabification algorithm (without the new rules) and the new version of the same algorithm, with the new rules implemented.

Table 3 shows the results of the syllabification tests for each source. The divergences between the syllabifications performed by the sources and the standards for syllable separation in BP, described in Bisol [3], were considered as errors encountered during the syllabification process of these sources.

Sources	Words	Errors	Error rates
Portuguese web dictionary	170	1	0.58%
Syllabification algorithm (old)	170	29	11.17%
Syllabification algorithm (new)	170	2	1.17%

Table 3. Error percentage analysis of the syllabification sources.

The new version of the syllabification algorithm achieved a very low amount of errors, compared to its previous version. The mentioned errors were detected in two words in the context of the falling diphthongs: "eufonia" and "ousadia". The syllable divisions "eu-fo-nia" and "ou-sa-dia" are incorrect because each one presents two vowels that should be separated to compose nuclei for two different syllables. The accepted syllabifications are: "eu-fo-ni-a" and "ou-sa-di-a".

5.2. Evaluation of the language model

This experiment evaluates the language model perplexity against the number of sentences used to train it (Figure 7). The SRILM tookit was used to build the trigram ARPA format language models. The number of sentences used to train the language models ranged between 255,830 and 1,534,980 extracted from CETENFolha and LapsStory corpora. The vocabulary was kept constant with the 65,532 distinct words present in UFPAdic.

The phrases used to measure the perplexity were separated into three test sets of ten thousand sentences each one, unseen during the training phase. The first test set was designed solely with sentences extracted from the CETENFolha corpus, the second set with sentences collected by crawling newspapers available on the Internet and the last one encompasses the phrases present in the previous sets. Note that, in terms of sentences, the CETENFolha and crawling corpus can be considered disjoint.

As expected, the perplexity tends to diminish as the number of sentences used in the training increases. This is related to the fact that the statistics of the trained models get improved as more occurrences of triples of words are registered in the database of written texts. It is important to observe, in Figure 7, the difference of perplexities measured for the data test sets. The perplexity was higher when the sentences used to evaluate the language model were collected from a different text corpus that was used to train it. It can be verified with the presented CETENFolha and crawling curves, since the crawling corpus was not used for training the models. With one thousand sentences this difference is 37%.

5.3. Evaluation of the acoustic model

The HTK software was used to build the acoustic models, according to the steps described in Young et al. [55]. Estimating a good acoustic model is considered the most challenging part of the design of an ASR system. For training an acoustic model, it is required a corpus with

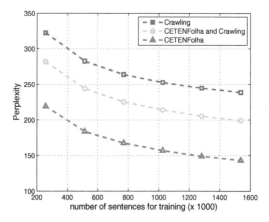

Figure 7. Perplexity against the number of sentences used to train the language model.

digitized voice, transcribed at the level of words (orthography) and/or at the level of phones. Below is a list with details about the configuration used:

- Window length: 25ms.
- Time to capture speech segments: at each 10ms (also knows as shift).
- Computed coefficients for each segment: Mel Cepstral.
- Total of coefficients: energy + 12 Mel Cepstral coefficients + first and second derivatives. On total, the computed vector for each segment has 39 coefficients.
- Acoustic modeling: continuous HMMs with 3 states left-right.
- Acoustic units (HMMs): cross-word triphone models that were built from 38 monophones and a silence model and tied with a decision tree.
- Decoder: Viterbi beam search.

The speaker independent acoustic model was initially trained using the LapsStory and West Point corpora, which corresponds to 21.65 hours of audio, and the UFPAdic. After that, the HTK software was used to adapt the acoustic model, using the maximum likelihood linear regression (MLLR) and maximum a posteriori (MAP) techniques with the Spoltech corpus, which corresponds to 4.3 hours of audio. This adaptation process was used to combat acoustic mismatches and is described in Silva et al. [41]. Both MAP and MLLR were used in the supervised training (offline) mode.

For decoding, the experiments performed in this work adopts the Julius rev.4.1.5 [?] and HDecode (part of HTK) [55] softwares. It was used the trigram language model trained before with 1,534,980 sentences and 14 Gaussians modeled the output distributions of the HMMs. The LapsBenchmark corpus was used to evaluate the models.

Several tests were conducted in order to evaluate the best decoding parameters for both HDecode and Julius. It was observed that the increasing on the xRT factor and recognition accuracy can be linked to a more effective pruning of the decoder at the acoustic level. The pruning process is implemented at each time step by keeping a record of the best hypotheses overall and de-activating all hypotheses whose log probabilities fall more than a beam width below the best. Setting the beam width is thus a compromise between speed and avoiding search errors, as showed in Figure 8.

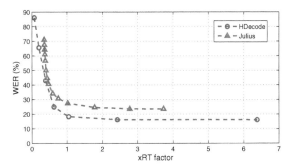

Figure 8. WER against xRT factor using the Julius and HDecode recognizers.

The tests were performed varying the beam width value from 100 to 400 and 15,000 for HDecode and Julius, respectively. It was because the WER stopped to evolve, while the xRT factor increased significantly. It was perceived that Julius can implement more aggressive pruning methods than HDecode, without significantly increasing the xRT factor. On the other hand, Julius could not achieve the same WER obtained with HDecode.

Thus the best decoding parameters for both HDecode and Julius are described in Table 4 and Table 5, respectively. For convenience, the xRT factor value was kept around one.

Parameter	Value
Pruning beam width	220
Language model scale factor	20
Word insertion penalty	22
Word end beam width	100
Number of tokens per state	8
Acoustic scale factor	1.5

Table 4. Parameters used for testing with HDecode.

5.4. Using different number of Gaussians within the acoustic model

In this test, it was considered the same acoustic and language configurations as before. However, the number of Gaussians used in the state output distributions is varied, from a single Gaussian up to 20 Gaussians, as showed in Figure 9. The LapsBenchmark corpus was used to evaluate the models.

Parameter	Value
Pruning beam width for the first pass	2,000
Pruning beam width for the second pass	200
Language model weight for the first and second passes	15
Word insertion penalties for the first and second passes	10
Score envelope width	300

Table 5. Parameters used for testing with Julius.

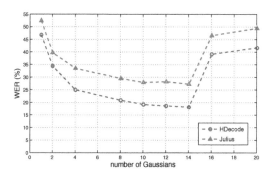

Figure 9. WER against the number of Gaussians used for training the acoustic model.

It was perceived that the computational costs added for increasing the number of Gaussians is compensated by an improvement in the decoder performance. The WER with 14-component Gaussian mixtures is 18.24% and 27.33% for HDecode and Julius, respectively. As the WER increased above 14 Gaussians, the next experiment will consider this number as a default.

5.5. Speaker dependent speech recognition

Preliminary decoding tests with the independent acoustic model adopted before were made using part of the LapsBenchmark corpus, which corresponds to 1.55 minutes of audio recorded with a selected male speaker voice. The results are showed in Figure 10.

In the sequel, a speaker dependent evaluation was performed. The same speaker acessed the VOICECONET platform and contributed with 10.8 minutes of his voice. Thus, the collected audio was used to adapt the independent acoustic model, using the MLLR and MAP adaptation techniques, according to the steps described in Young et al. [55]. The results are presented in Figure 11.

As expected, the speaker adaptation process increased the performance of all decoders. The goal of this experiment was to show that is possible to use the Internet as a collaborative network for improving the engines accuracy.

VOICECONET: A Collaborative Framework for Speech-Based Computer Accessibility with a
Case Study for Brazilian Portuguese

321

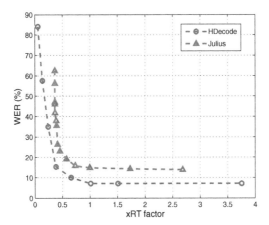

Figure 10. WER and xRT factor observed on tests of speaker independent recognition.

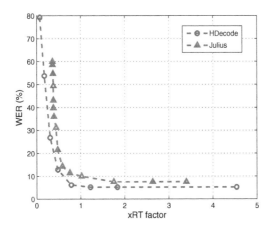

Figure 11. WER and xRT factor observed on tests of speaker dependent recognition.

5.6. Evaluation of the TTS system

This experiment evaluates the TTS system developed in this work. Experiments were also
made with two other BP TTS systems: Liane and Raquel. Liane is a MBROLA synthesizer [13]
and Raquel is a state-of-art commercial software of Nuance [29]. Both are concatenative
diphone synthesizers and were used only for comparison purposes.

The evaluation process was carried out in two stages: segmental intelligibility and
pleasantness. The pleasantness of speech was analyzed in respect of the MOS protocol and
the WER was used to mensure the intelligibility. Twenty sentences (about 5 seconds each one)
collected from the Internet were used to perform the tests. Thus, the sixty audio files were

randomly played and the listener had to give a note for pleasantness and repeat what he/she heard. On total, ten people were interviewed, and none of which has formal education in speech area. The results are showed in Figure 12 and 13.

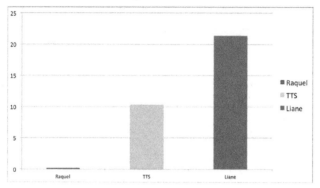

Figure 12. WER observed for each TTS software.

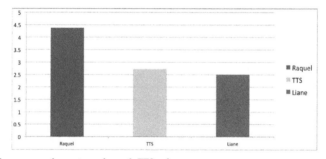

Figure 13. The average pleasantness for each TTS software.

In pleasantness evaluation, the developed TTS system and Liane were considered slightly annoying, while Raquel was evaluated as a good synthesizer. It was observed that even the most developed systems still are less natural than the human voice. In objective test, the TTS system (with WER around 10%) outperforms Liane. Raquel achieved again the best result.

6. Conclusions

This chapter advocates the potential of using speech-enabled applications as a tool for increasing social inclusion and education. This is specially true for users with special needs. In order to have such applications for underrepresented languages, there is still a lot of work to be done. As discussed, one of the main problems is the lack of data for training and testing the systems, which are typically data-driven. So, in order to minimize cost, this work presents the VOICECONET, a collaborative framework for building applications using speech recognition and synthesis technologies. Free tools and resources are made publicly available [15], which include a complete TTS and ASR systems for BP.

VOICECONET: A Collaborative Framework for Speech-Based Computer Accessibility with a
Case Study for Brazilian Portuguese

323

Future work includes expanding both the audio and text databases, aiming at reaching the performance obtained by ASR for English and Japanese, for example. The phonetic dictionary refinement is another important issue to be addressed, considering the existing dialectal variation in Brazil. In parallel, improving the free TTS for BP and develop prototypes for groups of people that are not usually the main target of the assisting technology industry and that require special attention. And finally, one important goal is to help groups that use the network for developing resources for languages other than BP.

Acknowledgements

This work was supported by Conselho Nacional de Desenvolvimento Científico e Tecnológico (CNPq), Brazil, project no. 560020/2010-4.

Author details

Nelson Neto, Pedro Batista and Aldebaro Klautau
*Federal University of Pará (UFPA), Signal Processing Laboratory (LaPS) – http://www.laps.ufpa.br,
Belém – PA – Brazil*

7. References

[1] Agranoff, R. [2006]. Inside collaborative networks: Ten lessons for public managers, *Public Administration Review, 66* pp. 56–65.

[2] Antoniol, G., Fiutem, R., Flor, R. & Lazzari, G. [1993]. Radiological reporting based on voice recognition, *Human-computer interaction. Lecture Notes in Computer Science, 753* pp. 242–253.

[3] Bisol, L. [2005]. *Introdução a Estudos de Fonologia do Português Brasileiro*, Porto Alegre: EDIPUCRS.

[4] Black, A., Taylor, P. & Caley, R. [1999]. *The Festival Speech Synthesis System*, The University of Edinburgh, System Documentation, Edition 1.4.

[5] Calado, A., Freitas, J., Silva, P., Reis, B., Braga, D. & Dias, M. S. [2010]. Yourspeech: Desktop speech data collection based on crowd sourcing in the internet, *International Conference on Computational Processing of Portuguese - Demos Session* .
URL: *http://pt.yourspeech.net*

[6] Caseiro, D., Trancoso, I., Oliveira, L. & Viana, C. [2002]. Grapheme-to-phone using finite-state transducers, *IEEE Workshop on Speech Synthesis* pp. 215–218.

[7] CET [2012]. CETENFolha Text Corpus. Visited in March.
URL: *www.linguateca.pt/CETENFolha/*

[8] Cirigliano, R., Monteiro, C., Barbosa, F., Resende, F., Couto, L. & Moraes, J. [2005]. Um conjunto de 1000 frases foneticamente balanceadas para o Português Brasileiro obtido utilizando a abordagem de algoritmos genéticos, *XXII Simpósio Brasileiro de Telecomunicações* pp. 544–549.

[9] Damper, R. [2001]. *Data-Driven Methods in Speech Synthesis*, Kluwer Academic.

[10] Davis, S. & Merlmestein, P. [1980]. Comparison of parametric representations for monosyllabic word recognition in continuously spoken sentences, *IEEE Transactions on Acoustics, Speech, and Signal Processing, 28* (4): 357–366.

[11] Deshmukh, N., Ganapathiraju, A. & Picone, J. [1999]. Hierarchical search for large-vocabulary conversational speech recognition, *IEEE Signal Processing Magazine* pp. 84–107.

[12] Dic [2012]. Portuguese Web Dictionary. Visited in March.
URL: *www.dicionarioweb.com.br*

[13] Dutoit, T., Pagel, V., Pierret, N., Bataille, F. & Vrecken, O. [1996]. The MBROLA project: Towards a set of high quality speech synthesizers free of use for non commercial purposes, *Proceedings of the 4th International Conference of Spoken Language Processing* pp. 1393–1396.

[14] Eskenazi, M. [2009]. An overview of spoken language technology for education, *Speech Communication, 51* (10): 832–844.

[15] Fal [2012]. Research Group FalaBrasil. Visited in March.
URL: *www.laps.ufpa.br/falabrasil/index_en.php*

[16] Fidalgo-Neto, A., Tornaghi, A., Meirelles, R., Berçot, F., Xavier, L., Castro, M. & Alves, L. [2009]. The use of computers in Brazilian primary and secondary schools, *Computers & Education, 53* (3): 677–685.

[17] Godfrey, J., Holliman, E. & McDaniel, J. [1992]. SWITCHBOARD: Telephone speech corpus for research and development, *IEEE International Conference on Acoustics, Speech and Signal Processing, 1* pp. 517–520.

[18] Huang, X., Acero, A. & Hon, H. [2001]. *Spoken Language Processing*, Prentice Hall.

[19] Huggins-Daines, D., Kumar, M., Chan, A., Black, A. W., Ravishankar, M. & Rudnicky, A. [2006]. Pocketsphinx: A free, real-time continuous speech recogntion system for hand-held devices, *Proceedings of ICASSP* pp. 185–188.

[20] IBG [2010]. Census Demographic Profiles.
URL: *www.ibge.gov.br/home/estatistica/populacao/censo2010/*

[21] JSA [2012]. Java Speech API. Visited in March.
URL: *java.sun.com/products/java-media/speech/*

[22] Juang, H. & Rabiner, R. [1991]. Hidden Markov models for speech recognition, *Technometrics, 33* (3): 251–272.

[23] Kornai, A. [1999]. Extended Finite State Models of Language, Cambridge University Press.

[24] Lee, A., Kawahara, T. & Shikano, K. [2001]. Julius - an open source real-time large vocabulary recognition engine, *Proc. European Conf. on Speech Communication and Technology* pp. 1691–1694.

[25] Lee, C. & Gauvain, J. [1993]. Speaker adaptation based on MAP estimation of HMM parameters, *IEEE International Conference on Acoustics, Speech and Signal Processing, 2* pp. 558–561.

[26] Maia, R., Zen, H., Tokuda, K., Kitamura, T. & Resende, F. [2006]. An HMM-based Brazilian Portuguese speech synthetiser and its characteristics, *Journal of Communication and Information Systems, 21* pp. 58–71.

[27] Mea [1996]. P.800 - ITU: Methods for Subjective Determination of Transmission Quality.
URL: *www.itu.int/rec/T-REC-P.800-199608-I/en*

[28] MLD [2012]. Microsoft Development Center. Visited in March.
URL: *www.microsoft.com/portugal/mldc/default.mspx*

VOICECONET: A Collaborative Framework for Speech-Based Computer Accessibility with a
Case Study for Brazilian Portuguese

325

[29] Nua [2012]. Nuance Communications, Inc. Visited in March.
      URL: *www.nuance.com*
[30] O'Harea, E. & McTearb, M. [1999]. Speech recognition in the secondary school classroom:
      an exploratory study, *Computers & Education, 33* (1): 27–45.
[31] Sabau, G., Bologa, R., Bologa, R. & Muntean, M. [2009]. Collaborative network for
      the development of an informational system in the SOA context for the university
      management, *International Conference on Computer Technology and Development, 1*
      pp. 307–311.
[32] SAM [2012]. SAMPA Phonetic Alphabet. Visited in March.
      URL: *www.phon.ucl.ac.uk/home/sampa/*
[33] SAP [2012]. Microsoft Speech API. Visited in March.
      URL: *www.microsoft.com/speech/*
[34] Saz, O., Yin, S.-C., Lleida, E., Rose, R., Vaquero, C. & Rodríguez, W. [2009]. Tools and
      technologies for computer-aided speech and language therapy, *Speech Communication, 51*
      (10): 948–967.
[35] Schramm, M., Freitas, L., Zanuz, A. & Barone, D. [2000]. A Brazilian Portuguese
      language corpus development, *International Conference on Spoken Language Processing, 2*
      pp. 579–582.
[36] Schröder, M. & Trouvain, J. [2001]. The German text-to-speech synthesis system MARY:
      A tool for research, development and teaching, *International Journal of Speech Technology,
      6* (4): 365–377.
[37] Sealea, J. & Cooperb, M. [2010]. E-learning and accessibility: An exploration of the
      potential role of generic pedagogical tools, *Computers & Education, 54* (4): 1107–1116.
[38] Silva, D., Braga, D. & Resende, F. [2008]. Separação das sílabas e determinação da
      tonicidade no Português Brasileiro, XXVI Simpósio Brasileiro de Telecomunicações
      pp. 1–5.
[39] Silva, D., de Lima, A., Maia, R., Braga, D., de Moraes, J., de Moraes, J. & Resende, F.
      [2006]. A rule-based grapheme-phone converter and stress determination for Brazilian
      Portuguese natural language processing, *VI International Telecommunications Symposium*
      pp. 992–996.
[40] Silva, P., Batista, P., Neto, N. & Klautau, A. [2010]. An open-source speech recognizer for
      Brazilian Portuguese with a windows programming interface, *Computational Processing
      of the Portuguese Language, Springer, 6001* pp. 128–131.
[41] Silva, P., Neto, N. & Klautau, A. [2009]. Novos recursos e utilização de adaptação de
      locutor no desenvolvimento de um sistema de reconhecimento de voz para o Português
      Brasileiro, *XXVII Simpósio Brasileiro de Telecomunicações* pp. 1–6.
[42] Siravenha, A., Neto, N., Macedo, V. & Klautau, A. [2008]. Uso de regras fonológicas com
      determinação de vogal tônica para conversão grafema-fone em Português Brasileiro, *7th
      International Information and Telecommunication Technologies Symposium* pp. 1–6.
[43] Siravenha, A., Neto, N., Macedo, V. & Klautau, A. [2009]. A computer-assisted learning
      software using speech synthesis and recognition in Brazilian Portuguese, Interactive
      Computer Aided Blended Learning pp. 1–5.
[44] Stolcke, A. [2002]. SRILM - an extensible language modeling toolkit, *International
      Conference on Spoken Language Processing* pp. 901–904.
[45] Taylor, P. [2009]. *Text-To-Speech Synthesis*, Cambridge University Press.

[46] Teixeira, A., Oliveira, C. & Moutinho, L. [2006]. On the use of machine learning and syllable information in European Portuguese grapheme-phone conversion, *Computational Processing of the Portuguese Language, Springer, 3960* pp. 212–215.

[47] UFR [2012]. Accessibility Projects of NCE/UFRJ. Visited in March.
URL: *http://intervox.nce.ufrj.br/*

[48] Vandewalle, P., Kovacevic, J. & Vetterli, M. [2009]. Reproducible research in signal processing - what, why, and how, *IEEE Signal Processing Magazine, 26* pp. 37–47.

[49] Voi [2012]. VOICECONET. Visited in March.
URL: *www.laps.ufpa.br/falabrasil/voiceconet/*

[50] Vox [2012]. VoxForge.org. Visited in March.
URL: *www.voxforge.org*

[51] Walker, W., Lamere, P., Kwok, P., Raj, B., Singh, R., Gouvea, E., Wolf, P. & Woelfel, J. [2004]. *Sphinx-4: A Flexible Open Source Framework for Speech Recognition*, Sun Microsystems, TR-2004-139.

[52] Wang, T.-H. [2010]. Web-based dynamic assessment: Taking assessment as teaching and learning strategy for improving students' e-learning effectiveness, *Computers & Education, 54* (4): 1157–1166.

[53] Ynoguti, C. A. & Violaro, F. [2008]. A Brazilian Portuguese speech database, *XXVI Simpósio Brasileiro de Telecomunicações* pp. 1–6.

[54] Yoshimura, T., Tokuda, K., Masuko, T., Kobayashi, T. & Kitamura, T. [1999]. Simultaneous modeling of spectrum, pitch and duration in HMM-based speech synthesis, *Proc. of EUROSPEECH, 5* pp. 2347–2350.

[55] Young, S., Ollason, D., Valtchev, V. & Woodland, P. [2006]. *The HTK Book*, Cambridge University Engineering Department, Version 3.4.

Permissions

The contributors of this book come from diverse backgrounds, making this book a truly international effort. This book will bring forth new frontiers with its revolutionizing research information and detailed analysis of the nascent developments around the world.

We would like to thank S. Ramakrishnan, for lending his expertise to make the book truly unique. He has played a crucial role in the development of this book. Without his invaluable contribution this book wouldn't have been possible. He has made vital efforts to compile up to date information on the varied aspects of this subject to make this book a valuable addition to the collection of many professionals and students.

This book was conceptualized with the vision of imparting up-to-date information and advanced data in this field. To ensure the same, a matchless editorial board was set up. Every individual on the board went through rigorous rounds of assessment to prove their worth. After which they invested a large part of their time researching and compiling the most relevant data for our readers. Conferences and sessions were held from time to time between the editorial board and the contributing authors to present the data in the most comprehensible form. The editorial team has worked tirelessly to provide valuable and valid information to help people across the globe.

Every chapter published in this book has been scrutinized by our experts. Their significance has been extensively debated. The topics covered herein carry significant findings which will fuel the growth of the discipline. They may even be implemented as practical applications or may be referred to as a beginning point for another development. Chapters in this book were first published by InTech; hereby published with permission under the Creative Commons Attribution License or equivalent.

The editorial board has been involved in producing this book since its inception. They have spent rigorous hours researching and exploring the diverse topics which have resulted in the successful publishing of this book. They have passed on their knowledge of decades through this book. To expedite this challenging task, the publisher supported the team at every step. A small team of assistant editors was also appointed to further simplify the editing procedure and attain best results for the readers.

Our editorial team has been hand-picked from every corner of the world. Their multi-ethnicity adds dynamic inputs to the discussions which result in innovative outcomes. These outcomes are then further discussed with the researchers and contributors who give their valuable feedback and opinion regarding the same. The feedback is then collaborated with the researches and they are edited in a comprehensive manner to aid the understanding of the subject.

Apart from the editorial board, the designing team has also invested a significant amount of their time in understanding the subject and creating the most relevant covers. They scrutinized every image to scout for the most suitable representation of the subject and create an appropriate cover for the book.

The publishing team has been involved in this book since its early stages. They were actively engaged in every process, be it collecting the data, connecting with the contributors or procuring relevant information. The team has been an ardent support to the editorial, designing and production team. Their endless efforts to recruit the best for this project, has resulted in the accomplishment of this book. They are a veteran in the field of academics and their pool of knowledge is as vast as their experience in printing. Their expertise and guidance has proved useful at every step. Their uncompromising quality standards have made this book an exceptional effort. Their encouragement from time to time has been an inspiration for everyone.

The publisher and the editorial board hope that this book will prove to be a valuable piece of knowledge for researchers, students, practitioners and scholars across the globe.

List of Contributors

R. Thangarajan
Department of Computer Science and Engineering, Kongu Engineering College, Perundurai, Erode, Tamilnadu, India

Chung-Hsien Wu and Chao-Hong Liu
Department of Computer Science and Information Engineering, National Cheng Kung University, Tainan, Taiwan, R.O.C.

Ronan Flynn
School of Engineering, Athlone Institute of Technology, Athlone, Ireland

Edward Jones
College of Engineering and Informatics, National University of Ireland, Galway, Ireland

Aleem Mushtaq
School of ECE, Georgia Institute of Technology, Atlanta, USA

Santiago Omar Caballero Morales
Technological University of the Mixteca, Mexico

Longbiao Wang, Kyohei Odani and Atsuhiko Kai
Shizuoka University, Japan

Norihide Kitaoka
Nagoya University, Japan

Seiichi Nakagawa
Toyohashi University of Technology, Japan

Jozef Juhár and Peter Viszlay
Technical University of Košice, Slovakia

Alfredo Victor Mantilla Caeiros
Tecnológico de Monterrey, Campus Ciudad de Mexico, México

Hector Manuel Pérez Meana
Instituto Politécnico Nacional, México

Shunsuke Ishimitsu
Hiroshima City University, Japan

Masashi Nakayama
Kagawa National College of Technology, Japan
National Institute of Advanced Industrial Science and Technology (AIST), Japan

Seiji Nakagawa
National Institute of Advanced Industrial Science and Technology (AIST), Japan

Komal Arora and Richard Dowell
Department of Otolaryngology, The University of Melbourne, Australia

Pam Dawson
The Hearing CRC, Australia

Dia AbuZeina, Husni Al-Muhtaseb and Moustafa Elshafei
King Fahd University of Petroleum and Minerals, Dhahran, Saudi Arabia

Ján Staš, Daniel Hládek and Jozef Juhár
Department of Electronics and Multimedia Communications, Technical University of
Košice, Slovakia

Nelson Neto, Pedro Batista and Aldebaro Klautau
Federal University of Pará (UFPA), Signal Processing Laboratory (LaPS), Belém – PA
– Brazil

Printed in the USA
CPSIA information can be obtained
at www.ICGtesting.com
JSHW011504221024
72173JS00005B/1201